Lectures on the Relation between Law and Public Opinion in England during the Nineteenth Century

A. V. DICEY

Lectures on the Relation between Law and Public Opinion in England during the Nineteenth Century

BY A. V. DICEY

Edited and with an Introduction by Richard VandeWetering

 Liberty Fund INDIANAPOLIS

𒀀𒈦𒄄

New introduction, editor's note, new annotations, translations, index © 2008 by Liberty Fund, Inc.

The Liberty Fund edition is based on the 1917 printing of the second edition, published by Macmillan in 1914.

Frontispiece: Courtesy of Richard A. Cosgrove

1 3 5 7 9 C 10 8 6 4 2
1 3 5 7 9 P 10 8 6 4 2

Library of Congress Cataloging-in-Publication Data
Dicey, Albert Venn, 1835–1922.
Lectures on the relation between law and public opinion in England during the nineteenth century / A.V. Dicey ; edited and with an introduction by Richard VandeWetering.
p. cm.
Originally published: London : Macmillan, 1917.
Includes bibliographical references and index.
ISBN 978-0-86597-699-3 (alk. paper) — ISBN 978-0-86597-700-6 (pbk. : alk. paper)
1. Law—England—History.   2. Public opinion—England—History—
19th century.   3. England—Politics and government—19th century.   I. Title.
KD626.D5 2008
349.4209'034—dc22   2006052871

Liberty Fund, Inc.
8335 Allison Pointe Trail, Suite 300
Indianapolis, Indiana 46250-1684

Contents

LECTURE III. *Democracy and Legislation*

LECTURE IV. *The Three Main Currents of Public Opinion*

Preface to the First Edition

IN 1898 I ACCEPTED an invitation to deliver to the students of the Harvard Law School a short course of lectures on the History of English Law during the last century. It occurred to me that this duty might best be performed by tracing out the relation during the last hundred years between the progress of English law and the course of public opinion in England. This treatment of my subject possessed two recommendations. It enabled me to survey the law of England as a whole, without any attempt to go through the whole of the law; it opened, as I hoped, to my hearers a novel and interesting view of modern legislation; a mass of irregular, fragmentary, ill expressed, and, as it might seem, illogical or purposeless enactments, gains a new meaning and obtains a kind of consistency when seen to be the work of permanent currents of opinion.

The lectures delivered at Harvard were the basis of courses of lectures which, after having undergone sometimes expansion and sometimes curtailment, have been during the last five years delivered at Oxford. Of the lectures originally given in America, and thus reconsidered and rewritten, this book is the outcome. To them it owes both its form and its character.

The form of lectures has been studiously preserved, so that my readers may not forget that my book pretends to be nothing but a course of lectures, and that a lecture must from its very nature present a mere outline of the topic with which it deals, and ought to be the explanation and illustration of a few elementary principles underlying some subject of interest.

The character of my book may require some explanation, since it may easily be misconceived. Even for the nineteenth century the book is not a history of English law; still less is it a history of English opinion. It is an attempt to follow out the connection or relation between a century of English legislation and successive currents of opinion. The book is, in fact, an endeavour to bring the growth of English laws during a hundred years into connection with the course of English thought. It cannot claim to be a work of research; it is rather a work of inference or reflection. It is written with the object, not of discovering new facts, but of drawing from some of the best known facts of political, social, and legal history certain conclusions which, though many of them obvious enough, are often overlooked, and are not without importance. If these lectures should induce a student here and there to study the development of modern law in connection with the course of modern thought, and to realise that dry legal rules have a new interest and meaning when connected with the varying current of public opinion, they will have attained their object.

If this end is to any extent reached its attainment will be due in no small measure to the aid I have received from two authors.

To Sir Roland K. Wilson I am indebted for the conception of the way in which the growth of English law might during the last century be linked with and explained by the course of public opinion. Thirty years have passed since, on its appearance in 1875, I read with care his admirable little manual, *The History of Modern English Law.* From its pages I first gained an impression, which time and study have deepened, of the immense effect produced by the teaching of Bentham, and also a clear view of the relation between the Blackstonian age of optimism or, to use an expression of Sir Roland Wilson's, of "stagnation," and the Benthamite era of scientific law reform. In 1875 the progress of socialism or collectivism had hardly arrested attention. It had already begun, but had only begun, to enter the sphere of legislative opinion; Sir Roland Wilson could not, therefore, describe its effects. It would be a happy result of my book should it suggest to him to perform the public service of re-editing his treatise and bringing it up to date, or at any rate to the end of the nineteenth century.

To my cousin, Leslie Stephen, I am under obligations of a somewhat different character. For years past I have studied all his writings with care and admiration, and, in common, no doubt, with hundreds of other readers, have derived from them invaluable suggestions as to the relation between the thought and the circumstances of every age. Ideas thus suggested have aided me in almost every page of my book. Of his *English Utilitarians*

I have made the utmost use, but, as the book was published two years after my lectures at Harvard were written and delivered, and the lines of my work were finally laid down, I gained less direct help from his analysis of utilitarianism than I should have done had it appeared at an earlier date. The fact, however, that I found myself in substantial agreement with most of his views as to the utilitarian school, much strengthened my confidence in already-formed conclusions. There is a special satisfaction in dwelling on the help derived from Leslie Stephen's thoughts, for I feel there is some danger lest his skill and charm as a biographer should for the moment conceal from the public his originality and profundity as a thinker. But it is a pain to reflect that delays in the completion of my task have prevented me from expressing my obligation to him at a time when the expression might have given him pleasure.

To the many persons who have in various ways furthered my work I tender my thanks. To one friend for the service rendered by reading the proofs of this work, and by the correction of errors and the suggestion of improvements, whilst it was going through the press, I owe an obligation which it was as pleasant to incur as it is impossible to repay. I have special reason to feel grateful to the kindness of Sir Alfred de Bock Porter for information, courteously given and hardly to be obtained from books, about the history and the working of the Ecclesiastical Commission; to my friend Mr. W. M. Geldart for reading pages of my work which refer to parts of the law of which he is in a special sense a master; to Mr. E. H. Pelham, of the Board of Education; to Mr. G. Holden, Assistant Librarian at All Souls; and to Mr. H. Tedder, Secretary and Librarian of the Athenaeum Club, for the verification of references which during an absence from books I could not verify for myself.

A. V. DICEY.
OXFORD, *May* 1905.

Preface to the Second Edition

THE BODY OF THIS WORK is a second edition, or a corrected reprint of the first edition, of my treatise on *Law and Public Opinion in England during the Nineteenth Century*. It is accompanied by a new Introduction, the object of which is to trace and to comment upon the rapid changes in English law and in English legislative opinion which have marked the early years of the twentieth century. In the attempt to perform a somewhat difficult task I have been much assisted by aid from many friends. Acknowledgments for such help are specially due to Professor Geldart, my successor as Vinerian Professor of English Law in the University of Oxford; to Professor Kenny, of Cambridge; and to Mr. A. B. Keith, of the Colonial Office. Nor can I omit to mention suggestions as to alterations in the modern law of France made to me by and also derived from the writings of Professor Duguit, and Professor Jéze. More information about recent French enactments than I have been able to use in a treatise which touches only incidentally on French law, has been obtained for me by my friend, Mr. André Colanéri, who has carefully examined recent French legislation in so far as it illustrates the development of socialistic ideas.

A. V. DICEY.
OXFORD, 1914.

LECTURES

ON

THE RELATION BETWEEN

LAW & PUBLIC OPINION
IN ENGLAND

DURING THE NINETEENTH CENTURY

BY

A. V. DICEY, K.C., Hon. D.C.L.

OF THE INNER TEMPLE; FORMERLY VINERIAN PROFESSOR OF ENGLISH LAW

FELLOW OF ALL SOULS COLLEGE, OXFORD; HON. LL.D. CAMBRIDGE, GLASGOW, AND EDINBURGH

AUTHOR OF 'INTRODUCTION TO THE STUDY OF THE LAW OF THE CONSTITUTION'

MACMILLAN AND CO., LIMITED
ST. MARTIN'S STREET, LONDON
1917

The Relation between Law and Public Opinion

MY AIM IN THESE LECTURES is to exhibit the close dependence of legislation, and even of the absence of legislation, in England during the nineteenth century upon the varying currents of public opinion.[1]

The fact of this dependence will be assumed by most students with even too great readiness. We are all of us so accustomed to endow public opinion with a mysterious or almost supernatural power, that we neglect to examine what it is that we mean by public opinion, to measure the true limits of its authority, and to ascertain the mode of its operation. Surprise may indeed be felt, not at the statement that law depends upon opinion, but at this assertion being limited to England, and to England during the last century. The limitation, however, is intentional, and admits of full justification.

True indeed it is that the existence and the alteration of human institutions must, in a sense, always and everywhere depend upon the beliefs or feelings, or, in other words, upon the opinion of the society in which such institutions flourish.

"As force," writes Hume,

is always on the side of the governed, the governors have nothing to support them but opinion. It is, therefore, on opinion only that government is founded; and this maxim extends to the most despotic and most military governments, as well as to the most free and most popular. The Soldan of Egypt, or the Emperor of Rome, might drive his harmless subjects, like brute beasts, against

---

1. "Opinion rules everything." Napoleon, cited in *Life* by Fournier, Eng. trans. vol. ii. p. 446.

their sentiments and inclination; but he must, at least, have led his mame-lukes, or praetorian bands, like men, by their opinion.[2]

And so true is this observation that the authority even of a Southern planter over his slaves rested at bottom upon the opinion of the negroes whom he at his pleasure flogged or killed. Their combined physical force exceeded the planter's own personal strength, and the strength of the few whites who might be expected to stand by him. The blacks obeyed the slave-owner from the opinion, whether well or ill founded, that in the long run they would in a contest with their masters have the worst of the fight; and even more from that habit of submission which, though enforced by the occasional punishment of rebels, was grounded upon a number of complicated sentiments, such, for example, as admiration for superior abil-ity and courage, or gratitude for kindness, which cannot by any fair analysis be reduced to a mere form of fear, but constitute a kind of prevalent moral atmosphere. The whites, in short, ruled in virtue of the opinion, enter-tained by their slaves no less than by themselves, that the slave-owners possessed qualities which gave them the might, and even the right, to be masters. With the rightness or wrongness of this conviction we are not here in any way concerned. Its existence is adduced only as a proof that, even in the most extreme case conceivable, Hume's doctrine holds good, and the opinion of the governed is the real foundation of all government.

But, though obedience to law must of necessity be enforced by opinion of some sort, and Hume's paradox thus turns out to be a truism, this statement does not involve the admission that the law of every country is itself the result of what we mean by "public opinion." This term, when used in reference to legislation, is merely a short way of describing the belief or conviction prevalent in a given society that particular laws are beneficial, and therefore ought to be maintained, or that they are harmful, and therefore ought to be modified or repealed. And the assertion that public opinion governs legislation in a particular country, means that laws are there maintained or repealed in accordance with the opinion or wishes of its inhabitants. Now this assertion, though it is, if properly understood, true with regard to England at the present day, is clearly not true of all

2. Hume, *Essays*, vol. i., Essay iv. p. 110: Green and Grose.

countries, at all times, and indeed has not always been true even of England.

For, in the first place, there exist many communities in which public opinion—if by that term be meant speculative views held by the mass of the people as to the alteration or improvement of their institutions—can hardly be said to have any existence. The members of such societies are influenced by habits rather than by thoughts. Their mode of life is determined by customary rules, which may indeed have originated in the necessities of a given social condition, or even in speculative doctrines entertained by ancient law-givers, but which, whatever be their origin, assuredly owe their continuance to use and wont. It is, in truth, only under the peculiar conditions of an advanced civilisation that opinion dictates legislative change. In many Eastern countries, opinion—which is better described as traditional or instinctive feeling—has for ages been, in general, hostile to change and favourable to the maintenance of inherited habits. There, as in the West, opinion, in a very wide sense of that word, rules; but such aversion to change as for ages keeps a society within the limits of traditional action, is a very different thing from the public opinion which in the England of the nineteenth and twentieth centuries has demanded constant improvements in the law of the land.

It is possible, in the second place, to point to realms where laws and institutions have been altered or revolutionised in deference to opinion, but where the beliefs which have guided legislative reform have not been what we mean in England by "public" opinion. They have been, not ideas entertained by the inhabitants of a country, or by the greater part thereof, but convictions held by a small number of men, or even by a single individual who happened to be placed in a position of commanding authority. We must, indeed, remember that no ruler, however powerful, can stand completely alone, and that the despots who have caused or guided revolutions have been influenced by the opinion, if not of their own country, yet of their generation. But it may be asserted with substantial truth that Peter the Great laid the foundation of Russian power without much deference to the opinion of Russia, and that modern Prussia was created by Frederick the Great, who certainly drew his ideas of good government from other than Prussian sources. It was not, then, the public opinion of the Russian people or the public opinion of the Prussians, but the convictions of a single man which in each case moulded the laws and institutions of a powerful country. At this moment legislation in British India is the work of a body of English specialists who follow to a great extent the current of English opinion. They are, indeed, it is to be hoped, guided far more by their own experience and by their practical knowledge of India, than by English sentiment; but Anglo-Indian officials though they may not always obey the transitory feelings of the English public, certainly do not represent Indian public opinion.

In the third place, the law of a country may fail, for a time, to represent public opinion owing to the lack of any legislative organ which adequately responds to the sentiment of the age. A portion, at least, of that accumulation of abuses, which was the cause or the occasion of the French Revolution, may fairly be ascribed to the want of any legislative body possessing both the power and the will to carry out reforms which had long been demanded by the intelligence of the French nation. Some critics may, it is true, deny that a legislative organ was lacking: a French king held in his hands under the *ancien régime* an authority nearly approaching to sovereign power, and an enlightened despot might, it has been suggested, have conferred upon the country all the benefits promised by the Revolution. But the power of the French Crown was practically more limited than modern critics always perceive, whilst the circumstances no less than the character of Louis XV. and Louis XVI. disqualified these monarchs for performing the part of enlightened despots. The "Parliaments," again, which assuredly possessed some legislative power, might, it has been argued, have reformed the laws and institutions of the country. But the Parliaments were after all Courts, not legislatures, and represented the prejudices of lawyers, not the aspirations of reformers; Frenchmen, zealous for the removal of abuses, looked, as a matter of fact, with more hope to the action of the king than to the legislation of Parliaments which represented the antiquated conservatism of a past age. The want, then, of a legislative organ was in France a check upon the influence of public opinion. Nor can it be denied that even in England defective legislative machinery has at times lessened the immediate influence of opinion. The chief cause, no doubt, of the arrest of almost every kind of reform during the latest years of the eighteenth and the earlier part of the nineteenth century, was a state of feeling so hostile to revolution that it forbade the most salutary innovations. But "legislative stagnation," as it has been termed, lasted in England for at least ten or twenty years beyond the date when it ought naturally to have come to an end; and it can hardly be disputed that this delay in the improvement of English institutions was due in part to the defects of the unreformed Parliament—that is, to the non-existence of a satisfactory legislative organ.

The close and immediate connection then, which in modern England exists between public opinion and legislation is a very peculiar and noteworthy fact, to which we cannot easily find a parallel. Nowhere have changes in popular convictions or wishes found anything like such rapid and immediate expression in alterations of the law as they have in Great Britain during the nineteenth century, and more especially during the last half thereof. France is the land of revolution, England is renowned for conservatism, but a glance at the legal history of each country suggests the existence of some error in the popular contrast between French mutability and English unchangeableness. In spite of revolutions at Paris, the fundamental provisions of the Code Napoléon have stood to a great extent unaltered since its publication in 1804, and before 1900 the Code had become invested with a sort of legal sanctity which secured it against sudden and sweeping change. In 1804 George the Third was on the throne, and English opinion was then set dead against every legal or political change, yet there is now hardly a part of the English statute-book which between 1804 and the present day has not been changed in form or in substance; and the alterations enacted by Parliament have been equalled or exceeded by innovations due to the judge-made law of the Courts. The United States of America, again, have been under the government of a pure democracy, and in no country is the expression of opinion more free; but the whole history of the United States shows that federal legislation, at any rate, does not lend itself easily to large and sudden changes, nor do alterations introduced by State legislation appear to have been on the whole either fundamental or rapid.

This condition of legislative quiescence, it may be objected, is, in the case both of France and of the United States, due to a condition of opinion hostile to legal innovations, and therefore in no way shows that public opinion cannot as easily effect alterations in the law of the land as it can in England, and this suggestion contains a certain amount of truth. The

occasional outbreak of revolution has among Frenchmen been unfavourable to that habit of constantly and gradually amending the law, which has
become natural to Englishmen, whilst admiration for American institutions and a certain general satisfaction with things as they are, have in the
United States created a remarkable kind of legal conservatism. The condition of opinion is, however, not the only reason for the existence of
legislative quiescence both in the greatest of European and in the greatest
of American Republics. In neither country are there wanting critics of the
national institutions, but in neither has effective criticism usually led so
easily to legislation as in England. The difficulty imposed by many French
constitutions on meeting with rapidity the requirements of public opinion
has not only been an excuse for revolutionary violence, but has also hindered the gradual amendment of the law of France; nor is it irrelevant to
note that the constitution of the Third Republic renders the Parliament a
body which responds more easily to the immediate sentiment of the moment, than any legislature which has existed in France since the National
Assembly of 1789, and that simultaneously with this change, a tendency
towards the introduction of amendments into the law of the country has
begun to make itself apparent. In the United States the Federal Constitution limits the power both of Congress and of the State legislatures; and
the hands of any State legislature, be it noted, are tied by the articles, not
only of the Federal Constitution, but also of the State Constitution, whilst
throughout the United States there exists a tendency to restrict more and
more closely the authority of the State representative assemblies. The constitutionalism, then, of the United States, no less than of France, has told
against the promotion of that constant legislative activity which is a characteristic feature of modern English life. From whatever point of view, in
short, the matter be regarded, it becomes apparent that during the last
seventy-five years or more public opinion has exercised in England a direct
and immediate control over legislation which it does not even now exert
in most other civilised countries.

There are, then, to be found three different reasons why we cannot assert
of all countries, or of any country at all times, that laws are there the result
of public opinion. No "opinion," in the proper sense of that word, with
regard to the change of the law may exist; the opinion which does direct
the development of the law may not be "public opinion"; and lastly, there

may be lacking any legislative organ adapted for carrying out the changes of the law demanded by public opinion.

In England, however, the beliefs or sentiments which, during the nineteenth century, have governed the development of the law have in strictness been public opinion, for they have been the wishes and ideas as to legislation held by the people of England, or, to speak with more precision, by the majority of those citizens who have at a given moment taken an effective part in public life.

And here the obvious conclusion suggests itself that the public opinion which governs a country is the opinion of the sovereign, whether the sovereign be a monarch, an aristocracy, or the mass of the people.

This conclusion, however, though roughly true, cannot be accepted without considerable reservation. The sovereign power may hold that a certain kind of legislation is in itself expedient, but may at the same time be unwilling, or even unable, to carry this conviction into effect, and this from the dread of offending the feelings of subjects who, though they in general take no active share in public affairs, may raise an insuperable opposition to laws which disturb their habits or shock their moral sentiment; it is well indeed, thus early in these lectures, to note that the public opinion which finds expression in legislation is a very complex phenomenon, and often takes the form of a compromise resulting from a conflict between the ideas of the government and the feelings or habits of the governed. This holds good in all countries, whatever be their form of government, but is more manifest than elsewhere in a country such as England, where the legislation enacted by Parliament constantly bears traces of the compromise arrived at between enlightenment and prejudice. The failure of Parliament during the eighteenth century to introduce reasonable reforms, for instance, was due far less to the prejudices of members of Parliament, or even of the electorate, than to the deference which statesmen instinctively, and on the whole wisely, paid to the dulness or stupidity of Englishmen, many of whom had no votes, and were certainly not able to dictate by constitutional means to Parliament. Walpole and his Whig associates were utterly free from bigotry, yet Walpole would never consent to relieve Dissenters from the Test Act, though Dissenters were his most strenuous supporters. The Act facilitating the naturalisation of Jews was, in obedience to popular clamour, repealed in the next session after it had been passed. Even the amendment of the calendar was found to be a matter of great difficulty; the ignorance of the electors was imposed upon by the phrase that they had been robbed of eleven days. The moderate measure of 1778 for the mitigation of the penal laws against Roman Catholics gave rise in 1780 to an outbreak of revolutionary violence; and the Lord George Gordon Riots explain, if they do not justify, the long delay of Catholic Emancipation. But the Roman Catholic Relief Act of 1829 is itself the most striking monument of legislative compromise. The measure was carried by reformers who desired the removal of all the political disabilities under which the Roman Catholics of the United Kingdom suffered, but it contains stringent provisions on the face of them intended to banish from the United Kingdom "every Jesuit and every member of any other religious order, community, or society of the Church of Rome bound by monastic or religious vows."[3] How does it happen that a law restoring to Roman Catholics the rights of citizenship, contained penal laws against Jesuits and monks? The answer lies close at hand. The general scope of the Act represents the enlightenment of a governing class which, by favour of peculiar circumstances, carried through a scheme of religious toleration opposed to the prejudices of the people. Penal enactments threatening Jesuits and monks with a banishment, which had never in a single instance been put in force, are the monument of a concession made by parliamentary statesmanship to vulgar bigotry.[4]

The principle that the development of law depends upon opinion is, however, open to one objection.

Men legislate, it may be urged, not in accordance with their opinion as to what is a good law, but in accordance with their interest, and this, it may be added, is emphatically true of classes as contrasted with individuals, and therefore of a country like England, where classes exert a far more potent control over the making of laws than can any single person.

Now it must at once be granted that in matters of legislation men are

3. See Roman Catholic Relief Act, 1829, ss. 28–36. These enactments (which do not apply to religious orders of women, *ibid.* s. 37) have never been enforced.

4. So the Ecclesiastical Titles Act, 1851, prohibiting the assumption of ecclesiastical titles, is a record of popular panic caused by Papal aggression, whilst the absolute non-enforcement, and the subsequent repeal of the Act in 1871, mark the tolerant spirit of Parliament.

guided in the main by their real or apparent interest. So true is this, that from the inspection of the laws of a country it is often possible to conjecture, and this without much hesitation, what is the class which holds, or has held, predominant power at a given time. No man could cast a glance at the laws and institutions of the middle ages without seeing that power then went with ownership of land. Wherever agriculturalists are predominant you will find laws favouring the cultivators of the soil, and if you discover laws passed for the special benefit of manufacturers or artisans, you may be certain that these classes, in some way or other, are or were of political weight. Who could look into the statute-book of Jamaica or South Carolina without discovering that at one time the whites were despotic masters of the blacks? Who could contrast the English land law with the modern land law of France and fail to perceive that political authority has in England been in the hands of large landowners, and is in the France of to-day in the hands of small proprietors? The criminal law of the eighteenth century, and also many of its trade laws, bear witness to the growing influence of merchants. The free-trade legislation of 1846 and the succeeding years tells us that political authority had come into the hands of manufacturers and traders. Nor would any man, even though he knew not the history of our Parliamentary Reform Acts, hesitate, from the gist of modern statutes, to infer that during the nineteenth century, first the middle classes, then the artisans of our towns, and lastly the country labourers, had obtained an increase of political power. The connection, however, between legislation and the supposed interests of the legislators is so obvious that the topic hardly requires illustration.

The answer to the objection under consideration is, however, easy to find.

"Though men," to use the words of Hume, "be much governed by interest, yet even interest itself, and all human affairs, are entirely governed by *opinion*."[5] Even, therefore, were we to assume that the persons who have power to make law are solely and wholly influenced by the desire to promote their own personal and selfish interests, yet their view of their interest and therefore their legislation must be determined by their opinion; and

5. Hume, *Essays*, vol. i. Essay vii. p. 125.

hence, where the public has influence, the development of the law must of necessity be governed by public opinion.

But though this answer is sufficient, there exists so much misunderstanding as to the connection between men's interests and their beliefs that it is well to pursue the matter a step further. The citizens of a civilised country, such as England, are for the most part not recklessly selfish in the ordinary sense of that word; they wish, no doubt, to promote their own interests—that is, to increase their own pleasures and to diminish their own discomforts, but they certainly do not intend to sacrifice, to their own private advantage or emolument, either the happiness of their neighbours or the welfare of the State. Individuals, indeed, and still more frequently classes, do constantly support laws or institutions which they deem beneficial to themselves, but which certainly are in fact injurious to the rest of the world. But the explanation of this conduct will be found, in nine cases out of ten, to be that men come easily to believe that arrangements agreeable to themselves are beneficial to others. A man's interest gives a bias to his judgment far oftener than it corrupts his heart. The heir of an English landowner is convinced that the law of primogeniture is a blessing to the country, but, if he looks too favourably upon a scheme for the devolution of property, which most Frenchmen consider patently unjust, his "sinister interest" (to use a favourite term of Bentham's) affects him with stupidity rather than with selfishness. He overestimates and keeps constantly before his mind the strength of the arguments in favour of, and underestimates, or never considers at all, the force of the arguments against, the principle of primogeniture which, whatever its evils, confers upon him a large estate and an influential position. English manufacturers were sincere believers in protection as long as they thought it beneficial to trade, and became equally sincere enthusiasts for freedom of trade from the moment they were convinced that free trade in corn would be favourable to commerce and would give additional weight to the manufacturing interest. Landlords and farmers who found their gain in keeping up the price of corn were in general perfectly honest protectionists, and were convinced that protection, by rendering the country self-supporting and extending the sphere of agriculture, was of the greatest benefit to the nation. At this day an artisan who holds that the welfare of working men, in which his own prosperity is included, is promoted by trade-unionism, is honestly convinced that there can be little evil in practices which, though they certainly trench upon the personal freedom of individual workmen, enhance the authority of trade unions. It is well to insist upon the true relation between self-interest and belief, because ardent reformers, and notably Bentham and his disciples, have at times misunderstood it, and have used language which implied that every opponent of progress was, if not a fool, then a rogue, who deliberately preferred his own private advantage to the general benefit of mankind, whereas in reality he will be found in most cases to have been an honest man of average ability, who has opposed a beneficial change not through exceptional selfishness, but through some intellectual delusion unconsciously created by the bias of a sinister interest. Take the extreme case of American slave-owners. It will not be denied that, at the outbreak of the War of Secession, there were to be found in the South many fervent enthusiasts for slavery (or rather for the social system of which it was a necessary part), just as there were to be found in the North a far greater number of ardent enthusiasts for abolition. Some Southerners at least did undoubtedly hold the bona fide belief that slavery was the source of benefit, not only to the planters, but to the slaves, and indirectly to the whole civilised world. Such Southern fanatics were wrong and the Abolitionists were right. The faith in slavery was a delusion; but a delusion, however largely the result of self-interest, is still an intellectual error, and a different thing from callous selfishness. It is at any rate an opinion. In the case, therefore, of Southerners who resisted the passing of any law for the abolition of slavery, as in all similar instances, we are justified in saying that it is at bottom opinion which controls legislation.

Characteristics of Law-making Opinion in England

LET IT BE HERE NOTED once for all that these lectures have a very precise and limited scope; they are primarily concerned with public opinion only during the nineteenth century; they are concerned, directly at least, even for this period, only with that kind of public opinion which, since it has told on the course of legislation, may with strict propriety be called law-making or legislative public opinion, and is recorded either in the statute-book, which contains the laws enacted by Parliament, or in the volumes of the reports, which contain the laws indirectly but not less truly enacted by the Courts.[1]

The limited aim of these lectures explains, in the first place, why it is that I have attempted only a very general or broad account of different schools of opinion, *e.g.* either of individualism or of socialism;[2] fine and subtle distinctions, such as the speculative differences which divide the absolute individualism of Herbert Spencer on the one hand, from the practical or utilitarian individualism of J. S. Mill and H. Sidgwick on the other, have not materially affected legislation; they are therefore appropriate rather to a work dealing with political philosophy, than to lectures on the relation between the actual current of opinion and actual legislation in England during a given period, and may be dismissed from our consideration. The limited scope of these lectures explains, in the second place, why it is that they contain nothing about the extreme forms either of individualism or of socialism. Extreme and logically coherent theories have, during the nineteenth century, exerted no material effect on the law of

1. As to judicial legislation and public opinion, see Lect. XI., *post.*
2. In these lectures generally termed "collectivism." See Lect. IV. p. 46, *post.*

England. It is moderate, though it may be inconsistent individualism alone, as it is moderate, though it may be inconsistent socialism alone, which has told upon the making of English laws, and which therefore can claim to be legislative public opinion. With the individualism which all but demands the abolition of the national Post Office we need trouble ourselves as little as with the socialism which advocates the nationalisation of the land.

When we talk of legislative public opinion we should not forget that such opinion may bear a merely negative character, and operate not by making laws but by forbidding their enactment. It is, in short, a force which may act either, as it does nowadays, in favour of innovation, or, as it did in the early part of the nineteenth century, in favour of conservatism. In England, indeed, periods of legislative activity have always been exceptional. They may be reduced to four, namely, the era of Edward I., the age of the Tudors, the period of the Restoration, and the years which, commencing a little before, have followed the Reform Act of 1832. Nor need the fact that the absence of energetic legislation has been emphatically the rule, not the exception, cause us surprise. In any country which is governed in accordance with the wishes of its inhabitants there will in general exist no effective desire for change. And this is a consideration worth notice, since the legislative activity which has more or less prevailed for the last seventy years produces among Englishmen the delusion that popular sentiment always favours vigorous legislation. The experience, at any rate, of democratic countries where the constitution provides a regular mode of appeal from the legislature to the people, proves that the voice of the people may be just as ready to check as to stimulate the energy of parliamentary law-makers. It is at least possible that in England the legislative activity of Parliament may again decrease and the country enter upon another period of legislative inertia.

However this may be, public legislative opinion, as it has existed in England during the nineteenth century, presents several noteworthy aspects or characteristics. They may conveniently be considered under five heads— the existence at any given period of a predominant public opinion; the origin of such opinion; the development and continuity thereof; the checks imposed on such opinion by the existence of counter-currents and cross-currents of opinion; the action of laws themselves as the creators of legislative opinion.

First, There exists at any given time a body of beliefs, convictions, sentiments, accepted principles, or firmly-rooted prejudices, which, taken together, make up the public opinion[3] of a particular era, or what we may call the reigning or predominant current of opinion, and, as regards at any rate the last three or four centuries, and especially the nineteenth century, the influence of this dominant current of opinion has, in England, if we look at the matter broadly, determined, directly or indirectly, the course of legislation.

It may be added that the whole body of beliefs existing in any given age may generally be traced to certain fundamental assumptions which at the time, whether they be actually true or false, are believed by the mass of the world to be true with such confidence that they hardly appear to bear the character of assumptions. Before the Reformation, for example, the authority of the Church, and of the Papacy as its visible head, was generally admitted throughout Western Europe both by thinkers and by men of action. As to the nature and limits of this authority there were no doubt wide differences of belief, but the general opinion of the time recognised the authority of the Church and the Papacy in matters of religion as past dispute. A belief, in short, which in later ages has been rejected by many men and by the population of many countries, as not only untrue but even incredible, seemed at one period so well established that its truth was among statesmen and thinkers hardly matter of debate.

The large currents, again, of public opinion which in the main determine legislation, acquire their force and volume only by degrees, and are in their turn liable to be checked or superseded by other and adverse currents, which themselves gain strength only after a considerable lapse of time. For example, the whole way in which, during the sixteenth and the seventeenth centuries, men looked at the regulation of labour or the fixing of prices by the State—a view which finds expression in Tudor legislation, and has the closest connection with the Elizabethan poor law—is the result of a body of beliefs favouring State intervention in matters of trade no less than in

---

3. Peel in a letter to Croker (March 23, 1820) describes public opinion as "the tone of England—of that great compound of folly, weakness, prejudice, wrong feeling, right feeling, obstinacy, and newspaper paragraphs, which is called public opinion." See Thursfield's *Peel,* p. 19. [Editor's note: This footnote was added in the second edition.]

matters of religion, and had been growing up during many generations. This confidence in the authority of the State was in the seventeenth and eighteenth centuries superseded by a different body of beliefs which pointed at any rate towards the conclusion that the chief, though not the sole, duty of the State is to protect men's persons and property,[4] so as to secure the maximum of freedom for each man compatible with the existence of the like freedom on the part of others. All that need here be noted is that any fundamental change of convictions which inevitably affects legislation in all directions has, in England at least, always gone on slowly and gradually, and has been in this respect like the gradual rising of the tide. Nor does the likeness end here, for an alteration in the condition of opinion more often than not, begins just at the very time when the predominant beliefs of a particular age seem to exert their utmost power. The height of the tide immediately precedes its ebb.

Secondly, The opinion which affects the development of the law has, in modern England at least, often originated with some single thinker or school of thinkers.

No doubt it is at times allowable to talk of a prevalent belief or opinion as "being in the air," by which expression is meant that a particular way of looking at things has become the common possession of all the world. But though a belief when it prevails, may at last be adopted by the whole of a generation, it rarely happens that a widespread conviction has grown up spontaneously among the multitude. "The initiation," it has been said, "of all wise or noble things, comes and must come, from individuals; generally at first from some one individual;"[5] to which it ought surely to be added that the origination of a new folly or of a new form of baseness comes, and must in general come, at first from individuals or from some one individual. The peculiarity of individuals, as contrasted with the crowd, lies neither in virtue nor in wickedness but in originality. It is idle to credit minorities with all the good without ascribing to them most at least of the evils due to that rarest of all human qualities—inventiveness.

The course of events in England may often at least be thus described: A new and, let us assume, a true idea presents itself to some one man of

---

4. Compare Macaulay's essay on "Gladstone on Church and State."
5. Mill, *On Liberty,* p. 119.

originality or genius;[6] the discoverer of the new conception, or some follower who has embraced it with enthusiasm, preaches it to his friends or
disciples, they in their turn become impressed with its importance and its
truth, and gradually a whole school accept the new creed. These apostles
of a new faith are either persons endowed with special ability or, what is
quite as likely, they are persons who, owing to their peculiar position, are
freed from a bias, whether moral or intellectual, in favour of prevalent
errors. At last the preachers of truth make an impression, either directly
upon the general public or upon some person of eminence, say a leading
statesman, who stands in a position to impress ordinary people and thus
to win the support of the nation. Success, however, in converting mankind
to a new faith, whether religious, or economical, or political, depends but
slightly on the strength of the reasoning by which the faith can be defended,
or even on the enthusiasm of its adherents. A change of belief arises, in
the main, from the occurrence of circumstances which incline the majority
of the world to hear with favour theories which, at one time, men of
common sense derided as absurdities, or distrusted as paradoxes.[7] The
doctrine of free trade, for instance, has in England, for about half a century,[8] held the field as an unassailable dogma of economic policy, but an
historian would stand convicted of ignorance or folly who should imagine
that the fallacies of protection were discovered by the intuitive good sense
of the people, even if the existence of such a quality as the good sense of

6. It may very well, owing to the condition of the world, and especially to the progress
of knowledge, present itself at the same time to two or more persons who have had no
intercommunication. Bentham and Paley formed nearly at the same date a utilitarian system
of morals. Darwin and Wallace, while each ignorant of the other's labours, thought out
substantially the same theory as to the origin of species.

7. To take an historic instance of world-wide celebrity, it is certain that the destruction
of Jerusalem must have done at least as much as Pauline or other teaching towards winning
over to Christianity Jews or Jewish proselytes.

8. Written 1898. [Editor's note: The following was added in the second edition.] Carlyle
was in 1846 a convinced Free Trader. He thought he had found his strong man in Peel. The
Repeal of the Corn Laws seemed to prove it. "Whatever," said he, "were the spoken unve-
racities of Parliament—and they are many on all hands, lamentable to Gods and men—here
has a great veracity been *done* in Parliament, considerably our greatest for many years past;
a strenuous, courageous, and needful thing." Cromwell's *Letters and Speeches,* Firth's Introduction, p. xlix.

the people be more than a political fiction. The principle of free trade may, as far as Englishmen are concerned, be treated as the doctrine of Adam Smith. The reasons in its favour never have been, nor will, from the nature of things, be mastered by the majority of any people. The apology for freedom of commerce will always present, from one point of view, an air of paradox. Every man feels or thinks that protection would benefit his own business, and it is difficult to realise that what may be a benefit for any man taken alone, may be of no benefit to a body of men looked at collectively. The obvious objections to free trade may, as free traders conceive, be met; but then the reasoning by which these objections are met is often elaborate and subtle, and does not carry conviction to the crowd. It is idle to suppose that belief in freedom of trade—or indeed any other creed—ever won its way among the majority of converts by the mere force of reasoning. The course of events was very different. The theory of free trade won by degrees the approval of statesmen of special insight, and adherents to the new economic religion were one by one gained among persons of intelligence. Cobden and Bright finally became potent advocates of truths of which they were in no sense the discoverers. This assertion in no way detracts from the credit due to these eminent men. They performed to admiration the proper function of popular leaders; by prodigies of energy, and by seizing a favourable opportunity, of which they made the very most use that was possible, they gained the acceptance by the English people of truths which have rarely, in any country but England, acquired popularity. Much was due to the opportuneness of the time. Protection wears its most offensive guise when it can be identified with a tax on bread, and therefore can, without patent injustice, be described as the parent of famine and starvation. The unpopularity, moreover, inherent in a tax on corn is all but fatal to a protective tariff when the class which protection enriches is comparatively small, whilst the class which would suffer keenly from dearness of bread and would obtain benefit from free trade is large, and having already acquired much, is certain soon to acquire more political power. Add to all this that the Irish famine made the suspension of the corn laws a patent necessity. It is easy, then, to see how great in England was the part played by external circumstances—one might almost say by accidental conditions—in determining the overthrow of protection. A student should further remark that after free trade became an established principle of English policy, the majority of the English people accepted it mainly on authority. Men, who were neither land-owners nor farmers, perceived with ease the obtrusive evils of a tax on corn, but they and their leaders were far less influenced by arguments against protection generally than by the immediate and almost visible advantage of cheapening the bread of artisans and labourers. What, however, weighed with most Englishmen, above every other consideration, was the harmony of the doctrine that commerce ought to be free, with that disbelief in the benefits of State intervention which in 1846 had been gaining ground for more than a generation.[9]

It is impossible, indeed, to insist too strongly upon the consideration that whilst opinion controls legislation, public opinion is itself far less the result of reasoning or of argument than of the circumstances in which men are placed. Between 1783 and 1861 negro slavery was abolished, one might almost say ceased of itself to exist, in the Northern States of the American Republic; in the South, on the other hand, the maintenance of slavery developed into a fixed policy, and before the War of Secession the "peculiar institution" had become the foundation-stone of the social system. But the religious beliefs and, except as regards the existence of slavery, the political institutions prevalent throughout the whole of the United States were the same. The condemnation of slavery in the North, and the apologies for slavery in the South, must therefore be referred to difference of circumstances. Slave labour was obviously out of place in Massachusetts, Vermont, or New York; it appeared to be, even if in reality it was not, economically profitable in South Carolina. An institution, again, which was utterly incompatible with the social condition of the Northern States harmonised, or appeared to harmonise, with the social conditions of the Southern States. The arguments against the peculiar institution were in themselves equally strong in whatever part of the Union they were uttered, but they

9. It has been argued, by critics entitled to respect, that Cobden, when he entered into a commercial treaty with France, compromised, for the sake of a limited extension of free trade, the principles on which alone free trade admits of complete defence. Cobden was a keen logician, and more nearly a systematic thinker than most politicians; this criticism, therefore, on the treaty with France, if it be to any extent sound, affords a striking example of the slight effect which the abstract arguments against protection might produce on the mind even of a leading free trader.

carried conviction to the white citizens of Massachusetts, whilst, even when heard or read, they did not carry conviction to the citizens of South Carolina. Belief, and, to speak fairly, honest belief, was to a great extent the result not of argument, nor even of direct self-interest, but of circumstances. What was true in this instance holds good in others. There is no reason to suppose that in 1830 the squires of England were less patriotic than the manufacturers, or less capable of mastering the arguments in favour of or against the reform of Parliament. But every one knows that, as a rule, the country gentlemen were Tories and anti-reformers, whilst the manufacturers were Radicals and reformers. Circumstances are the creators of most men's opinions.

Thirdly, The development of public opinion generally, and therefore of legislative opinion, has been in England at once gradual, or slow, and continuous.

The qualities of slowness and continuity may conveniently be considered together, and are closely interconnected, but they are distinguishable and essentially different.

Legislative public opinion generally changes in England with unexpected slowness.

Adam Smith's *Wealth of Nations* was published in 1776; the policy of free exchange was not completely accepted by England till 1846. All the strongest reasons in favour of Catholic emancipation were laid before the English world by Burke between 1760 and 1797; the Roman Catholic Relief Act was not carried till 1829. On no point whatever was Bentham's teaching more manifestly sound than in his attack on rules unnecessarily excluding evidence, and, *inter alia,* the evidence of the parties to an action or prosecution. His *Rationale of Judicial Evidence specially applied to English Practice* was published in 1827, and his principles had been made known before that date, yet even the restrictions on the evidence of the parties to proceedings at law were not completely removed till 1898. Nor is this slow growth of opinion peculiar to the legislation advocated by any one school. The line of Factory Acts begins in 1802; the movement of which they are the outward result achieved its first decided triumph in 1847, and received its systematic, though assuredly not its final development in the labour code known as the Factory and Workshop Act, 1901. Owing to the habitual conservatism to be found even among ardent reformers when leaders of

Englishmen, and to the customs of our parliamentary government, the development of legislative opinion is rendered still slower by our inveterate preference for fragmentary and gradual legislation. Only in exceptional cases and under the pressure of some crisis can English legislators be induced to carry out a broad principle at one stroke, to its logical and necessary consequences. Before the end of the eighteenth century Englishmen of intelligence had ceased to believe that Roman Catholicism could be rightly treated as a crime, and come to doubt whether it was a fair ground of political disability. But the penal laws against Roman Catholics were relaxed only by degrees; they were mitigated in 1778 (18 Geo. III. c. 60), and again in 1791 (31 Geo. III. c. 32). It was not till 1829 that professors of the old faith were granted substantial political equality, and since the passing of the Catholic Relief Act, 1829, more than one Act of Parliament has been needed in order to remove the remnants of the old penal laws. The broad principle that religious belief or disbelief ought not in any way to deprive a man of political rights or civil rights, has at last been in the main accepted by the English people, but it has needed a whole line of enactments from the Toleration Act, 1688, to the Oaths Act, 1888,[10] to give all but complete effect to this accepted idea. The modern labour code[11] is the fruit of more than forty enactments extending over the greater part of the nineteenth century. The mitigation of our criminal law has been carried out by a long series of separate Acts, each dealing with special offences. Even the gross brutality of the pillory was not got rid of at one blow. In 1816 it was reserved for a limited number of crimes (56 Geo. III. c. 138); in 1837 it was at last abolished (7 Will. IV. & 1 Vict. c. 23). If capital offences have been reduced from at least 160 to 2, this humanisation of our law is the consequence of a series of Acts dating from the beginning of the nineteenth century, and passed for the most part between 1827 and 1861. Here, as elsewhere, exceptions prove the rule. The early energy of the generation which, wearied with toryism, carried the Reform Act, effected for a short

10. See Anson, *Law and Custom of the Constitution,* Part I. Parliament (3rd ed.), pp. 96, 97.

11. See for list of Factory Acts, extending from the Health and Morals Act, 1802, 42 Geo. III. c. 73, to the Factory and Workshop Act, 1901, 1 Edw. VII. c. 22, Hutchins and Harrison, *History of Factory Legislation,* p. 323.

time legislation which to its authors seemed sweeping and thoroughgoing. The Reform Act itself startled the Whigs by whom it was carried. The Municipal Reform Act, 1836, swept away at once a mass of antiquated abuses; above all, the Poor Law Amendment Act, 1834, did in reality introduce, and introduce at once, a fundamental revolution in the social condition of England. But even these laws fell far short of giving full effect to the principles which they more or less embodied; the Reform Act had no finality, and the Municipal Corporations Act, 1882,[12] bears witness in its list of sixty-eight repealed enactments to the gradual procedure by which modern municipal government has received its development.[13]

The slowness with which legislative opinion acts is not quite the same thing as its continuity, though the bit by bit or gradual system of law-making dear to Parliament, does in truth afford strong evidence that the course of opinion in England has certainly during the nineteenth century, and probably ever since parliamentary government became to any degree a reality, been continuous, *i.e.* has been rarely marked by sudden breaks.[14] In any case it is certain that during the nineteenth century the legislative opinion of the nation has never veered round with sudden violence.

To this general statement an objection may possibly be taken, based on the history of the great Reform Act. In 1832, it may be said, passionate enthusiasm for parliamentary reform and all the innovations to which it gave birth, displaced, as it were, in a moment the obstinate toryism which for nearly half a century had been the accepted creed, if not of the whole nation, yet assuredly of the governing classes; here we have a revolution in popular opinion of which the violence was equalled by the suddenness.

The objection is worth consideration, but can easily be met.

The true answer is, that there exists an important distinction between a change of public opinion and an alteration in the course of legislation. The one has in modern England never been rapid; the other has sometimes,

---

12. The best specimen of consolidation to be found in the statute-book.

13. To appreciate to the full the nature of this method one must remember that the sphere of municipal government has to a great extent been moulded by a vast number of private bills. See Clifford, *Private Bill Legislation.*

14. Nor does the apparent suddenness of the revolution in public sentiment at the time of the Restoration afford any real exception to the rule here laid down.

though rarely, been sudden; the history of the Reform Act admirably illustrates this difference. The spirit of Benthamite liberalism,[15] which in 1832 put an end to the reign of toryism, had developed slowly and gradually during a period of more than thirty years. We have here no sudden conversion of the people of England from one political faith to another; the really noteworthy fact is the length of time needed in order to convince Englishmen that their ancient institutions stood in need of alteration. Even when this conviction had been adopted by the mass of the middle classes, public opinion, owing to the constitution of the unreformed Parliament, could not be immediately transformed into legislative opinion. The very need for the reform of Parliament of itself prolonged for some years the period of legislative inactivity. At last the dominant opinion of the country, strengthened no doubt by external circumstances, such as the French Revolution of 1830, became the legislative opinion of the day. Liberalism of the Bethamite [sic] type was the political faith of the time. Its triumph was signalised by the Reform Act. Then, indeed, there did take place a startling change in legislation, but the suddenness of this change was due to the fact that a slowly developed revolution in public opinion had been held in check for years, and had, even when it became general, not been allowed to produce its proper effect on legislation; hence such an accumulation of abuses as made their rapid removal desirable, and in some cases possible. For, after all, the rapidity and the suddenness of the change in the course of legislation may easily be exaggerated. A critic who traces the history of special reforms which followed the Reform Act, is far more often struck by the slowness and the incompleteness, than by the rapidity of their execution. In any case the history of the Reform Act in reality supports the doctrine, that the development of legislative opinion has been throughout the nineteenth century slow and continuous.

This continuity is closely connected with some subordinate characteristics of English legislative opinion.

The opinion which changes the law is in one sense the opinion of the time when the law is actually altered; in another sense it has often been in England the opinion prevalent some twenty or thirty years before that time;

15. See Lect. VI., *post.*

it has been as often as not in reality the opinion not of to-day but of yesterday.

Legislative opinion must be the opinion of the day, because, when laws are altered, the alteration is of necessity carried into effect by legislators who act under the belief that the change is an amendment; but this law-making opinion is also the opinion of yesterday, because the beliefs which have at last gained such hold on the legislature as to produce an alteration in the law have generally been created by thinkers or writers, who exerted their influence long before the change in the law took place. Thus it may well happen that an innovation is carried through at a time when the teachers who supplied the arguments in its favour are in their graves, or even—and this is well worth noting—when in the world of speculation a movement has already set in against ideas which are exerting their full effect in the world of action and of legislation. Bentham's Defence of Usury[16] supplied every argument which is available against laws which check freedom of trade in money-lending. It was published in 1787; he died in 1832. The usury laws were wholly repealed in 1854, that is sixty-seven years after Bentham had demonstrated their futility; but in 1854 the opponents of Benthamism were slowly gaining the ear of the public, and the Money-lenders' Act, 1900, has shown that the almost irrebuttable presumption against the usury laws which was created by the reasoning of Bentham has lost its hold over men who have never taken the pains or shown the ability to confute Bentham's arguments. Nor is there anything mysterious about the way in which the thought or sentiment of yesterday governs the legislation or the politics of to-day. Law-making in England is the work of men well advanced in life; the politicians who guide the House of Commons, to say nothing of the peers who lead the House of Lords, are few of them below thirty, and most of them are above forty years of age. They have formed or picked up their convictions, and, what is of more consequence, their prepossessions, in early manhood, which is the one period of life when men are easily impressed with new ideas. Hence English legislators retain the prejudices or modes of thinking which they acquired in their youth; and when, late in life, they take a share in actual legislation,

---

16. Quaritch's *Catalogue*, No. 250, p. 84, contains a copy of Bentham on Usury, dated 1787. [Editor's note: This footnote was added in the second edition.]

they legislate in accordance with the doctrines which were current, either generally or in the society to which the law-givers belonged, in the days of their early manhood. The law-makers, therefore, of 1850 may give effect to the opinions of 1830, whilst the legislators of 1880 are likely enough to impress upon the statute-book the beliefs of 1860, or rather the ideas which in the one case attracted the young men of 1830, and in the other the youth of 1860.[17] We need not therefore be surprised to find that a current of opinion may exert its greatest legislative influence just when its force is beginning to decline. The tide turns when at its height; a school of thought or feeling which still governs law-makers has begun to lose its authority among men of a younger generation who are not yet able to influence legislation.

In England during the last three or four centuries, and especially during the nineteenth century, there has always at any given era existed some prevalent or dominant body of public opinion which in its turn has been succeeded by some different, it may be by some distinctly opposed, school of thought, but the periods during which each body of opinion has been more or less supreme, cannot be marked off from one another by any strict or rigid line. Currents of opinion have a tendency to run into one another; periods of opinion overlap.

Historians tell us that if we survey the era of the Reformation it is all but impossible to fix the exact date at which Englishmen definitely accepted Protestantism, and that the difficulty of fixing the date at which the country could be finally ranged among Protestant rather than Roman Catholic communities, arises from the fact that the change of belief, which ultimately became perfectly marked, was, in the case of individuals, if we study their personal history, and therefore in the case of the indefinite number of persons who made up the whole English nation, vague, partial, and ill-defined. Elizabeth carried through the Reformation, but Elizabeth entertained beliefs or sympathies which belonged rather to Roman Catholicism than to Protestantism. Of many among her courtiers and servants it is hardly possible to say whether they were Catholics or Protestants. Self-

---

17. One, though of course merely a minor, reason for the violence exhibited by the revolutionary legislation of the National Assembly was, it is said, that the leaders of that body were comparatively young men.

interest, no doubt, had a good deal to do with the easy transition of am-
bitious statesmen from one creed to another, in accordance with the wishes
of the reigning monarch or the exigencies of the time; a revolutionary era
is unfavourable to conscientious scrupulosity and promotes shiftiness. But
the conduct of a whole nation is governed by something better than sordid
views of self-interest. The instability of men's religious professions was, we
may be sure, in the main due to the uncertainty and indefiniteness of their
own convictions. The merit, or the demerit, of the ecclesiastical system
established by the Tudors was that it made easy the blending of old with
new beliefs; and the indefiniteness of the line which, even at epochs of deep
and violent revolutions in belief, divides one body of opinion from another
is still more marked when we come to consider the bodies of legislative
opinion which have been dominant during the nineteenth century; for
there was during that century nothing violent in the opposition between
different schools of thought, and every man of average courage and independence was at liberty to obey the natural and therefore, in many cases,
most illogical developments of his own convictions. An ardent reformer of
1832 could as a "conservative" of 1838 mingle traditions inherited from old
toryism with ideas derived from new and Benthamite liberalism.

Fourthly, The reigning legislative opinion of the day has never, at any
rate during the nineteenth century, exerted absolute or despotic authority.
Its power has always been diminished by the existence of counter-currents
or cross-currents of opinion[18] which were not in harmony with the prevalent opinion of the time.

A counter-current here means a body of opinion, belief, or sentiment
more or less directly opposed to the dominant opinion of a particular era.

Counter-currents of this kind have generally been supplied by the survival of ideas or convictions which are gradually losing their hold upon a
given generation, and particularly the youthful part thereof. This kind of
"conservatism," which prompts men to retain convictions which are losing
their hold upon the mass of the world, is found, it should be remarked, as
much among the adherents of one religious or political creed as of another.
Any Frenchman who clung to Protestantism during the reign of Louis the
Fourteenth; any north-country squire who in the England of the eighteenth

18. See Lect. X., *post.*

century adhered to the Roman Catholicism of his fathers; Samuel Johnson, standing forth as a Tory and a High Churchman amongst Whigs and Free Thinkers; the Abbé Grégoire, retaining in 1830 the attitude and the beliefs of a bishop of that constitutional church of France whereof the claims have been repudiated at once by the Church and by the State; James Mill, who, though the leader in 1832 of philosophic Radicals, the pioneers as they deemed themselves of democratic progress, was in truth the last "of the eighteenth century"[19]—are each and all of them examples of that intellectual and moral conservatism which everywhere, and especially in England, has always been a strong force. The past controls the present.

Counter-currents, again, may be supplied by new ideals which are beginning to influence the young. The hopes or dreams of the generation just coming into the field of public life undermine the energy of a dominant creed.

Counter-currents of opinion, whatever their source, have one certain and one possible effect.

The certain effect is that a check is imposed upon the action of the dominant faith. Thus, from 1830 to 1850 the Benthamite liberalism of the day, which then exerted its highest authority, was held in check by the restraining power of the older and declining toryism. Hence the progress of parliamentary reform, that is, the advance towards democracy, was checked. The Reform Act remained unchanged for more than thirty years, though it did not satisfy the philosophic Radicals who desired the ballot, nor the democratic artisans who agitated for the People's Charter. Reformers, no less than Tories, felt the influence of the counter-current. Some of the ablest among the Reform Ministry of 1832 had by 1834 turned Conservatives, and became in 1841 members of a Conservative Cabinet.

The possible, but far less certain, result of a strong counter-current may be to delay a reform or innovation[20] for so long a time that ultimately it cannot be effected at all, or else, when nominally carried out, becomes a measure of an essentially different character from the proposal put forward

19. See Mill, *Autobiography,* p. 204.

20. A legislative innovation demanded by the opinion of a particular time may of course be of a reactionary character, and may be resisted and deferred by the strength of a counter-current of liberal opinion.

by its original advocates. Delay thus caused, while it hinders the growth or application of the dominant political or social faith, may introduce into this faith itself an essential modification. The toryism, for instance, which in 1785 rejected Pitt's proposal to disfranchise thirty-six rotten boroughs, with compensation to their owners, and to give additional members to the counties and to London, did much more than arrest the reform of Parliament for all but half a century. The Reform Act of 1832 was different in principle from the measure proposed by Pitt; the Whig reformers of 1832 were unlike the democrats or the Tories of 1785. The liberalism of 1830 again found its authority and effective power diminished even in the heyday of its triumph by surviving toryism, and progress towards democracy was, in a sense at any rate, checked till 1867. But this check meant much more than the mere postponement of liberal reforms. Ancient toryism died hard. It lived long enough to leave time for the rise of a new toryism in which democratic sentiment deeply tinged with socialism, blends with that faith in the paternal despotism of the State which formed part of the old Tory creed. Liberalism itself has at last learned to place no small confidence in the beneficent effects of State control; but this trust, whether well founded or not, is utterly foreign to the liberalism of 1832.[21]

The assertion that to delay the action of a political creed may introduce into it essential modification, is opposed to the superstition, propagated by many eminent writers, that reformers, though baffled during their lifetime by the opposition of ignorance, prejudice, or selfishness, may count on their efforts being crowned with success in some subsequent age. This is the notion which underlies such an assertion as that "the failure of the [philosophic] Radicals of the second quarter of the nineteenth century was a failure which may be considered equivalent to success. The causes which they espoused triumphed so completely that the Tories of this generation are more Liberal than the Liberals of 1832."[22] But history lends no countenance to the optimism which it is alleged to encourage. Neither the

---

21. If any one doubts this statement let him consider one fact, and ask himself one question. In 1834 the Whigs and Radicals who reformed the poor law expected the speedy abolition of out-door relief; they hoped for and desired the abolition of the poor law itself. Do the Radicals of 1905 share these expectations and hopes?

22. *Life of Sir William Molesworth,* by Mrs. Fawcett, LL.D., p. 81.

democratic toryism nor the socialistic liberalism of to-day is the philosophic radicalism of Bentham, of Grote, or of Molesworth. The strong
counter-current of ancient toryism has, by delaying their action, modified
all the political beliefs of 1832.

A cross-current of opinion may be described as any body of belief or
sentiment which, while strong enough ultimately to affect legislation, is,
yet in a measure independent of, though perhaps not directly opposed to,
the dominant legislative creed of a particular era.[23] These cross-currents
arise often, if not always, from the peculiar position or prepossessions of
particular classes, such as the clergy, the army, or the artisans, who look
upon the world from their own special point of view. Such a cross-current
differs from a counter-current in that it does not so much directly oppose
the predominant opinion of a given time as deflect and modify its action.
Thus ecclesiastical legislation since 1832 will never be understood by any
historian who does not take into account both the general current of public
opinion, the trend whereof has been more or less anti-clerical, and also
the strong cross-current of clerical opinion which, favouring, as it naturally
has done, the authority of the established Church, has affected legislation,
not only as to ecclesiastical matters, but also in spheres such as that of
national education, which appear at first sight to lie somewhat outside the
operation of ecclesiastical beliefs.

Fifthly, Laws foster or create law-making opinion.

This assertion may sound, to one who has learned that laws are the
outcome of public opinion, like a paradox; when properly understood it
is nothing but an undeniable though sometimes neglected truth.

Every law or rule of conduct must, whether its author perceives the fact
or not, lay down or rest upon some general principle, and must therefore,
if it succeeds in attaining its end, commend this principle to public atten-

---

23. Cross-currents of opinion, as also the predominant public opinion of a given time,
may, it is true, be found, on careful examination, to be due to some general or common
cause. Whether this be so or not is a question to be answered by the historian of opinion,
but does not immediately concern a student occupied in ascertaining the relation between
law and opinion. He accepts the existence of a cross-current of opinion as a fact, and devotes
his attention to ascertaining the mode in which the influence on legislation of the general
current of public opinion was thereby modified.

tion or imitation, and thus affect legislative opinion.[24] Nor is the success of a law necessary for the production of this effect. A principle derives prestige from its mere recognition by Parliament, and if a law fails in attaining its object the argument lies ready to hand that the failure was due to the law not going far enough, *i.e.* to its not carrying out the principle on which it is founded to its full logical consequences.[25] The true importance, indeed, of laws lies far less in their direct result than in their effect upon the sentiment or convictions of the public.

The Reform Act of 1832 disfranchised certain corrupt boroughs, and bestowed on a limited number of citizens belonging mainly to the middle class, the right to vote for members of Parliament. But the transcendent importance of the Act lay in its effect upon public opinion. Reform thus regarded was revolution. It altered the way in which people thought of the constitution, and taught Englishmen, once and for all, that venerable institutions which custom had made unchangeable could easily, and without the use of violence, be changed. It gave authority to the democratic creed, and fostered the conviction or delusion that the will of the nation could be expressed only through elected representatives. The arguments in favour of practical conservatism which, put forward by Burke or Paley, satisfied at least two generations, so lost their popular force that modern Conservatives, no less than modern Liberals, find it hard to understand the attitude towards reform of men as able as Canning or Sir Walter Scott.[26]

---

24. A law which obviously fails in attaining its end may at times turn public opinion against the principle on which the law rests.

25. If whipping does not suppress theft, let it be turned into severe flogging; if this be not enough, add exposure in the pillory; and if this will not do, try capital punishment. This is the sort of argument which, as long as men believed in the principle that severity of punishment is the best mode of hindering crime, continually increased the cruelty or harshness of our criminal law.

26. Contrast Scott's satisfaction at taking a Russian prince to Selkirk in 1826 "to see our quiet way of managing the choice of a national representative" (Scott, *Journals,* July 1, 1826) with the comments thereon of modern Liberals. Scott could not see that a system of representation which, formally at any rate, misrepresented the Scotch people could not, even though in some ways it worked well, be permanently maintained. Modern critics cannot see that a system of representation, which contradicted the most elementary principles of democracy, did in Scotland, at the beginning of the nineteenth century, in many respects work

The new poor-law did much more than apply a drastic remedy to a dangerous social disease: it associated pauperism—a different thing from poverty—with disgrace; it revived, even among the poor, pride in independence, and enforced upon the whole nation the faith that in the battle of life men must rely for success, not upon the aid of the State, but upon self-help.

The Divorce Act of 1857 on the face of it did no more than increase the facilities for obtaining divorce. It in reality gave national sanction to the contractual view of marriage, and propagated the belief that the marriage contract, like every other agreement, ought to be capable of dissolution when it fails to attain its end. This Act and the feelings it fostered are closely related to the Married Women's Property Acts, 1870–1893. Nor can any one doubt that these enactments have in their turn given strength to the belief that women ought, in the eye of the law, to stand substantially on an equality with men, and have encouraged legislation tending to produce such equality. In this matter laws have deeply affected not only the legislative but also the social opinion of the country as to the position of women. It is further clear that the statutes to which reference has here been made, and others like them, have all tended to strengthen that faith in *laissez-faire* which is of the very essence of legislative Benthamism. Law and opinion, indeed, are here so intermixed that it is difficult to say whether opinion has done most to produce legislation or laws to create a state of legislative opinion.

That law creates opinion is plain enough as regards statutes which obviously give effect, even though it may be imperfectly, to some wide principle, but holds at least equally true of laws passed to meet in the readiest and often most offhand manner some pressing want or popular demand. People often, indeed, fancy that such random legislation, because it is called "practical," is not based on any principle, and therefore does not affect legislative opinion. But this is a delusion. Every law must of necessity be based on some general idea, whether wise or foolish, sound or unsound,

---

well, and, even, strange though the statement sounds, give effect to the wishes of the Scotch people. See Porritt, *The Unreformed House of Commons*, chap. xxxi.

and to this principle or idea it inevitably gives more or less of prestige. A member of Parliament is garotted;[27] a demand is made that garotters shall be flogged; a law is passed to meet this wish. The Act, whether wise or not, rests upon and countenances the notion, combated by the wisest philanthropists of an earlier generation, that severity rather than certainty of punishment is the best check on crime. It also strengthens the belief, as to the truth whereof moralists are not agreed, that a main object of punishment is the satisfaction of the feeling which, according to one's point of view, may be described as either the natural sentiment of justice or the natural sentiment of vindictiveness. The Garotters Act, 1863, therefore clearly did affect legislative opinion. The Money-lenders Act, 1900, again, may well be called an Act for the suppression of Isaac Gordon, since it was to a great extent the outcome of indignation against the rapacity and cruelty of that particular usurer. But this Act, though produced by temporary feeling, not only revives the usury laws, but gives expression and authority to beliefs supposed to have been confuted by reason.

It is far, indeed, from being true that laws passed to meet a particular emergency, or to satisfy a particular demand, do not affect public opinion; the assertion is at least plausible, and possibly well founded, that such laws of emergency produce, in the long run, more effect on legislative opinion than a law which openly embodies a wide principle. Laws of emergency often surreptitiously introduce or reintroduce into legislation, ideas which would not be accepted if brought before the attention of Parliament or of the nation. Is it certain that the legislators who passed the Money-lenders Act, 1900, might not have hesitated formally to re-enact the usury laws which Parliament deliberately repealed in 1854? Laws, indeed, passed for a limited or practical purpose—described as they are by the far too complimentary term of "tentative"[28] legislation—exert the greater moral influence

---

27. See Hansard, vol. clxix. p. 1305.

28. The word "tentative" is too complimentary. Parliament favours gradual legislation not from the desire, which would often be wise, to try an experiment in legislation by applying a wide principle to a very limited extent, *e.g.* within a small area, but from failure to perceive that a law which produces at the moment a very limited effect may involve the recognition of a principle of unlimited application. Indolence and ignorance, rather than any desire for scientific experiment, are the causes of hand-to-mouth legislation.

because they fall in with our English preference for dealing only with the special matter actually in hand, and with our profound reverence for precedent. Yet this apparent prudence is, in reality, often no better than the height of rashness. A principle carelessly introduced into an Act of Parliament intended to have a limited effect may gradually so affect legislative opinion that it comes to pervade a whole field of law.

In 1833 the House of Commons made for the first time a grant of something less than £20,000 to promote the education of the people of England. The money, for want of any thought-out scheme based on any intelligible principle, was spent on a sort of subscription to two societies which, supported by voluntary contributions and representing, the one the Church of England and the other, in effect, the Dissenters, did what they could in the way of affording to the English poor elementary education, combined with religious instruction. This niggardly,[29] haphazard subscription has proved to contain within it all the anomalies of the system which, now costing the country some £18,000,000 a year, is embodied in the Education Acts 1870–1902, with their universal, State-supported, and compulsory, yet to a great extent denominational, scheme of national education.[30]

So much as to the influence of law on opinion, which, after all, is merely one example of the way in which the development of political ideas is influenced by their connection with political facts. Of such facts laws are among the most important; they are therefore the cause, at least, as much as the effect of legislative opinion.[31]

It is a plausible theory, though one which is perhaps oftener entertained than explicitly stated, that the growth of English law has been governed by

29. The whole parliamentary grant for education in the United Kingdom in 1834 was less than a third of what was granted annually by the single State of Massachusetts with a population of less than a million. See *Life of Sir William Molesworth*, pp. 55, 56.

30. In dealing with laws as the creators of opinion, I have, for the sake of clearness, referred only to laws enacted by Parliament, but it is certain that judicial legislation affects opinion quite as strongly as does parliamentary legislation. See "Judicial Legislation," Lecture XI., *post*.

31. "The development of political ideas is influenced in a different way by their connection with political facts. The ideas are related to the facts of political history, not only as effect to cause, but also as cause to effect."—H. Sidgwick, *Development of European Polity*, p. 346.

a tendency towards democracy. Our best plan therefore will be to examine the relation between the advance of democracy and the course of legislation during the nineteenth century,[32] and then to consider what have been the main currents of predominant opinion during that period, and trace the influence of each of these[33] on the history of the law.

32. See Lecture III., *post.*
33. See Lectures IV. to IX., *post.*

LECTURE III *Democracy and Legislation*

DOES NOT THE ADVANCE of democracy afford the clue to the development of English law since 1800?

This inquiry is suggested by some indisputable facts. In England, as in other European countries, society has, during the last century, advanced in a democratic direction. The most ordinary knowledge of the commonest events shows us that in 1800 the government of England was essentially aristocratic,[1] and that the class which, though never despotic, was decidedly dominant, was the class of landowners and of large merchants; and that the social condition, the feelings and convictions of Englishmen in 1800, were even more aristocratic than were English political institutions. No one, again, can doubt that by 1900, and, indeed, considerably before 1900, the English constitution had been transformed into something like a democracy. The supremacy of the landowners had passed away; the destruction by the great Reform Act of rotten boroughs had been the cause and the sign of a thorough change in the system of government. The electorate, which had in the main represented the landed interest, was extended in 1832 so as to give predominant power to the middle classes and to the manufacturers. In 1867 the artisans of the towns acquired the parliamentary suffrage. Subsequent legislation, ending with the Reform Acts[2] of 1884–1885, admitted householders in counties to the same rights as the artisans, and finally established the system of so-called household suffrage, under

1. See this stated forcibly, though with great exaggeration, Ostrogorski, *Democracy and Organization of Political Parties,* chap. i.

2. The Representation of the People Act, 1884, 48 Vict. c. 3; the Redistribution of Seats Act, 1885, 48 & 49 Vict. c. 23.

which England is, in theory at least, governed by a democracy of house-holders. Of the real extent and the true nature of this advance towards democracy it is hardly necessary here to speak. All that need be noted is that alterations in parliamentary and other institutions have corresponded with an even more remarkable change, in a democratic direction, of public sentiment. Paley was a Whig, and an acute and liberal thinker, but the whole tenor of his speculations concerning the English constitution, with their defence of rotten boroughs, and their apology for "influence," or, in plain terms, for the moderate use of corruption, is not more remarkable for its opposition to the political doctrines, than for its contrast with the whole tone of political thought prevalent at and indeed before the close of the nineteenth century. The transition, then, from an aristocracy to a democracy is undeniable. May we not, then, find in this transition the main and simple cause of all the principal changes in the law of the land?

The true and general answer to this question is that the expression "advance of democracy," or rather the idea which this and similar phrases embody, is vague and ambiguous, and that, whatever be the sense in which the term is used, the advance of democracy affords much less help than might have been expected, in the attempt to account for the growth and evolution of the modern law of England.

This reply, however, both needs and repays explanation.

The word "democracy" has, owing in great measure to the popularity and influence of Tocqueville's *Democracy in America,* acquired a new ambiguity. It may mean either a social condition or a form of government.

In the writings of Alexis de Tocqueville, "democracy" often means, not a form of government or a particular kind of constitution, but a special condition of society—namely, the state of things under which there exists a general equality of rights, and a similarity of conditions, of thoughts, of sentiments, and of ideals. Democracy in this sense of the word has no necessary connection either with individual freedom or even with popular government. It is indeed opposed to every kind of aristocratic authority, since aristocracy or oligarchy involves the existence of unequal rights and of class privileges, and has for its intellectual or moral foundation the conviction that the inequalities or differences which distinguish one body of men from another are of essential and permanent importance. But democracy in this sense, though opposed to privilege, is, as Tocqueville insists, as compatible with despotism or imperialism as with popular government or republicanism. Now, if democracy be thus used as a name for a social condition, the expression "advance towards democracy," or any like phrase, can, it is clear, mean nothing but the progress among the inhabitants of a country towards a condition of general equality and, still more truly, of similarity. Hence Tocqueville and his followers trace back the progress of democracy to times long anterior to the revolutionary movements which marked the close of the eighteenth century, and see in Richelieu and in Frederick the Great, no less than in Napoleon I. and in Napoleon III., the promoters of the democratic regime. But if the progress of democracy, though it may often involve a change in the form of government, is in itself little else than the approach towards a given social condition, then the progress of democracy gives little or no help towards accounting for the particular development of the law of England. Grant, for the sake of argument—though the concession is one which, if we have regard to facts, must be accompanied by a large number of reservations—that the history of English, as of European civilisation generally, is the record of the continuous, though unconscious progress of mankind towards a condition of equality and similarity, and that every change which has taken place, including alterations in the law, is connected with, or rather is a part of the advance of democracy, and we arrive, after all, only at the true but barren conclusion that the growth of English law, as of every other English institution, during the nineteenth century is due to the general condition of English society. This is one of those explanations which, as it is true of everything, is for that very reason the adequate explanation of nothing.

"Democracy" in its stricter and older sense, in which it is generally employed by English writers, means, not a state of society, but a form of government; namely, a constitution under which sovereign power is possessed by the numerical majority of the male citizens; and in this sense, the "advance of democracy" means the transference of supreme power from either a single person, or from a privileged and limited class, to the majority of the citizens; it means, in short, the approach to government by numbers, or, in current, though inaccurate phraseology, by the people.

Now, the "advance of democracy," if thus understood, does in truth, in so far as it has really taken place, explain, though only to a limited extent, the alterations made in the English constitution, and a student must, in trying to estimate the character of these alterations, take into account the influence of definitely democratic opinions. Nor must he confine his attention merely to changes in what is technically called the constitution— such, for example, as the modification in the English representative system produced by the various Parliamentary Reform Acts, which begin with the great Reform Act of 1832: he must also note every important change in any of the organs of government. He will then assuredly find that the advance of democracy does explain the noteworthy fact that throughout the nineteenth century every permanent change of a constitutional character has been in a democratic direction, and shows how it has happened that every Act for the reform of Parliament has extended, and has been meant to extend, the influence of mere numbers. Even, however, in the province of constitutional law, democratic progress fails to explain several remarkable phenomena. How, for example, does it happen that the constitution of England, which is more readily responsive to the force of opinion than is any other existing polity, remains far from absolutely democratic, and is certainly not nearly as democratic as the constitutions of France, of Switzerland, of the United States, or (what is even more noteworthy) of the self-governing English colonies, such as the Dominion of Canada or the Australian Commonwealth? Nor, again, does the tendency towards democracy explain how it is that the demand for universal suffrage, which made itself heard with great force during the Chartist agitation towards the middle of the last century, is now almost unheard. But if the progress of democracy fails to explain at all perfectly the development or the condition of the English constitution, still less does it elucidate the course of legislation, in matters which have no reference to the distribution of political power.

Nor need this negative result cause any surprise. The idea that the existence of or the advance towards popular government in any country will of itself explain the course which legislation there takes, rests on the assumption that every democracy favours the same kind of laws or of institutions. This assumption is constantly made, but it rests on a very small foundation of fact. It has a certain amount of validity within the narrow sphere of constitutional law, but its plausibility depends on the confusion between the powers and the tendencies of a democracy, and it is grounded on a curious illusion which is contradicted by the most notorious facts.

Let us first examine the exceptional case of constitutional law, using that term in its very widest sense.

From the progress of democracy—which, be it remembered, we are here considering simply as a change in the form of government—we may with some confidence infer that, while this change is going on, no alteration in a constitution will take place which obviously, and upon the face of it, diminishes the authority of the people. It is necessary, however, when trying to apply this conclusion, to recollect that the mass of mankind often fail to perceive or appreciate the effect of gradual and apparently petty changes. Hence, even in democratic countries, habits or institutions may come into existence which in reality curtail the power of the people, though not apparently threatening that power.[3] It is probably true, for instance, that the elaborate party system of the United States does actually, though not in form, bestow on party managers and wirepullers a large amount of power, which is subtracted from the just authority of the mass of the citizens. But this party system exists just because the majority of the people do not perceive its anti-democratic tendency. Still, though we should keep in mind the possibility that the members of a democracy may fail to perceive the true character of laws or institutions which limit the authority of the people, it may fairly be assumed that where opinion has become democratic, or is becoming democratic, and where the mass of the people have obtained, or are obtaining sovereign power, each change in the constitution will probably increase the authority of numbers.

Let us now see how far the advance of democracy is likely to affect laws which have not a constitutional character, or, in other words, which do not tell upon the distribution of sovereign power.

In respect of the influence of democracy on such laws, we can draw with some confidence one probable conclusion. We may with high probability assume that no law will be carried, or at any rate that no law will long

3. The Chandos clause, introduced into the Reform Act by the Tory Opposition, but supported by some Radicals, gave a vote in the counties to tenants from year to year, mainly tenant farmers, paying a yearly rent of £50. This clause increased the number of voters, and seemed, therefore, democratic; but as such tenant farmers were dependent on their landlords, it really increased the power of the land-owners, and robbed the counties of their independence. It was supported, however, by democrats, who did not perceive the real tendency of the so-called amendment.

remain in force, which is opposed to the wish of the people, or, in other words, to the sentiment prevailing among the distinct majority of the citizens of a given country. It is, however, absolutely impossible from the advance of democracy to draw, with regard to laws which do not touch the balance of political power, anything more than this merely negative inference. The impossibility arises from the patent fact that, though in a democratic country the laws which will be passed, or at any rate will be put into effect, must be the laws which the people like, it is absolutely impossible to predict on any *a priori* ground what are the laws which the people of a country will at any given time wish to be passed or put in force.

The reason why the truth of a conclusion which is hardly disputable is not universally admitted, is to be found in a singular illusion which affects alike the friends and the opponents of democratic change. Democracy is a comparatively new form of government. Reformers, or revolutionists, who have attempted to achieve definite changes, *e.g.* the disestablishment of the Church, the abolition of primogeniture, the creation of peasant proprietorship, or, it may be, the regulation of public labour by the State for the advantage of artisans and labourers, stand in a position like that of men who look for immense blessing to the country from the accession to the throne of a new monarch; they tacitly or openly assume that the new sovereign—in this case the democracy—will carry out the ideas of beneficent legislation and good government entertained by the reformers who have placed the sovereign in power. The Whigs of 1830 supposed that a reformed Parliament would carry out the ideas which the Whigs had advocated in the *Edinburgh Review*. Radicals, such as the two Mills, Joseph Hume, or Francis Place, held that reform meant the triumph of unadulterated Benthamism. The Free Traders of 1846, even with the experience of France and America before their eyes, identified the progress of democracy with the acceptance of free trade. Many are the Englishmen who, in our own day, have found it impossible to believe that the old watchwords of peace, retrenchment, and reform might have as little attraction for a sovereign people as for a despotic monarch; and there are men still living who can recall the confidence with which ardent reformers anticipated that the predominance of British householders would ensure the adoption of exactly the policy which the reformers themselves deemed beneficial. Nor have the opponents of democratic innovation been free from a delusion strictly analogous to the error which has falsified the forecasts of democrats. Tories or Conservatives, who looked with terror and aversion on democratic progress, have for the most part assumed that the sovereign people would of necessity support legislation which is hateful to every man of conservative instincts. During the debates on the great Reform Bill the attacks made upon it by Tory zealots teemed with anticipations of iniquitous legislation. Men who hated revolution could not believe that democrats might be conservatives. At the bottom, in short, of all speculations about the effects of the advance of democracy, constantly lies the assumption that there exists such a thing as specially democratic legislation which every democracy is certain to favour. Yet there never was an assumption more clearly at variance with the teaching of history.

Democracy in modern England has shown a singular tolerance, not to say admiration, for the kind of social inequalities involved in the existence of the Crown and of an hereditary and titled peerage; a cynic might even suggest that the easy working of modern English constitutionalism proves how beneficial may be in practice the result of democracy tempered by snobbishness. The people of England have certainly shown no hostility to the existence either of large fortunes or of large estates, and during the nineteenth century have betrayed no ardent desire for that creation of a large body of peasant proprietors, or yeomen, which enlightened Liberals have thought would confer untold benefits on the country. In truth, the equal division of a man's property among his descendants or his nearest relatives at his death, though almost essential to the maintenance of small estates, is thoroughly opposed to that absolute freedom of testamentary disposition to which Englishmen have so long been accustomed that they have come to look upon it as a kind of natural right. The English ecclesiastical establishment, opposed as it is to many democratic ideas or principles, has not been the object of much popular attack. The Established Church is more influential and more popular in 1904, than it was in 1830, and the influence of Non-conformists is, under the democratic constitution of to-day, apparently less considerable than was the influence some sixty or seventy years ago of what was then called the Dissenting interest. English democracy, in short, whilst caring somewhat for religious freedom, exhibits indifference to religious equality. From another point of view the position of the English democracy is peculiar. Almost alone among popular governments of the world, it has hitherto supported complete freedom of trade, and has on the whole, though on this matter one must speak with less certainty, favoured everything that promotes freedom of contract. Now the point to be specially noted is that the attitude of the English people (and this holds true of the attitude and legislative action of the people of every great country) is determined much less by the mere advance of democracy than by historical, and, even what one may fairly term, accidental circumstances. Democracy in England has to a great extent inherited the traditions of the aristocratic government, of which it is the heir. The relation of the judiciary to the executive, to the Parliament, and to the people, remains now much what it was at the beginning of the century, and no man dreams of maintaining that the government and the administration, are not subject to the legal control and interference of the judges. Our whole system of government, lastly, is, as it has been since 1689, essentially parliamentary. And the supremacy of Parliament involves in England constant modification of the law of the land. The English Parliament is now a legislative machine which, whatever the party in office, is kept constantly in action.

Turn now by way of contrast to France.

French democracy is opposed to differences of rank involving political inequality. The very foundation of the French political and social system is the existence of a large body of small landed proprietors, or, to use English expressions, of small freeholders. Testamentary freedom, in the English sense of the word, is unknown. The systematic and equal division of a deceased person's property among his family thoroughly corresponds with French ideas of justice, and prohibits that formation of large hereditary estates which has long been a marked feature of English social life. For personal liberty, and for what we should call religious freedom, by which I mean the effective right of every man to advocate and propagate any theological or religious dogma which he pleases to adopt, and generally for the right of association, French democracy has hitherto shown little care. The whole relation of the Courts to the executive is one which Englishmen find it hard to realise; the dogma of the separation of powers which, be it noted, still remains one of the sacred principles of 1789, is, as the doctrine is interpreted in France, absolutely inconsistent with interference by the judges with the action either of the government or of the administration. In matters of trade and commerce, again, the French democracy has been as zealous for protection as the English democracy for free trade. The French democracy, in short, has inherited and accepted the traditions of the monarchy, and still more of the Napoleonic Empire; and democratic France, though tolerant of revolutions which hardly affect the ordinary life of the people is, as I have already pointed out,[4] as compared with England, the home of legislative conservatism.

A glance at the democracies, either of the United States or of Switzerland, would show us in each case types of legislation differing alike from each other, and from the laws either of democratic England or of republican France. But for our present purpose it is unnecessary to carry the comparison further. The annals of a century show that the mere advance of democracy does not, important as in many ways it is, of necessity produce in different countries one and the same kind of changes in the law. That this is so has of recent years been acknowledged both by Conservatives and by social reformers or revolutionists. Both in England and abroad, so-called conservatism has, under its ablest leaders, shown itself very tolerant of an extended or even a universal suffrage, and zealots for social change see in the Referendum, which, whatever its merits or demerits, is an essentially democratic institution, a device for retarding socialistic innovations. But if the progress of democracy does not of itself, except as regards the distribution of sovereign power, necessarily determine the character of legislation, we cannot expect that it should explain the development of the law of England. The explanation must be found, if at all, in the different currents of opinion, bearing more or less directly on legislation, which have, during different parts of the nineteenth century, been predominant in England.

4. See p. 7, *ante.* Note that divorce has with great difficulty been established in France; though existing under the First Republic and the Empire, it was abolished in 1816, and not again legalised till 1884.

The Three Main Currents of Public Opinion

THE NINETEENTH CENTURY falls into three periods, during each of which a different current or stream of opinion was predominant, and in the main governed the development of the law of England.

I. The Period of Old Toryism or Legislative Quiescence (1800–1830)[1]

This was the era of Blackstonian optimism reinforced, as the century went on, by Eldonian toryism or reaction; it may be termed the period of legislative quiescence, or (in the language of censors) stagnation. Political or legislative changes were first checked by that pride in the English constitution, and intense satisfaction with things as they were, which was inherited from a preceding generation, and is best represented by the studied optimism of Blackstone; they were next arrested by that reaction against Jacobinism and revolutionary violence which is represented by the legislative timidity of Lord Eldon; he devoted his great intellectual powers (which hardly receive justice from modern critics) at once to the cautious elaboration of the doctrines of equity, and to the obstruction of every other change or improvement in the law. The reactionary character of this period increased rather than diminished as the century advanced. The toryism of 1815 or 1817 was less intelligent and more violent than the toryism of 1800.

---

1. See R. K. Wilson, *Modern English Law*, chap. iii., and Lect. V., *post*.

It is for our present purpose convenient to treat 1800, in accordance with popular phraseology, as belonging to the nineteenth century.

Laws[2] passed during this period, and especially during the latter part thereof, assumed a deliberately reactionary form, and were aimed at the suppression of sedition, of Jacobinism, of agitation, or of reform. But though it is easy to find examples of reactionary legislation, the true characteristic of the time was the prevalence of quiescence or stagnation. Optimism had at least as much to do with the condition of public sentiment as had the dread of revolutionary propagandism.

II. The Period of Benthamism or Individualism (1825–1870)[3]

This was the era of utilitarian reform. Legislation was governed by the body of opinion, popularly, and on the whole rightly, connected with the name of Bentham.[4] The movement of which he, if not the creator, was certainly the prophet, was above all things a movement for the reform of the law. Hence it has affected, though in very different degrees, every part of the law of England. It has stimulated the constant activity of Parliament, it has swept away restraints on individual energy, and has exhibited a deliberate hostility to every historical anomaly or survival, which appeared to involve practical inconvenience, or in any way to place a check on individual freedom.

III. Period of Collectivism (1865–1900)[5]

By collectivism is here meant the school of opinion often termed (and generally by more or less hostile critics) socialism, which favours the in-

2. *E.g.* the great Combination Act, 1800, 40 Geo. III. c. 106; the Act of 1817, 57 Geo. III. c. 19, for the prevention of seditious meetings.

3. See Lecture VI., *post.*

4. In the whole field of economics Adam Smith and his disciples exerted a potent influence, but it is not necessary for our purpose to distinguish between the influence of jurists and the influence of economists: they both represented the individualism of the time.

5. See Lects. VII.–IX., *post.* Murray's Dictionary gives no authority for the use of the word collectivism earlier than 1880. It is there defined as "the socialistic theory of the collective

tervention of the State, even at some sacrifice of individual freedom, for the purpose of conferring benefit upon the mass of the people. This current of opinion cannot, in England at any rate, be connected with the name of any one man, or even with the name of any one definite school. It has increased in force and volume during the last half of the nineteenth century, nor does observation justify the expectation that in the sphere of legislation, or elsewhere, its strength is spent or its influence on the wane. The practical tendencies of this movement of opinion in England are best exemplified in our labour laws, and by a large amount of legislation which, though it cannot be easily brought under one head, is, speaking broadly, intended to regulate the conduct of trade and business in the interest of the working classes, and, as collectivists believe, for the benefit of the nation.

Our study of each of these currents of opinion in its bearing on legislation will be facilitated by attention to certain general observations.

First. Each of these three schools of thought has, if we look at the nineteenth century alone, reigned for about an equal number of years.

This statement, however, needs qualification if we take into account the years which preceded the commencement, and the years, few as they are, which have followed the end of the nineteenth century. We then perceive that while the unquestioned supremacy of Benthamism lasted for a more or less assignable and limited time—that is to say, for the thirty-five or possibly forty years which begin with 1828 or 1830—it is impossible to fix with anything like equal precision the limit either of the period of quies-

---

ownership or control of all the means of production, and especially of the land, by the whole community or State, *i.e.* the people collectively, for the benefit of the people as a whole." H. Sidgwick, in his *Elements of Politics* (2nd ed.), p. 158, uses the word to denote an extreme form of socialism. These are not exactly the meanings given to collectivism in these lectures. It is used as a convenient antithesis to individualism in the field of legislation. This use appears to be etymologically correct, and to be justified by the novelty and vagueness of the term. The very indefiniteness of the expression collectivism is for my purpose a recommendation. A person may in some respects be a collectivist—that is to say, entertain views which are not in harmony with the ideas of individualism—and yet not uphold or entertain any general belief which could fairly be called socialism; but though the vague term collectivism is for my present purpose preferable to socialism, I shall on occasion use the more popular and current expression socialism as equivalent to collectivism.

cence or of the period of collectivism. The intimate connection between the name of Blackstone and the optimism which was one main cause of legislative inaction, suggests that the period of quiescence must be carried back to a date earlier than the end of the eighteenth century, and that it may possibly at any rate be forced back to the accession of George the Third (1760), if not even to an earlier time. On this way of looking at the matter the age of legal quiescence covers some seventy years (1760–1830).

There is no possibility of fixing with any precision the limits to the period of collectivism. Socialistic ideas were, it is submitted, in no way a part of dominant legislative opinion earlier than 1865,[6] and their influence on legislation did not become perceptible till some years later, say till 1868 or 1870, or dominant till say 1880. This influence is still, however, not apparently on the decline, and may well, for years to come, leave its impress on the statute-book. The very dates assigned to each of our three periods bear witness to the fact that periods of belief run into one another and overlap. It is absolutely impossible to fix with precision the date at which a body of opinion begins to exert perceptible influence or even to become predominant.

Secondly. The relation to legislation of each of the three currents of opinion is markedly different.

The legislative inertia which, at the beginning of the nineteenth century, discouraged changes in the law was no theory of legislation. It was a sentiment of conservatism which, whether due to optimism or to hatred of revolution, opposed innovation in every province of national life.

Benthamism was a definite body of doctrine directly applied to the reform of the law. It was a legal creed created by a legal philosopher. Hence its direct and immense influence upon the development of English law.

Collectivism has been, during the nineteenth century, rather a sentiment than a doctrine, and in so far as it might be identified with socialism has been rather an economical and a social than a legal creed.

Thirdly. The examination into the character and the influence of collectivism presents certain peculiar difficulties which do not meet us when

---

6. An early example of such influence may be found in the Metropolitan Commons Act, 1866. It reversed that policy of breaking up commons which met with the enthusiastic approval of Bentham. See Bentham, *Works,* i. p. 342.

studying either the old toryism of Blackstone or Eldon, or the Benthamite individualism which, in accordance with popular phraseology, may often be conveniently called liberalism.

The general characteristics of the age of toryism are well-ascertained historical facts which have become the object of common knowledge. Benthamism is a definite creed. Its formulas are easily discoverable in the works of Bentham and his disciples; its practical results are visible in one statute after another. Collectivism, on the other hand, is even now rather a sentiment than a doctrine; hence it is a term which hardly admits of precise definition, and collectivism, in so far as it may be considered a doctrine, has never, in England at least, been formulated by any thinker endowed with anything like the commanding ability or authority of Bentham; its dogmas have not been reduced to the articles of a political or a social creed, still less have they been applied even speculatively to the field of law with the clearness and thoroughness with which Bentham and his followers marked out the application of utilitarianism to the amendment of the law. Hence a curious contrast between the mode in which an inquirer must deal with the legislative influence on the one hand of Benthamism, and on the other hand of collectivism. He can explain changes in English law by referring them to definite and known tenets or ideas of Benthamite liberalism; he can, on the other hand, prove the existence of collectivist ideas in the main only by showing the socialistic character or tendencies of certain parliamentary enactments.

The difficulties of the investigation, moreover, are increased by a peculiarity of the mode in which the ideas of collectivism have gradually entered into or coloured English legislation. The peculiarity is this: a line of Acts begun under the influence of Benthamite ideas has often, under an almost unconscious change in legislative opinion, at last taken a turn in the direction of socialism. A salient example[7] of this phenomenon is exhibited by the effort lasting over many years to amend the law with regard to an employer's liability for damage done to his workmen in the course of their employment. Up to 1896 reformers, acting under the inspiration of Benthamite ideas, directed their efforts wholly towards giving workmen the same right to compensation by their employer for damage inflicted through

7. See Lect. VIII., *post.*

the negligence of one of his workmen as is possessed by a stranger. This endeavour was never completely successful; but in 1897 it led up to and ended in the thoroughly collectivist legislation embodied in the Workmen's Compensation Acts, 1897 and 1900,[8] which (to put the matter broadly) makes an employer the insurer of his workmen against any damage incurred in the course of their employment.

The difference in the spirit of the three great currents of opinion may be thus summarised: Blackstonian toryism was the historical reminiscence of paternal government; Benthamism is a doctrine of law reform; collectivism is a hope of social regeneration. Vague and inaccurate as this sort of summary must necessarily be, it explains how it happened that individualism under the guidance of Bentham affected, as did no other body of opinion, the development of English law.

---

8. Workmen's Compensation Act, 1897, 60 & 61 Vict. c. 37; 1900, 63 & 64 Vict. c. 22. [Editor's note: This footnote was added in the second edition.]

The Period of Old Toryism or
Legislative Quiescence (1800–1830)

FOUR POINTS MERIT special attention: the state of opinion during the era of legislative quiescence—the resulting absence of legal changes during the first quarter of the nineteenth century—the inquiry, why some considerable innovations took place even during this period—and the causes which brought the era of legislative quiescence to its close.

(A) State of Opinion (1760–1830)

These seventy years constitute a period of legislative quiescence; the changelessness of the law is directly traceable to the condition of opinion.[1]

The thirty years from 1760 to 1790 may be well termed as regards their spirit, the age of Blackstone.[2] English society was divided by violent though superficial political conflicts, but the tone of the whole time, in spite of the blow dealt to English prestige by the successful revolt of the Thirteen Colonies, was after all a feeling of contentment with, and patriotic pride in, the greatness of England and the political and social results of the Revolution Settlement. Of this sentiment Blackstone was the typical representative; every page of his *Commentaries* is pervaded by aggressive optimism.

> Of a constitution, so wisely contrived, so strongly raised, and so highly finished, it is hard to speak with that praise, which is justly and severely its due:—the thorough and attentive contemplation of it will furnish its best

1. The distaste for legal changes which prevailed between 1800 and 1830 is distinctly traceable in part at least to the condition of opinion between 1760 and 1800.
2. Birth 1723; publication of *Commentaries*, 1765–69; death 1780.

panegyric. It hath been the endeavour of these commentaries, however the execution may have succeeded, to examine its solid foundations, to mark out its extensive plan, to explain the use and distribution of its parts, and from the harmonious concurrence of those several parts, to demonstrate the elegant proportion of the whole. We have taken occasion to admire at every turn the noble monuments of ancient simplicity, and the more curious refinements of modern art. Nor have its faults been concealed from view; for faults it has, lest we should be tempted to think it of more than human structure; defects, chiefly arising from the decays of time, or the rage of unskilful improvements in later ages. To sustain, to repair, to beautify this noble pile, is a charge intrusted principally to the nobility, and such gentlemen of the kingdom as are delegated by their country to parliament. The protection of THE LIBERTY OF BRITAIN is a duty which they owe to themselves, who enjoy it; to their ancestors, who transmitted it down; and to their posterity, who will claim at their hands this, the best birthright, and the noblest inheritance of mankind.[3]

These words sum up the whole spirit of the *Commentaries;* they express the sentiment not of an individual, but of an era. Some twenty-five years or so later Burke noted, with undisguised sympathy, the conservatism of English thinkers.

"Many of our men of speculation," he writes,

instead of exploding general prejudices, employ their sagacity to discover the latent wisdom which prevails in them. If they find what they seek, and they seldom fail, they think it more wise to continue the prejudice, with the reason involved, than to cast away the coat of prejudice, and to leave nothing but the naked reason; because prejudice, with its reason, has a motive to give action to that reason, and an affection which will give it permanence.[4]

Blackstone, it may be thought, though not a Tory, was an Old Whig of a pre-eminently conservative character. Burke had always in constitutional matters leaned strongly towards historical conservatism; in 1790, when the words just cited were published, hatred of Jacobinism had transformed

---

3. Blackstone, *Commentaries,* iv. p. 443 (end of Book iv.).

4. Burke, ii. p. 169. See also *Appeal from the New to the Old Whigs,* Burke, vi. pp. 263–265; Hallam, *Middle Ages,* ii. (12th ed.) p. 267; and Goldsmith, *Works,* iii., *Citizen of the World,* Letter iv.

him into a reactionist. But Paley was a man of a calm and judicial temperament. He felt no reverence for the historic dignity and pomp of English constitutionalism. Of the anomalies presented by the institutions which lie at the basis of civilised society he could write with extraordinary freedom. The famous illustration of the pigeons,[5] to be found in the chapter "Of Property" in his Moral Philosophy got for him the nickname of "Pigeon-Paley," and the warning of his friend, Law, justified by the event, that it would exclude him from a bishopric, only elicited the retort, "Bishop or no Bishop, it shall go in." But this hard-headed and honest moralist who sacrificed his chance of promotion rather than suppress a sarcasm aimed at the evils of our own social system, and at monarchy itself, was at bottom as much a defender of the existing state of things as was Blackstone. A few sentences from Paley's excellent chapter on the British Constitution reveal his whole position.[6]

> Let us, before we seek to obtain anything more, consider duly what we already have. We have a House of Commons composed of 548 members, in which number are found the most considerable landholders and merchants of the kingdom; the heads of the army, the navy, and the law; the occupiers of great offices in the State; together with many private individuals, eminent by their knowledge, eloquence, or activity. Now, if the country be not safe in such hands, in whose may it confide its interests? If such a number of such men be liable to the influence of corrupt motives, what assembly of men will

---

5. "If you should see a flock of pigeons in a field of corn; and if (instead of each picking where, and what it liked, taking just as much as it wanted, and no more) you should see ninety-nine of them gathering all they got into a heap; reserving nothing for themselves, but the chaff and refuse; keeping this heap for one, and that the weakest perhaps and worst pigeon of the flock; sitting round, and looking on all the winter, whilst this one was devouring, throwing about and wasting it; and, if a pigeon more hardy or hungry than the rest, touched a grain of the hoard, all the others instantly flying upon it, and tearing it to pieces; if you should see this, you would see nothing more than what is every day practised and established among men."—Paley, *Moral Philosophy*, Book iii. chap. i. (12th ed.), pp. 105, 106.

6. See especially Paley, *Moral Philosophy*, ii. (12th ed. 1799), pp. 217 and following. Paley's account of the unreformed Parliament is specially valuable because it was published by a man of judicial intellect at a date (1785) when his judgment was unaffected alike by the excitement of the French Revolution and by the vehement controversies which forty-five or forty-seven years later preceded or accompanied the passing of the Reform Act.

be secure from the same danger? Does any new scheme of representation promise to collect together more wisdom, or to produce firmer integrity? In this view of the subject, and attending not to ideas of order and proportion (of which many minds are much enamoured), but to effects alone, we may discover just excuses for those parts of the present representation, which appear to a hasty observer most exceptional and absurd.[7]

And Paley's view of the unreformed House of Commons is in substance his view of the whole British constitution,[8] and was shared by most statesmen of his day.

Blackstone, Burke, and Paley were, it may be thought, political philosophers who represent the speculative views of their time. Turn then to a writer the charm of whose style does not conceal the superficiality of his ideas, and whose whole aim as a man of letters was to express in graceful English the ideas current among ladies and gentlemen of average intelligence. Goldsmith, in his *Citizen of the World,* has precisely reproduced the tone of his day. The cosmopolitan Chinaman talks much of English law;[9] he maintains, among other fanciful notions, the paradox that it was the height of wisdom to fill the statute-book with laws threatening offenders with most severe penalties which were rarely or never exacted.

> In England, from a variety of happy accidents, their constitution is just strong enough, or if you will, monarchical enough, to permit a relaxation of the severity of laws, and yet those laws still to remain sufficiently strong to govern the people. This is the most perfect state of civil liberty, of which we can form any idea; here we see a greater number of laws than in any other country, while the people at the same time obey only such as are *immediately* conducive to the interests of society; several are unnoticed, many unknown; some kept to be revived and enforced upon proper occasions, others left to grow obsolete, even without the necessity of abrogation.
>
> There is scarcely an Englishman who does not almost every day of his life offend with impunity against some express law, and for which in a certain conjuncture of circumstances he would not receive punishment.

7. Paley, *Philosophy,* ii. pp. 220, 221.

8. See G. Lowes Dickinson, *The Development of Parliament,* ch. i.

9. This by the way is a curious illustration of the interest felt towards the end of the eighteenth century in legal speculations.

Gaming-houses, preaching at prohibited places, assembled crowds, nocturnal amusements, public shows, and an hundred other instances are forbid and frequented. These prohibitions are useful; though it be prudent in their magistrates, and happy for their people, that they are not enforced, and none but the venal or mercenary attempt to enforce them.

The law in this case, like an indulgent parent, still keeps the rod, though the child is seldom corrected. Were those pardoned offences to rise into enormity, were they likely to obstruct the happiness of society, or endanger the State, it is then that justice would resume her terrors, and punish those faults she had so often overlooked with indulgence. It is to this ductility of the laws that an Englishman owes the freedom he enjoys superior to others in a more popular government; every step therefore the constitution takes towards a democratic form, every diminution of the legal authority is, in fact, a diminution of the subject's freedom; but every attempt to render the government more popular not only impairs natural liberty, but even will at last dissolve the political constitution.[10]

The feebleness of our Chinaman's, or rather of Goldsmith's, reasoning adds to its significance. When pleas in support of an obvious abuse, which are not plausible enough to be called fallacies, pass current for solid argument, they derive their force from the sympathy of the audience to which they are addressed.

The optimism, indeed, of the Blackstonian age is recognised by moralists of a later generation, among whom it excites nothing but condemnation. "Then followed," writes Dr. Arnold,

one of those awful periods in the history of a nation which may be emphatically called its times of trial. I mean those tranquil intervals between one great revolution and another, in which an opportunity is offered for profiting by the lessons of past experience, and to direct the course of the future for good. From our present[11] dizzy state, it is startling to look back on the deep calm of the first seventy years of the eighteenth century. All the evils of society were yet manageable; while complete political freedom, and a vigorous state of mental activity, seemed to promise that the growth of good would more than keep pace with them, and that thus they might be kept down for ever. But tranquillity, as usual, bred carelessness; events were left to take their own

10. Goldsmith, *Works*, iii., *Citizen of the World*, pp. 194, 195.
11. 1833.

way uncontrolled; the weeds grew fast, while none thought of sowing the good seed.[12]

These are the words of a censor who points a lesson intended for his own generation by condemnation of a past age with the virtues and defects whereof he has no sympathy; but to a critic who wishes to understand rather than to pass judgment upon a bygone time, it is easy to discover an explanation or justification of the optimism represented by Blackstone.

The proper task of the eighteenth century was the work of pacification. The problem forced by the circumstances of the time upon thinkers and upon statesmen was, how best to terminate feuds originally generated by religious differences, and to open, if possible, a path for peaceful progress. This problem had in England received an earlier and a more complete solution than in any other European State. The Revolution Settlement had given the death-blow to arbitrary power, and had permanently secured individual freedom. The Toleration Act might appear contemptible to teachers who, like Arnold, wished to realise an ideal—we may now surely say an unattainable and mistaken ideal—of the identification of State and Church, but to men of sense who test the character of a law by its ultimate tendency and result, the celebrated statute will appear to be one of the most beneficial laws ever passed by any legislature. For the Toleration Act gave from the moment it was enacted substantial religious freedom to the vast majority of the English people; in reality, though not in theory, it made active persecution an impossibility. It formed the foundation on which was built up such absolute freedom of opinion and discussion as has never hitherto existed, for any length of time, in any other country than England, or at any rate in any other country the institutions whereof have not been influenced by the principles latent, though not expressed, in the Toleration Act.

The Revolution Settlement, moreover, while establishing theological peace, laid the basis of national greatness. It made possible the union with Scotland. And the union doubled the power of Great Britain. When, in

12. Dr. Arnold, *Miscellaneous Works* (ed. 1845), p. 276. It seems clear that though Arnold refers definitely only to the first seventy years of the eighteenth century, he really has in his mind the tone of the whole of that century—at any rate till near the outbreak of the French Revolution.

1765, Blackstone published the first volume of his *Commentaries,* there were men still living who remembered the victories of Marlborough, and no one had forgotten the glories of the last war with France.

It is well known that the administration of the first William Pitt was a period of unanimity unparalleled in our annals: popular and antipopular parties had gone to sleep together, the great minister wielded the energies of the whole united nation; France and Spain were trampled in the dust, Protestant Germany saved, all North America was the dominion of the British Crown, the vast foundations were laid of our empire in India. Of almost instantaneous growth, the birth of two or three years of astonishing successes, the plant of our power spread its broad and flourishing leaves east and west, and half the globe rested beneath its shade.[13]

The Blackstonian era moreover was, in comparison with the past, an age of philanthropy. The laws were antiquated, the statute-book was defaced by enactments condemned by the humane feeling of later times. But humanity had greatly developed during the eighteenth century; the subjects of George III. had tenderer hearts than the subjects of Cromwell. Goldsmith's childish paradox[14] has no value as argument but much as history; it reminds us that the severity of the law was tempered by compassion. The rules of the common law[15] and the statute-book contained survivals

---

13. Arnold, *Lectures on Modern History,* pp. 262, 263 (2nd ed. 1843). It is intelligible enough that Arnold, who was essentially a moralist and only accidentally an historian, should add, "yet the worm at its root was not wanting." But never did the convictions of a preacher more completely misrepresent an age which he knew only by reading or tradition. The Blackstonian era was a period of national strength and of most reasonable national satisfaction.

14. See p. 54, *ante.*

15. If a prisoner accused of felony stood mute, he could not be tried without his own consent. "To extort that consent he was (until 12 Geo. III. c. 20) subjected to the *peine forte et dure,* by being laid under a heavy mass of iron, and deprived almost entirely of food. Many prisoners deliberately preferred to die under this torture rather than be tried; because, by dying unconvicted, they saved their families from that forfeiture of property which a conviction would have brought about." Kenny, *Outlines of Criminal Law,* p. 467. As late as 1772, when Mansfield and Blackstone were on the Bench, pedantry and callousness to suffering still kept alive torture which might end in death, and could not be defended on the ground, inadequate as it is, that torture may lead to the discovery of truth.

which were at variance with the actual humanity of the age; the law was often so savage as to shock every man of common kindliness. But the law was tempered by technical though absurd rules which gave a criminal undue chances of escape from conviction by the practical revolt of jurymen against the immorality of penalties out of all proportion to moral guilt, and by the constant commutation of capital for some lighter punishment. Legislators were stupid, but they were not intentionally cruel, and the law itself was more severe in theory than in practice.[16]

Penal laws against the Roman Catholics were, at any rate till 1778, outrageously oppressive. The Relief Act, 1778, 18 Geo. III. c. 60, however, taken together with the Relief Act, 1791, 31 Geo. III. c. 32, deprived the laws against Papists of their most oppressive features, and after 1778, or indeed before that date, a Roman Catholic gentleman in practice suffered, we may conjecture, no great grievance other than the exclusion (in itself a bitter wrong) from public life,[17] and long before the passing of the Relief Acts the position of a Roman Catholic in England was enviable when compared with the lot of Protestants in France, till near the outbreak of the French Revolution. Here we touch upon the circumstances which in the eighteenth century gave a peculiar zest to an Englishman's enjoyment of his liberties. He gloried in them because they were, in his eyes, the special privileges of Englishmen. Liberty is never so highly prized as when it is contrasted with the bondage of our neighbours; English freedom has received the warmest adoration not when most complete, but when it has shone by contrast with the intolerance and despotism which were bringing ruin upon France.[18]

16. See on this whole matter, L. Stephen, *English Utilitarians*, i. pp. 25, 26, who points out that "The number of executions in the early part of this [*i.e.* the nineteenth century] varied apparently from a fifth to a ninth of the capital sentences passed," and refers to the Table in Porter's *Progress of the Nation* (1851), p. 635. [Editor's note: The following was added in the second edition.] "Not one in twenty of the sentences was carried into execution." May, *Constit. Hist.* ii. (1863 ed.) c. xviii. p. 597.

17. Compare Burke, speech at Bristol, previous to the election 1780, *Works*, iii. (ed. 1808) p. 389, which makes it apparent that, even prior to the Act of 1778, judges and juries threw every difficulty in the way of informers who proceeded against Roman Catholics for penalties. See Lecky, *Hist.* (1882) iii. p. 587.

18. The free citizens of a state where the majority of the population were slaves have always been fanatical assertors of their own right to freedom.

The optimism which may well be called Blackstonianism, was then the natural tone of the age of Blackstone. It led in the sphere of law to contented acquiescence with the existing state of things, but it would be a grave mistake to suppose that the educated men of Blackstone's generation were, until they were influenced by the course of the French Revolution, bigoted Tories, or in any sense reactionists. Lord Mansfield was in his judicial character an enlightened reformer. Ideas of progress and improvement do not easily associate themselves with the name of Lord Thurlow, yet to Thurlow is ascribed a most ingenious and beneficial device for securing the property rights of married women, and to his energetic interposition is due the recognition in 1801 by the House of Lords, of the right of a wife when suffering from outrageous ill-usage at the hands of her husband to obtain divorce by Act of Parliament.[19] The Commentator was an active humanitarian. He would have called himself a Revolution Whig, and was devoted to the Whig doctrines of civil and religious liberty. Nor was there any inconsistency between a conservative turn of mind and that conception of freedom in accordance with law which the Whigs of the age of George the Third had inherited from their predecessors. The Whig Revolution of 1689, and even the Puritan Rebellion of 1642, were from one point of view conservative movements. Their aim was to preserve the law of the land from either innovations or improvements introduced by arbitrary power. Coke was the legal hero of the Puritans, and Coke was the stiffest of formalists. A devotee of the common law, he detested the reforming ideas of Bacon fully as much as the despotic arbitrariness of James. The Revolution of 1689 was conducted under the guidance of Whig lawyers; they unwittingly laid the foundations of a modern constitutional monarchy, but their intention was to reaffirm in the Bill of Rights and in the Act of Settlement, not the innate rights of man but the inherited and immemorial liberties of Englishmen. This is the basis of truth which underlies the paradox exaggerated by the rhetoric of Burke that the statesmen who carried through the Revolution of 1689 were not revolutionists. They assuredly believed that the liberties of Englishmen were bound up with the maintenance of the common law. The conservatism then of the English Revolution found its natural representatives in English lawyers. If they

---

19. Campbell, *Lives of Lord Chancellors*, vii. (5th ed.), pp. 154, 155.

demurred to the introduction of wide reforms, their hesitation was due in part to the sound conviction that fixity of law is the necessary condition for the maintenance of individual rights and of personal liberty.

Under the horror excited by the excesses of the French Revolution, the mild and optimistic conservatism of Blackstone mingled, within twenty years after his death, with that strenuous and almost reactionary toryism of Eldon which not only retarded but for a time prohibited the removal of abuses. But it should be remembered that at the beginning of the nineteenth century the two different sentiments of optimism as regards English institutions, and of hatred of innovation co-existed, and together constituted the public opinion of the age. Blackstonianism, indeed, not only co-existed with, but survived the reactionary toryism which attained its height between, say, 1790 and 1820. To judge, indeed, from the expressions of Benthamite reformers, we may conclude, and probably with truth, that exaggerated satisfaction with English institutions retarded liberal reforms long after the panic excited by Jacobinism had passed away.[20] In any case, it was this mixture of Blackstonian content with everything English, and Eldonian dread of any change which panic-stricken prejudice could term foreign or Jacobinical, that coloured the whole public opinion of 1800, and determined the course of legislation during the first twenty-five or thirty years of the nineteenth century.

(B) Absence of Changes in the Law

The first quarter of the nineteenth century belongs to the era of legislative stagnation, and is till towards its close characterised (with rare exceptions which require special explanation)[21] by the absence of essential change in the law of the land.

The constitution was then as now what modern writers call flexible; any

---

20. Note the tone of the Benthamite school with regard to Blackstone. "He truckled," writes Austin, "to the sinister interests and to the mischievous prejudices of power; and he flattered the overweening conceit of their national or peculiar institutions, which then was devoutly entertained by the body of the English people, though now [1826–32] it is happily vanishing before the advancement of reason." Austin, *Jurisprudence*, i. (4th ed.), p. 71.

21. See p. 68, *post*.

part thereof might in theory be altered by an Act of Parliament, but the constitution though theoretically liable to be modified, was, owing to the condition of opinion, all but unchangeable by legislation. The English constitution, looked at from a merely legal point of view, remained in 1827 almost exactly what it had been in 1800. If indeed we leave out of sight the Acts of Union with Scotland and Ireland, we might assert, without much exaggeration, that to a mere lawyer who recognised no change which was not recorded in the statute-book or the law reports, the constitution rested in 1827 on the foundation upon which it had been placed by the Revolution of 1689. In the daily working of parliamentary government, it is true, vast alterations had been made during the lapse of more than a century, but these alterations were the result of political conventions or understandings,[22] which left untouched the law of the constitution.

In every sphere of law this absence of change is equally visible;[23] no one looked for active legislation. In truth, the functions of the Cabinet have since 1830 undergone a tacit revolution. From the beginning of the eighteenth century till pretty nearly the time of the Reform Bill, the chief duty of the Ministry was not the passing of laws, but the guidance of national policy. Chatham was the leading statesman of his time and country, but we cannot, it is said, attribute to him a single material amendment of the law. His son, when at the height of power, did not feel himself bound to retire from office, though unable to carry legislation which he proposed to the House of Commons. His attitude with regard to parliamentary reform, and his return to office, though prevented from conferring the full rights of citizenship upon Roman Catholics, can be understood only when we remember that the passing of Acts was not in his time a primary function of the Cabinet. All this is now changed. Every speech from the throne on the opening of Parliament has, for some seventy years and more, contained a legislative programme. Amendment of the law is supposed to be the chief duty of a Ministry. A Conservative no less than a Liberal Cabinet is expected to make, or at any rate to promise, improvements or alterations in

22. See Dicey, *Law of Constitution* (7th ed.), pp. 22–29.

23. An analysis of the contents of any ordinary volume of the statutes enacted during the reign of George III. will support the truth of this statement. Compare Ilbert, *Montesquieu*, pp. 37, 38, for an analysis of parliamentary legislation in 1730.

the law. Lord Halsbury is not counted a very ardent reformer; he has not held the seals for the length of time during which they were retained by Lord Eldon, but he has, we may be sure, carried through, proposed or sanctioned, legal innovations far more numerous and far more fundamental than were suggested or enacted by Lord Eldon during his twenty-seven years of office. Legislative quiescence belongs to the past.

This immutability of the law during the earlier part of the nineteenth century may be regarded from different points of view. We may note the easy tolerance of large public abuses; we may, looking at the matter from a different side, observe the general acquiescence in legal fictions and survivals, which, while they admitted of no logical defence, constituted either the grave defects or, sometimes, the oddities of the law of England. We must, further, while carrying out this survey, remember that none but a few theorists, who did not till, say 1825, command any general confidence, thought it practicable to amend defects which, though they now possess an interest for antiquarians, often caused the gravest inconvenience to the generation which had practical experience of their actual results.

As to Abuses. In 1820 appeared the notorious *Black Book*,[24] which in its day made some noise and stimulated the demand, which in 1830 became irresistible, for retrenchment and reform. This book purports to prove by facts and figures, that every branch of the State and of the Church was full of abuses, and that in every department of public life the nation's money, wrung from an overtaxed people, was wasted on pensions, on sinecures, or, to speak plainly, on corruption. There is no need to place implicit confidence in the allegations of a party pamphlet, but we must believe that the *Black Book* contains a broadly true, if rough and unfair, picture of the system of government as it existed during the first quarter of the nineteenth century. The mass of the people felt the pinch of poverty and were filled with deep discontent, yet heavy taxes were squandered on pensioners and sinecurists. One fact was established past a doubt. In the service neither of the State nor of the Church was reward in any way proportioned to merit. A favoured few connected by relationship or interest with the rich and the

---

24. It was the work of John Wade; it appeared in 1820–23 and was republished in 1831, 1832, and 1835. See *Dictionary of National Biography,* vol. lviii. p. 416.

powerful, received huge salaries for doing nothing, whilst the men who actually did the work of the nation were in many cases grossly underpaid.[25]

Legislative stagnation, or rather the prevalent dislike to all innovation of which it was the result, is indeed exemplified by the toleration of such public abuses as are denounced in the *Black Book;* but a far more striking illustration is presented by the indifference both of legislators and of the public to the maintenance of laws or customs which seriously affected private life, and might work obvious and palpable wrong or injustice. Land-owners, for example, made free use of spring-guns and man-traps; they protected their game at the cost of occasionally killing innocent trespassers. Yet the use of these instruments of death or grievous bodily harm (though declared criminal in Scotland) was sanctioned by English Courts, and not prohibited by Parliament till 1827. A prisoner on trial for felony—*e.g.* for murder or larceny—was denied defence by counsel. This rule was, on the face of it, unjust. The wit of Sydney Smith, one would have fancied, was hardly needed, though it was freely used,[26] to expose the cruelty of depriving a prisoner, whose life may be at stake, of help just at the moment when he most needed it. This denial of legal help assuredly led to the conviction of men innocent of any crime. It had not even the merit of consistent application; for the law allowed counsel to any man who was on trial for a misdemeanour or for treason, or who was impeached before the House of Lords. Yet, in 1824, and again in 1826, the House of Commons refused leave to bring in a bill for the remedy of this monstrous abuse. It was not till four years after the passing of the Reform Act that the Felony Act, 1836,[27] allowed to every person on trial the right to defence by counsel. The

---

25. On the abuses which flourished during the first thirty years of the nineteenth century, see Sydney Smith's *Works,* and Brougham's *Speeches, e.g.* vol. ii., Speech on Law Reform, 7th February 1828, p. 319; Speech on Local Courts, 29th April 1830, *ibid.* p. 489; and note specially the costliness of legal proceedings, *ibid.* pp. 495–499; Speech on Parliamentary Reform, 7th October 1831, p. 559; which shows the practical abuses resulting from the existence of rotten boroughs. An admirable account of the general condition of things under the unreformed Parliament is given in L. Stephen, *English Utilitarians,* chaps. i.–iii.

26. See articles on "Spring-Guns," and on "Man-Traps and Spring-Guns," Sydney Smith's *Works* (ed. 1869), pp. 365, 385.

27. 6 & 7 Will. IV. c. 114. Will not a reformer at the end of the twentieth century wonder that the law continued till 1903 to deny counsel to prisoners on their trial whose poverty

existence of unjust and foolish laws is less remarkable than the grounds
on which these laws were defended. Better, it was argued, that honest men,
who had never fired a gun, should be exposed to death by spring-guns or
man-traps than that a country gentleman should fail in preserving his
game. A prisoner, it was suggested, though he might occasionally through
inability to employ counsel be convicted of a murder or theft which he
had never committed, had no reason to complain, for the very absence of
an advocate turned the judge into counsel for the prisoner. This plea was
notoriously untrue; but, had it been founded on fact, it would have implied
that injustice to a prisoner could be remedied by neglect of duty on the
part of a judge.

Consider, again, the nature of one only of the many irrational restrictions placed by the common law upon the admissibility of evidence. The
party to an action, or the husband or wife of such party, was not competent
to be a witness at the trial.[28] Note what this restriction meant. A brought
an action against X, e.g. for breach of contract or for an assault. The persons
most likely to know—and perhaps the only persons who did know the
facts of the case—might well be A, the plaintiff, and X, the defendant; yet
neither A nor X was allowed to tell his story to the jury.[29] At the present
day we wonder not that under such a rule there should have been frequent
failures of justice, but that in spite of it the ends of justice should often
have been attained. But Parliament did not modify this irrational exclusion
of necessary evidence until well after the end of the period of stagnation.
The chief steps for its abolition are worth notice. Under the influence of
Benthamite teaching it was, in 1846, abolished as regards proceedings in

---

prevented them from paying the necessary fee, and that the Poor Prisoners' Defence Act,
1903 (3 Edw. VII. c. 38), s. 1, did not completely remedy this obvious injustice? [Editor's
note: The last half of this footnote was added in the second edition.]

28. See Taylor On Evidence (6th ed.), s. 1210.

29. The result might occasionally, at any rate, be that a person who had suffered a grievous
wrong was in effect deprived of any civil remedy. X assaults A. No other persons are present.
Neither X nor A could give evidence. It might possibly happen that A had no means of
proving the assault. Counsel, who lived when this exclusion of evidence was in force, have
sometimes attributed a large part of the extraordinary successes achieved by Erskine or
Scarlett to the impossibility of bringing the real facts of a case before a jury, and the wide
scope thus given to a skilful advocate of suggesting imaginary accounts of transactions which,
in the absence of evidence, admitted of more than one interpretation.

the County Courts;[30] five years later it was done away with as regards most actions in the Superior Courts;[31] in 1869 it was abolished as regards all civil actions, and also as regards all proceedings instituted in consequence of adultery.[32]

At the time, further, when the common law courts made oral evidence the basis of their inquiries, but deprived this mode of investigation of half its worth by excluding from the witness-box the parties to the cause, who naturally knew most about the truth, the Court of Chancery allowed a plaintiff to search the conscience of the defendants, and the defendants, by a cross bill, to perform a similar operation upon their antagonist, but only permitted the inquiry to be on paper.[33] In other words, whilst the common law courts took the right method for ascertaining the truth, they excluded the evidence of the persons to whom alone the truth was likely to be known, whilst the Court of Chancery admitted the evidence of the persons most likely to know the truth, but would receive it only in the form of written answers, which give little or no security that the witnesses who know the truth should tell it; and this anomaly in the procedure of the courts of equity was not substantially altered until the middle of the nineteenth century,[34] and was completely removed only by the Judicature Act, 1875.

---

30. 9 & 10 Vict. c. 95, s. 83.

31. The Evidence Act, 1851 (14 & 15 Vict. c. 99), s. 2. Even then the parties to an action for a breach of promise of marriage still were excluded from giving evidence, and were not made competent witnesses till 1869.

32. The Evidence Further Amendment Act, 1869, 32 & 33 Vict. c. 68. The principle or prejudice that persons interested in the result of a trial, whether civil or criminal, ought on account of their temptation to lie, even when on oath, not only to be heard as witnesses with a certain suspicion, but also to be held incompetent to give evidence, lingered on in the sphere of criminal law till nearly the close of the nineteenth century. Only in 1898 was a person charged with a criminal offence at last allowed to give evidence on his own behalf. (Criminal Evidence Act, 1898, 61 & 62 Vict. c. 36.) The truth, that is to say, of Bentham's doctrine that, "in the character of objections to competency no objections ought to be allowed," was not fully admitted till sixty-six years after his death. Before 1898, however, persons charged with crime had, in the case of special offences, been allowed to give evidence under various different enactments.

33. See Bowen, *Reign of Queen Victoria,* i. p. 290.

34. The Chancery Procedure Act, 1852 (15 & 16 Vict. c. 86), s. 39. See Ashburner, *Principles of Equity,* pp. 30–32.

As to Legal Fictions and Survivals. Every branch of the law teemed with fictions and survivals; they constituted the oddities of our legal system, and, whether simply useless or actually noxious, were specially typical of an age which acquiesced in things as they were.

The ordinary civil jurisdiction of the Court of King's Bench rested upon the absurd fiction that the defendant in an action, *e.g.* for a debt, had been guilty of a trespass.[35] The ordinary civil jurisdiction of the Court of Exchequer rested upon the equally absurd fiction that the plaintiff in an action was a debtor to the king, and, owing to the injury or damage done him by the defendant, was unable to pay his debt to the king.[36] If A brought an action for a wrong done him abroad[37] by X, as, for instance, for an assault committed at Minorca, his right to sue was justified by the fiction that the assault had taken place "at Minorca, (to wit) at London, in the parish of St. Mary-le-Bow; in the ward of Cheap." If A brought an action of ejectment[38] against X to establish A's title to land of which X was in possession, the whole proceeding was based on a purely fictitious or imaginary action brought by a plaintiff, John Doe, who had no existence, against a defendant, Richard Roe, who had no existence, for an assault committed upon the said John Doe on the land claimed by A, which assault had never been committed by any one, either on such land or elsewhere. If a tenant

35. Blackstone, *Comm.* iii. p. 43.

36. *Ibid.* p. 46.

37. *Mostyn* v. *Fabrigas,* 1775, Cowp. 161.

38. "The action was commenced (without any writ) by a declaration, *every word of which was untrue:* it alleged a *lease* from the claimant to the nominal plaintiff *(John Doe):* an *entry* by him under and by virtue of such lease; and his subsequent *ouster* by the nominal defendant *(Richard Roe):* at the foot of such declaration was a notice addressed to the *tenants in possession,* warning them, that, unless they appeared and defended the action within a specified time, *they would be turned out of possession.* This was the only comprehensible part to a non-professional person: it generally alarmed the tenants sufficiently to send them to their attorney, whereby one main object of the proceeding was attained: but the tenants were not permitted to defend the action, nor to substitute their names as defendants in lieu of that of the casual ejector *(Richard Roe),* except upon entering into a 'consent rule,' whereby they bound themselves to admit the alleged *lease, entry,* and *ouster,* and to plead the general issue 'not guilty,' and to insist on the title only."—Cole, *Law and Practice in Ejectment* (1857), p. 1. For a popular account of the action of ejectment as it still existed in 1840, see Warren's *Ten Thousand a Year.*

in tail wished to bar the entail, he could indeed do so in 1800 as a tenant in tail can do it to-day, but, whereas now the result is achieved by an ordinary deed of conveyance duly enrolled,[39] in 1800, and for many years later, it was attained by an action which was a fiction from beginning to end, and an action under which the tenant in tail nominally lost the very estate over which, by barring the entail, he, in fact, obtained complete control.

These long labyrinths of judge-made fictions, which were far more intricate than can be made apparent without giving details unsuitable for the purpose of these lectures, seem to a lawyer of to-day as strange as the most fanciful dreams of *Alice in Wonderland*. They sometimes, indeed, led by a most roundabout path to the attainment of desirable ends, but, while they were hardly defensible, even by the ardent optimism of Blackstone,[40] they were, as experience has now proved, absolutely unnecessary. They were nevertheless tolerated, or rather held unobjectionable, by the public opinion of 1800, just as were other survivals and fictions which were as noxious as they were obviously ridiculous. Under the proceeding, in itself anomalous, of an appeal of murder, the appellee might, through his right to claim trial by battel, sometimes escape conviction, as he certainly did as late as 1818, by reliance not on proof of his innocence, but on the strength of his arm.[41] Benefit of clergy, as regulated by law in 1800, though it no doubt mitigated the monstrous severity of punishments for crime, did in certain instances give an unjustifiable privilege or protection to criminals who happened to be clerks in orders.[42] Privilege of Peerage was simply a nuisance and an injustice. In 1765 it saved the Lord Byron of the day from the punishment due to manslaughter;[43] in 1776 it saved the Duchess of Kingston from punishment for bigamy.[44] In 1841 Lord Cardigan, when on

---

39. Stephen, *Comm.* i. (14th ed.), pp. 347, 348.

40. Blackstone, *Comm.* ii. p. 361.

41. See Blackstone, *Comm.* iii. pp. 337, 341; *ibid.* iv. pp. 340–342; *Ashford* v. *Thornton,* 1818, 3 B. & Ald. 485; 19 R. R. 349; Campbell, *Chief Justices,* iv. (3rd ser.), pp. 232, 233. Appeal of murder and trial by battel were abolished in 1819. 59 Geo. III. c. 46.

42. Stephen, *Hist.* i. p. 463.

43. *19 State Trials,* 1177.

44. *20 State Trials,* 379.

trial before the peers in respect of a duel, might, it was thought, if he had been found guilty, have escaped punishment by pleading his privilege.[45]

The existence of these fictions, survivals, and abuses, during a period of legal stagnation, is hardly more noteworthy than the fact that many of them were not abolished till well after the commencement of the era of Benthamite reform. Benefit of clergy remained in force till 1827.[46] Entails were barred by fictitious actions up to 1833.[47] Privilege of Peerage was not abolished till 1841.[48] John Doe and Richard Roe, with all the fictions which used to give an antiquarian interest to the action of ejectment, haunted our courts till 1852,[49] that is, till well within the memory of lawyers now living. Slow, indeed, even in the days of legislative activity, was the effective movement of opinion in favour of reform.

(C) Why considerable changes took place during the Period of Quiescence

How did it happen that the period of quiescence is nevertheless marked by several far-reaching changes in the law?

The answer in general terms is this: These innovations are of two different classes and due to two different causes; some of them are reactionary laws, the fruit of and congenial to the panic-stricken toryism which had cast into the background the Blackstonian optimism of an earlier date; others are reforms either necessitated (as was to all appearance the Act of Union with Ireland) by the irresistible requirements of the day, or else demanded by, and a concession to, the humanitarianism which from 1800 onwards exerted an ever increasing influence.

Reactionary Laws. Of such legislation let us take two examples. The first is the Combination Act of 1800,[50] which derives special importance from its intimate connection with the subsequent development of the combi-

45. See Stephen, *Hist.* i. p. 462.
46. 7 & 8 Geo. IV. c. 28.
47. 3 & 4 Will. IV. c. 74.
48. 4 & 5 Vict. c. 22.
49. Common Law Procedure Act, 1852, 15 & 16 Vict. c. 76.
50. See Lects. VI. and VIII., *post.*

nation law—a branch of the law which has been affected in a very marked degree by changes in public opinion. The second is the body of laws known as the Six Acts.

The Combination Act, 1800, 40 Geo. III. c. 106,[51] which must be read in connection with the law of conspiracy as then interpreted by the judges, aimed in reality at one object, namely, the suppression of all combinations of workmen, whether transitory or permanent, of which the object was to obtain an advance of wages or otherwise fix the terms of employment; it was an Act for the suppression of strikes and of trade unions. The severity of the statute can be realised only by a minute examination, which would be alien to my present purpose, of its different provisions. Two illustrations may suffice. Under the Act it is made an offence (if we put the matter shortly) to assist in maintaining men on strike:[52] persons guilty of this or any other offence under the Act are made liable to conviction on summary procedure before justices of the peace.[53]

One feature of the great Combination Act is sometimes (because of its small practical importance) overlooked. The statute imposes a penalty upon combinations among masters for the reduction of wages or for an increase in the hours or the quantity of work. To an historian of opinion this provision is of importance. It shows that in 1800 Parliament was in theory opposed to every kind of trade combination.

Behind the Combination Act—and this is a matter of primary importance—there stood the law of conspiracy. As to the exact nature of this

---

51. It re-enacts in substance the Combination Act of 1799, 39 Geo. III. c. 81. See generally as to the Combination Act, 1800, Stephen, *Hist.* iii. 306; Wright, 12.

52. Stephen, *Hist.* iii. 208.

53. The maintenance of this summary jurisdiction is a feature of subsequent Combination Acts (5 Geo. IV. c. 95, s. 7; 6 Geo. IV. c. 129, s. 6; Conspiracy and Protection of Property Act, 1875, s. 10). Under the last Act, however, the accused has the option of trial on indictment before a jury (see, for the reasons in favour of this summary jurisdiction, *Report of Committee on Combination Laws*, 1875, pp. 10, 11). The desirability of obtaining a ready method for the punishment of trade offences, which could only be effected by Act of Parliament, should be noted. It invalidates the argument that conduct made an offence under *e.g.* the Combination Act, 1800, could not be an offence at common law, since if punishable at common law it would not have been made an offence by statute.

law, as then understood, it would be rash to express one's self with dogmatic assurance.[54] There are one or two features, however, of the combination law, as it stood in 1800, of which it may be allowable to speak with a certain degree of confidence.

The law of conspiracy had by the end of the eighteenth century received under judicial decisions a very wide extension.[55]

A conspiracy, it is submitted, included in 1800 a combination for any of the following purposes; that is to say:

1. For the purpose of committing a crime.[56]

2. For the purpose of violating a private right in which the public has a sufficient interest,[57] or, in other words, for the purpose of committing any tort or breach of contract which materially affects the interest of the public.[58]

54. Sir William Erle, Sir Robert S. Wright, Sir J. F. Stephen, all eminent judges, have each published on this subject books of authority. A study of their writings leaves on my mind the impression that these distinguished authors have each arrived at somewhat different conclusions.

55. Wright's *Law of Criminal Conspiracies*—published before, but not republished after he was raised to the bench—contains elaborate arguments to show that this extension was illegitimate, and was not really supported by the authorities on which it is supposed to rest. From a merely historical point of view these arguments have great force, but from a legal point of view their effect is diminished by the reflection that similar arguments if employed by a lawyer of as wide historical information and of as keen logical acumen as Sir R. S. Wright, would shake almost every accepted principle of English law, in so far as it does not depend upon statute. In any case Wright's arguments are for my present purpose irrelevant; my object is to state, as far as may be, not what the law of conspiracy ought to have been, but what it was in 1800.

56. "It is undisputed law that a combination for the purpose of committing a crime is a crime" (Erle, *Trade Unions*, 31), and this whether the crime is known to the common law or is created by statute.

57. Erle, 32.

58. It is arguable in spite of Turner's case, 13 East, 228, that a combination to commit any tort, or for the breach of any contract, with a view to damage any person, is a conspiracy, but it is not necessary for our purpose to state the law as widely as this. See Kenny, *Outlines of Criminal Law*, 288–290.

3. For any purpose clearly opposed to received morality or to public policy.[59]

Since a combination to commit a crime is *ipso facto* a conspiracy, it follows that a combination for any purpose made or declared criminal by the Combination Act, 1800, *e.g.* a combination to collect money for the support of men on strike, was in 1800 an undoubted conspiracy.

If we bear these features of the law of conspiracy in mind and recollect that the Combination Act was not intended to render unlawful any bargaining, *e.g.* as to the rate of wages, between an employer and an individual workman, the combined result of the Combination Act, 1800, and the law of conspiracy, or, in other words, of the combination law as it stood at the beginning of the nineteenth century, may be thus broadly summed up: Any artisan who organised a strike or joined a trade union was a criminal and liable on conviction to imprisonment; the strike was a crime, the trade union was un [sic] unlawful association. The whole idea on which the law rested was this:

> Workmen are to be contented with the current rate of wages, and are on no account to do anything which has a tendency to compel their employers to raise it. Practically, they could go where they pleased individually and make

---

59. Erle, 33, 34.

The agreements which at the present day may be held to constitute a conspiracy have been thus summarised:

1. Agreements to commit a substantive crime (*R. v. Davitt*, 11 Cox, 676; *R. v. White-church*, 24 Q.B.D., 420), *e.g.* a conspiracy to steal or to incite one to steal.
2. Agreements to commit any tort that is malicious.
3. Agreements to commit a breach of contract under circumstances which are peculiarly injurious to the public.
4. Agreements to do certain other acts which, unlike those hitherto mentioned, are not breaches of law at all, but which nevertheless are outrageously immoral, or else in some way extremely injurious to the public.

See Kenny, 288–290.

The definition attributed to Lord Denman of a conspiracy as a "combination for accomplishing an unlawful end, or a lawful end by unlawful means" (see Wright, 63) is, it is submitted, sound, though too vague to be of much use. Its importance lies in the emphasis it lays on the *object* or *purpose*—a very different thing from the motive—of a combination as a test of its criminal character, and in the light which it throws on the wide extension given by the law to the idea of conspiracy.

the best bargains they could for themselves, but under no circumstances and by no means, direct or indirect, must they bring the pressure of numbers to bear on their employers or on each other.[60]

To a reader of the twentieth century this state of the law seems no less incomprehensible than intolerable, and indeed within twenty-five years after the passing of the Combination Act, appeared utterly indefensible to so rigid an economist as McCulloch, a man whose good sense and genuine humanity have been concealed from a later generation by the heavy and brutal satire of Carlyle. Who, we ask, were the tyrants who deprived working-men of all freedom, and what was the state of opinion which sanctioned this tyranny? The answer is that the men who passed the great Combination Act were not despots, and that the Act precisely corresponded with the predominant beliefs of the time.

The Parliament of 1800 acted under the guidance of Pitt. It contained among its members Fox and Wilberforce; it was certainly not an assembly insensible to feelings of humanity. The ideas of the working classes were, it may be said, not represented. This is roughly true, but artisans were no better represented in the Parliament of 1824 than in the Parliament of 1800, yet the Parliament of 1824 repealed the Combination Act and freed trade combinations from the operation of the law of conspiracy. The mere fact that the Combination Act of 1799 and the Combination Act of 1800, which re-enacted its provisions, passed through Parliament without any discussion of which a report remains, is all but decisive. The law represented in 1800 the predominant opinion of the day.

The public opinion which sanctioned the Combination Act (which was to a great extent a Consolidation Act)[61] consisted of two elements.

The first element, though not in the long run the more important, was a dread of combinations, due in the main to the then recent memories of the Reign of Terror. Nor are we justified in asserting that this fear was nothing better than unfounded panic. Englishmen who, though from a distance, had witnessed the despotism of the Jacobin Club, which towards

---

60. Stephen, *Hist.* iii. 209.

61. *I.e.* the Combination Act generalised provisions which had been long enforced under special Acts in respect of workmen engaged in particular kinds of manufacture. See Stephen, *Hist.* iii. 206.

the close of its tyranny sent weekly, in Paris alone, an average of nearly 200[62] citizens to the guillotine, may be excused for some jealousy of clubs or unions. The existence, at any rate, of this fear of combinations is certain; it is proved by a body of Acts—37 Geo. III. c. 123 (1797); 39 Geo. III. c. 79 (1799); 57 Geo. III. c. 19 (1817)—which were directed against any treasonable or seditious society, or against any society which might possibly foster treason or sedition. The presence in one at least of these enactments of exceptions in favour of meetings of Quakers, and of meetings assembled for the purposes of a religious or charitable nature only,[63] betrays the width of their operation and the fears of their authors. Clubs of all kinds were objects of terror.

The second element of public opinion in 1800 was the tradition of paternal government which had been inherited from an earlier age, and was specially congenial to the toryism of the day. This tradition had two sides. The one was the conviction that it was the duty of labourers to work for reasonable, that is to say, for customary, wages. The other side of the same tradition was the provision by the State (at the cost, be it noted, of the well-to-do classes, and especially of the landowners) of subsistence for workmen who could not find work. The so-called "Speenhamland Act of Parliament," by which the Justices of Berkshire granted to working-men relief in proportion to the number of their families, or, to use the political slang of to-day, tried to provide for them a "living wage," is the fruit of the same policy which gave birth to the Combination Act, 1800. The sentiment of the day was indeed curiously tolerant of a crude socialism. Whitbread introduced a bill authorising justices to fix a minimum of wages, and complained of the absence of any law to compel farmers to do their duty. Fox thought that magistrates should protect the poor from the injustice of grasping employers. Pitt introduced a bill for authorising allowances out of the public rates, including the present of a cow. Burke ap-

---

62. During a period of seven weeks, between June 10 and July 27 (9 Thermidor), 1794, at least 1376 individuals were sent by the Revolutionary Tribunal in Paris to the guillotine. This gives an average for that period of more than 196 victims a week. See Morse Stephens, *French Revolution*, ii. p. 548.

63. 57 Geo. III. c. 19, s. 27; Wright, 23, 24.

proved a plan for enabling the "poor" to purchase terminable annuities on the security of the rates.[64]

The Combination Act, then, of 1800 represented the public opinion of 1800.[65]

The Six Acts of 1819[66] were certainly the work of Tories who, filled with dread of sedition and rebellion, wished to curtail the right of public discussion, and these enactments which aimed, among other objects, at the prevention and punishment of blasphemous and seditious libels, and at effectually preventing seditious meetings and assemblies out of doors, aroused grave fears among all friends of freedom. But the Six Acts were not, after all, quite so reactionary as they appeared to Liberals who anticipated an attack upon the liberties of Englishmen. Some of these famous Acts—such, for example, as the Act to prevent delay in the administration of justice in cases of misdemeanour, or the Act, still in force, to prevent the training of persons to the use of arms and to the practice of military evolutions—were salutary; one at least was never intended to be more than temporary. The attempt—known as the Cato Street conspiracy—of a few democratic desperadoes to assassinate the whole of the Cabinet marks the

64. Fowle, *Poor Law* (2nd ed.), 66, 67.

65. Oddly enough the Code Napoléon of 1804, which, as regards the right of association, embodies the ideas of French revolutionists or reformers, is at least as strongly opposed to trade combinations, whether among employers or workmen, as the Combination Act, 1800.

66. The Six Acts were:

 1. An Act to prevent the training of persons to the use of arms and to the practice of military evolutions and exercise (60 Geo. III. & 1 Geo. IV. c. 1).

 2. An Act to authorise justices of the peace to seize arms, etc., to continue in force only till 1822 (c. 2).

 3. An Act to prevent delay in the administration of justice in cases of misdemeanour (c. 4).

 4. An Act for more effectually preventing seditious meetings, etc. [out of doors], to continue in force for only a limited time (c. 6).

 5. An Act for the effectual prevention and punishment of blasphemous and seditious libels (c. 8).

 6. An Act to subject certain publications to duties of stamps upon newspapers, and to restrain abuses arising from the publication of blasphemous and seditious libels (c. 9).

prevalent discontent of the time, and proves that the Six Acts were not the result of absolutely groundless panic.

The repressive legislation of 1819 may have been unwise, but it was an attempt to meet a serious crisis and was the natural outcome of the public opinion which in 1819 and 1820 determined the action of Parliament. The Six Acts, however, and other enactments of the same class, in so far as they were reactionary, produced little permanent result.

Reforms. Innovations which were, or were intended to be reforms, such, for example, as the Act of Union with Ireland, or the Health and Morals Act, 1802, are exceptions to the immutability of the law which characterised the period of quiescence, but they are exceptions which, though they need, admit of explanation; these Acts will indeed be found on careful consideration to be striking confirmations of the dependence of legislation upon opinion.

The Union with Ireland Act, 1800, was carried, as regards England at any rate, without any great difficulty; it was the work of a Tory Government; it was opposed, though not very vigorously, by a certain number of Whigs; the Act, moreover, as experience has proved, made a change in the constitution of Parliament not less fundamental and important than the alteration effected by the Reform Act of 1832. How are we to explain the paradox, that a revolutionary alteration of the constitution took place, and took place with ease, at a date when the public opinion of the day was opposed to every kind of innovation? The explanation lies on the surface of history.

The Union with Ireland was sanctioned by English opinion because it was enforced by the immediate and irresistible pressure of events. It was dictated by the logic of facts. Grattan's constitution had broken down; the Rebellion of 1798, the savagery of loyalists no less than of rebels, the severities of the Irish Parliament, the all but successful attempt at invasion by France, rendered some fundamental change in the government of Ireland a necessity. Any Englishman of common sense must have felt that things could not remain as they were. The choice lay between the amendment of the Irish parliamentary system[67] and the abolition of the Irish

---

67. This, as I understand Lecky's *History of England during the Eighteenth Century,* is the

Parliament by its absorption in the Parliament of the United Kingdom. To English statesmen at any rate such abolition must have appeared both the easier and the safer course. The precedent of the Union with Scotland seemed decisive, and the success of the legislation of 1707 concealed not only the dangers but the extent of the change involved in the legislation of 1800. The anticipation was natural that the introduction into the Parliament at Westminster of members from Ireland would work no greater alteration in its character than had the introduction of members from Scotland. Nor till the passing of the Catholic Relief Act, 1829, was the anticipation falsified. The Union, dissevered as it was from the emancipation of the Roman Catholics, failed to confer anything like the whole of its promised benefit on the United Kingdom, but the curtailment of Pitt's statesmanlike design soothed the alarms of Englishmen and fell in with English public opinion. If some change then in the government of Ireland was needed, and few were the Englishmen or Irishmen who could doubt the existence of such necessity, the Act of Union must have appeared to its supporters the least revolutionary of all possible changes. It was justified by precedent, and precedent, which always tells much with Englishmen, told for more in 1800 than it does in 1905.[68]

---

policy which that eminently well informed and pre-eminently just historian thinks ought to have been adopted. One must, however, remark that this policy if honestly carried out would have been marked by two characteristics which it is hardly possible to believe would have been accepted by Englishmen at the beginning of the nineteenth century. The one was the concession of full political rights to the Irish Roman Catholics, to which many zealots for Irish parliamentary independence—such, for instance, as Lord Charlemont—were opposed; the other was the creation of an Irish Executive really dependent upon the support of the Irish Houses of Parliament, and therefore truly, as well as in name, uncontrolled by the English Cabinet.

68. This is not the place in which to discuss the character of George III. His sentiments or prejudices afford, however, an admirable index to the public opinion of England during his reign. His errors were some of them great enough, but his opinion was always, or almost always, the opinion of the average English elector. It is impossible to show that as regards either the war with the colonies, the hatred to the Coalition, the distrust of parliamentary reform, the maintenance of the war with France, or the opposition to Catholic Emancipation, the feelings of George III. were not on the whole the feelings of the English people. In his support of the Act of Union with Ireland and in his refusal to couple it with Catholic Emancipation, George III. represented the opinion of the English electorate.

Many of the reforms belonging to the era of legislative quiescence bear a humanitarian character. Such, for example, are the prohibition of the slave trade (1806),[69] the partial abolition of the pillory (1816),[70] the abolition of the whipping of women (1820),[71] the earliest attempt to forbid cruelty to animals (1822),[72] the abolition of State lotteries (1826–1827),[73] the prohibition of the use of spring guns (1827).[74]

All these measures humanised the law of England. They are all distinctly due to the increasing development of humanitarianism,[75] by which term is here meant that hatred of pain, either physical or moral, which inspires the desire to abolish all patent forms of suffering or oppression. This passionate humanitarianism, opposed though it was to much popular indifference as regards various forms of cruelty,[76] was shared by philanthropists of every school, with many men whose fear of Jacobinical principles made them shun the name of reformers. In the detestation of cruelty, Benthamite free-thinkers, Whig philanthropists, such as Fox, Tory humanitarians, such as Pitt, and Evangelicals who followed Wilberforce, were substantially at one. On this subject, men divided by the widest political and theological differences stood side by side; there was here no difference between Burke and Bentham, or between Wesley and his biographer Southey. Common humanitarianism was a strong bond of union between men who on other

69. 46 Geo. III. c. 119.

70. 56 Geo. III. c. 138.

71. 1 Geo. IV. c. 57.

72. 3 Geo. IV. c. 71.

73. 6 Geo. IV. c. 60; 7 & 8 Geo. IV. c. 28.

74. 7 & 8 Geo. IV. c. 18.

75. That humanitarianism was a marked characteristic of the first half of the nineteenth century, and especially of the era of Benthamite reform, is certain. Whether this desire to avoid the infliction of pain has not in England diminished in force since the middle of the nineteenth century, admits at least of doubt. Note as example of increased humanitarianism between 1736 and 1818 that while the imaginary Jeanie Deans is sent home in a carriage by her patron, her real prototype, Ellen Walker (1736), was allowed to walk back to Scotland, and brought the pardon only just in time to save her sister's life. See Scott's note, *Heart of Midlothian,* Waverley Novels, xii., Introduction, pp. i–xi.

76. *E.g.* sports, such as bull-baiting or prize fights, of which the one was defended by Windham, the friend and disciple of Burke and of Johnson, and the other was patronised on principle by a statesman so kindly and so religious as Lord Althorp.

matters were stern opponents; William Smith, a leading Unitarian, or, in the language of the time, a Socinian, and the representative, in the words of a satirist, of "all the opinions of all the Dissenters," was the esteemed friend of the Tories and orthodox Churchmen who made up the Clapham Sect. James Mill, whom the religious world of his generation knew to be a free-thinker, and would, had they been aware of his true opinions, have termed an atheist, was the ally, if not the friend, of Zachary Macaulay, an enthusiastic, not to say fanatical, Evangelical.[77] These facts are of infinite importance to all persons engaged in the study of public opinion; they remind us that in an age disgraced by much general brutality, reformers of every school were united in the crusade against cruelty; they remind us further that a period of political reaction might also be a time during which humane feeling is constantly on the increase.[78] Between 1800 and 1830 Benthamism laid the foundations of its future supremacy. Though not yet dominant it exerted towards 1830 marked influence in public life; and the era of Benthamism coincided to a great extent with the Evangelical revival. It was the age of Wilberforce (1759–1833), of Clarkson (1760–1846), of Zachary Macaulay (1768–1838), of Simeon (1759–1836), of Henry Martin (1781–1812), of Elizabeth Fry (1780–1845), of Hannah More (1745–1833). These names, to which might be added a score of others, tell their own tale; they show at a glance that at the beginning of the nineteenth century Evangelicalism was among religious Englishmen supreme, and Evangelicalism, no less than Benthamism, meant as a social creed the advocacy of every form of humanity. The crusade against cruelty owes its success in an almost equal degree to philosophic philanthropy and to religious compassion for suffering. Humanitarianism in alliance with religious enthusiasm was assuredly the force which in 1806 abolished the slave trade, as twenty-eight years later it gave freedom to the slaves.[79]

No better example of philanthropic legislation during the supremacy of Tory statesmanship can be found than the Health and Morals Act, 1802.[80]

---

77. Cowper, the friend and disciple of John Newton, inveighed against the Bastille, that "house of bondage," with its horrid "towers," its "dungeons," and "cages of despair," with an indignation which would have become a disciple of Rousseau.

78. The reign of Nero is contemporaneous with the spread of Christianity.

79. For the intellectual relation between Benthamism and Evangelicalism as different forms of individualism, see Lect. XII., *post.*

80. 42 Geo. III. c. 73.

Up to that date there existed no factory[81] legislation whatever.[82] This earliest Factory Act was carried through Parliament by Sir Robert Peel (the father of the celebrated minister), himself a manufacturer and a Tory. The measure was suggested not by any general principle, but by the needs of the moment. An epidemic had broken out in Manchester, and had caused the death of many apprentices employed in the cotton mills. The plague was attributed to their scanty diet, and to the wretched conditions under which the apprentices, mostly pauper children, sent up to the north of England by the parochial authorities of the south, worked out their time of bondage. The Act of 1802 regulated, to a limited extent, the employment of these apprentices in cotton and woollen factories. It contained a few sanitary and moral rules; as, for example, that the rooms of any factory within the Act should be washed twice a year with quicklime and water; that each apprentice should receive two suits of clothes; that no apprentice should be kept at work more than twelve hours a day; that the apartments of male and female apprentices should be kept distinct; that not more than two should sleep in one bed; that every apprentice should on Sunday for the space of one hour "be instructed and examined in the principles of the Christian religion by a qualified person."

This law, which deserves special attention on account of its connection with the factory legislation of a later time,[83] is in complete correspondence with the ideas of an era when reform of all kinds was checked by dread of innovation, and humanitarianism could best obtain a hearing when allied with the promotion of sound churchmanship. A reader versed in the religious literature of 1800 might well believe that Sir Robert Peel had drafted the Health and Morals Act after consultation with Hannah More. This earliest Factory Act was the work of benevolent Tories; it sprung from the needs of the moment, and owed nothing either to the advance of democracy or to socialism. The means provided for its enforcement (*e.g.* the inspection of the mills, which come within its scope, by visitors who owed their appointment to justices of the peace) were ridiculously inadequate.

---

81. The word "factory" or "manufactory" does not, as far as I have observed, occur in Blackstone's *Commentaries;* the book certainly contains no reference to what we now understand by factory legislation.

82. See Hutchins and Harrison, *History of Factory Legislation,* ch. ii. pp. 16–18.

83. See Lect. VII., *post.*

The Act was a moral protest against cruelty, but practically produced no effect. These remarks apply more or less to enactments of a similar character which followed the Health and Morals Act, 1802,[84] and were passed in 1819,[85] in 1825,[86] in 1829,[87] and, to a great extent, even to the more effective Act of 1831.[88]

(D) Close of the Period of Quiescence

From 1815 to 1820, or even to 1825, Toryism was supreme in State and Church, reform was identified with revolution, and legislative reaction, in the judgment of Whigs and Radicals, menaced the hereditary liberties of Englishmen. In 1830 legislative inertia came with apparent suddenness[89] to an end. The activity of Parliament, which has lasted, though, with varying force, till the present day, evinced for a short time a feverish energy which alarmed tried reformers. "All gradation and caution," murmured Sydney Smith, "have been banished since the Reform Bill—rapid high-pressure wisdom is the only agent in public affairs."[90]

Whence this sudden outburst of legislative activity?

The answer may be given in one sentence: The English people had at last come to perceive the intolerable incongruity between a rapidly changing social condition and the practical unchangeableness of the law.

This general reply itself needs explanation. We must examine a little further what were the slowly operating causes of a noteworthy revolution in opinion. Our task will be lightened if we bear in mind that men's beliefs are in the main the result of circumstances[91] rather than of arguments, and that a policy, or rather the public opinion from which it derives its au-

84. 42 Geo. III. c. 73.

85. 39 Geo. III. c. 66.

86. 6 Geo. IV. c. 63.

87. 10 Geo. IV. c. 51.

88. 1 & 2 Will. IV. c. 39. This last Act was of a wider scope and comes within the period of individualism.

89. See pp. 23–24, *ante*.

90. Sydney Smith, *Works* (ed. 1879), p. 340 (n.).

91. See pp. 20, 21, *ante*.

thority, is often in the greatest danger of overthrow at the moment of its apparent triumph.[92]

The conditions which terminated the era of legislative quiescence, or (what is the same thing looked at from another point of view), which promoted the growth of Benthamite liberalism, may be conveniently brought under four heads: *First,* the rapid change in the social condition of England between 1800 and 1830; *secondly,* the increasing unsuitability of unchanging institutions for a quickly developing society; *thirdly,* the lapse of time, which of itself obliterated the memories of the French Revolution; *fourthly,* the existence of the Benthamite school.

(1) *As to the Change in the Social Condition of England.* It is somewhat difficult for a student to realise the indisputable fact that a period of legal stagnation was in other respects a period of great moral and intellectual activity.[93] The termination, indeed, of the great war opened a season of popular distress, which, however, slowly passed, as the century went on, into a time of mercantile and manufacturing prosperity. It was an era of social change. Population was constantly on the increase. In 1801 the population of England and Wales was, in round numbers, 8,000,000; in 1811 it was 10,000,000; in 1821 it was 12,000,000; and in 1831 it was 13,000,000. There was no reason to suppose that an increase which came very near to 2,000,000 in every decade would be arrested. Sagacious observers might conjecture that, as has already happened, the inhabitants of England and Wales would be quadrupled[94] by the end of the century. This increase belonged in the main to the operative or industrial classes. It was stimulated by inventions in machinery, by the making of canals, by the use of steam, by the opening of coal mines and the like. England was in fact changing from an agricultural into a manufacturing country, and in the north at any rate was becoming a vast industrial city. And this increase in the numbers of the people coincided with a shifting of the centres of population. Till towards the end of the eighteenth century the majority of the

---

92. See p. 17, *ante.*

93. The introduction of fast coaches towards the end of the eighteenth and the beginning of the nineteenth century is analogous to the introduction of railways at a later date. [Editor's note: This footnote was added in the second edition.]

94. *Statesman's Year-Book,* 1904, p. 16.

English people lived in the south and the west of England; Bristol was, next to London, the most important of our cities. From the beginning of the nineteenth century, manufactures, population, and wealth kept flowing from the south to the north of England; new cities sprung up in Lancashire and the northern counties where there had formerly been nothing but wastes dotted with townlets and villages. Towns such as Birmingham, Manchester, and Liverpool acquired a new importance, and with this change the influence of employers of labour begun to overshadow the authority of squires and merchants. The country, moreover, it is perfectly clear, was full of energetic life. The gigantic and lasting effort by which victory was at last secured in the great war with France proved the strength of the nation. It has been well noted that deficient, or rather non-existent, as was any system of national education, "there is probably no period in English history at which a greater number of poor men have risen to distinction,"[95] than at the end of the eighteenth and in the earlier part of the nineteenth century.

The greatest beyond comparison of self-taught poets was Burns (1759–1796). The political writer who was at the time producing the most marked effect was Thomas Paine (1737–1809), son of a small tradesman. His successor in influence was William Cobbett (1762–1835), son of an agricultural labourer, and one of the pithiest of all English writers. William Gifford (1756–1826), son of a small tradesman in Devonshire, was already known as a satirist and was to lead Conservatives as editor of *The Quarterly Review.* John Dalton (1766–1842), son of a poor weaver, was one of the most distinguished men of science. Porson (1759–1808), the greatest Greek scholar of his time, was son of a Norfolk parish clerk, though sagacious patrons had sent him to Eton in his fifteenth year. The Oxford professor of Arabic, Joseph White (1746–1814), was son of a poor weaver in the country, and a man of reputation for learning, although now remembered only for a rather disreputable literary squabble. Robert Owen and Joseph Lancaster, both sprung from the ranks, were leaders in social movements."[96]

95. Leslie Stephen, *English Utilitarians,* i. pp. 111, 112.

96. *Ibid.* p. 112. This list, to which might be added Francis Place and many others, reminds us of the difference between the extension of knowledge and the extension of education. Receptivity of information which is cultivated and rewarded in schools and also in Univer-

This was in literature the age of Coleridge (1772–1834), of Sir Walter Scott (1771–1832), of Wordsworth (1770–1850), of Charles Lamb (1775–1834), of Hazlitt (1778–1830), of Miss Austen (1775–1817), of Miss Edgeworth (1767–1849), of Byron (1788–1824), of Shelley (1792–1822), of Sydney Smith (1771–1845), of Jeffrey (1773–1850), and of the whole body of Edinburgh Reviewers.[97] Add to this, that between 1800 and 1832 a younger body of writers, such as Macaulay (1800–1859), John Mill (1806–1873), Arnold of Rugby (1795–1842), J. H. Newman (1801–1890), Tennyson (1809–1892), who belong in influence to a somewhat later generation, were coming to manhood. Consider, at the same time, the existence of men of science such as Sir Humphrey Davy (1778–1829), or Sir John Herschell (1792–1871), and note the appearance of inventors such as Watt (1736–1819), and Stephenson (1781–1848). Imperfect and irregular as this list is, it affords irresistible evidence that, at a time when from special causes public opinion is opposed to legal or political innovation, a country may be full of vigour and of life.

(2) *As to the incongruity between the social condition and the legal institutions of England.* At any date after 1815 thoughtful men must have perceived the existence of a want of harmony between changing social conditions and unchanged laws. Year by year theoretical anomalies were by the mere course of events transformed into practical grievances.

Our system of parliamentary representation had long been full of absurdities. The House of Commons, before the Union with Ireland, consisted of 548 members, of whom 200 were elected by 7000 constituents.[98] A majority of this 7000 might therefore decide a question against the opinion of many millions. The political power which a man possessed varied in the most capricious manner; if his estate is situate in one part of the kingdom he might possess a ten-thousandth part of a single representative; if in another a thousandth; if in a particular district he might be one of

---

sities, is a totally different thing from the education, sometimes conferred even by adverse circumstances, which trains a man to seize opportunities either of learning or of advancement. It has been well said that failures in life arise far less often from mere want of knowledge than from want of skill in the seizing of such favourable opportunities.

97. The *Edinburgh Review* was started in 1802.

98. As to the state of parliamentary representation in 1799, see Paley, *Moral Philosophy*, ii. (12th ed.) pp. 217, 218.

twenty who chose two representatives; if in a more favoured spot he might possess the right of appointing two members himself; if he lived in one town he might have no representative at all, and might, as was remarked by Paley, take no more part in electing the persons who made the law by which he was governed than if he had been a subject of the Grand Signior; whilst forty-two members were lavished upon Cornwall, neither Birmingham nor Manchester had any representative whatever; and whilst about one-half of the House of Commons obtained their seats in that assembly by something like popular election, the other half obtained them by purchase, or by the nomination of single proprietors of great estates. Boroughs, or, in other words, seats in the House of Commons, were bought and sold as openly as any article of commerce, and the King was at times himself the great purchaser of boroughs. "This flagrant incongruity in the constitution," to use the words of Paley, had existed for centuries, and continued to exist up to 1832. The objections to it were patent, and had often been pointed out. They were already felt in the time of the Commonwealth, and were more or less remedied by the constitution of 1654.[99] But, though the existence of members of Parliament nominated by borough owners had towards the end of the eighteenth century provoked theoretical censure, it was not apparently felt by the mass of the people to be a pressing grievance. In 1825, and still more in 1830, the incongruities of an unreformed Parliament had become in the eyes of many Englishmen an intolerable abuse. The reason for this change of feeling is easy enough to discover. As long as the power of the State was centred in the south and west of England, a system which denied representatives to Birmingham or Manchester or Sheffield, whilst it showered representatives on petty Cornish boroughs, might be defended on grounds of expediency by ingenious thinkers such as Paley, or by practical statesmen such as Lord Liverpool or Peel; any constitution which gives real representation, in however strange a manner, to the classes which are powerful in the State, achieves one main end of representative government. But when population, wealth, trade, and power shifted towards the north, apologies for the vices of our representative system, even

99. This reform excited no enthusiasm: it did not last even till the Restoration. The Parliament summoned by Richard Cromwell was elected in England by the old constituencies.

from the mouths of eminent statesmen, began to sound like dishonest pleas suggested by antiquated prejudice, and put forward to preserve the predominance of the Tory party. No doubt Sir Walter Scott, with all his sound judgment, and others who possessed his good sense without his genius, defended institutions struck with decay, on the true plea that under these institutions the English had become the freest and the most wealthy among the nations of the earth; but apology came perilously near to condemnation when it was, in effect, the admission that aged institutions had not been modified in accordance with the growth and development of England. The best defence for the unreformed Parliament—namely, that it represented all that was most powerful in the State—became weaker year by year. The manufacturers and the artisans of the towns had become a power in the land, but they manifestly received no adequate recognition in Parliament.

The defects, moreover, of parliamentary representation were not compensated for by the activity or flourishing condition of local authorities. No part of the administrative system had suffered so complete a collapse as municipal government. On this point the report of the Commission of 1834 is absolutely decisive. The municipal corporations of England were marked by almost every defect which such bodies could exhibit. They did not represent the inhabitants of the towns whose affairs they were supposed to administer. They were inefficient: they were corrupt. Duties which ought to have been discharged by a corporation were, if discharged at all, placed in the hands of separate bodies—*e.g.* improvement commissioners—created to perform some special service. The following facts are significant. The prosperity of Birmingham was attributed by observers to that rising town being still in theory a village and free from the disadvantage of being a corporation;[100] the general distrust of corporate government led the authors of the Municipal Reform Act, 1836, to bestow astonishingly narrow powers even upon the reformed corporations. The counties, with the affairs whereof their inhabitants had for the most part little to do, were in reality governed by the justices of the peace. The rule of the justices had its defects, but it was not marred by corruption, and was better than the government of the towns under the old municipal system.

Consider, again, in the most general way, the position of the Established

100. See Leslie Stephen, *English Utilitarians*, i. pp. 99, 100.

Church, or rather the way in which, as the first quarter of the nineteenth century was drawing to its close, the Established Church came to be regarded by thousands of Englishmen.

In 1825, when the evangelical movement was at its height, and Simeon was reputed to have more authority than any bishop, the clergy were assuredly a more zealous and more devoted body of men than were their predecessors of 1725, and (though eminently pious clergymen occasionally acquiesced in arrangements as to the holding of pluralities and the like which every one would now condemn as scandals) some real, though ineffectual, efforts had been made towards the reform of patent ecclesiastical abuses. Nobody in short can doubt that the character and moral weight of the clergy had risen with the advance of the nineteenth century. Yet the defects of the Establishment met in 1825 with severer censure than in 1725, or even in 1800. Here, again, we see the effect of the obvious want of harmony between the institutions and the needs of the time. In 1725 a clergyman might possibly minister to the spiritual and moral wants of a large northern parish, which, though extensive in size, contained a scanty and scattered population of yeomen and farmers. But how could a clergyman by anything short of a miracle discharge his duties in the same parish when it was turned into a huge town, crowded with miners or manufacturing hands? In truth, the very face of the country had changed; northern villages were being transformed into cities. Yet, in an altering world, the Church establishment remained much what it had been in 1689.

If the course of trade and the growth of manufactures altered the position without altering the arrangements of the Established Church, it also revolutionised, without in any way improving, the relation of masters and workmen. This fact was visible to observers who detested Jacobinical principles.

"The unhappy dislocation," writes Sir Walter Scott,

> which has taken place betwixt the employer and those in his employment has been attended with very fatal consequences. Much of this is owing to the steam-engine. When the machinery was driven by water, the manufacturer had to seek out some sequestered spot where he could obtain a suitable fall of water, and then his workmen formed the inhabitants of a village around him, and he necessarily bestowed some attention, less or more, on their morals and on their necessities, had knowledge of their persons and char-

acters, and exercised over them a salutary influence as over men depending on and intimately connected with him and his prospects. This is now quite changed; the manufacturers are transferred to great towns, where a man may assemble five hundred workmen one week and dismiss them next, without having any further connection with them than to receive a week's work for a week's wages, nor any further solicitude about their future fate than if they were so many old shuttles. A superintendence of the workers considered as moral and rational beings is thus a matter totally unconnected with the employer's usual thoughts and cares. They have now seen the danger of suffering a great population to be thus entirely separated from the influence of their employers, and given over to the management of their own societies, in which the cleverest and most impudent fellows always get the management of the others, and become bell-wethers in every sort of mischief. Some resolutions have been adopted respecting the employing only such men as have been either uniformly of loyal character or acknowledge their errors and withdraw from all treasonable meetings, associations, and committees.

The banks and monied men should use their influence, which is omnipotent with the manufacturers, to enforce the observance of these resolutions, so necessary for the general quiet. That such regulations would secure tranquillity is quite certain, for notwithstanding the general influence of example, the workmen in some of the greatest manufactures did not furnish a single recruit to Radicalism.[101]

This want of harmony between the needs and the institutions of the time reappears in matters which, though of less importance than the condition of the working-classes, affected the comfort of thousands of Englishmen.

Nothing can be more necessary for the happiness of ordinary citizens than protection against robbery and physical violence. Yet even in London the protection was not adequately supplied. Until 1829 the capital of England did not possess a regular body of police.[102] The welfare, again, of a

---

101. Scott's *Familiar Letters*, vol. ii., Letter to Morritt, 19th May 1820.

102. The slowness with which necessary reforms have been carried out in England is curiously illustrated by the history of the police force during the nineteenth century. The creation of the Metropolitan police in 1829 (10 Geo. IV. c. 14) is due to Peel's administrative genius; it was a stroke of intensely unpopular but very beneficent statesmanship; but even in the metropolis the police force was not put on a satisfactory basis till 1839 (2 & 3 Vict. c.

mercantile community is dependent on the existence of a fair and effective law of bankruptcy, yet the state of the bankruptcy law shocked every man versed in business. There was an absolute opposition on this matter between the law of the land and the feelings of the mercantile world. The state of things as late as the beginning of the reign of Victoria (1837) is thus described by Lord Bowen:

> The great commercial world, alienated and scared by the divergence of the English bankruptcy law from their own habits and notions of right and wrong, avoided the court of bankruptcy as they would the plague. The important insolvencies which have been brought about by pure mercantile misfortune were administered to a large extent under private deeds and voluntary compositions, which, since they might be disturbed by the caprice or malice of a single outstanding creditor, were always liable to be made the instruments of extortion. "To the honest insolvent the bankruptcy court was a terror." To the evil-doer it afforded means of endlessly delaying his creditors, while the enormous expenses of bankruptcy administrations rendered it the interest of few to resort to the remedy, except with the object of punishing the fraudulent or vexing the unfortunate.[103]

From whatever direction then we examine the condition of England between 1800 and 1830, and especially between 1815 and 1830, we can perceive the discord between a changing social condition and unchanging laws.

(3) *As to the lapse of time.* Before the outbreak of the French Revolution intelligent Englishmen of all classes were prepared to welcome natural and gradual reforms. Blackstone, though an optimist, was not opposed to reasonable changes; Pitt, Burke, and Fox were all of them in different ways

---

47). In the boroughs reform went on slowly, and was not anything like complete until 1839. In the counties reform progressed at even a slower pace. The so-called Permissive Act of 1839 (2 & 3 Vict. c. 93) made the organisation of a good county police possible. In 1842 an attempt was made to infuse new life into the decrepit system of parish constables. Fourteen years later the County and Borough Police Act, 1856 (19 & 20 Vict. c. 69), known as the Obligatory Act, for the first time provided every part of England with stipendiary police, and thus completed a police system for the whole country. See Melville, *History of Police in England,* chaps. xiii.–xv.

103. Bowen, *Reign of Queen Victoria,* i. p. 315.

reformers; and the men we have named are representatives of that large class of Englishmen who at most times have been quite willing to abolish abuses or grievances of a practical character. In the ordinary course of things the law of England would have been amended before the end of the eighteenth, or soon after the beginning of the nineteenth century. The obstacle to reasonable reform is to be found in the revolutionary excesses of France. In England the French Revolution worked nothing but evil; it delayed salutary changes for forty years, and rendered reforms, when at last they came, less beneficial than they might have been if gradually carried out as the natural result of the undisturbed development of ideas suggested by English good sense and English love of justice.[104] But to the men who began to take part in public life, or to take an interest in national affairs, between 1815 and 1830, the horrors of the Reign of Terror were mere traditions. They knew by experience the narrow-mindedness of the Tories who had governed England since the beginning of the century, and toryism had by a strange fatality grown less reasonable and more reactionary from the very time when Waterloo, and the permanent peace which it established, had deprived the resistance to all innovation and restrictions on individual liberty of such justification as was afforded by a life and death struggle for national independence. In 1819 or 1820 the Six Acts, the so-called Manchester massacre, the sordid scandals of the quarrel between George IV. and his Queen were present realities. The horrors of a *Regicide Peace*[105] were ancient history. Sensible men perceived that the state of England would soon necessitate a choice between revolution and reform.

(4) *As to the existence of Benthamism.* The work of Bentham and his school forms the subject of the next lecture; thus much may here be said:

104. The delay, however, in reform by Eldon and his school conferred some benefit on the country. It postponed action until in 1832 it took the shape of reform instead of revolution. [Editor's note: This footnote was added in the second edition.]

105. The very title of Burke's celebrated *Three Letters on the Proposals for Peace with the Regicide Directory of France,* 1796, is a curious example of the difference between the feelings of his times and of our own. Would suggestions of peace with France (or for that matter with any other civilised country) now excite horror simply on the ground that the French Government had put their king to death? The Directory, by the way, had not as a government executed Louis XVI. Would Burke, one wonders, have blamed Louis XIV. for recognising Cromwell, who was in the strictest sense a regicide?

reformers who had escaped from the panic caused by revolutionary excesses, and prolonged by Napoleonic aggression, had inherited the distrust of Jacobinical principles. The need of the day was, they felt, thoroughgoing but temperate reform, thought out by teachers who, without being revolutionists, had studied the faults of English law, and elaborated schemes for its practical amendment. Such teachers were found in Bentham and his disciples; they provided for reformers an acceptable programme. Utilitarian individualism, which for many years under the name of liberalism, determined the trend of English legislation, was nothing but Benthamism modified by the experience, the prudence, or the timidity of practical politicians. The creation of this liberalism was the death-blow to old toryism, and closed the era of legislative stagnation.

*The Period of Benthamism
or Individualism*[1]

INDIVIDUALISM AS REGARDS legislation is popularly, and not without reason, connected with the name and the principles of Bentham. The name of one man, it is true, can never adequately summarise a whole school of thought, but from 1825 onwards the teaching of Bentham exercised so potent an influence that to him is fairly ascribed that thorough-going though gradual amendment of the law of England which was one of the main results of the Reform Act.[2]

Bentham's genius and position were fully understood by his contemporaries.

> The age of law reform and the age of Jeremy Bentham are one and the same. He is the father of the most important of all the branches of reform, the leading and ruling department of human improvement. No one before him had ever seriously thought of exposing the defects in our English system of jurisprudence. All former students had confined themselves to learn its principles—to make themselves masters of its eminently technical and artificial rules; and all former writers had but expounded the doctrines handed down from age to age. . . . He it was who first made the mighty step of trying the whole provisions of our jurisprudence by the test of expediency, fearlessly examining how far each part was connected with the rest; and with a yet more undaunted courage, inquiring how far even its most consistent and

1. See Bentham, "Memoirs and Correspondence," *Works,* x. xi.; Montague, Bentham's *Fragment on Government;* L. Stephen, *English Utilitarians,* i., especially chaps. i.–iii.; Elie Halévy, *La formation du radicalisme philosophique;* G. Wallas, *Life of Francis Place,* ch. iii.; Bowen on "Administration of the Law, from 1837–1887," *Reign of Queen Victoria,* i. 281.

2. The influence even on law reform of Adam Smith and his disciples ought, of course, not to be forgotten, but in 1830 the economists and the Benthamites formed one school.

symmetrical arrangements were framed according to the principle which should pervade a code of laws—their adaptation to the circumstances of society, to the wants of men, and to the promotion of human happiness.

Not only was he thus eminently original among the lawyers and the legal philosophers of his own country; he might be said to be the first legal philosopher that had appeared in the world.[3]

These are the words of Brougham, published in 1838; they strike the right note. Bentham was primarily neither a utilitarian moralist nor a philanthropist: he was a legal philosopher and a reformer of the law. The object of his lifelong labours was to remodel the law of England in accordance with utilitarian principles. These labours were crowned by extraordinary success, though the success was most manifest after the end of Bentham's life. This is Bentham's title to fame. His life cannot here be told, but it is well to insist upon the circumstances or conditions which favoured his success as a law reformer.

Both the date and the length of Bentham's life are important.

He was born in 1748, two years after the failure of the last attempt to restore the Stuarts; he died immediately before the passing of the Reform Act, 1832. The eighty-four years of his life thus span over the period which divides the last endeavour to establish in England the real supremacy of the Crown from the commencement in England of modern democratic government. This era stretched indeed beyond the limits of the eighteenth century, but though Bentham lived till the first third of the nineteenth century had nearly come to an end, he was in spirit entirely a child of the eighteenth century, and in England was the best representative of the humanitarianism and enlightenment of that age. Length of days was no small aid in the performance of his life's work. Bentham, like Voltaire,[4] ultimately owed much of his authority to the many years for which he was able to press his doctrines upon the world. Iteration and reiteration are a great force; when employed by a teacher of genius they may become an irresistible power. For well nigh sixty years, that is to say to two generations, Bentham preached the necessity, and explained the principles, of law reform. He began his career as an unknown youth whose ideas were scouted

3. Brougham's *Speeches*, ii. pp. 287, 288.
4. Voltaire, born 1694, died 1778. Each lived to the age of eighty-four.

by men of the world as dangerous paradoxes: he ended it as a revered teacher who numbered among his disciples lawyers and statesmen of eminence, and had won over to his leading ideas the most sensible and influential of English reformers.

Bentham was the son of a wealthy London attorney.

He thus formed one of that body of tradesmen, merchants, and professional men who, as the "middle class," had at the beginning of the nineteenth century long exercised great influence in public life, and at the moment of his death were about to become the true sovereign of England. And Bentham, though distinguished among his fellows by his genius, his enlightenment, and his zeal for the public good, belonged, to a far greater extent than he or his opponents perceived, in spirit no less than in position, to the middle classes. He shared their best ideals. When he taught that the aim of law as of life was to promote the greatest happiness of the greatest number, he meant by happiness no far-fetched conception of well-being, but that combination of an honest and industrious life with the enjoyment of modest wealth and material comfort, which is felt to be an object of desire by an ordinary Englishman. He spoke the language of his countrymen, and the men of the middle class whom he addressed understood his meaning. The character and the wealth of Bentham's father are circumstances not to be overlooked. The elder Bentham recognised his son's extraordinary gifts and set his heart on seeing him rise to the position of Mansfield or of Eldon. This commonplace ambition was the torment of Jeremy's youth, but it had one good effect. It induced or compelled Bentham to study with care the actual law of England; he was saved from being one of those jurists who know a little of every law but their own. His father's wealth even more profoundly affected Bentham's career. He never had to rely upon fees for his support. At his father's death he became possessed of ample means. Thus he was able to follow, as he did follow through life, the bent of his own genius.[5]

His genius was of the rarest quality.

In Bentham's intellect were united talents seldom found in combination; a jurist's capacity for the grasp of general principles and the acumen of a

---

5. Bentham in this matter resembled Darwin. Each of these eminent men owed to inherited wealth the possibility of wholly dedicating his whole life to its appropriate work.

natural born logician were blended with the resourcefulness of a mechanical inventor. In studying Bentham's intellectual character we are reminded that, if he was the follower of Hobbes and of Locke, he was the contemporary of Arkwright[6] and of Watt.[7] How near Bentham's turn of mind lay to that of men renowned for mechanical inventions may be seen from a transaction which has perplexed and sometimes amused his admirers. He devoted trouble, money, thought, and time to the creation of the "Panopticon" or "Inspection-house"—that is, a model prison so planned that from one point in the building could be seen all that was going on in every other portion of the establishment. Of the mixed ingenuity and weakness of Bentham's plan nothing need here be said; the point to be noticed is the light which the scheme throws on the nature of Bentham's intellect. The Panopticon was a mechanical contrivance from which, if rightly used, he, after the manner of ingenious projectors, expected untold benefits for mankind; "morals reformed, health preserved, industry invigorated, instruction diffused, public burdens lightened, economy seated as it were upon a rock, the Gordian knot of the poor-law not cut but untied—all by a simple idea in architecture!"[8] He was in truth created to be the inventor and patentee of legal reforms. It is in this inventiveness that he differs from and excels his best known disciples. Austin may have equalled him in the capacity for analysing legal conceptions, James Mill may have surpassed him in metaphysical subtlety, John Mill had acquired under a course of elaborate training a more complete philosophical equipment, and was endowed by nature with wider sympathies than Bentham; but neither Austin, nor James Mill, nor John Mill, possessed any touch of Bentham's inventive genius, nor in fact made any suggestion, which was at once original and valuable, for the amendment of the law of England.

The course of Bentham's life was, however, finally determined, neither by the opportuneness of circumstances, nor by the possession of wealth, nor even by the peculiarity of his intellectual gifts, but by the nature and the development of his moral character.

6. b. 1732, d. 1792.
7. b. 1736, d. 1819.
8. Bentham, *Works,* iv. p. 39.

In early manhood he was "converted"[9]—I use the term deliberately, as it better gives my meaning than does any other expression—to an unshakeable faith in that form of utilitarianism which places the object of life in the promotion of "the greatest happiness of the greatest number." When about twenty years of age he found this formula in a pamphlet of Priestley's[10] and accepted it as the guide of his life.

"It was by that pamphlet and this phrase in it," writes Bentham,

> that my principles on the subject of morality, public and private, were determined. It was from that pamphlet and that page of it that I drew the phrase, the words and import of which have been so widely diffused over the civilised world. At the sight of it, I cried out as it were in an inward ecstasy, like Archimedes on the discovery of the fundamental principle of hydrostatics, Εὕρηκα. Little did I think of the corrections which within a few years on a closer scrutiny I found myself under the necessity of applying to it.[11]

With this combine the following expressions taken from Bentham's notebooks.

"Would you appear actuated by generous passion? be so.—You need then but show yourself as you are."

"I would have the dearest friend I have to know, that his interests, if they come in competition with those of the public, are as nothing to me. Thus I will serve my friends—thus would I be served by them."

"Has a man talents? he owes them to his country in every way in which they can be serviceable."[12]

This creed, however, which we should now term the enthusiasm of humanity, need not have impelled Bentham to labour at the reform of the

---

9. "The name of Jeremy Bentham, one of the few who have wholly lived for what they held to be the good of the human race, has become even among educated men a byword for what is called his 'low view' of human nature. The fact is that, under its most important aspect, he greatly overrated human nature. He overestimated its intelligence."—Maine, *Popular Government*, pp. 85, 86. These sentences contain an appreciation which is rare, not only of Bentham's virtues but of his enthusiasm.

10. Apparently the formula was originally derived not from Priestley, but from Beccaria (see *Crimes and Punishments*, Introduction, p. 2, where the expression is found. "This sole end the greatest happiness of the greatest number").

11. Montague, Bentham's *Fragment on Government*, p. 34.

12. Bentham's *Works*, x. ("Extracts from Bentham's Commonplace Book"), p. 73.

law. That his passion for the furtherance of human happiness took this particular form, arose from his becoming possessed by the two convictions that legislation was the most important of human pursuits, and that Jeremy Bentham was born with a genius for legislation.

> "Have I," he asked, "a *genius* for anything? What can I *produce?*" That was the first inquiry he made of himself. Then came another. "What of all earthly pursuits is the most important?" "Legislation," was the answer Helvetius gave. "Have I a genius for legislation?" Again and again was the question put to himself. He turned it over in his thoughts; he sought every symptom he could discover in his natural disposition or acquired habits. "And have I indeed a genius for legislation?" I gave myself the answer, fearfully and tremblingly, "Yes."[13]

Of these convictions the first was shared by the best thinkers of the eighteenth century, and contained an immense amount of relative truth; the need of the time was the reform of the institutions of Europe. The second was absolutely true, and its truth has been recognised by the wisest men of the generations which have followed Bentham; he was in very truth the first and greatest of legal philosophers.

My objects in this lecture are, first, to sketch in the merest outline the ideas of Benthamism or individualism, in so far as when applied by practical statesmen they have affected the growth of English law; next to explain and describe the general acceptance of Benthamism as the dominant legislative opinion of a particular era; and, lastly, to illustrate by examples the general trend of Benthamite or individualistic legislation.

(A) Benthamite Ideas as to the Reform of the Law

Bentham considered exclusively as a reformer of the law of England achieved two ends.

He determined, in the first place, the *principles* on which reform should be based.

He determined, in the second place, the *method, i.e.* the mode of legislation, by which, in England, reform should be carried out.

---

13. Sir Roland Knyvet Wilson, Bart., *History of Modern English Law* (ed. 1875), p. 136.

As to the Principles[14] of Law Reform. The ideas which underlie the Benthamite or individualistic scheme of reform may conveniently be summarised under three leading principles and two corollaries.

I. Legislation is a Science.

English law, as it existed at the end of the eighteenth century, had in truth developed almost haphazard, as the result of customs or modes of thought which had prevailed at different periods. The laws actually in existence had certainly not been enacted with a view to any one guiding principle. They had, indeed, for the most part never been "enacted" (in the strict sense of that word) at all. They were, as they still indeed to a great extent are, the result of judicial legislation built up in the course of deciding particular cases. English law had in fact grown, rather than been made, and the language used by Paley with regard to the constitution might, with the change of one word, be applied to the whole law of England.

> The [law] of England, like that of most countries in Europe, hath grown out of occasion and emergency; from the fluctuating policy of different ages; from the contentions, successes, interests, and opportunities of different orders and parties of men in the community. It resembles one of those old mansions, which, instead of being built all at once, after a regular plan, and according to the rules of architecture at present established, has been reared in different ages of the art, has been altered from time to time, and has been continually receiving additions and repairs suited to the taste, fortune, or conveniency of its successive proprietors. In such a building we look in vain for the elegance and proportion, for the just order and correspondence of parts, which we expect in a modern edifice; and which external symmetry, after all, contributes much more perhaps to the amusement of the beholder than the accommodation of the inhabitant.[15]

14. These principles, it should be remembered, are not so much the dogmas to be found in Bentham's Works as ideas due in the main to Bentham, which were ultimately, though often in a very modified form, accepted by the reformers or legislators who practically applied utilitarian conceptions to the amendment of the law of England.

15. Paley ("Of the Constitution"), *Moral Philosophy,* ii. (12th ed. 1799), pp. 193, 194.

But Bentham saw clearly several facts which Paley failed to recognise. The revered mansion was not only antiquated, but in many respects so unsuited to the requirements of the times, that it was to its numerous inhabitants the cause not only of discomfort but even of misery. In order to amend the fabric of the law we must, he insisted, lay down a plan grounded on fixed principles; in many instances not amendment but re-construction was a necessity; and even gradual improvements, if they were to attain their object, must be made in accordance with fixed rules of art. Legislation, in short, he proclaimed is a science based on the characteristics of human nature, and the art of law-making, if it is to be successful, must be the application of legislative principles. Of these ideas Bentham was not the discoverer but the teacher; he may be described as the prophet who forced the faith in scientific legislation upon the attention of a generation of Englishmen by whom its truth or importance was denied or forgotten.

> II. The right aim of legislation is the carrying out of the principle of utility, or, in other words, the proper end of every law is the promotion of the greatest happiness of the greatest number.

This principle, obtained as we have seen from Priestley, is the formula with which popular memory has most closely connected the name of Bentham.

With the objections to which the principle of utility is open, either as a standard or as a source of morality, any person at all interested in ethical discussions is now well acquainted. In these lectures we are concerned with the utilitarian dogma as an axiom not of morals but of legislation, and one may with confidence assert that the principle of utility is far more easily applicable to law than to morals, and this for at least two reasons:

First. Legislation deals with numbers and with whole classes of men; morality deals with individuals. Now it is obviously easier to determine what are the things which as a general rule constitute, or rather promote, the happiness or well-being of a large number of persons, or of a State, than to form even a conjecture as to what may constitute the happiness of an individual. To ensure the happiness of a single man or woman even for a day is a task impossible of achievement; for the problem wherein may lie the happiness of one human being is, though narrow, so infinitely complex that it admits not of solution. To determine, on the other hand, the general conditions which conduce to the prosperity of the millions who make up a State is a comparatively simple matter. Let it be noted, also, that whilst ethical maxims may aim at directly benefiting or ensuring the welfare of individuals, a law never attempts more than the production of a state of things favourable to the welfare of the citizens of a State. When it is said, in accordance with Benthamite phraseology, that a good law is a law productive of the greatest happiness of the greatest number, what is meant is not that a law really makes men happy, but that it favours the existence of the conditions under which it is likely that the persons subject to it may prosper, and obtain the happiness open to human beings. But here we come across another distinction.

Secondly. Law is concerned primarily with external actions, and is only in a very secondary and indirect manner concerned with motives. Morality, on the other hand, is primarily concerned with motives and feelings, and only secondarily and indirectly with actions. But it is far easier to maintain that the principle of utility is the proper standard or criterion of right action than that it supplies the foundation, or, at any rate, the whole of the foundation, on which rests the conviction that one feeling or motive is right and another wrong.

However this may be, the generality and the externality of law are the circumstances which enable us to test the goodness or the badness, the wisdom or the folly, of a given law by the criterion of utility. Indeed, if once the meaning of this standard be understood, it is hard to see how any one can deny its applicability, without involving himself in something like absurdity or self-contradiction. How can it be maintained that a law which on the whole increases human happiness is a bad law, or that a law which on the whole diminishes it is a good law? But if these questions supply their own answer, the principle of utility is admitted to be a good test, as far as it goes, of the character of a law; and half the plausibilities by which during the age of Blackstone the anomalies or absurdities of English law were defended turn out, when submitted to Bentham's criterion, to be nothing better than hollow fallacies.

Ideas of happiness, it has been objected, vary in different ages, in different countries, and among different classes or races; a legislator therefore gains no real guidance from the dogma that laws should aim at promoting the greatest happiness of the greatest number.

To this objection, which assumes many different forms, there exist at least two answers.

The first is that, even if the variability of men's conceptions of happiness be admitted, the concession proves no more than that the application of the principle of utility is conditioned by the ideas of human welfare which prevail at a given time in a given country. Nor, in truth, is there any reason why a convinced utilitarian should refuse to accept this conclusion. It embodies a principle of practical importance. In legislating for any country we must take into account the habits, the feelings, or the prejudices, of its inhabitants, and allow for their ideas of what constitutes happiness. Freedom of testamentary disposition is a right or a privilege which few Englishmen desire to surrender. The compulsory division into more or less equal shares of a deceased person's property among his heirs is a fundamental principle of the law of France, and one which receives the approval of the French people. But testamentary freedom and the equal division of a deceased person's property are at bottom inconsistent institutions. Must we therefore say that one or other of them is bad—*i.e.* is opposed to the principle of utility? Surely not. The reply both of good sense and of sound logic is that the law supporting testamentary freedom may be a good law for Englishmen, and the law supporting the equal division of a dead man's property may be a good law for Frenchmen. Each law may promote the happiness of the people among whom it exists; the reason is that Englishmen and Frenchmen form in this matter different conceptions of happiness.

The second reply is that, as regards the conditions of public prosperity, the citizens of civilised states have, in modern times, reached a large amount of agreement. Who can seriously doubt—whatever be the idle contentions of paradox-mongers—that a plentiful supply of cheap food, efficient legal protection against violence or fraud, and the freedom of all classes from excessive labour conduce to the public welfare? What man out of Bedlam ever dreamed that a country was the happier for the constant recurrence of pestilence, famine, and war; but who then can deny that laws which promote the cultivation of the soil, ensure the public health, keep the country at peace, and avert invasion, are, as far as they go, good laws? To all these and similar questions the inhabitants of every country which enjoys European civilisation will give one and the same reply. Their general agreement, indeed, goes much further than this. Nowhere is it doubted by men of average intelligence that the reintroduction of torture or the re-establishment of slavery would be the gravest of calamities. We all have learned by this time that every kind of punishment which causes more pain than it averts is an evil. We all admit that the due and regular administration of justice, the promotion of education, the opening of various careers to the majority of the people, the extension of the innocent enjoyments of life among all classes, promote human happiness, and that laws which confer these benefits are good laws. In matters of legislation, in short, subtle refinements as to the nature of happiness are misplaced. The homely saying, that you ought not to weigh butcher's meat in diamond scales, has a practical weight which is overlooked by paradoxical thinkers. Laws deal with very ordinary matters, and deal with them in a rough and ready manner. The character therefore of a law may well be tested by the rough criterion embodied in the doctrine of utility.

There exists, however, a good reason for examining with care an objection to which it is easy to supply conclusive answers. Bentham and his disciples have displayed a tendency to underestimate the diversity between human beings. Hence they have too easily supposed that the ideas of happiness prevailing at a given time throughout the civilised countries of Europe were entirely uniform; and have fallen into the further error of assuming that the same notion of happiness prevails in all countries, and has more or less prevailed in all ages. This supposition facilitates legislation, but, like all assumptions which are not strictly true, has led both to speculative and to practical mistakes. The weakness of the Benthamites as legislators has been, not their devotion to the principle of utility, but their feeling that laws which in the nineteenth century promoted the happiness of Englishmen must, with rare exceptions, promote at all times the happiness of the inhabitants of all countries.[16]

16. Bentham almost certainly held that laws against usury were always bad; yet strong reasons have been produced by Grote—a most zealous utilitarian—for the belief that in ancient Athens and Rome such laws were beneficial. Sir J. F. Stephen, though a pronounced

The foundation then of legislative utilitarianism is the combination of two convictions. The one is the belief that the end of human existence is the attainment of happiness,[17] or in other words, faith in the principle of utility; the other is the assurance that legislation is a science and that the aim of laws is the promotion of human happiness. Neither of these convictions entertained separately will make a man a legislative utilitarian.

A person may be a strict utilitarian and hold that the attainment of happiness is the true end and object of existence, yet if he does not believe that law may do much to produce human happiness, or fails to perceive that law is a science, he will hardly concern himself with the systematic reform of the law. A man, again, who believes that good legislation is conducive to human prosperity, will hardly be a successful law reformer if he does not grasp the connection between legislation and the principle of utility.

Samuel Johnson was in morals a thorough-going utilitarian,[18] but he never displayed the remotest interest in the amendment of the laws of England. His nature was conservative, his turn of character, no less than his religious convictions, made him consider as slight the influence of laws on the happiness of mankind.

> How small of all that human hearts endure,
> That part which laws or kings can cause or cure.

Paley[19] stands in spirit nearer to Bentham. His theology and his moral philosophy are avowedly utilitarian. His writings betray a keen interest in legal problems. He possessed the intellect of an enlightened lawyer. But he probably did not believe that law could be treated as a science; he either had not grasped, or did not care to work out, the idea that the laws of

---

utilitarian, appears to incline towards the opinion that laws placing a check on usury might occasionally be useful as a means of preventing fraud. See Stephen, *Hist.* iii. pp. 195, 196.

17. See Principle No. 2, p. 98, *ante.*

18. "Review of a Free Enquiry," Johnson's *Works,* viii. p. 37.

19. "Virtue is, 'the doing good to mankind, in obedience to the will of God, and for the sake of everlasting happiness.'["]

"According to which definition, 'the good of mankind' is the subject; the 'will of God' the rule; and 'everlasting happiness' the motive of human virtue."—Paley, *Moral Philosophy,* i. bk. i. ch. vii. p. 41.

England might be systematically remodelled so as to promote the greatest happiness of the greatest number of Englishmen. His philosophy, utilitarian though it was, is, in so far as he applied it to law, an ingenious defence of things as they stood in 1786. He is neither an innovator nor a reformer, but like Blackstone an apologist.

A man, on the other hand, may have a fervent belief that the laws of a country are radically wrong and may be prepared to advocate their change even at the cost of violence. If, however, he is guided by some idea of abstract right,[20] as a thing independent of utility, he may, like Rousseau, popularise ideas which kindle a revolution, but he will hardly become a systematic law reformer. He is not possessed of any definite criterion by which to test the merits or defects of a law; he may perceive that things are wrong; he cannot perceive, as Bentham and his disciples saw, or thought they saw, a definite principle by the application whereof bad laws might in every case be either got rid of or amended. For utilitarianism in the field of legislation, whatever the speculative objections—and they are not small— which lie against it in the sphere of ethics, has one saving virtue. It directs a legislator's attention to the consequences of any proposed enactment. An innovator who recommends or denounces a law or institution, because of its conformity or opposition to the law of nature or the moral instincts of mankind, is under the greatest temptation to make his own feelings the test of expediency, and is certainly less inclined than a Benthamite, to weigh the actual or probable effects of legislation; and if it be objected that zealots for the law of nature have often advocated or carried out beneficial changes, the best reply is, that the law of nature has often been a name for the dictates of obvious expediency. The privileges, for example, of the nobles under the *Ancien Régime* were in 1789 palpably opposed to the welfare of

---

20. On the whole *a priori* systems of ethics will in general produce conservatism. "I suspect," writes Paley, "that a system of morality, built upon instincts, will only find out reasons and excuses for opinions and practices already established—will seldom correct or reform either."—Paley, *Moral Philosophy*, i. bk. i. ch. v.

This is not invariably true, as appeared during the French Revolution. In a country where the mode of government is on the whole liked, intuitional morality will promote conservatism; where the mode of government is detested, it may promote revolution. Its defect everywhere is that it fails to fix attention on the consequences of legislation and generally of men's actions.

the French people. Bentham would have said that they were opposed to the principle of utility. A French reformer would have alleged that they were opposed to the law of nature. But this difference of language was at bottom little more than a different way of describing one and the same fact, viz., that the welfare of France required the establishment of equal civil rights among Frenchmen. Towards the close, indeed, of the eighteenth century, appeals to the doctrine of utility, and appeals to the law of nature were often in reality, though not in words, appeals to one and the same principle. The failure to perceive this led to some strange results. Bentham sometimes came into conflict with men who in reality shared his principles. He dissected with merciless severity the patent fallacies contained in the American Declaration of Independence, with its enumeration as self-evident truths of the dogmas that all men are created equal, that they are endowed by their Creator with certain inalienable rights, and that among these are to be found the right to life, liberty, and the pursuit of happiness. To Bentham all these abstract statements of innate rights were as hateful as to Burke; they presented themselves to his mind as a mere "hodge-podge of confusion and absurdity."[21] But the American Declaration of Independence did, nevertheless, though in a form open to every logical objection, embody that faith in *laissez faire* which was in practice the most potent and vital principle of Benthamite reform.

> III. Every person is in the main and as a general rule the best
> judge of his own happiness. Hence legislation should aim at
> the removal of all those restrictions on the free action of an
> individual which are not necessary for securing the like
> freedom on the part of his neighbours.[22]

This dogma of *laissez faire* is not from a logical point of view an essential article of the utilitarian creed. A benevolent despot of high intelligence,

21. Bentham, x. p. 63. So he deplored the publication in France of the Declaration of Rights. "I am sorry," he writes to Brissot, "you have undertaken to publish a Declaration of Rights. It is a metaphysical work—the *ne plus ultra* of metaphysics. It may have been a necessary evil, but it is nevertheless an evil. Political science is not far enough advanced for such a declaration."—Cited Kent, *English Radicals*, p. 184. Compare Halévy, *La Formation du Radicalisme Philosophique*, ii. pp. 38–43, and pp. 47–51.

22. See, *e.g. Truth against Ashurst*, Bentham, v. p. 234, and generally Mill, *On Liberty,*

while admitting that the proper end of scientific legislation is to promote the greatest happiness of the greatest number, might contend that the mass of his people, owing to ignorance and prejudice, did not understand their own interests, and might go on to maintain and act on the principle, that as his subjects were neither the best judges of the conditions which constituted happiness, nor understood the means by which these conditions were to be attained, it was his duty to enforce upon them laws which, though they might diminish individual liberty, were likely nevertheless to ensure the well-being of his people. This position is not in itself illogical;[23] it was held by the benevolent despots of the eighteenth century, and would have commended itself to so acute a thinker as Voltaire, for we may assume with confidence that he would not have condemned a ruler who by severe legislation overthrew the reign of superstition or intolerance. But, though *laissez faire* is not an essential part of utilitarianism it was practically the most vital part of Bentham's legislative doctrine, and in England gave to the movement for the reform of the law, both its power and its character. At the time when Bentham became the preacher of legislative utilitarianism the English people were proud of their freedom, and it was the fashion to assert, that under the English constitution no restraint, which was not requisite for the maintenance of public order, was placed on individual liberty. Bentham saw through this cant, and perceived the undeniable truth, that, under a system of ancient customs modified by haphazard legislation,

---

which is throughout a defence, though not at bottom quite a consistent one, of this principle.

Herbert Spencer (who criticises Bentham, by the way, as unfairly as Bentham criticised Blackstone) argues in substance (*e.g. Social Statics*, pp. 7–10, *The Man versus The State*, pp. 372–383) that the *laissez faire* doctrine or something very like it, and not the dogma of the "greatest happiness for the greatest number," is the fundamental doctrine of sound legislation; and, whatever may be said on this point as a question of ethical theory, it is plain that it is the doctrine of *laissez faire* which has really governed Benthamite legislation.

23. "Despotism is a legitimate mode of government in dealing with barbarians, provided the end be their improvement, and the means justified by actually effecting that end. Liberty, as a principle, has no application to any state of things anterior to the time when mankind have become capable of being improved by free and equal discussion. Until then, there is nothing for them but implicit obedience to an Akbar or a Charlemagne, if they are so fortunate as to find one" (Mill, *On Liberty*, p. 23). This concession goes further than Mill seems to perceive. Its principle seems to apply to every case where a government is far more intelligent than the governed.

unnumbered restraints were placed on the action of individuals, and restraints which were in no sense necessary for the safety and good order of the community at large, and he inferred at once that these restraints were evils. Consider for a moment but one fragment of the Benthamite dialogue between Mr. Justice Ashurst (whose charge sums up the platitudes of toryism) and Truth, the defender of human liberty.

> ASHURST. *The law of this country only lays such restraints on the actions of individuals as are necessary for the safety and good order of the community at large.*
>
> TRUTH. I sow corn: partridges eat it, and if I attempt to defend it against the partridges, I am fined or sent to gaol: all this, for fear a great man, who is above sowing corn, should be in want of partridges.
>
> The trade I was born to is overstocked: hands are wanting in another. If I offer to work at that other, I may be sent to gaol for it. Why? Because I have not been working at it as an apprentice for seven years. What's the consequence? That, as there is no work for me in my original trade, I must either come upon the parish or starve.
>
> There is no employment for me in my own parish: there is abundance in the next. Yet if I offer to go there, I am driven away. Why? Because I *might* become unable to work one of these days, and so I must not work while I am able. I am thrown upon one parish now, for fear I should fall upon another, forty or fifty years hence. At this rate how is work ever to get done? If a man is not poor, he won't work: and if he is poor, the laws won't let him. How then is it that so much is done as is done? As pockets are picked— by stealth, and because the law is so wicked that it is only here and there that a man can be found wicked enough to think of executing it.
>
> Pray, Mr. Justice, how is the community you speak of the better for any of these *restraints?* and where is the necessity of *them?* and how is safety strengthened or *good order* benefited by them?
>
> But these are three out of this thousand: not one of them exists in France.[24]

Here we have Bentham's denunciation of the needless restraints imposed in 1823 upon individual activity. It may be termed the eulogy of *laissez faire*, but *laissez faire*, be it noted, was with Bentham and his disciples a totally different thing from easy acquiescence in the existing conditions of life. It

24. *Truth against Ashurst*, Bentham, v. p. 234.

was a war-cry. It sounded the attack upon every restriction, not justifiable by some definite and assignable reason of utility, upon the freedom of human existence and the development of individual character. Bentham assaulted restraints imposed by definite laws. John Mill carried the war a step further, and, in his treatise *On Liberty*, denounced restraints on the action of individuals imposed by social habits or conventions. This struggle for personal liberty, which means much more than mere resistance to obvious oppression, such as could be guarded against by the Habeas Corpus Act, gave to early Benthamism its whole spirit and life as a militant creed.

From these three guiding principles of legislative utilitarianism—the scientific character of sound legislation, the principle of utility, faith in *laissez faire*—English individualists have in practice deduced the two corollaries, that the law ought to extend the sphere and enforce the obligation of contract, and that, as regards the possession of political power, every man ought to count for one and no man ought to count for more than one. Each of these ideas has been constantly entertained by men who have never reduced it to a formula or carried it out to its full logical result; each of these ideas has profoundly influenced modern legislation; each deserves separate attention.[25]

(i.) *The Extension of the Sphere of Contract.* Once admit that *A, B,* or *C* can each, as a rule, judge more correctly than can any one else of his own interest, and the conclusion naturally follows that, in the absence of force or fraud, *A* and *B* ought to be allowed to bind themselves to one another by any agreement which they each choose to make—*i.e.* which in the view of each of them promotes his own interest, or, in other words, is conducive to his own happiness.

From one point of view, indeed, a contract between *A* and *B* whereby, for example, *A* agrees to sell and *B* to buy a horse for £20, places a limit upon the freedom of each of them, since *A* comes under a legal compulsion to sell, and *B* comes under a legal compulsion to pay for the horse; but, if the matter be fairly considered, it is easily seen that freedom of contract is an extension of an individual's power to do what he likes, *i.e.* of his freedom. As both *A* and *B* are at full liberty not to enter into a contract at all, it must be assumed that, at the moment of contracting, *A* wishes to have

25. See Sidgwick, *Elements of Politics*, ch. iv.

£20 instead of the horse, and *B* wishes to have the horse at the price of £20. For the law to give effect to the agreement by which this result is attained, as also to more complicated contractual engagements, is nothing else than an extension of each individual's power to get what he wants.[26]

To these abstract grounds for extending contractual freedom add the consideration that the substitution of relations founded on contract for relations founded on status was for individualists generally,[27] and especially for Benthamite liberals, the readiest mode of abolishing a whole body of antiquated institutions, which presented, during the eighteenth century, a serious obstacle to the harmonious development of society. Hence individualistic reformers opposed anything which shook the obligation of contracts, or, what at bottom is the same thing, limited the contractual freedom of individuals. It is no accident that Bentham very early in his career assailed the usury laws, or that freedom of trade in money, in goods, and in labour, has been the watchword of the statesmen who in their policy and their legislation have most closely followed the footsteps of Bentham. To individualism, again, is assuredly due that legalisation of divorce, which is itself a mere extension of the area of contractual freedom.

The very zeal, however, for freedom of contract, which is a note of individualism, raises questions which, on the principles of individualism, do not admit of an easy answer.

Ought a borrower to have the right to obtain a loan, which he urgently requires, by the promise to pay the most usurious interest? Ought a man, to take an extreme instance, to be allowed to make a contract binding

---

26. A contractual incapacity, such, for example, as the incapacity of an infant to bind himself by a contract to pay for things which are not necessaries, may be a desirable protection, but it assuredly, as far as it goes, limits an infant's power of obtaining luxuries on credit. The point is elementary, but it is worth insisting upon, since there is a constant tendency on the part both of theorists and of so-called practical men, to forget that protection invariably involves disability, *i.e.* limitations on the individual liberty of the protected person.

27. Respect for the obligation of contracts is embodied in the Constitution of the United States. The revolutionary, no less than the Napoleonic legislation of France is systematically hostile to the existence of guilds, corporations, or associations which might in any way limit the freedom of contract between individuals. Compare Hauriou, *Précis de Droit Administratif* (5th ed.), p. 100; Pic, *Traité Elémentaire de Législation Industrielle* (2nd ed.), ss. 336–343.

himself to be the servant of his neighbour for life?[28] To put the matter more generally, ought every person of full age, acting with his eyes open and not the victim of fraud, but who nevertheless is placed in a position in which from the pressure of his needs he can hardly make a fair bargain, to be capable of binding himself by a contract? If these and the like questions be answered in the affirmative an individual's full contractual capacity is preserved, but he is in danger of parting, by the very contract which he is allowed to make, with all real freedom. If, on the other hand, these questions are answered in the negative, then many men and women are protected against certain forms of hardship or injustice, but contractual freedom is sacrificed and the validity of the belief which underlies individualistic legislation, that men are on the whole the best judges of their own interest, is in effect denied. The difficulty is in all these cases, and in others which might easily be imagined, the same; there is a perpetual danger that unlimited contractual capacity, which is looked upon as an extension of individual freedom, may yet be so used by some individual as to deprive him of the very freedom of which it is assumed to be the exercise. To the particular questions here raised by way of illustration the older Utilitarians, at any rate, would generally have answered that each man being as a rule the best judge of his own interest, his right to bind himself by contract should be left untouched, even though he might sometimes use the right so as to do himself an injury.

This difficulty of fixing the right limit to contractual freedom suggests a theoretical inquiry which always raises, as it did raise in the time of Bentham, a question or problem of great practical importance.

Is it desirable to fix a limit on the right, which, though in England it has not received a technical name, is known in foreign countries as the "right of association"[29]—which is nothing else than the right of two or more citizens, *X, Y,* and *Z,* to combine together by agreement among themselves for the attainment of a common purpose?

This right has the peculiarity that it presents two different and even

---

28. A contract of service for life is legal (*Wallis* v. *Day* (1837), 2 M. & W. 273). But though damages might be recovered for the breach of the contract, the specific performance thereof would not be enforced. Compare Macdonell, *Law of Master and Servant,* pp. 31, 197.

29. See Appendix, Note I., Right of Association.

opposed aspects, according to the point of view from which it is regarded. It may, on the one hand, be looked upon as the mere extension of each citizen's individual freedom—that is, of his right to manage his own affairs in his own way so long as he does not trench upon the legal rights of his neighbours, whence it apparently follows that whatever course of action *X*, or *Y*, or *Z* may each lawfully pursue when acting without agreement, that course of action *X*, *Y*, and *Z* may all of them lawfully pursue when acting together under an agreement; but the right of association may, on the other hand, be looked upon as a right to a very special character, in that the exercise thereof may under certain circumstances greatly restrict the freedom of individuals.[30] That this is so is due to the fact, which has received far too little notice from English lawyers, that, whenever men act in concert for a common purpose, they tend to create a body which, from no fiction of law, but from the very nature of things, differs from the individuals of whom it is constituted. *Esprit de corps* is a real and a powerful sentiment which drives men to act either above, or, still more often, below the ordinary moral standard by which they themselves regulate their conduct as individuals. A body, moreover, created by combination—a natural corporation, if the expression may be allowed—whether a political league, a church, or a trade union, by its mere existence limits the freedom of its members, and constantly tends to limit the freedom of outsiders. Its combined power is created by some surrender of individual liberty on the part of each of its members, and a society may from this surrender acquire a strength far greater than could be exercised by the whole of its members acting separately; a disciplined regiment of a thousand men, acting under command, is a far more formidable assailant than a thousand men who, even though armed, act without discipline and combination. An association may in this way constantly acquire powers which curtail the freedom of outsiders. A private citizen has often found it impossible to disobey the commands of a political association or of a church. Hence the right of association has, even when considered from a merely speculative point of view, a paradoxical character. A right which seems a necessary extension of individual freedom may, it would seem, become fatal to the individual freedom which it seems to extend. And this speculative paradox leads to a

30. And also may menace the authority of the State.

practical question which has in England perplexed the whole combination law.

May *X, Y,* and *Z* lawfully bind themselves by agreement to act together for every purpose which it would be lawful for *X,* or *Y,* or *Z* to pursue if he were acting without concert with others?

If this question be answered in the affirmative then contractual freedom, and therefore individual liberty of action, receives what appears to be a legitimate extension, but thereupon from the very nature of things two results immediately ensue. The free action of *X,* or *Y,* or *Z* is, in virtue of the agreement into which they have entered, placed for the future under strict limits, and their concerted action may grievously interfere with the liberty of some third party, *T.* Thus if *X, Y,* and *Z,* being employers of labour, bind themselves never to employ a workman who has taken part in a strike, or, being workmen, bind themselves never to work with any man who is not a member of a trade union, then both the liberty of the individual *X* to manage his business or to do his work on such terms as he thinks fit is gone, and the liberty of *T,* who has been the leader of a strike, or, as the case may be, has refused to join a trade union, may be reduced to nothing, and he may be deprived of the means of earning an honest livelihood. If, on the other hand, the question before us be answered in the negative, and, in the interest of individual freedom, the law forbids *X, Y,* and *Z* to combine for purposes which they might each lawfully pursue if acting without concert, then the contractual power of *X, Y,* and *Z,* or, in other words, their liberty of action, suffers a serious curtailment.

What, on the principles of individualism, is the true reply to our problem?

To this inquiry Benthamites have never, it is submitted, given a perfectly consistent or satisfactory reply.

In truth they never fully realised the extent and the difficulty of the problems which, during the last fifty or sixty years, have been raised as to the limits which ought to be placed on the right of association. Individualists tacitly assumed that each man if left to himself would in the long run be sure to act for his own true interest, and that the general welfare was sufficiently secured if each man were left free to pursue his own happiness in his own way, either alone or in combination with his fellows. On the application, however, of this doctrine there existed much difference of opinion. Some Benthamites, such as Place, believed that trade unionism would disappear if only the laws against trade combinations were repealed; but, whilst the elder Benthamites were as a rule anxious to extend the right of association as a part of individual freedom, some of them were prepared to cut down rigorously the right of combination whenever it in fact menaced the right of each individual to manage his trade or dispose of his labour on such terms as he himself thought good. From this point of view the report produced by Nassau Senior, a typical economist of 1830, is important. A commission, of which he was the principal member,

> recommend that a law should be passed clearly reciting the common law prohibitions of conspiracy and restraint of trade. The law should go on to forbid, under severe penalties, "all attempts or solicitations, combinations, subscriptions, and solicitations to combinations" to threaten masters, to persuade blacklegs, or even simply to ask workmen to join the union. Picketing, however peaceful, was to be comprehensively forbidden and ruthlessly punished. Employers or their assistants were to be authorised themselves to arrest men without summons or warrant, and hale them before any justice of the peace. The encouragement of combinations by masters was to be punished by heavy pecuniary penalties, to be recovered by any common informer. "This," say the commissioners, "is as much as we should recommend in the first instance. But if it should be proved that the evil of the combination system cannot be subdued at a less price ... *we must recommend the experiment of confiscation*"—confiscation, that is, of the funds "subscribed for purposes of combination and deposited in savings banks or otherwise."[31]

But if in 1830 some individualists were prepared to cut down the right of combination as stringently as might be required for the absolute protection of each individual's freedom of action, others have taken a different view.

Turn to the treatise, *On Liberty*.

"Thirdly," writes Mill in 1859, "from this liberty of each individual follows the liberty, within the same limits, of combination among individuals; freedom to unite, for any purpose not involving harm to others: the per-

---

31. Webb, *History of Trade Unionism* (1894), p. 125.

sons combining being supposed to be of full age, and not forced or deceived."[32]

Unless these words be understood in a very non-natural sense, the Benthamites of 1859, as represented by their most authoritative exponent, were apparently ready, with a view to securing the right of combination, to curtail the free action of individuals.

However this may be, the utilitarians, whether in 1830 or 1859, had not given sufficient attention to the difficulty of combining the contractual freedom of each individual when acting alone with that unlimited right of association which, from one point of view, is a main element of individual freedom.

This gap in the Benthamite creed is of untold importance. It is closely connected with the tendency of all individualists to neglect the social aspect of human nature. In the sphere of legislation, as elsewhere, confusion of thought has led, as it always will lead, to confusion of action.

(ii.) *Every Man to count for one and no Man for more than one.* This deduction from the axioms of utilitarianism forms the intellectual link between Benthamism and democracy.

The idea that each man ought to receive the same share of political power stands manifestly in close connection both with the assumption that the differences which divide man from man are insignificant in comparison with the characteristics which all men have in common, and with the conviction that every man is on the whole the best judge of his own interest. These conceptions, which receive their embodiment in the maxim that every man should count for one and no man for more than one, led Bentham (in later life[33] at least) and most of his immediate disciples to the practical conclusion that the best form of government is a democracy. "Every man," as they argued,

> follows his own interest as he understands it, and the part of the community which has political power will use it for its own objects. The remedy is to transfer political power to the entire community. It is impossible that they

32. Mill, *On Liberty*, p. 27. Compare pp. 157, 158, and 176–180.

33. See Halévy, ii. pp. 34–51, as to Bentham's want of sympathy with the democratic aspect of the Revolution.

should abuse it, for the interest which they will try to promote is the interest of all, and the interest of all is the proper end and object of all legislation.[34]

Nor, on strict utilitarian principles, was it to be expected than [sic] any other government than a democracy would legislate with a view to the happiness of the whole community; a true monarch would look to his own interest, an oligarchy would administer public affairs with a view to the interests not of all but of a part of the citizens, viz. of the oligarchy. Force, moreover, was added to these logical considerations by the actual condition of the European world, and especially of England. That the reformers of Bentham's day were unfair and one-sided critics of English institutions is past denial, but it is equally certain that England did at the moment suffer greatly from the predominance of particular classes and from the influence of sinister interests. There was scarcely a department of the law, whether public or private, the state of which did not prove the truth of this assertion.[35] The Benthamites, therefore, were as a rule democrats, and the English democrats[36] of 1830 were as a rule Benthamites, yet for all this there was no necessary connection between Benthamism and the democratic creed.[37] The doctrine, in short, that beneficial legislation was impossible[38] under any form of government except a democracy, was no fundamental article of utilitarianism. It was in truth a practical conclusion drawn from

34. Maine, *Popular Government,* p. 83, and see pp. 82–86.

35. Lect. V., *ante.* Compare *Creevy Papers,* edited by the Rt. Hon. Sir Herbert Maxwell, for illustrations of the worst side of English government between 1800 and 1832.

36. Even if not Benthamites they were with rare exceptions imbued with individualism.

37. Whether the precept that every one should count for one included women, was in 1830 a question outside the sphere of practical politics, but it divided the Benthamites. The language of Bentham himself was somewhat uncertain. James Mill condemned the government of women as decisively, if not as consistently, as in an earlier age did John Knox. John Mill was throughout his life the ardent advocate of the political equality of the sexes, but John Mill, though honestly basing all his political views on the principle of utility, entertained, though unconsciously, a sentiment in favour of equality which belongs to the school rather of Rousseau than of Bentham.

38. James Mill's *Essay on Government* aims apparently at establishing this conclusion, but a student who reads between the lines will see that James Mill in reality advocates the political supremacy of the middle class. See *Government,* pp. 31, 32.

the actual condition of the European world, but was capable of modification.

It might be modified by at least two considerations. A sound utilitarian might, in the first place, hold that, under a constitution which was not a democracy, power might be placed in the hands of a class so wide that the interests of that class would, in general, coincide with the interest of the whole people. Under such a condition of things there was no necessity for insisting upon the constitution being made strictly democratic. This was substantially the attitude of the philosophic Radicals with regard to the Reform Act of 1832. The Act, they believed, would transfer political supremacy to the middle classes, and the English middle classes they thought were so numerous and so varied in character as to share the feelings and, what to a utilitarian was of more consequence, pursue the true interest, of the majority of the nation; a Parliament elected by the ten-pound householders would study to promote the greatest happiness of the greatest number, *i.e.* of the whole community.

A sound utilitarian might in the second place doubt whether the citizens of a given country were sufficiently enlightened to understand their own interest, and entertaining this doubt might, with the utmost consistency, prefer for such a country the rule of an intelligent despot or of an intelligent minority to the rule of an unintelligent democracy.

As to the capacity of the people to recognise their own interest, there was among the Benthamites themselves a division of opinion.

The predominant belief of the school was represented by the democratic utilitarianism of James Mill.

> In politics, an almost unbounded confidence in the efficacy of two things: representative government, and complete freedom of discussion. So complete was my father's reliance on the influence of reason over the minds of mankind, whenever it is allowed to reach them, that he felt as if all would be gained if the whole population were taught to read, if all sorts of opinions were allowed to be addressed to them by word and in writing, and if by means of the suffrage they could nominate a legislature to give effect to the opinions they adopted. He thought that when the legislature no longer represented a class interest, it would aim at the general interest, honestly and with adequate wisdom; since the people would be sufficiently under the guidance of educated intelligence, to make in general a good choice of persons

to represent them, and having done so, to leave to those whom they had chosen a liberal discretion. Accordingly aristocratic rule, the government of the Few in any of its shapes, being in his eyes the only thing which stood between mankind and an administration of their affairs by the best wisdom to be found among them, was the object of his sternest disapprobation, and a democratic suffrage the principal article of his political creed, not on the ground of liberty, rights of man, or any of the phrases, more or less significant, by which, up to that time, democracy had usually been defended, but as the most essential of "securities for good government." In this, too, he held fast only to what he deemed essentials; he was comparatively indifferent to monarchical or republican forms—far more so than Bentham, to whom a king, in the character of "corruptor-general," appeared necessarily very noxious.[39]

The other aspect of the relation between utilitarianism and democracy was represented by John Austin.

He attached much less importance than formerly to outward changes; unless accompanied by a better cultivation of the inward nature. He had a strong distaste for the general meanness of English life, the absence of enlarged thoughts and unselfish desires, the low objects on which the faculties of all classes of the English are intent. Even the kind of public interests which Englishmen care for, he held in very little esteem. He thought that there was more practical good government, and (which is true enough) infinitely more care for the education and mental improvement of all ranks of the people, under the Prussian monarchy, than under the English representative government; and he held, with the French *Economistes,* that the real security for good government is "un peuple éclairé," which is not always the fruit of popular institutions, and which if it could be had without them, would do their work better than they. Though he approved of the Reform Bill, he predicted, what in fact occurred, that it would not produce the great immediate improvements in government which many expected from it. The men, he said, who could do these great things, did not exist in the country. There were many points of sympathy between him and me, both in the new opinions he had adopted and in the old ones which he retained. Like me, he

---

39. J. S. Mill, *Autobiography,* pp. 106, 107. It is arguable that many utilitarians were in their estimate of the "people" more influenced than they were aware of by the teaching of Rousseau, or rather by the prevalent sentiment to which this teaching gave expression.

never ceased to be an utilitarian, and with all his love of the Germans, and enjoyment of their literature, never became in the smallest degree reconciled to the innate-principle metaphysics. He cultivated more and more a kind of German religion, a religion of poetry and feeling with little, if anything, of positive dogma; while in politics (and here it was that I most differed with him) he acquired an indifference, bordering on contempt, for the progress of popular institutions; though he rejoiced in that of Socialism, as the most effectual means of compelling the powerful classes to educate the people, and to impress on them the only real means of permanently improving their material condition, a limitation of their numbers. Neither was he, at this time, fundamentally opposed to Socialism in itself as an ultimate result of improvement. He professed great disrespect for what he called "the universal principles of human nature of the political economists," and insisted on the evidence which history and daily experience afford of the "extraordinary pliability of human nature" (a phrase which I have somewhere borrowed from him); nor did he think it possible to set any positive bounds to the moral capabilities which might unfold themselves in mankind, under an enlightened direction of social and educational influences. Whether he retained all these opinions to the end of life I know not. Certainly the modes of thinking of his later years, and especially of his last publication, were much more Tory in their general character than those which he held at this time.[40]

In this passage we have the explanation of the curious historical phenomenon that after the middle of the nineteenth century Austin, Bowring, W. R. Greg, Robert Lowe, and other rigid utilitarians adopted, without any fundamental change of principles, a peculiar type of conservatism. They felt that a Parliament constituted under the Reform Act of 1832 was more likely to legislate in accordance with utilitarian principles than would be any more democratic assembly. Their forecast of the future has been justified by subsequent events. A House of Commons representing the householders of the United Kingdom has shown far less inclination than did a House elected by the £10 householders to respect either the dogmas or the sentiment of Benthamism.

As to the Method of Law Reform. Bentham's influence in setting before reformers an ideal to be attained by the amendment of the law has re-

---

40. Mill, *Autobiography*, pp. 177, 178, 179. "This time" apparently means from about 1830 to 1840.

ceived general and due acknowledgment;[41] his influence in determining the method, *i.e.* the legislative means, by which the amendment of the law might be best affected, deserves equal acknowledgment, but has received less notice.

To appreciate the effect of his authority in this matter we must bear in mind that laws are with us created and changed in two different ways— that is, either by Act of Parliament, or by judicial legislation arising from the action of the Courts in deciding the particular cases which come before them. Even at the present day the greater part and the most important of the laws by which Englishmen are governed are in reality judge-made law, and this was much more obviously the case at the beginning of the nineteenth century.[42] When, therefore, in the latter part of the eighteenth century jurists and philanthropists perceived that the law of England stood in need of amendment and expansion, it was apparent that this end might conceivably be attained either by the free use of judicial authority or by the employment of parliamentary sovereignty. Two reformers arose of equal though of different genius. The one was Lord Mansfield, the other Bentham. The Chief-Justice adopted the judicial, the utilitarian philosopher advocated and adopted the parliamentary, method of legislation and reform.

Lord Mansfield,[43] as Chief-Justice of England, presided over the King's Bench for twenty-four years; he was not only in name but in reality the head of the English common law; he was a jurist of genius; he filled a position of unrivalled authority; he achieved as much in the way of reform as was achievable by the means at his disposal. Yet his labours, taken as a whole, were not crowned with success. In some of his innovations he distinctly failed—as notably in the endeavour to reduce within narrow limits

41. See Maine, *Ancient Law*, pp. 78, 79.

42. An intelligent reader of Blackstone's *Commentaries* is astonished at the slightness of the reference made by the commentator to statutes. Contrast on this matter the first edition of the *Commentaries*, completed in 1765, with the last edition of Stephen's *Commentaries* (based as they are on Blackstone's work), edited by Mr. Jenks in 1903.

43. For Lord Mansfield's attempted reform by way of introduction of equitable principles into the common law, and the way in which the attempt was afterwards rendered abortive by Kenyon, see Ashburner, *Principles of Equity*, pp. 15, 16. [Editor's note: This footnote was added in the second edition.]

the rule that a promise not under seal needed a consideration for its validity—and even where he was to a certain extent successful, successors,
who did not inherit his spirit, limited the operation of the principles which
he had introduced into the law. Lord Mansfield lived at least two centuries
too late. If the body of English law was to be remodelled or amended the
work could be done by Parliament, and by Parliament alone.

Bentham learned the lesson of Lord Mansfield's career; he learned it the
more easily because the element of fiction, which is an almost essential
feature of judicial innovation, shocked his logical understanding, and was
in his eyes little better than a fraud by which judges usurped authority,
which, when they had wrongfully obtained it, they had not the intelligence
to use with wisdom. The importance, moreover, which he attached to the
publication of law increased his enthusiasm for codification, and an English
code, it was clear, must be the work of Parliament. He determined or
assumed that the law must be reformed, if at all, by parliamentary enactment. His determination, justified by the circumstances of the age, was
decisive. It has been followed by every man, whether a utilitarian or not,
who since Bentham's time has wished to change systematically the law of
the land.

But, if the legislature was the only body which possessed the power to
carry through a utilitarian reformation of the law, it became before Bentham's death apparent both to himself and his disciples—the philosophic
Radicals—that the unreformed Parliament, just because it mainly represented the interests and feelings of landowners and merchants, would not
sanction fundamental improvements in the law of England. Benthamism
thus led to the demand for such a reform in the constitution of Parliament
as should make it a fit instrument for carrying out Benthamite ideas.

(B) The Acceptance of Benthamism

The existence of a school of thinkers bent on the reform of the law in
accordance with utilitarian principles was, as already pointed out,[44] one of
the causes which brought the era of quiescence to its close.

44. See pp. 89, 90, *ante*.

Two questions remain for consideration, which to a student of opinion are of profound interest—*First.* Why did the Benthamite creed obtain ready acceptance? *Secondly.* What was the extent of that acceptance?

To the inquiry why the teaching of Bentham obtained from, say, 1825 onwards, ready acceptance among thoughtful Englishmen, the right reply, put in the most general terms, is, that when it became obvious to men of common sense and of public spirit that the law required thorough-going amendment, the reformers of the day felt the need of an ideal and of a programme.[45] Both were provided by Bentham and his school. The ideal was the attainment of the greatest happiness for the greatest number, the programme was to be found in the suggestions for the amendment of the law on utilitarian principles which, during a period of forty years, had been elaborated by Bentham and his disciples. Note, however, that the men who as legislators or writers actually guided the course of legislation were in many instances not avowed Benthamites, and that some of them would have certainly repudiated the name of utilitarians.[46] The law reformers, whether in or out of Parliament—Mackintosh, Brougham, Romilly, Joseph Hume, Grote, Roebuck, Macaulay, O'Connell, Peel, the body of Edinburgh

45. "It is impossible to overrate the importance to a nation or profession of having a distinct object to aim at in the pursuit of improvement. The secret of Bentham's immense influence in England during the past thirty years is his success in placing such an object before the country. He gave us a clear rule of reform. English lawyers of the last century were probably too acute to be blinded by the paradoxical commonplace that English law was the perfection of human reason, but they acted as if they believed it for want of any other principle to proceed upon. Bentham made the good of the community take precedence of every other object, and thus gave escape to a current which had long been trying to find its way outwards."—Maine, *Ancient Law*, pp. 78, 79. These words were published in 1861.

"German philosophers, indeed, have neglected Bentham. Even Robert von Mohl, who alone appreciates his genius, thinks Hill Burton's eulogy absurdly exaggerated, because Hill Burton declares that nearly all the great reforms of the first half of nineteenth-century England were originated by Bentham. The opinion of Sir Henry Maine might be quoted in support of Hill Burton's proposition, which is indeed strengthened by publications of a later date. But the best and most conclusive evidence of all is to be drawn from a comparison of Bentham's teaching with the legislation which followed it."—Redlich and Hirst, *Local Government in England*, i. p. 97.

46. This is certainly true of Sydney Smith. See Holland's *Memoir and Letters of Sydney Smith* (4th ed.), p. 386.

Reviewers, with their ablest representative Sydney Smith—were all at bottom individualists. They were all, consciously or unconsciously, profoundly influenced by utilitarian ideas. But these men were men of the world; they were, even when avowed Benthamites, occupied with and used to the transaction of public affairs; they were most of them members of Parliament; they loved practical compromises as much as Bentham loved logical deductions from strict principles; they were utilitarians, but they accepted not the rigid dogmas of utilitarianism, but that Benthamism of common sense which, under the name of liberalism, was to be for thirty or forty years a main factor in the development of English law. This liberalism was the utilitarianism not of the study but of the House of Commons or of the Stock Exchange. It modified the doctrines of Bentham, so that, when they were introduced into Acts of Parliament, they were not really carried out to their full extent,[47] and were thus made the more acceptable to the English people. The general answer, then, to the question why Benthamism obtained ready acceptance is that it gave to reformers, and indeed to educated Englishmen, the guidance of which they were in need; it fell in with the spirit of the time.[48]

47. For an illustration of the difference between systematic Benthamism and utilitarian liberalism contrast Bentham's *Book of Fallacies* with Sydney Smith's review thereof, containing the celebrated "Noodle's Oration," or James Mill's "Essay on Government," with Macaulay's articles on the utilitarian philosophy which appeared in the *Edinburgh Review* of 1829. With these articles should be read Macaulay's review of "Gladstone on Church and State."

48. To Benthamism it is owing that the pacific revolution of which the Reform Act, 1832, was the visible sign, did not, like many other pacific or violent attempts at improvement, fail in attaining its end. Puritanism, it has been well said, missed its mark. In no sphere is this more obviously true than in the sphere of legislation. Many Puritans perceived that the law needed reform, yet the Puritan revolution achieved but little for the amendment of the law. Chief-Justice Rolle could perfect the fictions on which rested the action of ejectment, and in so far he facilitated the recovery of land (Blackstone, *Comm.* iii. p. 202); but the Puritans did not perceive that the fictions which complicated the proceedings in ejectment ought to be abolished. The Puritan worship of the common law barred the path which might lead to its amendment. Their rightful dread of arbitrary power blinded them to the necessity for the changes which were gradually and awkwardly introduced by the development of equity through the Court of Chancery. A party who adored Coke could not possibly produce a reformer such as Bentham, or have understood him had he lived in the seventeenth century.

This answer, however, is very general, not to say indefinite. To state that a creed falls in with the spirit of the time is, after all, nothing but a vague way of asserting that its propagation is aided by favourable conditions. If we are to obtain anything like a definite answer to our inquiry we must ascertain the specific conditions which, say from 1825 onwards, favoured the reception of Benthamite doctrine. They were in part the transitory circumstances of a particular era, and in part certain permanent tendencies of English thought.

Benthamism exactly answered to the immediate want of the day.

In 1825 Englishmen had come to feel that the institutions of the country required thorough-going amendment; but Englishmen of all classes, Whigs and reformers, no less than Tories, distrusted the whole theory of natural rights, and shunned any adoption of Jacobinical principles. The dogmatism and the rhetoric of the French Revolution had even among Radicals lost their charm. The Jacobins or Terrorists,[49] some of whom were still living, had been apostles of the social contract, but the Jacobins were to Englishmen objects of horror—Robespierre was the confutation of Rousseau. The teacher who could lead England in the path of reform must not talk of the social contract, of natural rights, of rights of man, or of liberty, fraternity, and equality. Bentham and his disciples precisely satisfied this requirement; they despised and derided vague generalities, sentiments, and rhetoric; they thoroughly disbelieved in the social contract;[50] nowhere can you find a more trenchant exposure of revolutionary dogmatism than in Bentham's dissection of the "Declaration of the Rights of Man and the Citizen."

> "The things," he writes, "that people stand most in need of being reminded of are, one would think, their duties; for their rights, whatever they may be, they are apt enough to attend to themselves ... the great enemies of public peace are the selfish and dissocial passions. ... What has been the object, the perpetual and palpable object, of this declaration of pretended rights? To add as much force as possible to those passions, already but too strong, to burst the cords that hold them in; to say to the selfish passions—There, everywhere is your prey! to the angry passions, There, everywhere is your enemy!"[51]

49. Many of them had become the most servile of Napoleon's servants.

50. See for Bentham's criticisms on the theory of a social contract, Halévy, vol. i., appendix iii., p. 416.

51. Bentham, "Anarchical Fallacies," cited Kent, *English Radicals,* p. 184.

True it is that modern critics might attack Bentham's own teaching as a form of political metaphysics; but his practical ingenuity,[52] his reliance on argument, and his contempt for oratory, concealed from the English world no less than from Bentham himself, the *a priori* and abstract element which lies hid under Benthamite utilitarianism. Even the prosaic side of Bentham's doctrines, which checks the sympathy of modern readers, reassured sensible Englishmen who in 1830 had come to long for reform but dreaded revolution. Bentham and his friends might be laughed at as pedants, but were clearly not Jacobins; and, after all, whatever were the defects of Bentham as a jurist, critics who really understood his life and work knew that the first of legal philosophers was no agitator, but a systematic thinker of extraordinary power, and a thinker who kept his eyes fixed, not upon vague and indefinite ideals, but upon definite plans for the practical amendment of the law of England. Where could a teacher be found so acceptable to men of common sense as a lawyer who had studied the law of England more profoundly than had many Lord Chancellors, and had studied it only with a view to removing its defects? He was a teacher of a totally different stamp from a thinker like Godwin, whose revolutionary creed was already out of date; it had been confuted by Malthus, and the theories of Malthus were accepted with fervour by the utilitarians. Bentham was a guide whose speculations lawyers could take seriously, and on whose labours intelligent Englishmen could look with a respect which could not be accorded to the sincere but childish radicalism of Cartwright, to the theatrical bluster of Burdett, to the oratory and egotism of Hunt, or to the inconsistent doctrine and dubious character of Cobbett. Bentham, in short, was a man of wealth and of genius, who had worked out with the greatest logical acumen plans for law reform which corresponded to the best ideas of the English middle class.

About 1830 utilitarianism was, as the expression goes, "in the air."

Dr. Johnson, the moralist of the preceding generation, had admitted, and Paley, still the accepted English theologian of the day, had advocated, the fundamental dogma of Benthamism, that the aim of existence was the attainment of happiness. The religious teachers who touched the conscience of Englishmen tacitly accepted this doctrine. The true strength of Evangelicalism did not, indeed, lie in the fervour with which its preachers

52. See pp. 93–94, *ante.*

appealed, as they often did, to the terrors of hell as a sanction for the practice of virtue on earth, but the appeal was in fact a recognition of the principle of utility. When Bentham applied this principle to the amendment of the law he was in thorough harmony with the sentiment of the time; he gave no alarm to moderate reformers by applying to the appropriate sphere of legislation that greatest happiness principle which the public had long accepted as something like a dictate of common sense.

The essential strength, however, of utilitarianism lay far less in the transitory circumstances of a particular time than in its correspondence with tendencies of English thought and feeling which have exhibited a character of permanence.

Benthamism fell in with the habitual conservatism of Englishmen.

The Benthamites were, indeed, for the most part democrats, but the most democratic of the utilitarians did not attack any foundation of the English social system.[53] They entertained the prevalent conceptions of individual happiness and of national well-being. To socialism of any kind they were thoroughly opposed; they looked with disfavour on State intervention; they felt no sympathy with those Spencean philanthropists who alarmed the Government in the days of the Six Acts, and the Cato Street Conspiracy; they were more adverse to measures of latent socialism than the Tory philanthropists, represented in literature by Southey, and in the world of practical benevolence by Lord Shaftesbury. The philosophical Radicals proposed to reform the law of England, not by any root and branch revolution, but by securing for all Englishmen the rights of property and of individual liberty which all Englishmen in theory enjoyed, but which, through defects in the law, were in fact denied to large classes.[54] The

---

53. Francis Place was even in later life well described by an admirer as "an old firebrand," but fanatic as he was, he does not express the least hatred to English institutions. The moderation, again, of Bentham's objects may be inferred from this sentence in a letter to O'Connell: "Parliamentary Reform, Law Reform, Codification—all these *agenda* crowned with your approbation—nothing can be more satisfactory, nothing more glorious to me— nothing more beneficial to the so unhappily United Kingdom, from thence to the rest of the civilised world, and from thence, in God Almighty's good time, to the uncivilised."— Bentham, *Works*, x. p. 598.

54. Every man, for example, had a right to be paid the debts owing to him, but until the

English public then came to perceive that Benthamism meant nothing more than the attempt to realise by means of effective legislation the political and social ideals set before himself by every intelligent merchant, tradesman, or artisan. The architect who proposes to repair an existing edifice intends to keep it standing: he cannot long be confused with the visionary projector who proposes to pull down an ancient mansion and erect in its stead a new building of unknown design.

Legislative utilitarianism is nothing else than systematised individualism, and individualism has always found its natural home in England.[55]

During the long conflicts which have made up the constitutional history of England, individualism has meant hatred of the arbitrary prerogative of the Crown, or, in other words, of the collective and autocratic authority of the State, and has fostered the instinctive and strenuous effort to secure for the humblest Englishman the rule of law. Benthamism was, and was ultimately felt to be, little else than the logical and systematic development of those individual rights, and especially of that individual freedom which has always been dear to the common law of England. The faith indeed of the utilitarians in the supreme value of individual liberty, and the assumption on which that faith rests, owe far more to the traditions of the common law than thinkers such as John Mill, who was no lawyer, are prepared to acknowledge. Bentham is heavily indebted to Coke, and utilitarianism has inherited some of its most valuable ideas from Puritanism. This combination of innovation with essential conservatism gave to the utilitarian reformers the peculiar power which attaches to teachers who, whilst appearing to oppose, really express the sentiment of their time.

The strength of Benthamism lay then far less in its originality than in its being the response to the needs of a particular era, and in its harmony with the general tendencies of English thought. This consideration does not detract from the merit of Bentham and his disciples. That in 1830 the demand for reform should arise was a necessity, but a demand does not of itself create the means for its satisfaction. Had not Benthamism provided reformers with an ideal and a programme, it is more than possible that

---

creation of the County Courts it was often difficult, if not impossible, for any poor man to obtain payment of even an admitted debt.

55. See as to the relation between Evangelicalism and Benthamism, Lect. XII., *post.*

the effort to amend the law of England might, like many other endeavours to promote the progress of mankind, have missed its mark.

What then was the extent[56] to which the Benthamism of common sense or individualism, obtained acceptance?

The answer may be given with certainty and decision. From 1832 onwards the supremacy of individualism among the classes then capable of influencing legislation was for many years incontestable and patent.

This undoubted fact ought not to be concealed from modern students, either by the important consideration (to which attention is drawn in the next lecture), that there has always existed a minority who protested against the dogmas of dominant individualism, or by the comparatively unimportant fact that divisions between political parties constantly fail to correspond with real differences of opinion, and that after 1832 Conservatives were often as much imbued with individualism as were Whigs or Liberals. On the passing of the Reform Act, at any rate, the political movement of the day was under the guidance of leaders who, by whatever party name they were known, were in essence individualists and utilitarians. The philosophic Radicals, Grote, Roebuck, and Molesworth, were ardent disciples of Bentham. Brougham, Russell, and Macaulay, and other Whig statesmen, whether they disclaimed or not the name of Benthamites, were firm believers in common-sense utilitarianism. Nothing is more noteworthy in this matter than the attitude of O'Connell; it would be sufficient of itself to prove the immense authority possessed between 1830 and 1845 by Benthamite liberalism. O'Connell stands apart from English party leaders. His sincere Roman Catholicism, his alliance with the priests, and the revolutionary character of the Repeal movement, separate him in the eyes of most Englishmen from the philosophic Radicals. He stands out as an agitator rather than a thoughtful statesman. But for all this he might well be numbered among the Benthamites. He was certainly a more ardent admirer and a more genuine disciple of Bentham than were many Whigs. On most matters, except the policy of Repeal, he agreed with the philosophic Radicals.

He was one of the most prominent advocates of parliamentary reform of the most radical description, going as far as universal suffrage, the ballot, and

56. See p. 119, *ante.*

an elective House of Lords. He was an early and steady supporter of the emancipation of the Jews. He spoke with great force and knowledge on questions of legal reform; on the importance of cheapening, simplifying, and codifying the law, of multiplying local tribunals, of abolishing obsolete forms and phraseology. He was an ardent advocate of the abolition of capital punishment. He wished to change the law of bequest, so as to make it obligatory on parents to leave at least half their property among their children. He supported the abolition of the Usury Acts, and agreed with Bentham about the folly of attempting to regulate the rate of interest by law. He spoke in favour of the abolition of flogging in the army; of the abolition of the taxes on knowledge; of the complete abolition of the game laws.[57]

He was a vehement opponent of slavery when his opposition cost him the sympathy of Americans. He withstood trade unionism, and denounced outrages committed by trade unionists, though his denunciations aroused the hostility of the Dublin workmen. He was as enthusiastic a free trader as Bright; he opposed the corn laws as in themselves immoral, and used language on this point which Cobden possibly might have deemed exaggerated.[58] His enthusiasm for free trade is the more remarkable because of the belief certainly held by some patriotic and liberal Irishmen, that protection has been a benefit to Ireland.

---

57. Lecky, *Leaders of Public Opinion in Ireland*, ii. (ed. 1903), p. 91.

58. "He was also an uncompromising advocate of free trade in all its forms, including the complete abolition of the Corn Laws. His policy on this question is very remarkable, for Ireland had a special interest in the question, which O'Connell seems never to have understood. Nothing was more contrary to his desire than that her population should be greatly diminished and that she should be turned into a great pastoral country, yet nothing is more clear than that the abolition of the Corn Laws, depriving her of her preferential position in the corn market of England, made such a change inevitable. O'Connell argued the question on the crudest and also the most extreme lines, treating any tax on food as simply immoral. In his letter to Lord Shrewsbury he accused that Catholic nobleman of having 'stained Catholicity itself with the guilt of that sordid monopoly.' 'The provision tax,' he wrote, 'is in its nature most criminal. It is murderous. It is the most direct violation of the first principles of justice. . . . It is in itself so radically oppressive and unjust, that it is incapable of moral mitigation. . . . The protected person, by the voice of the Corn Laws, addresses the workmen: "You shall not buy your breakfast, though you have your own hard-earned money to buy it with, until you have first paid *me* a heavy tax for liberty to purchase."' "—Lecky, *Leaders of Public Opinion in Ireland*, ii. pp. 92, 93.

The leaders of the Manchester school, again, were not philosophic Radicals nor philosophers of any kind; they were enlightened men of business who desired reforms which were rather commercial than political or social. Yet in the world of politics they followed out the ideas of Bentham more nearly than did any other body of English Liberals.

Benthamism was not in reality the monopoly of Liberals. The Conservatives who followed Peel[59] would have derided the idea of being utilitarians, but in common with the men of their generation they had accepted to a great extent the doctrines of Bentham. They joined with the older Tories in resistance to further and large constitutional changes, but under the guidance of Peel they believed that the gradual removal of abuses, and the skilful administration of public affairs at home, combined with the preservation of peace abroad, would secure national prosperity. The men who in later years were known as Peelites were convinced individualists, no less than the Radicals of the Manchester school, and stood far nearer in their way of looking at politics to the older Benthamites than did a Whig such as Lord John Russell, or a nominally Liberal leader such as Palmerston. No Liberal and no Conservative betrayed, at any rate, the remotest leaning towards socialism. Lord Melbourne's "Why can't you let it alone?" was the expression not so much of indolence as of trust in *laissez faire.*

The guides, lastly, of the working classes were, in some cases, at any rate, Benthamites. Francis Place disbelieved in trade unionism, but believed heart and soul in Malthusianism, and in the saving virtues of the New Poor Law, if only it were administered with sufficient severity.[60] Trade unionists

59. Between 1835 and 1844 agricultural training schools and model farms were established in Ireland, but "a strong opposition to State-paid agricultural education arose among the English free-traders and greatly influenced the Government. They objected to training farmers at public cost; to the State paying for, and taking a part in agricultural operations. Peel and Cardwell sympathised with these views; the model farms were nearly all given up and the teaching of agriculture was almost restricted to mere book knowledge. In accordance with ideas that were then widely diffused, the inspectors positively discouraged practical agricultural instruction as not really education."—Lecky, *Leaders of Public Opinion in Ireland,* ii. pp. 125, 126. This illustrates both the *laissez faire* of the day and the attitude of Peel and the Peelites.

60. See generally Wallas, *Life of Francis Place,* and especially as to the reforms still desirable in 1832, pp. 326, 327. As to transitory character of trade combinations, pp. 217, 218; as to

themselves adopted the formulas, if not the principles of the political economists, and hoped that *laissez faire,* if rightly interpreted, would give to
wage-earners adequate means for working out their own social and political salvation.[61] Among the Chartists might be found some devotees of
socialistic ideals, but Chartism was not socialism. The People's Charter,
formulated in 1838,[62] was a strictly political programme which conformed
to the doctrine of democratic Benthamism.

Liberalism, indeed, of the Benthamite type was not only dominant during what may be termed the era of reform, but betrayed, in Parliament at
least, little sign of weakening authority till the nineteenth century had run
more than half its course. Consider for a moment the general condition
of opinion say in 1850 and 1852. The philosophic Radicals (whose fate it
was to advocate the cause of the people, and yet never to command the
people's confidence or affection) had almost ceased as a party to exist, but
practical individualism was the predominant sentiment of the time. It [sic]
there remained few ardent disciples of Bentham, such as were John Mill
and his friends, when twenty or thirty years earlier they were the fervent
propagandists of utilitarianism, Bentham had, in fact, triumphed, and moderate utilitarianism was the accepted and orthodox political faith. The optimism of Macaulay, the first two volumes of whose *History* appeared in
1849, expressed the tone of the day in the vigorous rhetoric of genius. At
about the same date (1849–50) the lucid dogmatism of Miss Martineau demonstrated that the progress of England during the Thirty Years' Peace was
due to liberalism of the Benthamite type; the learning of George Grote (1846–
56) was used, or misused, to deduce from the annals of the Athenian democracy conclusions in support of philosophic radicalism. The Exhibition
of 1851 had a significance which is hardly understood by the present generation. To wise and patriotic contemporaries it represented the universal
faith that freedom of trade would remove the main cause of discord among
nations, and open an era of industrial prosperity and unbroken peace. The

---

desire for the strict enforcement of the poor law, pp. 332–334; as to Malthusianism, pp. 174,
175.

61. See Webb, *History of Trade Unionism,* pp. 277–283; and 265, 266. I do not, of course,
forget that many artisans were deeply influenced by the principles of Robert Owen.

62. Walpole, *Hist.,* iv. p. 49.

ideas of the political economists, and above all the dogma of *laissez faire,* had, it was thought, achieved a final victory. The Reformed Parliament, though its legislation did not satisfy all the aspirations of philosophic radicalism, proved to be a suitable instrument for the gradual carrying out of utilitarian reform. Great political changes seemed to be at an end. Chartism had expired on the 10th April 1848, and the working classes had ceased to press for democratic innovations. Reform Bills were suggested or brought forward in deference to the pledges of statesmen, or the exigencies of party warfare, in 1852, 1854, 1859, and 1860, but excited no general interest. In 1859 Bright attempted an agitation in favour of household suffrage. His eloquence collected crowded audiences, but did not kindle popular emotion, and the orator is said to have compared his labours to the futile work of "flogging a dead horse." In truth the events of 1848 and of the years which immediately followed 1848 had discredited republicanism, and had in England checked the advance of democracy. They had done more than this; they had in the eyes of English common sense convicted socialism not only of wickedness but of absurdity.[63] Buckle in 1857 sounded forth throughout all England sonorous periods which embodied the principles or the platitudes of the then prevalent liberalism; whilst John Mill, the hereditary representative of Benthamism, published two years later that treatise *On Liberty,* which appeared, to thousands of admiring disciples, to provide the final and conclusive demonstration of the absolute truth of individualism, and to establish on firm ground the doctrine that the protection of freedom was the one great object of wise law and sound policy.[64] As a sign of the state of opinion it is noticeable that the only considerable legislative achievement which can be ascribed to Palmerston is the Divorce Act of 1857. And this measure, if opposed to the convictions of High Churchmen, was in perfect harmony with Benthamism. Add to all these

63. Note the violence of the language of the *Quarterly* in reference to Christian Socialists such as Maurice and Kingsley (see *Life of Maurice,* ii. pp. 71–73), and the protest against a sermon by Kingsley (supposed to contain socialist doctrine), uttered immediately after its delivery before the very congregation who heard it, by the Rector at whose request Kingsley had delivered the sermon (Kingsley, *Dictionary of National Biography,* xxxi. p. 177).

64. Notice Buckle's denunciation of everything which savoured of protection. As to John Mill's influence and also as to the relation between evangelicalism and individualism, see Lect. XII., *post.*

facts which lie on the very surface of recent history, the immense moral and intellectual effect produced by the uninterrupted course of Benthamite legislation, and above all by the repeal of the corn laws, and the subsequent prosperity of which this repeal was held to be the cause. This continuance, indeed, of Benthamite legislation is the main proof, as well as from one point of view a chief cause,[65] of the dominance of individualism throughout pretty nearly the whole existence of the reformed Parliament.

But here we pass to

(C) The Trend and Tendency of Benthamite Legislation

Benthamite individualism possessed, as already noted,[66] one peculiar characteristic. It was a movement which, under the influence of a teacher born with the genius of a law-maker, was immediately and intentionally directed towards the amendment of the law of England.

Hence a singular congruity or harmony in the whole trend of Benthamite legislation[67] which, if we look not at the gradual steps by which it was carried out, but at the nature of the objects which it systematically pursued, might seem to be dictated by the will of a despotic sovereign inspired with the spirit of Bentham. For this legislation has, speaking broadly, aimed at, and in England to a great extent attained, four objects—and four objects alone—the transference of political power into the hands of a class which it was supposed was large and intelligent enough to identify its own interest with the interest of the greatest number—the promotion of humanitarianism—the extension of individual liberty—the creation of adequate legal machinery for the protection of the equal rights of all citizens.

Transference of Political Power. The Reform Act of 1832 was actively supported by Bentham's disciples.[68] It was not, judged by a modern standard,

65. See pp. 30–34, *ante.*

66. See p. 46, *ante.*

67. This unity is concealed from casual observers by the gradual and fragmentary character of English legislation.

68. Notably by the utilitarian fanatic F[r]ancis Place, whose action, of an almost revolutionary nature, was countenanced by men richer and apparently more moderate than the Westminster tailor and wire-puller.

a very democratic measure.[69] Its aim was to diminish the power of the gentry, and to transfer predominant authority to the middle classes. This characteristic of the Reform Act was at the very crisis of the movement for reform—7th October 1831—pressed by Brougham on the House of Lords. It is the people who are to be admitted to political power. He scorns the "mob." He identifies the people with the middle classes.

"If there is the mob," he says,

> there is the people also. I speak now of the middle classes—of those hundreds of thousands of respectable persons—the most numerous, and by far the most wealthy order in the community; for if all your lordships' castles, manors, rights of warren and rights of chase, with all your broad acres, were brought to the hammer, and sold at fifty years' purchase, the price would fly up and kick the beam when counterpoised by the vast and solid riches of those middle classes, who are also the genuine depositaries of sober, rational, intelligent, and honest English feeling.[70]

"By the people, I repeat, I mean the middle classes, the wealth and intelligence of the country, the glory of the British name."[71] These are the men on whose political wisdom and conservatism Brougham, who at that moment was the popular hero, and was also closely connected with the Benthamites, relies.

> Unable though they be to round a period, or point an epigram, they are solid, right-judging men, and, above all, not given to change. If they have a fault, it is that error on the right side—a suspicion of State quacks, a dogged love of existing institutions, a perfect contempt of all political nostrums. . . . Grave, intelligent, rational, fond of thinking for themselves, they consider a subject long before they make up their minds on it; and the opinions they are thus slow to form they are not swift to abandon.[72]

The Reform Act achieved its end and gave predominant authority to the middle class. Why, we ask, did Benthamite democrats so zealously support a law which went such a little way on the path of democracy? A partial

---

69. As to the relation between Benthamism and democracy, see pp. 113–117, *ante*.
70. *Brougham's Speeches*, ii. p. 600.
71. *Ibid.* p. 617.
72. *Ibid.* p. 600.

answer is, that the Whigs had neither the wish nor the power to advance farther than they did in the democratic direction. The more complete answer is, as already suggested, that the Reform Act went very near to satisfying the desires and the sentiment of Benthamite liberalism. Benthamism was fundamentally a middle class creed,[73] and the middle classes were more likely to give effect to the aspirations of utilitarianism than any other part of the community. James Mill more or less distinctly perceived that this was so. The great Reform Act was not the handiwork of the Benthamites, but it was in the truest sense the outcome of political utilitarianism.

The Municipal Reform Act, 1836, was a further step in the development of democratic Benthamism; it abolished the mass of practical abuses which were specially hateful to utilitarians. It also gave to the middle class, and even to inhabitants of boroughs who fell below the middle rank, the government and management of the cities in which they lived. It is noteworthy, however, that the reform of local government, as carried out during the era of Benthamism, did nothing for the country labourers. The administration of the counties was left in the hands of the magistrates. Yet it must be remembered that the New Poor Law reformed the social condition of the labourers and placed poor relief under the supervision of the State.

Humanitarianism. The promotion of humanity—that is, the protection

---

73. "Another proposition may be stated, with a perfect confidence of the concurrence of all those men who have attentively considered the formation of opinions in the great body of society, or, indeed, the principles of human nature in general. It is, that the opinions of that class of the people, who are below the middle rank, are formed, and their minds are directed by that intelligent, that virtuous rank, who come the most immediately in contact with them, who are in the constant habit of intimate communication with them, to whom they fly for advice and assistance in all their numerous difficulties, upon whom they feel an immediate and daily dependence, in health and in sickness, in infancy and in old age; to whom their children look up as models for their imitation, whose opinions they hear daily repeated, and account it their honour to adopt. There can be no doubt that the middle rank, which gives to science, to art, and to legislation itself, their most distinguished ornaments, the chief source of all that has exalted and refined human nature, is that portion of the community of which, if the basis of representation were ever so far extended, the opinion would ultimately decide. Of the people beneath them, a vast majority would be sure to be guided by their advice and example."—James Mill, "Government," p. 32, reprinted from supplement to *Encyclopaedia Britannica*.

of human beings from unnecessary pain and suffering—was in accordance with the fundamental principle of Benthamite philosophy. Hence the attack by utilitarians on the infliction by law of any kind of pain[74] which appeared to be needless. To this source is due the mitigation of the criminal law which abolished the whipping of women,[75] the pillory,[76] and hanging in chains,[77] which between 1827[78] and 1861[79] reduced the number of crimes punishable with death till in effect capital punishment has been limited to cases of murder, which reformed our prisons, which at one time all but did away with whipping as a punishment for crime, and which, towards the end of the specially Benthamite period forbade the public execution of murderers.[80] From the same humanitarian movement sprung the various enactments for the protection of children, of which a good example is afforded by the laws prohibiting their employment as chimney sweeps,[81] and a whole series of Acts beginning in 1828,[82] and at last forming something like a complete code for the protection of lunatics, and for guarding sane men from the risk (under the old law or want of law not inconsiderable) of imprisonment in madhouses. Nor did Bentham and his school interest themselves solely in diminishing the sufferings of their fellow-men; their humanity extended to the lower animals. From 1822 onwards, laws for the prevention of cruelty to animals prohibited bull-baiting, cock-fighting, and ultimately cruelty to animals generally.[83] It has been well

74. Utilitarianism on this point coincided with, and was reinforced by Evangelicalism.

75. 1820, 1 Geo. IV. c. 57.

76. 1816, 56 Geo. III. c. 138; 1837, 7 Will. IV. & 1 Vict. c. 23.

77. 1834, 4 & 5 Will. IV. c. 26.

78. 7 & 8 Geo. IV. cc. 29, 30.

79. 24 & 25 Vict. cc. 96–100.

80. 1868, 31 & 32 Vict. c. 24.

81. 1840, 3 & 4 Vict. c. 85; 1864, 27 & 28 Vict. c. 37.

82. 9 Geo. IV. cc. 40, 41.

83. As to improper treatment of cattle, etc., 3 Geo. IV. c. 71 (1822), as to bull-baiting and cock-fighting, 3 & 4 Will. IV. c. 19 (1833): 5 & 6 Will. IV. c. 59 (1835), as to cruelty to domestic animals generally 12 & 13 Vict. c. 92 (1849): as to prohibition of use of dogs for draught, 17 & 18 Vict. c. 60 (1854); as to prohibition of vivisection, see Cruelty to Animals Act, 1876, 39 & 40 Vict. c. 77, and as to protection from cruelty of wild animals in confinement, see 63 & 64 Vict. c. 63, Wild Animals in Captivity Protection Act, 1900, and on whole subject compare Wilson, *Modern English Law*, 234, 235, and Stephen, *Comm.* iv. (14th ed.), 213–215.

remarked that the introduction into our legislation of a principle which had hardly received recognition, namely, that it was part of humanity to diminish as far as possible the pains inflicted by man on the lower animals, was, in the earlier legislation on the subject excused, so to speak, in the eyes of the public by the plea that the cruelties prohibited, *e.g.* bull-baiting or cock-fighting, promoted idleness and disorder, or otherwise demoralised the people.[84] Under the head of humanitarianism might be well brought the emancipation of the negroes, for the palpable cruelty of negro slavery assuredly excited the indignation of the English people as much as, if not more than the injustice of holding human beings in bondage. But negro emancipation properly belongs to another head of individualistic legislation, namely—

Extension of Individual Liberty. The term "individual liberty" or "personal freedom" must here be taken in a very wide sense. The extension of individual liberty as an object of Benthamite legislation includes, no doubt, that freedom of person or, in other words, that right of unimpeded physical movement which is protected by the Habeas Corpus Acts, and by an action, or it may be a prosecution, for assault or false imprisonment, but it includes also the striking off of every unnecessary fetter which law or custom imposes upon the free action of an individual citizen. The aim of Benthamite reformers was, in short, to secure to every person as much liberty as is consistent with giving the same amount of liberty to every other citizen.[85] In order to attain this end the men who guided English legislation for the forty years which followed the great Reform Act, introduced modifications into every branch of the law.

In the name of freedom of contract the crimes of forestalling and regrating (1844, 7 & 8 Vict. c. 24) and of usury (1833–1854) ceased to exist; in 1846 and in 1849 the Navigation Laws were repealed. By the Marriage Act, 1835, and succeeding legislation which reached for the moment its conclusion in 1898,[86] marriage has been treated as a contract in which the Church has no special concern, and by the Divorce Act of 1857, has been made, like other contracts, legally dissolvable, though from its peculiar

84. Wilson, *ibid.*
85. See Mill, *On Liberty,* p. 21.
86. 61 & 62 Vict. c. 58.

character dissolvable only under special circumstances, and by the action of the High Court.

To the desire to extend contractual freedom belongs the reform[87] in the Combination Law, effected under the direct influence of the Benthamite school in accordance with the principles of individualism by means of the two Combination Acts of 1824–1825.

In 1824 the Act 5 Geo. IV. c. 95 placed the whole Combination Law on a new basis. Its provisions have thus been summarised by Sir Robert Wright:

> In 1824 the Act of 5 Geo. IV. c. 95 repealed all the then existing Acts relating to combinations of workmen, and provided that workmen should not by reason of combinations as to hours, wages, or conditions of labour, or for inducing others to refuse work or to depart from work, or for regulating "the mode of carrying on any manufacture, trade, or business, or the management thereof," be liable to any criminal proceeding or punishment for conspiracy or otherwise under the statute or common law. By another section it extended a similar immunity to combinations of masters. On the other hand it enacted a penalty of two months' imprisonment for violence, threats, intimidation, and malicious mischief.[88]

This Act was repealed after a year's trial and was replaced by the Combination Act, 1825, 6 Geo. IV. c. 129, which also has been thus summarised by Wright:

> This Act again repealed the older statutes, but without mention of common law. It provided summary penalties for the use of violence, threats, intimidation, molestation, or obstruction by any person for the purpose of forcing a master to alter his mode of business, or a workman to refuse or leave work, or of forcing any person to belong or subscribe or to conform to the rules of any club or association. It did not expressly penalize any combination or conspiracy, and it exempted from all liability to punishment the mere meeting of masters or workmen for settling the conditions as to

87. The Combination Act, 1824, 5 Geo. IV. c. 95, and the Combination Act, 1825, 6 Geo. IV. c. 129. See Steph. *Hist.* iii. 221; Wright, 13.
88. Wright, 13.

wages and hours on which the persons present at the meeting would consent to employ or serve.[89]

Even a trained lawyer may fail at first sight to perceive wherein lies the difference between the two statutes, or to conjecture why the one was substituted for the other, yet it will be found that the similarity and the difference between the two enactments are equally important, and that, whilst the repeal of the earlier Act is perfectly explainable, the singular course of legislation in 1824 and 1825 is the exact reflection of the current of opinion.

As to the Points of Similarity. Both Acts aim at the same object; they both reverse the policy of 1800, and are intended to establish free trade in labour; they both, as a part of such freedom of trade, concede, to men and to masters alike, the right to discuss and agree together as to the terms on which they will sell or purchase labour; both give expression to the idea that the sale or purchase of labour should be as entirely a matter of free contract as the sale or purchase of boots and shoes. Both Acts therefore repeal the great Combination Act and all earlier legislation against trade combinations. Both Acts, lastly, impose severe penalties[90] on the use of violence, threats, or intimidation whereby the contractual freedom of an individual workman or an individual master may be curtailed, and both

89. Wright, 13.

90. "It is difficult," it has been said, "to see how, in the case of a conflict of interests, it is possible to separate the two objects of benefiting yourself and injuring your antagonist. Every strike is in the nature of an act of war. Gain on one side implies loss on the other; and to say that it is lawful to combine to protect your own interests, but unlawful to combine to injure your antagonist, is taking away with one hand a right given with the other."— Stephen, *Hist.* iii. 218, 219.

Surely this criticism, though often made, is fallacious. In every ordinary contract there is in one sense a conflict of interests. *A*, the seller, wishes to obtain the highest, *X*, the buyer, to give the lowest, price possible. Yet no one supposes that either *A* or *X* inflict an injury upon the other. The same thing might hold good of a strike where there was no coercion used towards third parties. *A*, *B*, and *C*, the masters, would offer what wages they chose, and *X*, *Y*, and *Z*, the workmen, would combine to accept the best wages they found they could get. If oppression be excluded there need be no injury inflicted on either side. The free haggling of the market would fix the rate of wages. This view, whether right or wrong, was entertained by the reformers of 1824–1825.

Acts provide the machinery whereby these penalties may be summarily enforced. The labour contract under each Act is intended to be perfectly free. Combinations to raise or lower wages and the like are no longer forbidden, but neither individuals nor combinations are to interfere with the right of each person freely to enter into any labour contract which may suit the contracting parties.

As to the Points of Difference. The Act of 1824 allows freedom of combination for trade purposes, both to men and to masters, in the very widest terms,[91] and (which is the matter specially to be noted) exempts trade combinations from the operation of the law of conspiracy. It then imposes penalties upon the use of violence, threats, or intimidation for certain definite purposes, *e.g.* the compelling a workman to depart from his work.

The Act of 1825, on the other hand, in the first place, imposes penalties upon the use of violence, threats, or intimidation for almost any purpose which could conceivably interfere with individual freedom of contract on the part of an individual workman or with the right of a master to manage his business in the way he thought fit. The Act, in the next place, confers indirectly[92] upon workmen and masters a limited right to meet together

---

91. Sect. 2 exempts from liability to any indictment or prosecution for conspiracy, or to any other criminal information or punishment whatever, under the common or the statute law, "journeymen, workmen, or other persons who shall enter into any combination to obtain an advance, or to fix the rate of wages, or to lessen or alter the hours or duration of the time of working, or to decrease the quantity of work, or to induce another to depart from his service before the end of the time or term for which he is hired, or to quit or return his work before the same shall be finished, or, not being hired, to refuse to enter into work or employment, or to regulate the mode of carrying on any manufacture, trade, or business, or the management thereof." Under this section a combination of *X, Y,* and *Z* to induce a workman to break a contract of work or to induce a master to dismiss all workmen who were not trade unionists, would *semble,* not have been a conspiracy. Sect. 3 gives an analogous exemption to masters.

92. Sect. 4. "Provided always . . . that this Act shall not extend to subject any persons to punishment, who shall meet together for the sole purpose of consulting upon and determining the rate of wages or prices, which the persons present at such meeting, or any of them, shall require or demand for his or their work, or the hours or time for which he or they shall work in any manufacture, trade, or business, or who shall enter into any agreement, verbal or written, among themselves, for the purpose of fixing the rate of wages or prices which the parties entering into such agreement, or any of them, shall require or demand

and come to agreements for settling the rate of wages, and the terms, which the persons persent at the meeting will accept or give. The Act, lastly, revives the law of conspiracy in regard to trade combinations.

The result, therefore, of the Combination Act, 1825 (at any rate, as interpreted by the courts), was this:

Any trade combination was a conspiracy, unless it fell within the limited right of combination given by the Act of 1825.[93]

A strike, though not necessarily a conspiracy, certainly might be so, and a trade union, as being a combination in restraint of trade, was at best a nonlawful society,[94] *i.e.* a society which, though membership in it was not a crime, yet could not claim the protection of the law.

The course of parliamentary legislation with regard to the Combination Law in 1824 and 1825 was singular, but in all its features it exactly represents the Benthamite individualism of the day. The Act of 1824 was the work of known Benthamites. McCulloch advocated its principles in the *Edinburgh Review;* Joseph Hume brought it as a Bill into Parliament; the astuteness of Francis Place, in whose hands Hume was a puppet, passed into law a Bill, of which the full import was not perceived, either by its advocates or by its opponents. The Act gives expression in the simplest and most direct form to two convictions pre-eminently characteristic of the Benthamites and the political economists. The one is the belief that trade in labour ought to be as free as any other kind of trade; the other is the well-grounded conviction that there ought to be one and the same law for men as for

---

for his or their work, or the hours of time for which he or they will work, in any manufacture, trade, or business, and that persons so meeting for the purposes aforesaid, or entering into any such agreement as aforesaid, shall not be liable to any prosecution or penalty for so doing; any law or statute to the contrary notwithstanding." Section 5 provides an analogous exemption for meetings of masters to settle the rate of wages, etc.

A comparison between the Act of 1824, section 2, and the Act of 1825, section 4, shows that the liberty of combination allowed under the first Act is a good deal wider than that allowed under the second.

93. This Act "left the common law of conspiracy in force against all combinations in restraint of trade, the combinations exempted from penalty under ss. 4 and 5 alone excepted."—Erle, 58. This is, it is submitted, the right view of the law. Contrast, however, Stephen, *Hist.* iii. 223.

94. *Farrer* v. *Close* (1869), L. R. 4 Q.B. 602.

masters; Adam Smith had, about fifty years earlier, pointed out that trade combinations on the part of workmen were blamed and punished, whilst trade combinations on the part of masters were neither punished nor indeed noticed.[95] Liberty and equality, each of which represent the best aspect of *laissez faire,* were the fundamental ideas embodied in the Benthamite reform.

Why, then, was the Act of 1824 repealed and replaced by the Act of 1825?

Something—even a good deal—was due to accidental circumstances. In spite of the sagacious advice of Francis Place, workmen, who for the first time enjoyed the right of combination, used their newly acquired power with imprudence, not to say unfairness. A large number of strikes took place, and these strikes were accompanied by violence and oppression. The artisans of Glasgow "boycotted," as we should now say, and tried to ruin an unpopular manufacturer. The classes whose voices were heard in Parliament were panic-struck, and their alarm was not unreasonable. Hence the demand for the repeal of the Combination Act, 1824. Place, after his manner, attributes the success of this demand to the baseness of parliamentary statesmen, to the bad faith of Huskisson, and, above all, to the machinations of one politician, who "lied so openly, so grossly, so repeatedly, and so shamelessly" as to astonish even the critic, who had always considered this individual "a pitiful shuffling fellow."[96] This pitiful, shuffling fellow was the well-known Sir Robert Peel.[97] He had, at any rate, as we might expect, something which was worth hearing to urge in support of his conduct. Peel has left on record the ground of his opposition to the Act of 1824. It is that "sufficient precautions were not taken in [that Act] . . . to prevent that species of annoyance which numbers can exercise towards individuals, short of personal violence and actual threat, but nearly as effectual for its object."[98]

Here we pass from the transitory events of a particular year and touch the true, if unperceived, cause of the reaction against the Combination Act of 1824. The right of combination which was meant to extend personal freedom was so used as to menace the personal freedom both of men and

95. See *Wealth of Nations,* ch. viii. pp. 97–102 (6th ed. 1791).
96. *Life of F. Place,* 236.
97. Then Mr. Peel.
98. Peel's *Private Correspondence,* 379 (London, 1891).

of masters. By the legislation of 1824 Benthamites and economists—that is, enlightened individualists—had extended the right of combination in order to enlarge the area of individual freedom; by the Act of 1825 sincere individualists, among whom Peel may assuredly be numbered, limited the right of trade combination in order to preserve the contractual freedom of workmen and of masters. The men who passed the Act of 1824 meant to establish free trade in labour; they did not mean to curtail the contractual capacity of persons who preferred not to join, or resisted the policy of, trade unions. The two Acts which seem contradictory are in reality different applications of that *laissez faire* which was a vital article of the utilitarian creed. The Liberals who in 1824 had begun to guide legislative opinion were the sincerest and most enthusiastic of individualists. It is hard for the men of 1905 to realise how earnest eighty years ago was the faith of the best Englishmen in individual energy and in the wisdom of leaving every one free to pursue his own course of action, so long as he did not trench upon the like liberty or the rights of his fellows. To such reformers oppression exercised by the State was not more detestable than oppression exercised by trade unions. Place was a Benthamite fanatic. His finest characteristic was passionate zeal for the interest of the working class whence he sprung. He knew workmen well: he had no love for employers. Yet Place, and we may be sure many wiser men with him, believed and hoped that the repeal of the Combination Law of 1800 would put an end to trade unions.

"The combinations of the men are but defensive measures resorted to for the purpose of counteracting the offensive ones of their masters. . . . When every man knew that he could carry his labour to the highest bidder, there would be less motive for those combinations which now exist, and which exist because such combinations are the *only* means of redress that they have."[99]

So Place in 1825. Eighteen years later thus writes Richard Cobden:

"Depend upon it nothing can be got by fraternising with trades unions. They are founded upon principles of brutal tyranny and monopoly. I would rather live under a Dey of Algiers than a trades committee."[100]

---

99. *Life of F. Place,* p. 217, and see further p. 218.
100. Morley, *Cobden,* i. ch. xiii. p. 299.

In 1849 Miss Martineau is well assured that the Act of 1825 was a necessary and salutary measure:

> By this Act [*i.e.* the Combination Act, 1825] combinations of masters and workmen to settle terms about wages and hours of labour are made legal; but combinations for controlling employers by moral violence were again put under the operation of the common law. By this as much was done for the freedom and security of both parties as can be done by legislation, which, in this matter, as in all others, is an inferior safeguard to that of personal intelligence.[101]

What is of even more consequence, the best and wisest of the judges who administered the law of England during the fifty years which followed 1825 were thoroughly imbued with Benthamite liberalism. They believed that the attempt of trade unions to raise the rate of wages was something like an attempt to oppose a law of nature. They were convinced—and here it is difficult to assert that they erred—that trade unionism was opposed to individual freedom, that picketing, for example, was simply a form of intimidation, and that, though a strike might in theory be legal, a strike could in practice hardly be carried out with effect without the employment of some form of intimidation either towards masters or non-unionists. No judges have ever deserved or earned more respect than Erle and Bramwell, yet Erle deliberately maintained that under the Act of 1825 any combination might be a conspiracy that interfered with "the free course of trade," whilst Bramwell enounced the doctrine that "the liberty of a man's mind and will to say how he should bestow himself and his means, his talents and his industry, is as much a subject of the law's protection as that of his body." His language is as wide as possible:

> Generally speaking, the way in which people have endeavoured to control the operation of the minds of men is by putting restraints on their bodies, and therefore we have not so many instances in which the liberty of the mind is vindicated as that of the body. Still, if any set of men agreed amongst themselves to coerce that liberty of mind and thought by compulsion and restraint, they would be guilty of a criminal offence, namely, that of conspiring against the liberty of mind and freedom of will of those towards whom

101. H. Martineau's *Thirty Years' Peace* (ed. 1877), i. 474.

they so conducted themselves. I am referring to coercion and compulsion—something that is unpleasant and annoying to the mind operated upon; and I lay it down as clear and undoubted law that, if two or more persons agree that they will by such means co-operate together against that liberty, they are guilty of an indictable offence.[102]

Bramwell's doctrine, moreover, laid down in 1867, harmonises with the general spirit of Mill's *On Liberty*, which was the final and authoritative apology for the Benthamite faith in individual freedom.

We may feel, therefore, assured that the legislation of 1824–1825 was not intentionally unjust. It represented even in its fluctuation the best and most liberal opinion of the time. The experiment of trying to establish absolute free trade in labour was a wise one. Whether reformers who were prepared to try this experiment would not have done wisely if they had left the Act of 1824 unrepealed, admits of discussion. The Act of 1825 remained in force for well-nigh fifty years. Two things are certain. The Act excited much dissatisfaction among artisans; the Benthamite Liberals, just because they were prone to neglect the social aspect of human nature, and had therefore hardly considered the characteristics of combined action, found it difficult to provide any consistent principle for the amendment of the combination law.[103]

Among the efforts of Benthamism to increase the sphere of contractual freedom stands the creation (1856–1862) of companies with limited liability. Here we have in reality an extension of freedom of contract, though at this point individualistic and collectivist currents of opinion blend together, for while the power of individuals to trade without at the same time exposing all their property to the risk of loss, does assuredly give them the opportunity to make contracts which the common law of England would not sanction, yet, the transference of business from individuals to corporate bodies favours the growth of collectivism.

Freedom in dealing with property, and especially property in land, forms an essential part of the Benthamite conception of individual liberty. To extend this freedom in one way or another is the aim and effect of legislation such as the Prescription Act, 1832, 2 & 3 Will. IV. c. 71; the Inheritance

---

102. *R. v. Druitt* (1867), 10 Cox, 600, per Bramwell, B., cited Steph. *Hist.* iii. 221, 222.
103. See pp. 111–113, *ante.*

Act, 1833, 3 & 4 Will. IV. c. 106; the Fines and Recoveries Act, 1833, 3 & 4 Will. IV. c. 74; the Wills Act, 1837, 1 Vict. c. 26; the Real Property Act, 1845, 8 & 9 Vict. c. 106; and all the statutes, none of them successful, by which it has been attempted to introduce a system of land registry[104] which should facilitate the transfer of land; the enactments for doing away with copyhold tenure or for diminishing the inconvenience arising from its peculiarities, which begin with the Copyhold Act, 1841, 4 & 5 Vict. c. 35, and have ended for the present with the Copyhold Act, 1894, 57 & 58 Vict. c. 46, and the Inclosure Acts between 1801, 41 Geo. III. c. 109, and the general Inclosure Act, 1845, 8 & 9 Vict. c. 118.[105] The same end is aimed at from another side by the whole series of Settled Estates Acts from 1856, 19 & 20 Vict. c. 120, to 1876, 39 & 40 Vict. c. 30, all of which, together with other enactments, increase the power of tenants for life and others to deal with land of which they are not the absolute owners. It is here worth noting that individualism in legislation, since it has for its object to free from unnecessary trammels the action of individuals who, at any given moment, are in existence, will tend, on the one hand, to liberate each generation from the control of the past, and on the other hand to restrain the attempt of each generation to fix the devolution of property in the future, and thus diminish the individual liberty of its successors.

It may appear to be a straining of terms if we bring under the head of freedom in dealing with property the most celebrated piece of legislation which can be attributed to the philosophic Radicals. The Poor Law of 1834 does not, on the face of it, aim at securing freedom of any kind; in popular imagination its chief result was the erection of workhouses, which, as prisons for the poor, were nicknamed Bastilles. Yet the object of the statute was in reality to save the property of hardworking men from destruction by putting an end to the monstrous system under which laggards who would not toil for their own support lived at the expense of their industrious neighbours, and enjoyed sometimes as much comfort as or even more comfort than fell to the lot of hardworking labourers. Whether a

---

104. Williams, *Real Property* (19th ed.), p. 616; Pollock, *Land Laws* (3rd ed.), pp. 171–178.

105. Compare Pollock, *Land Laws,* 3rd ed. pp. 180–186, and note particularly the change in policy as to the mode of dealing with commons from 1865 to 1876, which year is marked by the Commons Act, 1876, 39 & 40 Vict. c. 56.

poor law of any kind is consistent with the principles of thorough-going individualism is open to question. In England, however, the system of poor relief had existed for centuries. Instant abolition was an impossibility: all that reformers could do—and that at the cost of deep unpopularity—the reformers of 1834 achieved; they prevented an institution which was intended to save from starvation labourers who could not obtain work, from continuing to be a tremendous tax upon industry for the maintenance of indolence. This was the aim, and to a great extent the effect, of the New Poor Law.

Freedom of discussion, popularly, though inaccurately, called freedom of opinion, and religious liberty, which means the right of every man to avow and advocate any form of religious or non-religious belief without thereby exposing himself to legal penalties or disabilities, had long before 1830 become, under the name of civil and religious liberty, articles of the Whig creed;[106] but to these articles of faith Whig legislators had in practice given most imperfect application. The Benthamites aimed at carrying out their faith in freedom of opinion to its full logical results. Of this effort may be found ample illustrations in the extension of the Toleration Act to Unitarians (1813); in the Test and Corporation Act, 1828, 8 & 9 Geo. IV. c. 17; in the Roman Catholic Relief Act, 1829, 10 Geo. IV. c. 7; in the Nonconformists' Chapels Act, 1844, 7 & 8 Vict. c. 45; in the Marriage Acts extending from the Marriage Act, 1835, 5 & 6 Will. IV. c. 54, to the Marriage Act, 1898, 61 & 62 Vict. c. 58; and above all, in the long series of Oaths Acts, which have had the twofold effect of opening Parliament to any person otherwise eligible without any reference to his religious belief, and of enabling even avowed atheists to give evidence, and therefore enforce their rights, in a Court of Justice. Parliament has not, indeed, as yet established religious equality, but modern liberalism, which has in this matter inherited the ideas of the school of Bentham, had by the middle of the last century removed nearly all effective legal restraints on free discussion, and

---

106. See Paley, *Moral Philosophy*, ii. Bk. vi. c. x., with which contrast, on the one hand, Blackstone, *Comm.*, iv. p. 440, and on the other hand, the general tone of Macaulay's *Essays* and Sydney Smith's *Works passim*. The older Whigs justified the imposition of political disabilities upon Roman Catholics on the ground that in the case of Roman Catholics religious tenets were, for a time at least, the sign of political disloyalty.

has since that date practically established a liberty of opinion almost as wide as that demanded in 1859 by Mill in his treatise *On Liberty*.

The Adequate Protection of Rights. The labours of Bentham and of the lawyers who have followed in his steps, have been incessantly directed towards securing for every person the power to enforce his rights—that is, towards the amendment of everything which can be brought under the head of legal procedure, if that term be used in its very widest sense, so as to cover everything connected with the actual enforcement of a citizen's substantive rights, and thus to include the regulation of judicial evidence, the constitution and the jurisdiction of the courts, and all the steps in an action which English lawyers call practice, the reduction of the cost of legal proceedings, and a lot of other topics as dull and technical as any part of the law. Procedure, dreary though the matter seems, was the favourite object of Bentham's intense attention and prolonged study. Why, a student asks himself, was a legal philosopher so deeply concerned with a matter which seems to possess little speculative interest? The answer is, that in nothing did Bentham more markedly display his logical consistency and his sagacity as a reformer, than in the supreme importance which he attached to providing the means for the easy enforcement of every man's rights. A right which an individual cannot enforce is to him no right at all; the dilatoriness of legal proceedings, and their exorbitant cost, or the want of an easily accessible Court, work greater and far more frequent injustice than the formal denial of a man's due rights. The passion for amending procedure was only one side of Bentham's desire to protect individual freedom, and this passion, stirred up by Bentham, has now for more than seventy years led to constant attempts at improving the machinery of the law which have on the whole been crowned with marked success.[107]

107. The ardent wish to amend legal procedure connects Bentham more closely than he perceived with the greatest English judges. Our lawyers in and out of Parliament have instinctively felt that a right which cannot be enforced is no right at all. It is unfortunate for Bentham's reputation that the writers who in England have been the chief representatives of utilitarianism have either possessed little knowledge of law or else have lacked sympathy with Bentham's enthusiasm for law reform. Neither James nor John Mill was either a lawyer or a jurist. Austin had a firm grasp of a few most important legal conceptions, but nothing

Let us take a few typical examples of the scores of enactments which during the nineteenth century have reformed that system of legal procedure which, when Bentham made himself its critic, was full of patent faults. The Evidence Acts, beginning in 1833 with Denman's Act, 6 & 7 Vict. c. 85, and ending with the Act of 1898, which allows persons accused of crime to give evidence on their own behalf, have rationalised the whole of our law with regard to the competence of witnesses. The County Courts Acts from 1846[108] to 1888[109] have provided tribunals in every part of the country, to which persons may have recourse for the recovery of small debts which before 1846 were often in practice not recoverable because of the expense and difficulty of proceeding in the superior Courts. The Court of Chancery, which towards the middle of the nineteenth century was still a byword for dilatoriness and technicality, was, even before the passing of the Judicature Act, 1873, reformed to a great extent, though in a partial and fragmentary manner, by legislation subsequent to 1850.[110] Almost hand in hand with the reform of the Court of Chancery the procedure of the Common Law Courts was simplified, and everything which could be deemed useless in the technicality of pleadings was abolished by the Common Law Procedure Acts, 1852,[111] 1854,[112] and 1860.[113] At last that fundamental reform of procedure both in the Court of Chancery and in the Courts of Common Law,

---

in his writings betrays anything like systematic study of the laws of England. Sir J. F. Stephen was a considerable criminalist, but he hardly claimed to be, in the Benthamite sense of the term, a reformer of the law. Sir Leslie Stephen, who is by far the ablest of Bentham's critics, was not a lawyer, and did not pay as much attention as the matter deserved to Bentham's claim to be a legal philosopher.

108. 9 & 10 Vict. c. 95.

109. 51 & 52 Vict. c. 43, with which now read the County Courts Act, 1903, 3 Edw. VII. c. 42.

110. Ashburner, *Principles of Equity*, pp. 17, 18; Holdsworth, *History of English Law*, i. pp. 231–235; 14 & 15 Vict. c. 4 (1851); The Court of Chancery Acts, 1852 (15 & 16 Vict. cc. 80, 87); The Chancery Procedure Act, 1852 (15 & 16 Vict. c. 86); The Chancery Amendment Act, 1858 (21 & 22 Vict. c. 27); The Chancery Regulation Act, 1862 (25 & 26 Vict. c. 42); and see for earlier legislation of a reforming character, 53 Geo. III. c. 24 (1813), 3 & 4 Will. IV. c. 94 (1833); the Court of Chancery Acts, 1841, 1842 (5 Vict. c. 5; 5 & 6 Vict. c. 103).

111. 15 & 16 Vict. c. 76.

112. 17 & 18 Vict. c. 125.

113. 23 & 24 Vict. c. 126.

which had been the constant aim of Bentham and of every man imbued with his spirit, was with more or less completeness attained by the so-called fusion of law and equity under the Judicature Act of 1873,[114] which, taken together with the subsequent enactments which have amended it, has at last created an omni-competent Court in every Division of which every kind of right known to the law of England is recognised, and where every kind of remedy for the enforcement of rights may be obtained. Nor ought we to omit reference to the experiment of the new Commercial Court which in its absence of forms, in the wide discretion given to the judge, and in the rapidity of its proceedings, almost realises Bentham's ideal of a perfect tribunal. Compare now the defectiveness of English procedure in 1800[115] with the masterly picture of the actual administration of our law drawn in 1887 by one of the ablest and most enlightened of our judges. Thus writes the late Lord Bowen:

> A complete body of rules—which possesses the great merit of elasticity, and which (subject to the veto of Parliament) is altered from time to time by the judges to meet defects as they appear—governs the procedure of the Supreme Court and all its branches. In every cause, whatever its character, every possible relief can be given with or without pleadings, with or without a formal trial, with or without discovery of documents and interrogatories, as the nature of the case prescribes—upon oral evidence or upon affidavits, as is most convenient. Every amendment can be made at all times and all stages in any record, pleading, or proceeding that is requisite for the purpose of deciding the real matter in controversy. It may be asserted without fear of contradiction that it is not *possible* in the year 1887 for an honest litigant in her Majesty's Supreme Court to be defeated by any mere technicality, any slip, any mistaken step in his litigation. The expenses of the law are still too heavy, and have not diminished *pari passu* with other abuses. But law has ceased to be a scientific game that may be won or lost by playing some particular move.[116]

---

114. 36 & 37 Vict. c. 66. To understand the full extent of the change introduced under the Judicature Acts a student should read the fifteen Acts which make up the Judicature Acts, 1873–1899, and the Rules and Orders made thereunder. See Stephen, *Comm.* iii. (14th ed.), p. 352.

115. See pp. 62–68, *ante.*

116. Bowen, *The Administration of the Law, The Reign of Queen Victoria,* i. pp. 309, 310.

Any critic who dispassionately weighs these sentences, notes their full meaning, and remembers that they are even more true in 1905 than in 1887, will partially understand the immensity of the achievement performed by Bentham and his school in the amendment of procedure—that is, in giving reality to the legal rights of individuals.

Nor is it irrelevant to note that the more closely the renovation of English institutions under the influence of Bentham is studied, the more remarkably does it illustrate the influence of public opinion upon law. Nothing is effected by violence; every change takes place, and every change is delayed or arrested by the influence, as it may seem the irresistible influence, of an unseen power. The efforts of obstructionists or reactionists come to nothing, the toryism of Eldon, the military rigidity of the Duke of Wellington, the intelligent conservatism of Peel, at a later period the far less intelligent conservatism of Lord Palmerston, all appear, though the appearance is in some respects delusive, not in reality to delay for more than periods which are mere moments in the life of nations, the progress of change. On the other hand, the violence of democrats or the fervour of enthusiasts achieves little in hurrying on innovation. In the eighteenth century a duke was ready to recommend universal suffrage. It was demanded by the Chartists, who between 1830 and 1848 seemed destined to carry parliamentary reform to its logical conclusion. Yet now that England is far more democratic than in the middle of the nineteenth century, the electors, who could easily obtain any change which they eagerly desired, acquiesce in arrangements far less democratic than even unqualified household suffrage; and it is arguable (though, be it remembered, many things are arguable which turn out not to be true) that the reforms or changes of the last sixty years have considerably increased the popularity of the Crown, the Peerage, and the Church. If we look then to the changes which have been effected, and what is equally important, to the changes which have not been effected, in the law of the land, we trace everywhere the action of opinion, and feel as if we were in the hands of some mysterious influence which works with the certainty of fate. But this feeling or superstition is checked by the recollection that public opinion is nothing but the opinion of the public—that is, the predominant convictions of an indefinite number of Englishmen.

LECTURE VII   *The Growth of Collectivism*

WITH THE PASSING of the Reform Act began the reign of liberalism, and the utilitarianism of common sense acquired, in appearance at least, despotic power, but this appearance was to a certain extent delusive. At the moment of the Benthamite triumph there were to be found thinkers who, while insisting on the need for thorough-going reforms, denied the moral authority of individualism and denounced the dogma of *laissez faire.*

This vital difference between two opposed schools of thought had more than a merely speculative interest. It determined men's way of looking at by far the most pressing social problem of the day. The fifteen years from 1830 to 1845, which may well be termed the era of the Reform Act, were among the most critical in the history of England. The time was out of joint. The misery and discontent of city artisans and village labourers were past dispute. No Act of Parliament could remove at a stroke the wretchedness and pauperism created by the old poor law. The true cure contained in the new poor law of 1834, with its drastic severity, its curtailment of outdoor relief, and its detested Bastilles, increased for the moment the sufferings of the poorest amongst the poor, and excited intense popular resentment. The wages earned by labourers in the country were miserably low. The horrors connected with factory life were patent. Widespread was the discontent of the whole body of wage-earners. It is recorded in a series of state trials for sedition, for conspiracy, or for treason, extending from 1832 to 1843.[1] There was rick-

1. *R. v. Pinney* (1832), *R. v. Fursey* (1833), *R. v. Vincent* (1837), *R. v. Collins* (1839), *R. v. Feargus O'Connor, R. v. Cooper* (1843), to which add the notorious case of the Dorchester Labourers (1834); Webb, *History of Trade Unionism,* p. 129.

burning[2] by labourers in the country, there were acts of violence by trade unionists in the towns. The demand for the People's Charter was the sign of a social condition which portended revolution. To us who know that several points of the People's Charter have passed into law without causing social or political disturbance, the thought may occur that Chartism loomed too large in the eyes of contemporaries. But the men of 1832 understood the time in which they lived. The cry for the Charter told of bitter class hatreds and of widespread dissatisfaction with the whole constitution of society. Men who have known England only during the years of prosperity and of general good-will which have followed the repeal of the corn laws, can hardly realise the urgency with which the "state of England question" thrust itself upon the attention of the public between 1832 and 1840. It was a terrible question enough; it was nothing else than the inquiry, how, if at all, was it possible to alleviate the miseries and remove the discontent of the working classes?

The reply of utilitarian Liberals was in substance clear. The policy of wisdom was, they insisted, to make the nation, as the Reform Act was intended to do, master of its own destiny. Hence, it was argued, would follow the removal of every definite abuse and the repeal of every unjust law, and especially of any law which pressed unfairly and hardly upon the poor. This being done, law, it was assumed rather than stated, could do no more; for the ultimate cure of social diseases we must trust to general good-will, and above all to individual energy and self-help.

Nowhere is this doctrine better expressed than in the refutation by Sydney Smith of the argument familiar to the toryism of 1830, that the Reform Bill would bring no benefit to the hewer of wood and drawer of water.

"What good," says Sydney Smith in 1830,

> to the hewer of wood and the drawer of water? How is he benefited, if Old Sarum is abolished, and Birmingham members created? But if you ask this question of Reform, you must ask it of a great number of other great measures. How is he benefited by Catholic Emancipation, by the repeal of the Corporation and Test Act, by the Revolution of 1688, by any great political change, by a good government? In the first place, if many are benefited, and

2. As to the violent destruction of machinery in 1830, see "Letters to Swing," by Sydney Smith, *Memoir* by Lady Holland, i. (4th ed.), p. 287.

the lower orders are not injured, this alone is reason enough for the change. But the hewer of wood and the drawer of water *are* benefited by Reform. Reform will produce economy and investigation; there will be fewer jobs, and a less lavish expenditure; wars will not be persevered in for years after the people are tired of them; taxes will be taken off the poor and laid upon the rich; demotic habits will be more common in a country where the rich are forced to court the poor for political power; cruel and oppressive punishments (such as those for night-poaching) will be abolished. If you steal a pheasant you will be punished as you ought to be, but not sent away from your wife and children for seven years. Tobacco will be 2d. per lb. cheaper. Candles will fall in price. These last results of an improved government will be felt. We do not pretend to abolish poverty, or to prevent wretchedness; but if peace, economy, and justice are the results of Reform, a number of small benefits, or rather of benefits which appear small to us, but not to them, will accrue to millions of the people; and the connection between the existence of John Russell, and the reduced price of bread and cheese, will be as clear as it has been the object of his honest, wise, and useful life to make it.

Don't be led away by such nonsense; all things are dearer under a bad government, and cheaper under a good one. The real question they ask you is, What difference can any change of government make to you? They want to keep the bees from buzzing and stinging, in order that they may rob the hive in peace.[3]

Every one of these predictions has been fulfilled almost to the letter.

Turn now for illustrations of the protest against the dominant individualism of the day to the language of three men of genius who agreed in nothing but in their common distrust of *laissez faire,* and in their conviction that some great exertion of the authority of the State was needed for the cure of the diseases which afflicted the commonwealth.

"Moral evils," writes Southey (1829), "are of [man's] own making; and undoubtedly the greater part of them may be prevented, though it is only in Paraguay (the most imperfect of Utopias) that any attempt at prevention has been carried into effect."[4]

3. Sydney Smith's *Works* (ed. 1869), pp. 670, 671.

4. Southey's *Colloquies on the Progress and Prospects of Society,* i. p. 110.

"If there be," writes Macaulay, "in [Mr. Southey's] political system any leading principle, any one error which diverges more widely and variously than any other, it is that of which

And this prevention was, in Southey's judgment, to be effected by the moral authority of the Church and the action of the State.

"This neglect," writes Dr. Arnold (1838), namely, to provide a proper position in the State for the manufacturing population,

> is encouraged by one of the falsest maxims which ever pandered to human selfishness under the name of political wisdom—I mean the maxim that civil society ought to leave its members alone, each to look after their several interests, provided they do not employ direct fraud or force against their neighbour. That is, knowing full well that these are not equal in natural powers,—and that still less have they ever within historical memory started

---

his theory about national works is a ramification. He conceives that the business of the magistrate is not merely to see that the persons and property of the people are secure from attack, but that he ought to be a jack-of-all-trades,—architect, engineer, schoolmaster, merchant, theologian, a Lady Bountiful in every parish, a Paul Pry in every house, spying, eavesdropping, relieving, admonishing, spending our money for us, and choosing our opinions for us. His principle is, if we understand it rightly, that no man can do anything so well for himself as his rulers, be they who they may, can do it for him, and that a government approaches nearer and nearer to perfection, in proportion as it interferes more and more with the habits and notions of individuals.

"He seems to be fully convinced that it is in the power of government to relieve all the distresses under which the lower orders labour."—Macaulay, *Critical, etc. Essays* (1870 ed.), p. 110.

A reader of to-day finds it difficult to justify fully the strength of Macaulay's attack by citations from the *Colloquies*. But the Whig critic, who had the whole of Southey's writings before his mind, instinctively felt the opposition between Southey's whole view of society and the liberalism of 1832. This opposition is admitted by Southey's modern admirers, and by them considered his title to fame as a social reformer. "He looked forward to a time when, the great struggle respecting property over—for this struggle he saw looming not far off—public opinion will no more tolerate the extreme of poverty in a large class of the people than it now tolerates slavery in Europe; when the aggregation of land in the hands of great owners must cease, when that community of lands, which Owen of Lanark would too soon anticipate, might actually be realised."—Dowden, *Southey*, p. 154.

"The view of social evils to which Southey ... gave expression, often in anticipation of Mr. Ruskin, was in many respects deeper and truer than that of his optimistic critic [Macaulay]."—*Dictionary of National Biography*, vol. liii. p. 288.

Compare Thomas Hodgskin (1787–1869), *par* E. Halévy, for a combination of anarchism (based on ultra-individualism) with something like collectivism. [Editor's note: The last sentence was added in the second edition.]

with equal artificial advantages; knowing, also, that power of every sort has a tendency to increase itself, we stand by and let this most unequal race take its own course, forgetting that the very name of society implies that it shall not be a mere race, but that its object is to provide for the common good of all, by restraining the power of the strong and protecting the helplessness of the weak.[5]

"That the arrangements," writes Carlyle in 1839,

of good and ill success in this perplexed scramble of a world, which a blind goddess was always thought to preside over, are in fact the work of a seeing goddess or god, and require only not to be meddled with: what stretch of heroic faculty or inspiration of genius was needed to teach one that? To button your pockets and stand still is no complex recipe. *Laissez faire, laissez passer!* [Laissez faire, leave it be!][6] Whatever goes on, ought it not to go on. . . . Such at bottom seems to be the chief social principle, if principle it have, which the Poor Law Amendment Act has the merit of courageously asserting, in opposition to many things. A chief social principle which this present writer, for one, will by no manner of means believe in, but pronounce at all fit times to be false, heretical, and damnable, if ever aught was.[7]

Between 1830 and 1840 the issue between individualists and collectivists was fairly joined. Can the systematic extension of individual freedom and the removal of every kind of oppression so stimulate individual energy and self-help as to cure (in so far as they are curable by legislation) the evils which bring ruin on a commonwealth?

To this inquiry the enlightened opinion of 1832, which for some thirty or forty years, if not for more, governed the action of Parliament, gave, in spite of protests from a small body of thinkers backed more or less by the sympathy of the working classes, an unhesitating and affirmative answer. To the same inquiry English legislative opinion has from about 1870 onwards given a doubtful, if not a negative, reply.

My purpose in this lecture is to explain a revolution of social or political belief which forms a remarkable phenomenon in the annals of opinion. This explanation in reality is nothing else than an attempted analysis of

5. Arnold, *Miscellaneous Works*, pp. 453, 454.
6. [Editor's note: The translation was added in the Liberty Fund edition.]
7. Carlyle's *Works*, x. p. 340, "Chartism." See also *ibid.* chap. vi. p. 368.

the conditions or causes which have favoured the growth of collectivism, or, if the matter be looked at from the other side, have undermined the authority of Benthamite liberalism.[8]

A current explanation lies ready to hand. Under the Parliamentary Reform Acts 1867–1884 the constitution of England has been transformed into a democracy, and this revolution, it is argued, completely explains the increasing influence of socialism. The many must always be the poor, and the poor are by nature socialists. Where you have democracy there you will find socialism.

This reasoning, as already pointed out,[9] is essentially fallacious. Democracy cannot be identified with any one kind of legislative opinion. The government of England is far less democratic than is the government of the United States, but the legislation of Congress is less socialistic than the legislation of the Imperial Parliament. Nor in England are laws tending

---

8. Benthamite reformers have never had a perfectly fair chance of bringing their policy to a successful issue. Some of their proposals have never been carried into effect; outdoor relief, for example, has never been abolished. The realisation of some of them has been so delayed as to lose more than half its beneficial effect. If the first reformed Parliament had been able to establish free trade simultaneously with the enactment of the new poor law, and given to Dissenters in 1832 as complete political equality as they possess at the present day; if it had in reality opened to Roman Catholics in 1832 all careers as completely as they are open to them in 1905; if O'Connell had been first made Irish Attorney-General and then placed on the Bench; if the tithe war which harassed Ireland till 1838 had been terminated in 1834—is it not at least possible that a rapid increase in material prosperity and a sense of relief from oppression might have produced a general sentiment of social unity, which would have shown that the principles of individualism fitly met the wants of the time? Our habit of delaying reforms has its occasional advantages; these advantages are, however, much exaggerated. Sir Thomas Snagge, in his admirable *Evolution of the County Court,* thus writes of the County Court Act, 1846: "Its provisions were the outcome of nearly twenty years of resolute parliamentary effort, met by opposition no less persistent. Such struggles are wont to end, as this did, in a compromise. It was the old story of all sound English reform: hasty change was successfully withstood, and gradual evolution was happily accomplished." Can our esteemed author seriously maintain that opposition generated by partisanship brought a single compensation for the practical denial of justice to the poor during a period of twenty years? However this may be, the disadvantages of delay are often tremendous. It keeps alive irritation which constantly robs improvement itself of almost the whole of its legitimate benefit.

9. See Lect. III., *ante.*

towards socialism due to the political downfall of the wealthy classes. Under a democratic constitution they retain much substantial power—they determine in many ways the policy of the country. The rich have but feebly resisted, even if they have not furthered, collectivist legislation. The advance of democracy cannot afford the main explanation of the predominance of legislative collectivism.

The true explanation is to be found, not in the changed form of the constitution, but in conditions of which the advance of democracy is indeed one, but whereof the most important had been in operation before the Reform Act of 1867 came into force.

These conditions, which constantly co-operated, may be conveniently brought under the following heads: Tory Philanthropy and the Factory Movement[10]—the Changed Attitude after 1848 of the Working Classes—the Modification of Economic Beliefs—the Characteristics of Modern Commerce—the Introduction of Household Suffrage.

Tory Philanthropy and the Factory Movement

The age of individualism was emphatically the era of humanitarianism—it was the philanthropy of the day which, in the midst of the agitation for parliamentary reform, would not suffer the wrongs of the negroes to be forgotten. Now at the very time when the country was moved to passionate indignation at the horrors of West Indian slavery, public attention was suddenly directed, by the publication of Richard Oastler's *Slavery in Yorkshire*, to oppression, not in the West Indies, but in Yorkshire—to the bondage, not of negroes, but of English children. The horrors denounced by Oastler were of precisely the kind which most outraged the humanitarianism of the day. His appeal to the English public went home; it was the true beginning of the factory movement.[11]

That movement was in truth the fruit of humanitarianism.

10. The expression is obviously inaccurate, but I use it as a convenient and accepted name for the movement in favour of the regulation by law of labour in factories.

11. Factory legislation dates from 1802, but the factory movement aroused by Oastler's letters dates from 1830.

The earliest Factory Act belongs to an age (1802) when English statesmen had hardly heard of socialism. The strength of Oastler's appeal was public indignation at the physical sufferings brought, as it was believed, by the greed of manufacturers upon helpless infants. That English children were held in bondage, that to perform their task-work they were compelled under cruel punishment to walk as much as twenty miles a day, that their day's work lasted for from twelve to sixteen hours, were the facts or allegations which aroused the pity and the wrath of the nation. The vehemence of popular indignation had in its origin nothing to do with socialistic theories. The factory movement was in full accordance with the traditional principle of the common law that all persons below twenty-one had a claim to special protection. Nor was there anything in the early factory movement which was opposed either to Benthamism or to the doctrines of the most rigid political economy. Individualists of every school were only too keenly alive to the danger that the sinister interest of a class should work evil to the weak and helpless. They almost identified power with despotism. In 1836 Cobden was not only willing, but ready to exclude absolutely from labour in a cotton mill any child below the age of thirteen.

> As respects the right and justice by which young persons ought to be protected from excessive labour, my mind has ever been decided, and I will not argue the matter for a moment with political economy; it is a question for the medical and not the economical profession; I will appeal to —— or Astley Cooper, and not to McCulloch or Martineau. Nor does it require the aid of science to inform us that the tender germ of childhood is unfitted for that period of labour which even persons of mature age shrink from as excessive. In my opinion, and I hope to see the day when such a feeling is universal, *no child ought to be put to work in a cotton-mill at all so early as the age of thirteen years;* and after that the hours should be moderate, and the labour light, until such time as the human frame is rendered by nature capable of enduring the fatigues of adult labour. With such feelings as these strongly pervading my mind, I need not perhaps add that, had I been in the House of Commons during the last session of Parliament, I should have opposed with all my might Mr. Poulett Thomson's measure for postponing the operation of the clause for restricting the hours of infant labour.[12]

12. Morley, *Life of Cobden,* i. pp. 464, 465, Appendix. It is to be regretted that Cobden's

Nor need Cobden have hesitated to appeal to McCulloch. This econo-mist had already in 1833 thus expressed his sympathy with Lord Ashley's[13] philanthropic efforts:

> I hope your Factory Bill will prosper, and I am glad it is in such good hands. Had I a seat in the House it should assuredly have my vote. A notion is entertained that political economists are, in all cases, enemies to all sorts of interference, but I assure you I am not one of those who entertain such an opinion. I would not interfere between adults and masters; but it is absurd to contend that children have the power to judge for themselves as to such a matter. I look upon the facts disclosed in the late Report as most disgraceful to the nation; and I confess that, until I read it, I could not have conceived it possible that such enormities were committed. Perhaps you have seen the late work of M. Cousin, who was sent by the French Government to report on the state of education in Germany. It is well worth your Lordship's atten-tion. In Prussia, and most other German States, *all* persons are obliged to send their children to school from the age of seven to thirteen or fourteen years, and the education given to them is excellent; as much superior to anything to be had in this country as it is possible to conceive. This is the sort of interference that we ought gradually to adopt. If your Bill has any defect, it is not by the too great limitation, but by the too great extension of the hours of labour.[14]

Macaulay was at no time of his life fascinated by the ideals or tolerant of the weaknesses of socialism, yet under the influence of humanitarianism, as of common sense, he made by far the best defence delivered in Parlia-ment[15] of the Ten Hours Bill. Southey, anticipator though he was of so-cialistic ideas, denounced the employment of children in factories on the simple ground of humanity.

---

idea did not bear fruit. There might have been some advantage in trying the experiment whether the complete protection of children might not have been found compatible with the minimum of interference with the management of factories.

13. Afterwards known to the present generation as Lord Shaftesbury, and for the sake of convenience generally so described in these Lectures.

14. Hodder, *Life of Shaftesbury*, i. pp. 157, 158. McCulloch to Lord Ashley, 28th March 1833.

15. For speech on Ten Hours Bill, 22nd May 1846, see Macaulay, *Speeches* (ed. 1871), p. 718.

"There is one thing," he writes to Lord Ashley,

connected with these accursed factories which I have long intended to expose, and that is, the way in which Sunday Schools have been subservient to the merciless love of gain. The manufacturers know that a cry would be raised against them if their little white slaves received no instruction; and so they have converted Sunday into a *school-day,* with what effect may be seen in the evidences!

Thousands of thousands will bless you for taking up the cause of these poor children. I do not believe that anything more inhuman than the system has ever disgraced human nature in any age or country. Was I not right in saying that Moloch is a more merciful friend[16] than Mammon? Death in the brazen arms of the Carthaginian idol was mercy to the slow waste of life in the factories.[17]

Humanitarianism, then, was the parent, if socialism was the offspring, of the factory movement, and that movement from the first came under the guidance of Tories.

With this movement will be for ever identified the names of Southey, Oastler, Sadler, and above all of Lord Shaftesbury.

The character and the career of these leaders is the best illustration of the intimate connection between the attack on the iniquities of the factory system and toryism.

Southey (1774–1843) was in 1830 a Tory of the Tories. His whole career is paradoxical. He had once been a Jacobin, he had never been a Whig. He understood revolutionary enthusiasm; he had no desire for moderate reform or appreciation of its benefits. The foundation of his political creed

---

16. *Lege* "fiend"?

17. Hodder, i. pp. 156, 157. Southey to Lord Ashley, 7th Feb. 1833. Coleridge was one of those who (1802) took an interest in the factory children. He writes to a lawyer to know "'if there is not some law prohibiting, or limiting, or regulating the employment either of children or adults, or both, in the white lead manufactory? . . . Can your [sic] furnish us with any other instances in which the Legislature has directly, or by immediate consequence, interfered with what is ironically called "Free Labour"? (*i.e.* DARED to prohibit soul murder and infanticide on the part of the rich, and self-slaughter on that of the poor!)' The letter also alludes to circulars drawn up by S.T.C. in favour of Sir Robert Peel's Bill. It would be interesting to know if any of these circulars are in existence."—Hutchins and Harrison, *History of Factory Legislation,* p. 29 (*n.*).

was belief in the advantages to be derived from the free employment of the influence of the Church and the resources of the State for the benefit of the poor. This creed made it easy for the philanthropic Jacobin of 1794 to develop into the humanitarian Tory of 1830. It was natural for Whigs to see in Southey a weather-cock which, having turned rusty, had set up for a sign-post; it was equally natural that in Southey's own mind the essential identity of his sentiment in youth and in old age should conceal from him the apparent transformation of his political principles. His fame in his own day rested on his position as a man of letters. Even his friends could not have thought him a powerful reasoner; they must have expected that though his writings might be long remembered for their literary merits, he would never exert any memorable influence as a social reformer. But it is now manifest that while Southey's literary reputation has declined, his ideas on social questions exerted a permanent influence. He was a Carlyle without Carlyle's rhetorical genius and rough humour, but also without Carlyle's cynical contempt for humanitarianism. He was essentially a philanthropist. He is to us the prophetic precursor of modern collectivism. To his own generation he was the preacher of Tory philanthropy. The text on which he preached with the utmost vehemence was the duty of abolishing the cruelties of factory life.

Oastler (1789–1861) was a demagogue, but he was also a Churchman, a Tory, and a Protectionist. He hated the new poor law partly for the hardship it inflicted upon the poor, partly because he foresaw it would lead to the repeal of the corn laws, and believed that it would be fatal to the influence of the Church and of the landowners. A certain unity is given to the demagogic career of this "Factory king" by his denunciation of the whole system of factory labour. To him is due both the enthusiasm which ultimately carried the Ten Hours Bill and the gross exaggeration which identified the sufferings of children in English factories with the abominations of West Indian slavery, and thus excited the legitimate indignation even of manufacturers who were also philanthropists.

Michael Sadler (1780–1835) was born a member of the Church of England. Brought up in Tory principles, he remained throughout life a fervent Tory. He opposed Catholic Emancipation and Parliamentary reform. In 1823 the wrong done to children in factories enlisted his keenest sympathy. He was already interested in economical and social questions, and became not only the leader, but the theorist of the factory movement. As a sort of Christian and Tory socialist he attacked, though without any true grasp of political economy, the individualism which underlay the teaching of economists such as Ricardo. He thus introduced into the factory movement ideas which pointed towards socialism.

Sadler's public career represents dramatically the collision between Whig liberalism and Tory philanthropy. Twice he came into conflict with Macaulay, and twice he suffered defeat. In 1830 Sadler's ignorant and illogical attacks on Malthusianism involved him in a literary duel with the eloquent Whig reviewer. Party spirit ran high. Sadler's reasoning was full of flaws, and he suffered a disastrous argumentative overthrow; his critic did not care to consider whether inaccurately stated dogmas might not contain some element of neglected truth. In 1832 Sadler, who had sat in Parliament for a rotten borough abolished by the Reform Act, was a candidate for the representation of the newly created constituency of Leeds. His opponent was again Macaulay, and their second encounter ended in Sadler's defeat. This conclusion of the conflict was appropriate; it was fitting that the brilliant representative of liberalism should share the general triumph of individualism. It was also fitting that the representative of expiring toryism and as yet unrecognised collectivism, should suffer a repulse. That the humanitarian Whig and the Tory philanthropist, who were really at one on the necessity of protecting overworked children from ill usage, should in 1832 have understood one another was an impossibility. At the bottom of the literary and of the political battle lay the difference which divides liberalism from socialism.

Sadler's electoral defeat had one result of immense importance. It passed the leadership of the factory movement, then summed up in the demand for the Ten Hours Bill, into the hands of its most famous leader.

Lord Shaftesbury was the ideal Tory humanitarian.

To him we may apply Cowper's well-known line which eulogises or satirises a peer who lent dignity to the early evangelical revival as—

> One who wears a coronet, and prays.

In spirit Lord Shaftesbury always "wore a coronet"; he was, in the words of an American observer, the "complete beau-ideal of aristocracy." He inherited, together with the virtues, at least one of the faults often belonging to high lineage, he lacked all play of intellect or of fancy; he possessed neither subtlety nor versatility. At the foundation of his character lay moral and intellectual rigidity. Though an Oxford First Class man, he was in no way affected by the training which left indelible traces upon the minds, one might say upon the very natures of Cardinal Newman, Dr. Arnold, and Gladstone. If Lord Shaftesbury's collegiate career were at some future time to be inferred from his tastes and from his opinions, the obvious surmise of an historical inquirer would be that his Lordship graduated at Cambridge and never missed a sermon of Simeon's. In his purely political opinions he was all of a piece; he exhibits the stiffness of a Tory as rigid and thorough-going as could be a man of much sound sense and of a very sensitive conscience. He opposed Catholic Emancipation, and voted at last for the Catholic Relief Bill only when Peel's surrender made the concession of political rights to Roman Catholics a necessity. He came into Parliament as a protectionist, and when he saw that protection must be given up, resigned a seat which he had gained as an opponent of free trade. During his later life he placed much confidence in Palmerston, but when that most aristocratic of Liberal Premiers perceived what Bagehot has termed "the inestimable and unprecedented opportunity" of reforming the House of Lords without agitation, Lord Shaftesbury pronounced the proposal to create life peers to be as pernicious as it was specious, and foreboded that it would end in making the House of Lords like the American Senate. Ignorance, very characteristic of an English nobleman, was in this instance—not at all a solitary one—as remarkable as prejudice; for in 1857 to have given the House of Lords the position then held by the American Senate would have made the peers the most powerful body in the State. Lord Shaftesbury opposed throughout his career everything which he deemed a concession to Papal claims or to the High Church movement. But if he was an ardent Protestant, he was in theological matters intolerant of free thought[18] and of free discussion. Opposition to the results of Biblical criticism led him indeed into a curious alliance with Pusey.

Lord Shaftesbury, however, was primarily neither a politician nor a theologian, but a religious humanitarian. As he believed, and, as his critics, to

---

18. He was strongly opposed to the revision of the authorised version of the Bible.— Hodder, *Shaftesbury*, iii. p. 258.

whatever school they belong, may well believe also, it was implicit faith in a definite religious creed which compelled him to devote his life to philanthropic labours. One singularity at any rate of his career, and a singularity which for the purpose of these lectures proves to be of great importance, is that his defects no less than his virtues contributed to the success, and still more to the wide-reaching results of his work. Lord Shaftesbury formed no social theories. He never consciously advocated any measures which in his eyes savoured of socialism, a creed which he seemingly connected with infidelity.[19] At the same time he did not understand, as did Macaulay, the grounds on which factory legislation might be defended by men who distrusted all socialistic experiments. From Southey he had imbibed that opposition to *laissez faire* which is characteristic of every collectivist, and which falls in with the natural desire of an ardent philanthropist to save from immediate suffering any class of persons who are unable completely to protect themselves against oppression, and to do this by the means which lie nearest to hand, without deeply considering whether action which gives immediate relief to sufferers, *e.g.* women overworked in factories, may not possibly in the end produce evils of untold magnitude. Lord Shaftesbury, in short, was in practice, though not in theory, the apostle of governmental interference, and this, in part at least, because his intellectual limitations prevented him from realising the difficulty of reconciling paternal government with respect for individual freedom. Here we see how his very deficiencies increased his influence. They gained for him the support of two classes who do not in England often act together. The artisans were glad to follow a leader who shared their faith in the benefits to be derived from extending the authority of the State, and who with them felt no love whatever, to use the mildest terms, for manufacturers or mill-owners. If his latent and unconscious socialism conciliated

19. He writes to a socialistic ally: "You have been represented to me as a socialist and an advocate of principles that I regard with terror and abhorrence; and you will therefore readily believe the pleasure with which I observed the spirit and language of your letter. I could not but apply to you the words of that Book whose expressions you have borrowed, and say, as was said to Ananias of Saul, 'Behold, he prayeth.' I deeply rejoice in this, because I respect your talents, I admire your zeal, and I hope to find in you a true and faithful ally in these great and final efforts for the moral, social, and religious welfare of the working people."— Hodder, *Life of Lord Shaftesbury,* vol. i. pp. 407, 408. Conf. pp. 322, 323.

working men, his position and his defects enlisted for him the support of members of the middle-class who would never have followed a demagogue or a democrat. He was born heir to an English peerage—he became an English peer; he was a rigid Tory—he was not a theorist; he was a Low Churchman, he was the friend of Dissenters; he detested Roman Catholicism, Republicanism, socialism, and infidelity. How could any good and benevolent man belonging to the middle class fail in the middle of the nineteenth century to feel that his lordship was the safest of guides? Here and there a cold-blooded critic might note that the principles on which Lord Shaftesbury unconsciously acted were of wider application than the philanthropist perceived. A story is told, which may possibly be true, that Lord Melbourne introduced Lord Ashley—as he then was—to the young Queen as "the greatest Jacobin in your Majesty's dominions." The tale, if true, illustrates the keen insight of the easygoing Whig premier. But not one among Lord Shaftesbury's middle-class followers would have seen the true point of the joke. "No one goes so far as the man who doesn't know where he is going." This dictum, attributed to Cromwell, holds good both of men and of parties. The chief of the Tory philanthropists and his followers were not revolutionists, but they entered on a path which might well lead towards social revolution, and of which, apparently, they perceived neither the direction nor the goal. However this may be, the factory movement came from the first under the patronage and the guidance of Tories.

The factory movement gave rise to a parliamentary conflict between individualism and collectivism.

With the details of the agitation for the Ten Hours Bill which was not brought to a final close till 1850, with the various Acts passed in the course thereof, and with the ups and downs of the conflict between the opponents and the advocates of the Bill, we are not here concerned. The point here to be insisted upon is that the demand for the Ten Hours Act gave rise to a bitter conflict of which, owing to the circumstances of the day, the true character was concealed from the combatants. Everything was complicated by the accident that the agitation for the repeal of the corn laws covered nearly the same years as the early factory movement; repeal was obtained but one year before the Ten Hours Bill passed into law. In both contests Tories and protectionists were ranged against Radicals and free traders. As regards free trade the Tories played the unpopular part; they opposed the will of the people, and were liable to the charge (often grossly unjust) of starving the poor in order to raise the rents of landowners. The free traders meanwhile stood forward as friends of the people. Nor were the free trade orators in their attacks on protectionists careful to distinguish between economical heterodoxy and moral selfishness. In the battle over the Factory Bill the parts were reversed. Reasoners who insisted upon the indirect evils of State intervention were deemed heartless logicians smitten with a fatuous faith in the dismal science, and mill-owners, believed to wring huge profits out of the toil of overworked children, were placed on a level with slave-owners who refused to put an end to the tyranny from which they drew no small gain. Nor in popular estimation did the radicalism of the cotton lords do them any good. They looked like politicians who, after posing as the assertors of the rights of the people, had first by the new poor law deprived labourers of much-needed relief, and then in the name of *laissez faire* were claiming the right to overwork the children of artisans; the liberalism of such men might seem to add to cruelty a touch of hypocrisy. The Tory philanthropists, on the other hand, gained popularity, and even ordinary Tories stood forth in a more or less favourable light. They were honest gentlemen who had no liking for the new poor law, and who felt for the pangs of children and women held in bondage by greedy mill-owners. Who can wonder that Tories enjoyed the new sense of popularity, or that their leaders were not blind to the advantages of the situation? Disraeli, no doubt, honestly detested cruelties perpetrated in factories; but the author of *Sybil* knew well that his novel was a splendid party pamphlet fitted to show that the Tories were the true friends of the working-classes. On both sides there was nothing but misunderstanding and recrimination. If in the eyes of the Tory philanthropists their opponents seemed to be oppressors deficient in the ordinary feelings of humanity, to mill-owners and economists the promoters of the Ten Hours Bill were protectionists, who, under the cloak of philanthropy, tried to revive for their own advantage delusions exposed by the Anti-corn Law League, and who patronised socialism in order to revenge the overthrow of protection; their benevolence was at best stupidity, and at the worst hypocrisy supported by calumny.[20]

20. Compare, for Peel's attitude with regard to the factory movement, Martineau, *Thirty Years' Peace*, iii. p. 486.

If any one deems this description of animosities which have passed away an exaggeration, let him compare the sort of anathema pronounced by Lord Shaftesbury on the men who came not to his aid in the war against oppression with Bright's denunciation of the cant which, as he believed, had carried, and of the injustice which had been wrought by, the Ten Hours Act.

"I had," wrote Lord Shaftesbury in his private diary,

> to break every political connection, to encounter a most formidable array of capitalists, mill-owners, doctrinaires, and men who, by natural impulse, hate all "humanity-mongers." They easily influence the ignorant, the timid, and the indifferent; and my strength lay at first . . . among the Radicals, the Irishmen, and a few sincere Whigs and Conservatives. Peel was hostile, though, in his cunning, he concealed the full extent of his hostility until he took the reins of office, and then he opposed me, not with decision only, but malevolence, threatening, he and Graham, to break up his administration, and "retire into private life" unless the House of Commons rescinded the vote it had given in favour of my Ten Hours Bill. The Tory country gentlemen reversed their votes; but, in 1847, indignant with Peel on the ground of corn law repeal, they returned to the cause of the factory children. . . .
>
> In very few instances did any mill-owner appear on the platform with me; in still fewer the ministers of any religious denomination. . . .
>
> O'Connell was a sneering and bitter opponent. Gladstone ever voted in resistance to my efforts; and Brougham played the doctrinaire in the House of Lords.
>
> Bright was ever my most malignant opponent. Cobden, though bitterly hostile, was better than Bright. He abstained from opposition on the Collieries Bill, and gave positive support on the Calico Print-works Bill.
>
> Gladstone[21] is on a level with the rest; he gave no support to the Ten Hours Bill; he voted with Sir R. Peel to rescind the famous division in favour of it. He was the only member who endeavoured to delay the Bill which delivered women and children from mines and pits; and never did he say a word on behalf of the factory children, until, *when defending slavery in the West Indies,* he taunted Buxton with indifference to the slavery in England!

21. Note that in 1864 Gladstone more or less came round to the policy of the Factory Acts. Hodder, *Shaftesbury,* ii. p. 206.

Lord Brougham was among my most heated opponents. He spoke strongly against the Bill in 1847.

Miss Martineau also gave her voice and strength in resistance to the measure.[22]

"Why are we mill-owners," was Bright's retort,

to be selected as subjects of interference? Why is a Scotchman to be sent to see how I work my people, while the farmer, and the carpenter, and the builder, and the tailor is left to the ordinary responsibilities of law and public opinion? Are we worse educated than they are? Are our people less intelligent, more ready to submit to oppression, or more easy to manage? It was proposed the other day to force us to spend millions in boxing off our machinery. We have in our mills about a thousand work-people. In fifteen years we have had five accidents. We have three carters. In the same space of time two of them have been killed. I have no doubt that in agricultural employments accidents are a hundred times more frequent in proportion to the numbers employed, than those which occur in factories. But we are unpopular, we are envied, we are supposed to be rich, we are Radicals, and Whigs and Tories combine to gain popularity by calumniating us and robbing us. I have advised my partners, if this machinery Bill passes, to set the example of turning the key on the doors of our mills, and to throw on the legislators the responsibility of feeding the millions whom they will not allow us to employ with a profit.[23]

Such was the language used by men, each of whom was a Christian and a gentleman, each of whom was a staunch friend of the people, and each of whom was incapable of conscious slander or malignity; it was used, be it noted, not in the heat of conflict, but after the fight for the Ten Hours Bill had been won and lost.

All this invective was unjust. Bright was not a Legree; Peel was not a Bounderby, nor Gladstone a Gradgrind; Lord Shaftesbury was no political Pecksniff. The leading opponents, no less than the leading supporters of the factory movement, were men of high public spirit and undoubted humanity. What is the explanation of their antagonism? Lord Shaftesbury's list of opponents supplies the answer. They were all of them individualists,

22. Hodder, *Shaftesbury,* ii. pp. 209, 210.

23. Simpson, *Many Memories of Many People,* pp. 263, 264. Bright's words were apparently spoken Sept. 15, 1855.

whilst the Tory philanthropists were, though they knew it not, the leaders of a reaction; the factory movement was the battle-field of collectivism against individualism, and on that field Benthamite liberalism suffered its earliest and severest defeat. The bitterness of the conflict was probably increased by the consciousness of both of the parties to it that their own case had in it an element of weakness. Experience has proved that neither party was entirely in the right. The Ten Hours Act has not ruined British industry, and has put an end to much suffering. So far the policy of Lord Shaftesbury has been justified, and the resistance of the manufacturers has been condemned by experience. But the Ten Hours Act has tended towards socialism, and contains within it the germs of an unlimited revolution, of which no man can as yet weigh with confidence the benefits against the evils; and this revolution was one which Lord Shaftesbury did not intend to favour, and to the possibility whereof he was absolutely blind. Bright and his associates were far more keen sighted than the Tory philanthropists.

The factory movement introduced socialistic enactments into the law of England and gave prestige and authority to the ideas of collectivism.

The existing labour code,[24] which consolidates a whole line of Factory Acts, is the most notable achievement of English socialism.[25] The assertion, therefore, that the factory movement of which these Acts were the outcome, fostered the growth of socialism and gave authority to the ideas of collectivism, appears at first sight to involve the absurdity of putting the cart before the horse, and of treating legislation, which resulted from a particular state of opinion, as the cause of the state of opinion whence it sprung. But to a student who has grasped the true relation between law and opinion,[26] this apparent absurdity becomes an obvious truism. To him the history of the factory movement is of itself sufficient proof that laws may be the creators of legislative opinion.

The effect, indeed, of the factory legislation embodied in the Ten Hours Act[27] and the enactments which led up to it, may appear at first sight to

24. Embodied in the Factory and Workshop Act, 1901.

25. Written in 1905.

26. See p. 30, *ante.*

27. The Act must be taken together with the enactments leading up to it. There appears to be some little confusion in the use of the term the Ten Hours Act. The statute most

be nothing more than the protection from overwork of children, young persons, and women[28] employed in a limited number of manufactories. But this legislation had in reality far wider results. It recognised the principle that the regulation of public labour is the concern of the State and laid the basis for a whole system of governmental inspection and control. It fixed the hours of labour in the factories to which it applied for every woman,[29] whatever her age, and conferred upon her a protection, as well as imposed upon her a disability which is absolutely unknown to the common law of England, and is directly opposed to the fundamental assumptions of individualism. This factory legislation fixed, though not in so many words nor in all cases immediately, the normal day of work for all persons of whatever age or sex employed in the factories to which it extended. It applied, indeed, in the first instance only to a limited number of factories; but it contained principles of the widest scope, which were applicable and which were certain to be ultimately applied in the most general way to every kind of labour of which the public can take cognizance. It assuredly, therefore, has introduced socialistic enactments into the English labour law. But the factory legislation of 1848–50 did at once, or very nearly at once, far more than this. At the time when the repeal of the corn laws gave in

---

properly known by that name is 10 & 11 Vict. c. 29, passed in 1847 and coming into full force in 1848. But this statute was liable to evasion, and was rendered effective by an Act (13 & 14 Vict. c. 54) which received the Royal assent on July 26, 1850. This later Act seems to be sometimes treated as the Ten Hours Act. The general effect of the law on the passing of this Act has been thus stated in popular language:

"It reduced the legal working day for all young persons and women, to the time between six in the morning and six in the evening, with one and a half hours for meals. This permitted ten and a half hours' work on five days in the week; on Saturdays no protected person was to work after two. Such was the main feature of 13 & 14 Vict. c. 54, which has, since 1850, regulated the normal day in English factories."—Hodder, *Life of Lord Shaftesbury*, ii. p. 202. It will be observed that it made the time of labour on Saturdays less than ten hours, and on the five other working days of the week not ten hours, but ten hours and a half.

28. The definition of the ages of these protected persons has varied under different Acts. Under the present law "child" means any person under the age of thirteen, or in some cases under fourteen; "young person" means any person (not being a child) under eighteen; "woman" means any woman of the age of eighteen and upwards. See Factory and Workshop Act, 1901, s. 156.

29. The Factory Act, 1844 (7 & 8 Vict. c. 15), sec. 32.

the sphere of commerce what seemed to be a crowning victory to individualism, and when the prosperity following on free trade stimulated to the utmost in almost every department of life the faith in and the practice of *laissez faire,* the success of the Factory Acts gave authority, not only in the world of labour, but in many other spheres of life, to beliefs which, if not exactly socialistic, yet certainly tended towards socialism or collectivism.

Changed Attitude of the Working Classes

On the 10th April 1848 the Chartists fought their last fight, and suffered a crushing and final defeat.[30] The advocates of the Charter (who might, at this period, be identified with the artisans of the towns) abandoned chartism, and either gave up all interest in public affairs, or devoted their efforts to movements of which the object was not political, but social. Of these the chief was trade unionism.

This change of attitude told in more ways than one on the course of opinion.

The abandonment of the Charter was a distinct step away from democratic Benthamism; an increased interest in trade unionism was a step in the direction of collectivism. Trade unionism, which means collective bargaining, and involves practical restrictions on individual freedom of contract, could find no favour in the eyes of Liberals who belonged to the school of Bentham.[31] The most liberal judges had, as we have seen, under the influence of Benthamite ideas, interpreted the Combination Act of 1825[32]—in accordance, no doubt, with the real intention of Parliament—so as to put a check, not only upon all physical violence, but upon any so-called moral pressure which curtailed the right of an individual master to purchase, or of an individual workman to sell, labour upon such terms as might suit the contracting parties. To this view of the law trade unionists offered strenuous resistance. If some of them had at one time accepted the

30. For the Chartist demonstration meant to overawe Parliament and ensure the enactment of the People's Charter, see Walpole, *History of England,* iv. pp. 335–337.

31. See pp. 107, 135–146, *ante.*

32. See pp. 142, 143, *ante.*

doctrine of *laissez faire,* they interpreted this dogma as allowing the right of combination for any purpose, which would not be in the strictest sense unlawful, if pursued by an individual acting without concert with others. They maintained that trade unions, even though they aimed at the restraint of trade, should be treated as lawful societies, and that unionists were morally, and ought to be legally, entitled, as long as they made no use of physical violence or the threat thereof, to bring the severest moral pressure to bear upon the action, and thus restrain the freedom of any workman, who might be inclined to follow his own interest in defiance of union rules intended to promote the interest of all the workmen engaged in a particular trade. Here we have the essential conflict between individualism and collectivism.

The changed attitude of the working men facilitated the alliance between the artisans and men of the middle class who, on whatever ground, dissented from Benthamite liberalism.

Chartism had been discredited by the fact that some Chartists sought to attain their ends by the employment or menace of physical force.[33] Trade unionism had during its "revolutionary period" been linked with chartism, and had by acts of violence, and by the use of threatening language, secret oaths, and all the paraphernalia of revolution and conspiracy, excited the

33. In 1848 popular leaders and their opponents were the victims of a delusion fostered by the traditions of the French Revolution. Insurgents, it was supposed, were able to defeat disciplined troops. This notion rested in the main upon the successes achieved during the great Revolution, and again in 1830 and 1848, by the mob of Paris. No idea which has obtained general currency was ever less justified by fact. The belief in the mysterious force of popular enthusiasm was nothing better than a superstition. On no one occasion during the whole revolutionary history of France from 1789 up to the present day, have disciplined troops, when properly led, been defeated by insurgents. Nor has the army shown any special disposition to join the people. On this matter the events of 1848 and 1871 are decisive. In June 1848 the insurgents had every advantage, they had been arming for weeks, they fought with great enthusiasm, and they fought behind well-constructed barricades. Their opponents were to a great extent National Guards and the Garde Mobile, raised from the poorer classes of Paris, on whose absolute fidelity it was difficult to count. Yet the forces of insurrection were vanquished. In 1871 the troops employed by the Government were many of them men who had been vanquished in war. Among the defenders of the Commune there were many trained soldiers. Victory remained with the army.

opposition of all persons who valued the maintenance of law and order.[34] But between 1848 and 1868 unionism came under the guidance of capable, and, from their own point of view, moderate leaders. The abandonment, therefore, of the Charter, combined with the changed character of unionism, made it possible for men who were opposed to all violence or revolution to enter into an alliance with the artisans, or at any rate to sympathise with their policy. When Young England came under the guidance of Mr. Disraeli, Tories could afford at times to exhibit sentimental friendliness towards workmen engaged in conflict with manufacturers, whose mills offended the aesthetic taste, and whose radicalism shook the political authority of benevolent aristocrats.[35] Among young men, again, who though not Tories, dissented from the social and economic dogmas of utilitarianism, working men found lawyers willing and able to suggest changes in the law of the land fitted for the attainment of the ends aimed at by unionists.[36]

Modification in Economic and Social Beliefs

From somewhere about the middle of the nineteenth century (1840–1854) the unsystematic socialism of the artisans began, though it must be admitted in the most indirect way, to mingle with, and to influence and be influenced by, the opinions of thinkers or writers who adhered to very different schools, and though they were mostly opposed to utilitarianism,

34. See Lord Londonderry's Manifesto, Webb, *History of Trade Unionism*, p. 150.

35. Trade unionism came far oftener into conflict with manufacturers than with landowners. See, however, as to the case of the Dorchester labourers, Webb, pp. 123, 124; *R. v. Lovelace*, 6 C. & P. 596; *Law Magazine*, xi. pp. 460, 473; and Walpole, *History*, iii. pp. 229, 231.

36. The repeal of the corn laws, though the triumph of liberalism, had one indirect effect not looked for by philosophic Radicals. The repeal so completely removed the root of bitterness which had created animosity and distrust between the different classes of the community, that, like the abandonment of chartism by the artisans, it promoted the growth of goodwill, and therefore the formation of an alliance between all persons who, to whatever class or party they belonged, had common proclivities towards socialism.

belonged in some instances to the Benthamite school. It is no accident that Carlyle's *Latter Day Pamphlets* (1849–1850), filled with denunciations of *laissez faire*, the *Tracts on Christian Socialism* (1850), which turned men's hearts towards the duties of Christians as the members of society, Kingsley's *Alton Locke* (1850), which to many contemporaries seemed to preach rank socialism, Mrs. Gaskell's *Mary Barton* (1848), which painted sympathetically the position of workmen conducting a strike, and thereby earned the bitter censure of W. R. Greg, the representative of economists and mill-owners—all belonged to the years 1848–1850. It is no accident that at about the same time,[37] Comtism, with its distrust of political economy,[38] began to exert authority in England, and obtained disciples among men who interested themselves deeply in the welfare of the working classes. If *Alton Locke,* with its feeble and uninteresting tailor poet, and the *Latter Day Pamphlets,* with their bluster and bombast, redeemed here and there by flashes of insight, are in 1905 less readable than a volume of old sermons, the welcome which these books received is of deep import, for it displays a widespread distrust in the dominant liberalism of the day, and was a sure sign of a then approaching revolution in public opinion. Most significant of all was the publication in 1848 of Mill's *Political Economy;* the very title of this celebrated book—*Principles of Political Economy, with some of their Applications to Social Philosophy*—has a special meaning. The treatise is an attempt by the intellectual leader of the Benthamite school to bring accepted economic doctrines into harmony with the aspirations of the best men among the working classes.[39] It is to-day, at any rate, perfectly clear that from 1848 onwards an alteration becomes perceptible in the intellectual and moral atmosphere of England. A change we can now see was taking place in the current of opinion, and a change which was the more important, because it influenced mainly the then rising generation, and therefore was certain to tell upon the opinion of twenty or thirty years later—that is, of 1870 or 1880. Nor can we now doubt that this revolution of thought tended in the direction of socialism.

37. Publication of Miss Martineau's translation of Comte's *Philosophie Positive,* 1853.
38. Comte, *Cours de Philosophie Positive,* iv. 264–280.
39. See on Mill's position, Lecture XII. *post.*

Characteristics of Modern Commerce

The extension of trade and commerce is bound up with faith in unlimited competition, but it has, nevertheless, since the middle of the nineteenth century, shaken that confidence in the omnipotence of individual effort and self-help which was the very essence of the liberalism that ruled England during the existence of the middle class Parliament created by the first Reform Act. For combination has gradually become the soul of modern commercial systems. One trade after another has passed from the management of private persons into the hands of corporate bodies created by the State. This revolution may be traced in every volume of the statute-book which has appeared during the last seventy years or more, and especially in the long line of Railway Companies Acts passed since 1823,[40] and in the Joint Stock Companies Acts passed from 1856 to 1862. This legislation was favoured and promoted by Liberals,[41] but the revolution of which it is the sign has nevertheless tended to diminish, in appearance at least, the importance of individual action, and has given room, and supplied arguments for State intervention in matters of business with which in England the State used to have little or no concern. What, too, is of primary importance, this revolution has accustomed the public to constant interference, for the real or supposed benefit of the country, with the property rights of private persons. The truth of these statements may be shown by a comparison between the position of a coach-owner in 1830 as a carrier of passengers and goods, with the position in 1905 of our great modern carrier, a railway company. The coach-owner set up his business at his own will and carried it on, broadly speaking,[42] on his own terms; he possessed no legal monopoly, he asked for no legal privileges; he needed no Act of

40. The year in which was passed the Act under which was constructed the Stockton and Darlington Railway. See *Annual Register*, 1823, p. 241.

41. Here, as in other cases, a law favouring the power of combination has of necessity a twofold, and in a certain sense a contradictory effect. The Companies Acts, introducing the principle of partnerships with limited liability, create an extension of individual freedom. But the same Acts, in so far as they transfer the management of business from the hands of private persons into the hands of corporate bodies, substitute combined for individual action.

42. See for a carrier's common law liability, Leake, *Contracts*, 4th ed. p. 132, and for its modification by statute, the Carriers Act, 1830, 11 Geo. IV. & 1 Will. IV. c. 68.

Parliament which should authorise him to take the property of others on terms of compulsory purchase, or generally to interfere with the property rights of his neighbours. If his concern prospered his success was attributable to his own resources and sagacity, and enforced the homely lesson that wealth is the reward of a man's own talent and energy. There was nothing in the business of a coach-owner which even suggested the expediency of the Government undertaking the duties of carriers. A railway company, on the other hand, is the creature of the State. It owes its existence to an Act of Parliament. It carries on business on terms more or less prescribed by Parliament. It could not in practice lay down a mile of its railway, unless it were empowered to interfere with the property right of others, and above all, to take from landowners, under a system of compulsory purchase, land which the owners may deem worth much more than the price which they are compelled to take, or which they may be unwilling to sell at any price whatever. The success of a railway company is the triumph, not of individual, but of corporate energy, and directs popular attention to the advantages of collective rather than of individual action. The fact, moreover, that a business such as that of a railway company, the due transaction whereof is of the highest importance to the nation, must under the conditions of modern life be managed by a large corporation, affords an argument[43]—as to the force whereof there may be a wide difference of opinion—in favour of the control or even the management of railways by the State.

But the line of reasoning which may be urged in favour of the State management of railways applies to many other concerns,[44] for a railway company is after all only one among many corporations which carry on

43. "Whatever," writes Mill, "if left to spontaneous agency, can only be done by joint-stock associations, will often be as well, and sometimes better done, as far as the actual work is concerned, by the State. Government management is, indeed, proverbially jobbing, careless, and ineffective, but so likewise has generally been joint-stock management. . . . The defects . . . of government management do not seem to be necessarily much greater, if greater at all, than those of management by joint stock."—Mill, *Political Economy*, ch. xi. s. xi. p. 580.

44. See Leonard Darwin, *Municipal Trade*, for a careful examination of the cases in which a trade may or may not be carried on with advantage by the State, and remember that the State takes a part in trade as much when it acts through local bodies as when it acts through the central government.

business, and business in which the nation has a vital interest, in virtue of powers and privileges conferred upon them by Act of Parliament.

The modern development then of corporate trade has in more ways than one fostered the growth of collectivist ideas. It has lessened the importance of the individual trader. It has transformed the abstract principle that all property, and especially property in land, belongs in a sense to the nation, into a practical maxim on which Parliament acts every year with the approval of the country. It constantly suggests the conclusion that every large business may become a monopoly, and that trades which are monopolies may wisely be brought under the management of the State. The characteristics of modern commerce, looked at from this point of view, make for socialism.

Introduction of Household Suffrage, 1868–1884

From about the middle of the nineteenth century conditions unfavourable to the despotic authority of individualism operated by degrees on the opinion of wide classes, and especially of the artisans. But these conditions did not greatly modify legislative opinion, and therefore produced little effect on actual legislation till 1868.[45] Though the Metropolitan Commons Act, 1866,[46] which marks a reaction against the policy, ardently favoured by Bentham, of converting common land into private property, and one or two other isolated enactments, may be taken as a sign of approaching change even in law-making opinion, still by far the greater part of the reforms—such, for example, as the Common Law Procedure Acts, 1851–1862, or the Companies Acts, 1856–1862—passed between 1850 and 1868 are in harmony with Benthamite doctrine. The reason why the spirit of legislation remained on the whole unaltered was that till the Reform Act of

---

45. The passing of the Ten Hours Act, and subsequent Acts passed prior to 1868 which extend its operation, afford an apparent but not a real exception to this statement. See pp. 156–164, *ante.*

46. 29 & 30 Vict. c. 122. See Pollock, *Land Laws,* pp. 182–188.

1867[47] Parliament still represented the middle classes who were in the main guided by the Benthamism of common sense.

"In this country, . . ." writes Mill in 1861,

> what are called the working classes may be considered as excluded from all direct participation in the government. I do not believe that the classes who do participate in it, have in general any intention of sacrificing the working classes to themselves. They once had that intention; witness the persevering attempts so long made to keep down wages by law. But in the present day their ordinary disposition is the very opposite: they willingly make considerable sacrifices, especially of their pecuniary interest, for the benefit of the working classes, and err rather by too lavish and indiscriminating beneficence; nor do I believe that any rulers in history have been actuated by a more sincere desire to do their duty towards the poorer portion of their countrymen. Yet does Parliament, or almost any of the members composing it, ever for an instant look at any question with the eyes of a working man? When a subject arises in which the labourers, as such, have an interest, is it regarded from any point of view but that of the employers of labour? I do not say that the working man's view of these questions is in general nearer to truth than the other; but it is sometimes quite as near, and in any case it ought to be respectfully listened to, instead of being, as it is, not merely turned away from, but ignored. On the question of strikes, for instance, it is doubtful if there is so much as one among the leading members of either House who is not firmly convinced that the reason of the matter is unqualifiedly on the side of the masters, and that the men's view of it is simply absurd. Those who have studied the question know well how far this is from being the case; and in how different, and how infinitely less superficial a manner the point would have to be argued if the parties who strike were able to make themselves heard in Parliament.[48]

These words, though they refer to trade unionism, admit of a much wider application; they describe the attitude of a Legislature which, sharing the convictions of the middle classes, looked with little favour upon ideas entertained by wage-earners whose voice was scarcely heard in parliamentary debates.

47. The last Parliament elected under the Reform Act of 1832 came to an end on July 31, 1868.

48. Mill, *Representative Government*, pp. 56, 57 (ed. 1861).

Even when Mill wrote, however, a change in the constitution of Parliament was near at hand. The year 1865 brought to an end the War of Secession. This event opens a new era. During the nineteen years which followed, democracy, under the modified form of household suffrage, was established throughout the United Kingdom. First the artisans of the towns, and later the country labourers, were admitted to the parliamentary franchise. The details of these transactions belong to constitutional history. Here we note only their connection with, and their effect upon, legislative opinion. Two points are specially noticeable.

The first is that the laws establishing democratic government were themselves the fruit of opinion produced by and in turn influencing public events.

Progress towards democracy was in England immensely stimulated by the victory of the Northern States of America. The conflict between North and South was recognised as a contest between democracy and oligarchy; each had submitted to the ordeal of battle, and democracy came out the victor. This triumph increased the strength of democratic faith; it also, owing to the special circumstances of the day, added weight to the claim of English working men for admission to the full rights of citizens. The artisans had stood by the North, the landowners and the wealthy classes had as a body given moral support to the South. Popular sympathy or sagacity had, it might be argued, proved more far-sighted than educated conservatism, whilst the patience with which the Lancashire "hands" endured the sufferings arising from the cotton famine gained for them general respect. The current argument, too, that the workmen of England could not be denied votes which would soon be conceded to the negroes of the United States, though weak as logic, was irresistible as rhetoric. At the very moment when the moral authority of the artisans was thus increased they had, under the guidance of able counsellors, resumed their interest in politics, and especially in the reform of Parliament.[49] Their return to the political arena was no revival of Chartism. The old Chartists were dead or forgotten. In 1866–1867 the People's Charter and its six points were never mentioned. Little was heard of universal suffrage, nothing of republicanism. Toryism also came once more into strange, but not acci-

49. See Webb, *History of Trade Unionism*, p. 231.

dental, alliance with democracy; the Reform Act of 1867 was carried, not by a Liberal, but by a so-called Conservative ministry. Of the manoeuvres, or diplomacy, or of the real or alleged sacrifices of principle, by which this result was attained, nothing need here be said. Even if the very harshest view possible were to be taken of the process by which Disraeli "educated" the Conservatives, the one matter which for the present purpose deserves consideration is the nature of that education, and its connection with the current of public opinion. The lesson which Disraeli taught his party was the possibility, which he had long perceived, of an alliance between the Tories and English wage-earners; and the true basis of this alliance was their common dissent from individualistic liberalism. It was no accident that Disraeli and his pupils were far less alarmed at the power which might, under a democratic Reform Bill, fall into the hands of the residuum than was John Bright; or that the last and by far the most effective opponent of any attempt to alter the settlement of 1832 was Robert Lowe, who, from the general tenor of his opinions and the character of his intellect, might be termed the last of the genuine Benthamites.[50] What in any case is certain is that the changes in the constitution of the House of Commons, begun by the Act of 1867 and completed by the Act of 1884, were strictly the result of a peculiar condition of opinion, and especially of the belief on the part of Tories, whether well or ill founded, that constitutional changes would in practice produce no revolutionary effect, but would diminish the influence of liberalism.

The second point is that the democratic movement of 1866–1884 was, if from one point of view more moderate, from another more far reaching than the Chartist movement 1838–1848.

The Chartists claimed universal suffrage; they demanded a share of political power as one of the natural rights of man; the artisans who resumed political agitation in 1866–1867, on the other hand, demanded household, not universal suffrage; they demanded electoral rights, not as one of the rights of man, but as a means for obtaining legislation (such, for example,

---

50. John Austin was as much opposed to any further advance towards democracy as was Lowe. See Austin's pamphlet on Reform (1859). Note, too, that, if John Mill assented to a democratic Reform Bill, he desired every advance in the democratic direction to be accompanied by checks which he fancied would protect the rights of minorities.

as a modification of the combination laws), in accordance with the desires of trade unionists. Looked at from the political side, therefore, the moderation of the new democracy contrasts conspicuously with the revolutionary spirit of chartism. But if the two movements be looked at from the social side the comparison presents a different aspect. The avowed wish for social change on the part of the new democracy stands in marked contrast with the desire for merely political change represented by chartism. The same contrast becomes even more marked if we compare, not the Chartists and the later democrats, but the Reform movement of 1832 with the Reform movement of 1866–1884. The great Reform Act was carried by and for the benefit of the middle classes.[51] It was the work of men who desired to change the constitution of Parliament because they wished for legislation in conformity with the principles of individualism.[52] The Reform Acts, 1867–1884, were carried in deference to the wishes and by the support of the working classes, who desired, though in a vague and indefinite manner, laws which might promote the attainment of the ideals of socialism or collectivism. Note, too, that whilst the reformers of 1832 possessed a programme of legislative reform created by the genius and designed to carry out the principles of Bentham, the new democracy came into power under the influence of vague aspirations and unprovided with any definite plan of legislation. If we substitute the word "desires" for "passions," we may apply to the working classes of England in 1868 the language applied by Tocqueville to the working classes of France in 1848:

"Les classes ouvrières . . . aujourd'hui, je le reconnais, sont tranquilles. Il est vrai qu'elles ne sont pas tourmentées par les passions politiques proprement dites, au même degré où elles en ont été tourmentées jadis; mais, ne voyez-vous pas que leurs passions, de politiques, sont devenues sociales?" [Today the working classes . . . are quiet. I recognise that. It is true to say that they no longer are stirred, as once they were, by true political

51. See Brougham's *Speeches*, ii. pp. 600 and 617.

52. Compare the language of Sydney Smith, cited, p. 151, *ante*, and the Benthamite programme of parliamentary reform, and of the ends to be attained thereby set forth in an article published by George Grote in 1831.

See *Minor Works of George Grote* (Bain's ed. 1873), pp. 1–55. [Editor's note: This last sentence was added in the second edition.]

passion, but do you not see that their passions, in politics, have become "social"?][53]

These aspirations may, to use the expression of another French writer, be described as *Le Socialisme sans doctrines*,[54] or a wish for socialistic laws without the conscious adoption of socialistic theory. Here, as elsewhere, law and speculation, action and thought react upon one another.[55] One example of such interaction may be seen in the writings and speeches of H. Fawcett. He was himself an economist and individualist after the school, not of Senior or McCulloch, but of John Mill. His essays published in 1872—that is within five years after the Reform Act, 1867—show that a writer, who criticised socialism in a moderate and not unsympathetic manner, felt that he was struggling against the sentiment of the time. When six years later, in 1878, Fawcett protested with vigour against restrictions imposed by the Factory Acts on the liberty of women, he is clearly the brave defender of a lost cause. In 1885 appeared the Radical Programme. It celebrated the complete establishment of the new democracy; it demanded reforms in the direction of socialism. These reforms, it is assumed, will sound the death-knell of the *laissez faire* system. Democracy is to advance, and "the goal towards which the advance will probably be made at an accelerated pace, is that in the direction of which the legislation of the last quarter of a century has been tending—the intervention, in other words, of the State on behalf of the weak against the strong, in the interests of labour against capital, of want and suffering against luxury and ease."[56] Under this programme free education—that is, education at the expense, not of the parent, but of the nation—"cottage farms and yeomanry holdings," also in some form or other to be provided at the cost of the nation, the complete reversal of the Benthamite policy embodied in the Inclosure Act 1845, the provision by the use of the resources of the State of good

53. *Souvenirs d'Alexis de Tocqueville,* publiés par Le Comte de Tocqueville, 1893, pp. 15, 16. [Editor's note: The translation was added in the Liberty Fund edition.]

54. Métin, *Le Socialisme sans doctrines.* The expression is used in reference to socialistic experiments in Australia. See W. P. Reeves, *State Experiments in Australia and New Zealand.*

55. See pp. 30–35, *ante.*

56. *The Radical Programme,* with a Preface by the Right Hon. J. Chamberlain, M.P. Reprinted, with additions, from the *Fortnightly Review:* Chapman and Hall, 1885. [Editor's note: This footnote was expanded in the second edition.]

houses in towns for the poor, and a graduated income-tax, as well as a considerable extension of the right of the State to take for the public use the land of individuals at the lowest market price, are advantages offered or promised to the electorate. No one can doubt the direction in which the current of legislative opinion was in 1885 assumed to be flowing by the Radical leaders; they believed it—and no one can say that their belief was erroneous—to be completely turned in the direction of collectivism.

If to any student the conditions referred to in this lecture appear, even when co-operating, insufficient to account for a remarkable revolution in legislative opinion, such doubts may be lessened by one reflection: The beneficial effect of State intervention, especially in the form of legislation, is direct, immediate, and, so to speak, visible, whilst its evil effects are gradual and indirect, and lie out of sight. If a law imposes a penalty on a shipowner who sends a vessel to sea before he has obtained a Board of Trade certificate of its seaworthiness, it is probable that few ships will set out on their voyage without a certificate, and it is possible that, for the moment, the number of ships which go to sea unfit to meet a storm may be diminished. These good results of State intervention are easily notice-able. That the same law may make a shipowner, who has obtained a cer-tificate, negligent in seeing that his ship is really seaworthy, and that the certificate will in practice bar any action for real negligence, are evil results of legislation which are indirect and escape notice. Nor in this instance, or in similar cases, do most people keep in mind that State inspectors may be incompetent, careless, or even occasionally corrupt, and that public confidence in inspection, which must be imperfect, tends to make the very class of persons whom it is meant to protect negligent in taking due mea-sures for their own protection; few are those who realise the undeniable truth that State help kills self-help. Hence the majority of mankind must almost of necessity look with undue favour upon governmental interven-tion. This natural bias can be counteracted only by the existence, in a given society, as in England between 1830 and 1860, of a presumption or prejudice in favour of individual liberty—that is, of *laissez faire*. The mere decline, therefore, of faith in self-help—and that such a decline has taken place is certain—is of itself sufficient to account for the growth of legislation tend-ing towards socialism. This consideration goes far to explain the peculiar development of English law during the later part of the nineteenth century.

LECTURE VIII *The Period of Collectivism*

THIS LECTURE DEALS with two topics: first, the principles of collectivism, as actually exhibited in, and illustrated by English legislation during the later part of the nineteenth century; and, secondly, the general trend of such legislation.

(A) Principles of Collectivism

The fundamental principle which is accepted by every man who leans towards any form of socialism or collectivism, is faith in the benefit to be derived by the mass of the people from the action or intervention of the State even in matters which might be, and often are, left to the uncontrolled management of the persons concerned.

This doctrine involves two assumptions: the one is the denial that *laissez faire* is in most cases, or even in many cases, a principle of sound legislation; the second is a belief in the benefit of governmental guidance or interference, even when it greatly limits the sphere of individual choice or liberty. These assumptions—the one negative, the other positive—are logically distinguishable, and, as a matter of reasoning, belief in the one does not of necessity involve belief in the other.[1]

1. A thinker may without inconsistency repudiate the faith of individualists in the unlimited benefits to be conferred on mankind by the extension of individual freedom, and yet rate very low the advantages which any community can derive from the action of the State. A doctor may have little trust in the recuperative power of nature as a cure for a serious malady, and yet may warn the sufferer that popular nostrums will hasten instead of arresting the progress of the disease. But statesmen or reformers can never permanently hold this attitude of balanced and unsanguine scepticism.

This fundamental doctrine, however, is of too abstract a nature to tell much upon the course of legislation, at any rate where the law-makers are Englishmen. The importance of its general, even though tacit, acceptance lies, as regards the development of English law, in the support which it has given to certain subordinate principles or tendencies which immediately affect legislation. These may conveniently be considered under four heads: the Extension of the idea of Protection; the Restriction on Freedom of Contract; the Preference for Collective as contrasted with Individual Action, especially in the matter of bargaining; the Equalisation of Advantages among individuals possessed of unequal means for their attainment. A given law, it should be remembered, may easily be the result of more than one of these tendencies, which indeed are so closely inter-connected that they ought never, even in thought, to be separated from one another by any rigid line of demarcation.

The extension of the idea and the range of protection.

The most fanatical of individualists admits the existence of persons, such as infants or madmen, who, because they are incapable of knowing their own interest, and, in the strictest sense, unable to protect themselves, need the special protection or aid of the State. The most thoroughgoing Benthamites, moreover, not only acknowledge, but strenuously insist upon[2] the principle that for certain purposes all persons need State protection, *e.g.* for the prevention of assault by robbers, or for the attainment of compensation for injuries done to them by the breaker of a contract or by a

---

2. The State often falls short, in the eyes of an individualist, of affording to a citizen all the protection which is justly due to him. If X breaks a contract made with A, or libels A, the latter is clearly entitled, assuming that he himself has done nothing unlawful, to compensation, as complete as possible, for the injury he has suffered. He ought to be paid damages, first, for the loss arising from, *e.g.* the breach of contract; next, for the costs he has incurred in bringing an action against X; and, lastly, for the loss of time and trouble involved in bringing the action. Under English law he may possibly recover, though he rarely does, complete compensation for the damage arising from the breach of contract; he never, or hardly ever, recovers the whole of the costs actually incurred in bringing the action; he receives no compensation for the loss of time and the trouble incurred in the assertion of his rights. The antiquated, though not even yet quite obsolete idea, that the law ought to discourage litigation, means in reality that a law-abiding citizen who has suffered an injury from the inability or neglect of the State to defend his rights, is rightly fined for trying to obtain compensation for the wrong he ought never to have suffered.

wrong-doer. But such protection or State aid, as understood by consistent individualists, is in reality nothing but the defence of individual liberty, and is, therefore, not an exception to, but an application of the individualistic creed. Protection, however, may, in the mouth of any man at all influenced by socialistic ideas, acquire a far wider signification. It is extended in two different ways.

"Protection," in the first place, is tacitly transformed into "guidance," and is applied to classes who, though not in any strictness "incapable" of managing their own affairs, are, in the opinion of the legislature, unlikely to provide as well for their own interest as can the community. An artisan, a tenant farmer, and a woman of full age, would each feel insulted, if told that they could not manage their own business; and they do, in fact, each of them possess on most matters the full legal capacity (as regards at any rate anything coming under the head of private law) which is possessed by other citizens, yet they are each on certain subjects treated as incapables. A workman cannot make a binding contract for the payment of his wages in goods instead of in money;[3] an artisan or a labourer cannot by contract give up the benefit of, or, as the expression goes, "contract himself out" of, the Workmen's Compensation Acts,[4] nor can a farmer contract himself out of the Agricultural Holdings Acts.[5] A woman's labour in factories, workshops, shops, or even in some cases at her home, is regulated by law.[6] She is excluded, as it is presumed for her own good, from work which she might personally be willing to undertake. All of these persons, therefore, represent large classes on whom the State confers protection or imposes disabilities. Nor is it doubtful that modern legislation tends to increase the number of protected classes.[7]

3. See the Truck Acts, 1831, 1 & 2 Will. IV. c. 37; 1887, 50 & 51 Vict. c. 46; 1896, 59 & 60 Vict. c. 44; and Stephen, *Comm.* ii. (14th ed.), p. 281.

4. See the Workmen's Compensation Acts, 1897, 60 & 61 Vict. c. 37; 1900, 63 & 64 Vict. c. 22.

5. See Acts, 1875, 38 & 39 Vict. c. 92; 1876, 39 & 40 Vict. c. 74; 1883, 46 & 47 Vict. c. 61; 1887, 50 & 51 Vict. c. 26; 1890, 53 & 54 Vict. c. 57; and 1895, 58 & 59 Vict. c. 27.

6. See the Factory and Workshop Acts, 1878 to 1895, and especially 1901, 1 Edw. VII. c. 22.

7. Note the provisions for the protection of sailors from imposition (Merchant Shipping Act, 1894, 57 & 58 Vict. c. 60, ss. 212–219). Note also the curious extension given to the doctrine long ago established by the Courts of Equity, that where *X* induces *A* to enter into

Protection, in the second place, is made to include arrangements for the safeguarding, not of special classes, but of all citizens against mistakes which often may be avoided by a man's own care and sagacity. Thus enactments to prevent the adulteration of food or to provide for its analysis by some State official, extending from the Adulteration of Food Act, 1860[8] down to the Sale of Food and Drugs Act, 1899,[9] defend all citizens from dangers which certainly might be warded off, though at the cost of a great deal of trouble, by individual energy and circumspection, and these enactments rest upon the idea (which is thoroughly congenial to collectivism) that the State is a better judge than a man himself of his own interest, or at any rate of the right way to pursue it.

Restrictions on Freedom of Contract

Collectivism curtails as surely as individualism extends the area of contractual freedom. The reason of this difference is obvious. The extension of contractual capacity enlarges the sphere of individual liberty. According as legislators do or do not believe in the wisdom of leaving each man to settle his own affairs for himself, they will try to extend or limit the sphere of contractual freedom. During the latter part of the nineteenth century

---

a contract through the use of undue influence, the contract is voidable at the instance of *A*. This doctrine was reasonable enough where *X* made an unconscientious use of authority or power over *A*, arising from the special relation between *X* and *A*, as, for instance, where *X* is *A*'s parent, or stands towards *A* *in loco parentis*, or is *A*'s spiritual adviser or doctor; but the doctrine has in one set of cases, at any rate, been extended far beyond this, and has been used as a means for enabling any person who expects, whether strictly as heir or merely on account of a relation's goodwill, to succeed to property, and being in want of money, makes a "catching bargain," as it is called, with regard to such expected property, to repudiate the contract, with the result that in some instances a man well past twenty-one is given the protection against the results of a hard bargain which the common law gives only to infants— that is, to persons below twenty-one (see *Aylesford* v. *Morris* (1873), L.R. 8 Ch. 484). There is thus constituted a new class of protected persons. It is not an unreasonable conjecture that the extension given to the idea of undue influence was originally suggested by the usury laws, and, after the repeal of the usury laws, was supported by the Courts, partly with a view to diminish the effect of the repeal.

8. 23 & 24 Vict. c. 84.

9. 62 & 63 Vict. c. 51.

the tendency to curtail such liberty becomes clearly apparent. With Irish legislation these lectures are not directly concerned, but, though that legislation has generally been dictated by exceptional circumstances due to the peculiar history of Ireland, it throws, at times, strong light on the condition of English opinion. The Landlord and Tenant (Ireland) Act, 1870, 33 & 34 Vict. c. 46, and still more the Land Law (Ireland) Act, 1881, 44 & 45 Vict. c. 49, are the negation of free trade in land, and make the rights of Irish landlords and of Irish tenants dependent upon status, not upon contract. Legislation of this character would in any year between 1830 and 1860 have been in reality an impossibility, owing to the absence in Parliament, and indeed among the electors who were then represented in Parliament, of the convictions to which the later Irish Land Acts give expression.

Let us here consider with a little further attention the increasing number of cases in which a person belonging to a particular class, *e.g.* the body of tenant farmers, has been forbidden by law to part under a contract with advantages, such as compensation for improvements, which Parliament intends to secure to the class of which he is a member.[10] Law-making of this sort generally passes through two stages. In the earlier stage the law places upon some kind of contract an interpretation supposed to be specially favourable to one of the parties, but allows them to negative such construction by the express terms of the agreement between them. In the later stage the law forbids the parties to vary, by the terms of their contract, the construction placed upon it by law. The difference between these two stages is well illustrated by the case of a lease made by a landlord to a tenant farmer. As the law originally stood the tenant had no right to compensation for improvements made by him during his tenancy, unless he was entitled thereto by an express term in his lease. This was felt to be a hardship. Parliament, therefore, enacted that it should be an implied term of every lease, unless the contrary were expressly stated therein, that the tenant should receive compensation for improvements. So far there was no interference with the contractual freedom either of the landlord or the tenant, for it was open to the parties by an express term of the lease to

10. See the Agricultural Holdings Acts, 1875 to 1895; the Workmen's Compensation Act, 1897, 60 & 61 Vict. c. 37.

exclude the tenant's right to compensation. It was found, however, that, upon this change in the law, the tenant's right was habitually excluded by the terms of the lease, and that he did not therefore receive the benefit which the legislature hoped to confer upon him. The next step was for Parliament absolutely to prohibit the bargaining away of his right by the tenant. Here the inroad upon contractual freedom is patent. The necessity for forbidding the tenant to contract himself out of the statute is no proof that the policy of conferring upon him an absolute right to compensation was unsound, but it is conclusive evidence that landlords were ready to purchase and tenants were ready to sell the rights conferred upon them by statute, and that the Act, which prevents the parties to a lease from making the bargain which they are willing to make, does curtail the freedom of contract. The transition from permissive to compulsory legislation bears witness to the rising influence of collectivism.

Preference for Collective Action

This preference rests on two grounds.

The one is the belief that whenever the interest of the wage-earners comes into competition with the interest of capitalists, and especially when a bargain has been struck as to the rate of wages payable by employers to workmen, an individual artisan or labourer does not bargain on fair terms; he seems powerless against a wealthy manufacturer, and still more so against a large company possessed of wealth, which, as compared with his own resources, may be regarded as unlimited. The sale of labour, in short, is felt to be unlike the sale of goods. A shopkeeper can keep back his wares until the market rises, whilst a factory hand, if he refuses low wages, runs the risk of pauperism or of starvation. The other ground is the sentiment or conviction which is entertained by every collectivist, that an individual probably does not know his own interest, and certainly does not know the interest of the class to which he belongs, as well as does the trade union, or ultimately the State of which he is a member. This belief that associations or communities of any kind are organisms, which may be wiser as well as stronger than the persons of whom they are composed, affects a man's whole estimate of the merit of combined as compared with individual action, and underlies much modern legislation.

As illustrations of this preference for collective action take the Combination Act of 1875 and the modern Arbitration Acts.

The Combination Act, 1875 (Conspiracy and Protection of Property Act, 1875).[11] This statute must be read in connection with the Trade Union Acts, 1871[12]–1876.[13] All these Acts taken together place trade combinations of every kind, whether they take the form of strikes or of trade unions, in a position totally different from that which they occupied under the Benthamite legislation of 1825.[14] From this point of view the following features of the existing combination law, which may well be described as the compromise of 1875, deserve special consideration.

First. A combination to do an act in furtherance of a trade dispute between employers and workmen is made, so to speak, privileged. For it is enacted that "an agreement or combination by two or more persons to do or procure to be done any act in contemplation or furtherance of a trade dispute between employers and workmen shall not be *indictable as a conspiracy*[15] if such act committed by one person would not be punishable as a crime."[16] Hence a distinction is made between trade combinations and other combinations, in virtue of which it is not a criminal conspiracy if in furtherance of a trade dispute a combination is made to do a particular thing (*e.g.* to break a contract), which would certainly not in general be a crime if done by a person acting alone, whilst a combination to do the same thing (viz. break a contract) in furtherance of some other object may be a criminal conspiracy. The effect, in short, of this enactment is that a combination among workmen to break a contract with their employer, *e.g.* to leave his service without due notice, with a view to compelling him to grant a rise in wages, is not a crime, whilst a combination by tenants to break a contract by refusing to pay rent due to their landlord, with a view to compelling him to lower their rents, is a crime.

Secondly. Something like a legal sanction is given to conduct which is

11. 38 & 39 Vict. c. 86.

12. 34 & 35 Vict. c. 31.

13. 39 & 40 Vict. c. 22.

14. See pp. 136–143, *ante*.

15. It may be "actionable" though not indictable. (But see now the Trade Disputes Act, 1906, 6 Edw. VII. c. 47.) [Editor's note: The previous sentence was added in the second edition.]

16. Conspiracy, etc. Act, 1875 (38 & 39 Vict. c. 86), s. 3, 1st par.

popularly known as picketing in connection with a trade dispute, as long as such conduct does not partake of intimidation or violence.[17]

Thirdly. A trade union—which under the legislation of 1825 was more or less an unlawful society,[18] on the simple ground that its object was the restraint of trade—is freed from this character of necessary illegality.[19] Hence a trade union is completely protected as regards its funds, and can no longer be defrauded with impunity by its officials. Thus too trade unions, though not corporate bodies, enjoy the protection of the law. Violation of the rules of a trade union by one of its members, however, is not allowed to give rise to a right of action for breach of contract.

Fourthly. Certain kinds of intimidation likely to be used by trade unions, or by workmen on strike, in order to interfere with the free action either of other workmen or of employers, are made criminal—that is to say, are forbidden under severe penalties.[20]

The combination law of 1875 is, on the face of it, a compromise between the desire of collectivists to promote combined bargaining and the conviction of individualists that every man ought, as long as he does not distinctly invade the rights of his neighbours, to enjoy complete contractual freedom. But the compromise marks a distinct change in the spirit of English legislation, and, though it contains some severe provisions for the

17. 38 & 39 Vict. c. 86, s. 7.

18. See p. 139, *ante.*

19. 34 & 35 Vict. c. 31. A trade union may, it is submitted, now be described as a semilegal association. It is not of necessity, or indeed in most cases a strictly unlawful society, since the only objection to its lawful character may be that its object is the restraint of trade, and this objection is, under the Conspiracy, etc. Act, 1875, no longer tenable; but a trade union may obviously pursue some other objects, *e.g.* the interference with the right of an individual workman to take service on such terms as he sees fit; and it is possible, at any rate, that the pursuance of such an object may make a trade union an unlawful society.

20. It is "enacted in general terms that every person who, with a view to compel any other person to abstain from doing, or to do any act which such person has a legal right to do or abstain from doing, wrongfully and without legal authority, uses violence to or intimidates such person, follows him about, hides his tools, watches or besets his house, or follows him through the streets in a disorderly way, shall be liable to three months' hard labour."—Stephen, *Hist.* iii. p. 226, and see 38 & 39 Vict. c. 86, s. 7. Certain specific breaches of contract which are likely to cause injury to persons or property are in like manner made criminal.—*Ibid.* ss. 4, 5.

protection of individual freedom, is, as compared with the combination law of the past, highly favourable to trade combinations.

The combination law of 1875 is the direct antithesis to the combination law of 1800.[21] The former favours as much as the latter condemns combinations among either workmen or employers. The law of 1875 treats a strike as a perfectly lawful proceeding, and gives to trade unions a recognised, though somewhat singular position; whilst the law of 1800 in effect treated a strike as a crime, and a trade union as little better than a permanent conspiracy.

The combination law of 1875 differs, again, in its whole spirit from the law of 1825. For the law of 1875 contemplates and facilitates combined bargaining on the part both of men and of masters; whilst the Benthamite legislation of 1825 was intended to establish free trade in labour, and allowed, or tolerated, trade combinations, only in so far as they were part of and conducive to such freedom of trade. The law of 1875 is primarily designed to extend, as regards bargaining between masters and workmen, the right of combination, and is only secondarily concerned with protecting the freedom of individuals in the sale or purchase of labour; whilst the law of 1825 was primarily concerned with protecting the contractual freedom of each individual, whether as a seller or purchaser of labour, and was only secondarily concerned with extending the right of combination, so far as seemed necessary for establishing genuine free trade in labour.

The combination law of 1875 has, indeed, been thought to go so far in the way of extending the right of association, that competent critics have doubted[22] whether it sufficiently secures the contractual freedom either of an individual workman or of an individual master. This doubt has, it is true, been to a great extent removed by cases decided during recent years,[23] which establish, first, that combinations having reference to a trade dispute,

---

21. *I.e.* the Combination Act, 1800, and the law of conspiracy as then interpreted. See pp. 68–74, *ante*.

22. Conf. Memorandum by Sir F. Pollock on Law of Trade Combinations, *Fifth and Final Report of Labour Commission*, 1894 [c. 7421], pp. 157–159.

23. *Quinn v. Leathem* [1901], A. C. 495; *Taff Vale Railway Co. v. Amalgamated Society of Railway Servants* [1901], A. C. 426; *Giblan v. National Amalgamated Labourers' Union* [1903], 2 K. B. (C. A.) 60. Compare *Allen v. Flood* [1898], A. C. 1, and *Mogul Case* [1892], A. C. 25.

though not indictable as conspiracies, may nevertheless expose the persons who take part in them to civil liability for damages thereby done to individuals; and next, that trade unions can be made responsible for wrongs done by their agents. One thing is at any rate clear. The authors of the compromise of 1875, and the public opinion by which that compromise was sanctioned, were very far from accepting the Benthamite ideal of free trade in labour.

The story of the combination law from 1800 to the present day illustrates with such singular accuracy the relation between law and opinion, that it is well at this point to cast a glance back over this tangled story, which has necessarily been told bit by bit, and survey it as a whole.

The combination law of 1800 represents the panic-stricken but paternal toryism of that date.[24]

The legislation of 1824–1825, even in its singular fluctuation, corresponds with and is guided by the Benthamite ideal of free trade in labour.[25]

The compromise of 1875 represents in the main the combined influence of democracy and collectivism—an influence, however, which was still balanced or counteracted by ideas belonging to individualistic liberalism.[26]

The interpretation of that compromise by the Courts was necessitated by the ambiguity of the law, and represents the belief which now, as heretofore, has great weight with Englishmen, that individual liberty must be held sacred, and that this liberty is exposed to great peril by an unrestricted right of combination. If we ask what were the causes which after 1875 revived the sense of this peril, they may all be summed up in the existence, or rather the creation, of the one word, "boycott." The term, which has obtained a world-wide acceptance, came into being during the autumn of 1880;[27] it spread far and wide, because it supplied a new name for an old disease, which had reappeared under a new form. It bore witness to the pressing danger that freedom of combination might, if unrestrained, give a death-blow to liberty.

The present state of the law, it is sometimes said, is confused, but this

24. See pp. 68–74, *ante.*
25. See pp. 136–143, *ante.*
26. See pp. 189–192, *ante.*
27. See Murray's *Dictionary,* "Boycott."

very confusion, in so far as it really exists, corresponds with and illustrates a confused state of opinion. We all of us in England still fancy, at least, that we believe in the blessings of freedom, yet, to quote an expression which has become proverbial, "to-day we are all of us socialists." The confusion reaches much deeper than a mere opposition between the beliefs of different classes. Let each man, according to the advice of the preachers, look within. He will find that inconsistent social theories are battling in his own mind for victory. Lord Bramwell, the most convinced of individualists, became before his death an impressive and interesting embodiment of the beliefs of a past age; yet Lord Bramwell himself writes to a friend, "I am something of a socialist."

The combination law, from whatever point of view and at whatever date it be examined, affords the clearest confirmation of the doctrine that in modern England law is the reflection of public opinion.[28]

The Modern Arbitration Acts. These enactments begin with the Arbitration Act, 1867,[29] and terminate for the moment with the Conciliation Act, 1896.[30] Earlier enactments known as Arbitration Acts[31] provided summary or expeditious modes for the settlement of definite disputes between a

28. See Appendix, Note 1, Right of Association.

29. 30 & 31 Vict. c. 105.

30. 59 & 60 Vict. c. 30. The Acts repealed by the latter Act are the Workman's Arbitration Act, 1824, 5 Geo. IV. c. 96; the Councils Conciliation Act, 1867, 30 & 31 Vict. c. 105; the Arbitration (Masters and Workmen) Act, 1872, 35 & 36 Vict. c. 46.

31. See Howell, *Labour Legislation,* etc. p. 436. "In all essential respects the questions adjudicated upon by justices of the peace relating to labour disputes were similar to those pertaining to trading and commercial disputes, though the conditions of reference, pleading, and adjudication were decidedly different. In the case of labour the dispute to be dealt with had reference to work actually done, and as to wages due therefor; or to lengths of work, in the case of silk, cotton, woollen, or other textiles; or to deductions for alleged bad work. Various other matters would often arise as to time of finish of work, delivery, and as to frame rents and other charges. But all these questions related to work done, not done, damaged, not delivered, and otherwise, at the date of complaint and arbitration. Future rates of wages—amounts to be paid—had no lot or part in legislation except possibly as to finishing a certain article in hand. It was not arbitration or labour questions, as we now understand the subject, but adjudication upon disputed points there and then at issue. How, indeed, could it be otherwise? Wages were arbitrarily fixed in very many industries."— Howell, p. 436.

master and his workmen, similar in character to the differences connected with trade or commerce which are determined by the ordinary law courts. The modern Conciliation Acts, as represented by the statute of 1896, aim at a new object and rest upon new ideas. Their object is not merely the settlement of definite disputes which have arisen between employers and their workmen, but also the prevention of such disputes in the future, and they seek to achieve this end through the moral influence of the State brought into play by the action of the Government. The ideas on which these enactments are based obviously tend in the direction of collectivism. True it is that, as the law now[32] stands, governmental intervention in labour disputes is restricted within narrow limits.[33] But the possibility of such intervention is sufficient to bring the full force of public opinion—an opinion which is never impartial—to bear upon the relation in a given case between a master and his workmen; the sphere, moreover, of the State's activity may any day receive extension. We have reached a merely transitory stage in the effort of the State to act as arbitrator. The attempt, if not given up, must be carried out to its logical conclusion, and assume the shape of that compulsory arbitration which is a mere euphemism for the regulation of labour by the State, acting probably through the Courts.[34]

32. 1905. [Editor's note: This footnote was added in the second edition.]

33. It must take the form either of mere inquiry into the circumstances of a particular dispute, or of arbitration on the application of *both* the parties to such dispute.

34. Compulsory arbitration must be carried through either by the Courts or by the Executive, but it may be doubted whether either of these bodies is fit for the work.

1. The judges are not by nature qualified for real arbitration, as regards matters of which they can have no special knowledge; and the Courts possess no proper machinery for enforcing their awards against the parties to a trade dispute. To put the judges, it may be added, to do work which is not judicial, is certain to deprive them of that repute for perfect impartiality which is in England their special glory.

2. The Executive is a more appropriate body than the Courts for the enforcement of an award, but a Parliamentary Cabinet does not and cannot possess that impartiality, which is the primary requisite for the performance of his duties by an arbitrator. A ministry called upon to adjudicate upon a dispute between an employer and his workmen will inevitably, in giving judgment, think a good deal of the effect which the judgment may produce at the next general election.

Equalisation of Advantages

The extension given by collectivists to the idea of protection makes easy the transition from that idea to the different notion of equalisation of advantages. Of the members of every community the greater number cannot obtain the comforts or the enjoyments which fall to the lot of their richer and more fortunate neighbours. Against this evil of poverty the State ought, it is felt by collectivists, to protect the wage-earning class, and in order to give this protection must go a good way towards securing for every citizen something like the same advantages, in the form of education, or of physical well-being, as the rich can obtain by their own efforts. This extension of the idea and practice of protection by the State has not, it is true, in England led as yet to anything like that enforced equality popularly known as communism, but, during the latter part of the nineteenth century, it has produced much legislation tending towards that equalisation of advantages among all classes which, in practice, means the conferring of benefits upon the wage-earners at the expense of the whole body of the tax-payers.

This tendency is traceable in the development of the law with reference to elementary education, to an employer's liability for injuries received by workmen in the course of their employment, and to municipal trading.[35]

As to Elementary Education. Up to 1832 the State recognised no national responsibility and incurred no expense for the elementary education of the people of England; nor did it impose upon parents any legal obligation to provide for the education of their children.[36]

---

35. No attempt is here made to give, even in outline, a history or a full statement of the law on these topics; they are dealt with only in so far as they illustrate the tendency towards the equalisation of advantages.

36. See Balfour, *Educational Systems of Great Britain and Ireland* (2nd ed.).

The statements made here as to education do not refer to Scotland or Ireland.

In 1807 Whitbread introduced a Bill, which passed the House of Commons, for the foundation of a school in every parish, with power to employ local rates.

In 1816 Brougham obtained a Select Committee to Inquire into the Education of the Lower Orders. In 1820 he brought in an Education Bill which did not pass into law. In 1811 was founded the National Society for Promoting the Education of the Poor in the Principles

From 1833 onwards, the State made grants, the earliest of which amounted to not quite £20,000, for the indirect promotion of the education of the English people, and thereby to a certain extent admitted its duty as a national educator, but the assumption of this duty was delayed by the distrust of State intervention which characterised the Benthamite era.[37]

In 1870 the education of the English poor became for the first time the direct concern of the nation, and the State attempted to enforce upon parents, though to a very limited extent, the obligation of providing their children with elementary knowledge, and in so far at the parents' own expense, that they were compellable to pay school fees. In 1876 this duty of the parents[38] received distinct legal recognition, and in 1880 the compulsory attendance of children at school was for the first time made universal.[39]

In 1891 parents of children compelled to attend school were freed from the duty of paying school fees, and elementary education became what is called free.[40]

This last change completely harmonises with the ideas of collectivism.

---

of the Established Church, and in 1808 the British and Foreign School Society, which in effect represented Dissenters. These facts, as also the foundation of Sunday Schools, show the gradual growth, since at any rate the beginning of the nineteenth century, of the conviction that it was the duty of the State or the public to provide education for the poor.

The mere fact that a country maintains a national system of education does not of itself necessarily prove the prevalence of socialistic ideas, as witness the history of popular education in Scotland and in New England. But it is true that the gradual development of the conviction that the nation must provide for the education of the people, and make such provision at the expense of the nation, may be, and certainly has been in England, connected with the development of collectivism.

37. Even as late as 1859, John Mill deprecated the direct assumption by the State of educational functions, and contended that it ought to do no more than compel parents to provide for the elementary education of their children.—Mill, *On Liberty,* pp. 188–194.

38. "It shall be the duty of the parent of every child to cause such child to receive efficient elementary instruction in reading, writing, and arithmetic, and if such parent fail to perform such duty, he shall be liable to such orders and penalties as are provided by the Act."—Elementary Education Act, 1876, 39 & 40 Vict. c. 79, s. 4. See Balfour, *Educational Systems,* 2nd ed. p. 24.

39. The Elementary Education Act, 1880, 43 & 44 Vict. c. 23.

40. 54 & 55 Vict. c. 56, s. 1.

It means, in the first place, that *A*, who educates his children at his own expense, or has no children to educate, is compelled to pay for the education of the children of *B*, who, though, it may be, having means to pay for it, prefers that the payment should come from the pockets of his neighbours. It tends, in the second place, as far as merely elementary education goes, to place the children of the rich and of the poor, of the provident and the improvident, on something like an equal footing. It aims, in short, at the equalisation of advantages. The establishment of free education is conclusive proof that, in one sphere of social life, the old arguments of individualism have lost their practical cogency. Here and there you may still hear it argued that a father is as much bound in duty to provide his own children at his own expense with necessary knowledge as with necessary food and clothing, whilst the duty of the tax-payers to pay for the education is no greater than the obligation to pay for the feeding of children whose parents are not paupers. But this line of reasoning meets with no response except, indeed, either from some rigid economist who adheres to doctrines which, whether true or false, are derided as obsolete shibboleths; or from philanthropists who, entertaining, whether consciously or not, ideas belonging to socialism, accept the premises pressed upon them by individualists, but draw the inference that the State is bound to give the children, for whose education it is responsible, the breakfasts or dinners which will enable them to profit by instruction. The State, moreover, which provides for the elementary education of the people, has now, in more directions than one, advanced far on the path towards the provision of teaching which can in no sense be called elementary.[41] If a student once realises that the education of the English people was, during the earlier part of the nineteenth century, in no sense a national concern, he will see that our present system is a monument to the increasing predominance of collectivism. For elementary education is now controlled and guided by a central body directly representing the State; it is administered by representative local authorities, it is based on the compulsory attendance of children

---

41. See Balfour, pp. xxi.–xxiii.; Stephen, *Comm.* iii. (14th ed.) 132, and compare generally as to the present state of the law relating to education, *ibid.* 127–144. The chapter on this subject has had the advantage of revision by F. W. Hirst.

at school, it is supported partly by parliamentary grants and partly by local rates.[42]

As to Employer's Liability. Before 1800 the Courts had established the principle, that an employer was liable to a third party for damage inflicted upon him through the negligence of the employer's servants or workmen in the course of their work. The moral justification for this obligation has been sometimes questioned by moralists no less than by judges.

"The law of this country," writes Paley,

goes great lengths in intending a kind of concurrence in the master [with the acts of his servant], so as to charge him with the consequences of his servant's conduct. If an innkeeper's servant rob his guests, the innkeeper must make restitution; if a farrier's servant lame a horse, the farrier must answer for the damage; and still farther, if your coachman or carter drive over a passenger in the road, the passenger may recover from you a satisfaction for the hurt

42. I have no wish to overlook the extent to which voluntary contributions, made by the members of different religious bodies, supply in part the means of national education, but it cannot be disputed that the education of the people is now in the main paid for by the nation.

The cost of elementary education to the Imperial Exchequer, as provided for in the Estimates, is for the financial year 1904–5, £10,998,000. This is made up as follows:

Grants	£10,688,400	} = Total, £10,998,000.
Administration and inspection	309,600	

The corresponding figures for the financial year 1903–4 were:

Grants	£9,798,512	} = Total, £10,114,126.
Administration and inspection	315,614	

In addition to this the cost of training of teachers and pupil teacher instruction, which is now a part of education other than elementary, is estimated at—

for	1904–5	£385,795
	1903–4	£335,215.

To the amounts here mentioned must, I conceive, be added the sums raised from the local rates, which in 1901 amounted in round numbers to £6,000,000. The sums paid in one shape or another by the nation to maintain the elementary education of the people of England cannot, therefore, apparently fall much short, if at all, of £18,000,000.

Legislation with regard to elementary education illustrates the influence exerted by the cross-current of ecclesiastical opinion.

he suffers. But these determinations stand, I think, rather upon the authority of the law than any principle of natural justice.[43]

This doubt whether legal liability could justly co-exist with the absence of moral responsibility contributed to a singular result. The Courts, between 1830 and 1840, curtailed the extent of an employer's liability by grafting upon it an anomalous limitation. An employer, they held, was not liable to pay compensation to one of his servants or workmen for damage suffered through the negligence of a fellow-servant or fellow-workman in the course of their common employment.[44] This rule is known as the "doctrine of common employment." It belonged to the era of individualism, and was supported by the economic theory, of dubious soundness, that when a person enters into any employment, *e.g.* as a railway porter, the risks naturally incident to his work are taken into account in the calculation of his wages.[45] However this may be, the doctrine of common employment caused much apparent hardship. If a railway accident occurred through the negligence of the engine driver, every passenger damaged thereby could obtain compensation from the railway company, but a guard or a porter, since they were injured through the negligence of their fellow-servant, could obtain no compensation whatever. A rule accepted in Massachusetts, no less than in England, could not be attributed to anti-democratic sentiment, but it excited frequent protests from workmen. The introduction, however, of household suffrage[46] did not lead to the immediate abolition

---

43. Paley, *Moral Philosophy,* book iii. part i. ch. xi. "Contracts of Labour" (12th ed. 1799), vol. i. p. 168.

The true basis of the liability of an employer for damage caused to others through the negligence of his servant or workman, is that every man must so conduct his affairs as not to injure third parties either by his own negligence or that of the agents whom he employs.

44. See *Priestley* v. *Fowler* (1837), 3 M. & W. 1, and the American case, *Farwell* v. *Boston Railroad Corporation* (1842), Bigelow, *Leading Cases,* 688.

45. This economic view was supplemented by the consideration that a servant or workman may be partially responsible for an accident from which he suffers, even though he may not contribute directly to its occurrence. Thus, if the workmen in a powder magazine habitually and contrary to orders smoke there, and *N,* who is one of their number, shares or tolerates this habit, he may well be responsible for the explosion of which he is the victim, even though it is not caused by a spark from his own pipe.

46. 1867–68.

of the doctrine of common employment.[47] In 1880 the Employers' Liability Act, 43 & 44 Vict. c. 42, greatly limited the operation of a rule which all wage-earners felt to be unjust, but did not do away with its existence.[48] In 1894 a Bill passed through the House of Commons which did away altogether with the doctrine of common employment, but the House of Lords struck out a clause which prohibited a workman from contracting himself out of the Act, and the Bill was dropped by its supporters. Thus far every actual or proposed amendment of the law aimed mainly at placing a workman, when injured through the negligence of his fellows, in the same position as a stranger.

In 1897, however, legislation took a completely new turn. The Workmen's Compensation Act of that year[49] (60 & 61 Vict. c. 67) introduced into the law the new principle that an employer must, subject to certain limitations, insure his workmen against the risks of their employment. At the same time the right of a workman to bargain away his claim to compensation was in reality, though not in form, nullified, since any contract whereby he foregoes the right to compensation secured him by the Workmen's Compensation Acts is effective only where a general scheme for compensation, agreed upon between the employer and the employed, secures to the workmen benefits at least as great as those which they would derive from the Compensation Acts; and this arrangement must be sanctioned by a State official.[50]

47. In 1868, indeed, the House of Lords forced the doctrine upon the reluctant Courts of Scotland, *Wilson* v. *Merry,* L.R., 1 Sc. Ap. 326.

48. It still in some instances remains in force. It applies to actions under the Employers' Liability Act, 1880, 43 & 44 Vict. c. 42, which do not fall within sec. 1. It applies also to actions by domestic servants, who do not fall within this Act. See Macdonell, *Master and Servant,* ch. xv. The fact that after the Compensation Acts have placed the rights of workmen and the liability of employers on a new basis, the Employers' Liability Act, 1880, which belongs to an older and abandoned view of the relation between employers and workmen, should not have been repealed, and that the doctrine of common employment should not have been abolished, is characteristic of the fragmentary and unsystematic manner in which the law is amended in England.

49. Extended three years later so as to apply to agricultural labourers. Workmen's Compensation Act, 1900, 63 & 64 Vict. c. 22. The principle of the Compensation Acts is not as yet [1905] extended to domestic servants. It may be conjectured with some confidence that this extension will sooner or later take place.

50. See the Workmen's Compensation Act, 1897 (60 & 61 Vict. c. 37), s. 3.

This legislation bears all the marked characteristics of collectivism. Workmen are protected against the risks of their employment, not by their own care or foresight, or by contracts made with their employers, but by a system of insurance imposed by law upon employers of labour. The contractual capacity both of workmen and of masters is cut down. Encouragement is given to collective bargaining. The law, lastly, secures for one class of the community an advantage, as regards insurance against accidents, which other classes can obtain only at their own expense, and, though it is true that the contract of employment is still entered into directly between masters and workmen, yet in the background stands the State, determining in one most important respect the terms of the labour contract. The rights of workmen in regard to compensation for accidents have become a matter not of contract, but of status.

As to Municipal Trading. At the beginning of the nineteenth century English municipal corporations[51] took little part in trade; they did not, in general, engage in business which otherwise would have been carried on for profit by private persons or companies.[52] In truth, the old corporations which were reformed by the Municipal Corporations Act, 1835,[53] were not adapted for entering into trade. As we have seen,[54] they were corrupt and inefficient, and shirked even the duties which generally belonged to civic authorities;[55] they were the object of deep distrust;[56] no one dreamed of increasing their sphere of action. It was not till municipal reform had

---

51. See Leonard Darwin, *Municipal Trade*, pp. 1–27; Redlich and Hirst, *Local Government in England*, i. pp. 111–133.

52. This statement may be disputed, but is (it is submitted) in substance true. Municipal corporations, or other local authorities created for a special purpose, did in some instances, long before the beginning of the nineteenth century, carry on concerns which might be called trades (*e.g.* the supply of water for a particular locality); but these concerns were closely connected with municipal administration, and could not fairly be described as municipal trading.

53. 5 & 6 Will. IV. c. 76.

54. See p. 85, *ante.*

55. In Bath "every quarter of the town was under the care of a separate board, except one quarter which was totally unprotected."—Redlich and Hirst, *Local Government*, i. p. 120.

56. The belief was widespread that a town without a charter was a town without a shackle. "Manchester," observes Aikin (in 1795), "remains an open town; destitute (probably to its advantage) of a corporation, and unrepresented in Parliament." See Leslie Stephen, *English Utilitarians*, i. pp. 99, 100.

worked its salutary effects that any popular feeling grew up in favour of the management of trades, which might concern the public interest, by municipal corporations. Nor was municipal trading during the Benthamite era in harmony with the liberalism of the day. A gradual change of public opinion may be dated from about the middle of the century. Since 1850 the extension of municipal trading has progressed with a rapidity which increased greatly as the nineteenth century drew towards its close; the market rights of private owners have been bought up by municipalities;[57] markets so purchased have often turned out lucrative properties, and "we find that the more recent developments [of municipal trading] in connection with municipal markets include slaughter-houses, cold-air stores, ice manufactories, and the sale of surplus ice, and that the right to sell the ice to the public without restriction has been demanded"[58] from Parliament. Municipal bathing establishments have become common, as well as the foundation of municipal water-works,[59] and since the middle of the century the supply of gas, which up to that date had been wholly in the hands of companies, has in many cases passed under the management of local authorities. Tramways (1868–1869) were first constructed and owned, and since a later date (1882–1892) have been worked by municipalities, whilst since 1889 electrical works have been carried on by municipalities, and the fact is now clearly recognised that all or the greater number of tramways will ultimately become municipal property. Before 1890 local authorities had little concern with house building, and the Labouring Classes' Lodging Houses Act, 1851,[60] remained a dead letter. Under the Housing of the Working Classes Act, 1890, local authorities now possess large powers of buying

57. Darwin, pp. 3, 4.

58. *Ibid.*

59. The extension of municipal business has been constantly accompanied and accomplished by the compulsory purchase on the part of local authorities, of land, or other property, belonging to private individuals. It is worth notice that compulsory purchase might more accurately be termed compulsory sale, and always involves the possibility, or probability, that a man may be compelled to sell property either which he does not wish to sell at all, or which he does not wish to sell on the terms that he is compelled to accept. Such compulsory sale is often justified by considerations of public interest, but it always means a curtailment of the seller's individual liberty.

60. 14 & 15 Vict. c. 34.

up insanitary areas, of demolishing insanitary buildings, of letting out land to contractors under conditions as to the rebuilding of dwellings for the poor, and of selling to private persons the buildings thus erected. Municipalities have at the same time received powers to build additional houses on land not previously built upon, and to erect, furnish, and manage dwellings and lodging-houses. They have also entered into various trades. They have employed themselves, *e.g.* in turning dust into mortar, in working stone quarries, in building tram-cars, in the provision of buildings for entertainments and for music, in laying out race-courses, in the manufacture of electrical fittings, in the undertaking of telephone services, in the sale and distribution of milk, and the like. The desires, moreover, of municipalities have outstripped the powers hitherto conceded to them by Parliament. They desire to run omnibuses in connection with tramways; they wish to construct bazaars, aquaria, shops, and winter gardens; they wish to attract visitors to a district by advertising its merits. No one, in short, can seriously question that, for good or bad, the existence of municipal trading is one of the salient facts of the day, and that it has since the middle of the nineteenth century acquired a new character. The trades, if so they are to be called, which were first undertaken by local authorities were closely connected with the functions of municipal government. At the present day municipal trading is becoming an active competition for business between municipalities supported by the rates, and private traders who can rely only on their own resources. The aim, moreover, of municipal trading is, on the face of it, to use the wealth of the ratepayers in a way which may give to all the inhabitants of a particular locality benefits, *e.g.* in the way of cheap locomotion, which they could not obtain for themselves. Here we have, in fact, in the most distinct form the effort to equalise advantages. The present state of things, indeed, can in no way be more vividly described than by using the words of an author, who is certainly no opponent of socialism, and who, if he expresses himself with satirical exaggeration, means honestly to depict matters passing before our eyes:

> The practical man, oblivious or contemptuous of any theory of the social organism or general principles of social organisation, has been forced, by the necessities of the time, into an ever-deepening collectivist channel. Socialism, of course, he still rejects and despises. The individualist town councillor will walk along the municipal pavement, lit by municipal gas, and cleansed by

municipal brooms with municipal water, and seeing, by the municipal clock in the municipal market, that he is too early to meet his children coming from the municipal school, hard by the county lunatic asylum and municipal hospital, will use the national telegraph system to tell them not to walk through the municipal park, but to come by the municipal tramway, to meet him in the municipal reading-room, by the municipal art gallery, museum, and library, where he intends to consult some of the national publications in order to prepare his next speech in the municipal town hall, in favour of the nationalisation of canals and the increase of Government control over the railway system. "Socialism, Sir," he will say, "don't waste the time of a practical man by your fantastic absurdities. Self-help, Sir, individual self-help, that's what's made our city what it is."[61]

But here we pass to the second subject of this lecture.

(B) Trend of Collectivist Legislation

"It cannot be seriously denied," wrote Mr. Morley in 1881,

that Cobden was fully justified in describing the tendencies of this legislation [*i.e.* the factory laws] as socialistic. It was an exertion of the power of the State, in its strongest form, definitely limiting in the interest of the labourer the administration of capital. The Act of 1844 was only a rudimentary step in this direction. In 1847 the Ten Hours Bill became law. Cobden was abroad at the time, and took no part in its final stages. In the thirty years that followed, the principle has been extended with astonishing perseverance. We have to-day a complete, minute, and voluminous code for the protection of labour; buildings must be kept pure of effluvia; dangerous machinery must be fenced; children and young persons must not clean it while in motion; their hours are not only limited, but fixed; continuous employment must not exceed a given number of hours, varying with the trade, but prescribed by the law in given cases; a statutable number of holidays is imposed; the children must go to school, and the employer must every week have a certificate to that effect; if an accident happens notice must be sent to the proper authorities; special provisions are made for bakehouses, for lace-making, for collieries, and for a whole schedule of other special callings; for the due

61. See Sidney Webb, *Socialism in England* (1890), pp. 116, 117.

enforcement and vigilant supervision of this immense host of minute pre-scriptions there is an immense host of inspectors, certifying surgeons, and other authorities, whose business it is "to speed and post o'er land and ocean" in restless guardianship of every kind of labour, from that of the woman who plaits straw at her cottage door, to the miner who descends into the bowels of the earth, and the seaman who conveys the fruits and materials of universal industry to and fro between the remotest parts of the globe. But all this is one of the largest branches of what the most importunate socialists have been accustomed to demand; and if we add to this vast fabric of labour legislation our system of Poor Law, we find the rather amazing result that in the country where socialism has been less talked about than any other country in Europe, its principles have been most extensively applied.[62]

Thus wrote Mr. Morley in 1881 in a passage from his *Life of Cobden* which has become classical; his words directly refer only to the factory laws, but they admit of a far wider application. Every year which has passed since their publication has confirmed their truth.

The labour law of 1878 (41 & 42 Vict. c. 16) has been superseded and widely extended by the code whereof the details are to be found in the Factory and Workshop Act, 1901, 1 Edw. VII. c. 22. Not only factories and workshops, in the ordinary sense of those terms, but also any place such as a hotel, which is the scene of public labour, and even places of domestic employment which may fairly be called homes, have been brought within the sphere of the labour code. The time is rapidly approaching when the State will, as regards the regulation of labour, aim at as much omnipotence and omniscience as is obtainable by any institution created by human beings. Wherever any man, woman, or child renders services for payment, there in the track of the worker will appear the inspector. State control, invoked originally to arrest the ill-usage of children in large factories, has begun to take in hand the proper management of shops. A shop-girl has already acquired a legal right to a seat.[63] The hours of shop closing may now in most cases be fixed by a local authority[64]—that is, be regulated, not

62. Morley, *Life of Cobden*, i. pp. 302, 303.

63. Seats for Shop Assistants Act, 1899 (62 & 63 Vict. c. 21), and compare the Shop Hours Acts, 1892–1895, and the Employment of Children Act, 1903 (3 Edw. VII. c. 45).

64. See the Shop Hours Act, 1904 (4 Edw. VII. c. 31).

by the wishes of the shopkeeper, of his customers, or of the shopmen, but by rules imposed under the authority of the State. The Public Health Acts, starting in 1848 from the modest attempt to get rid of palpable nuisances calculated to generate disease, have expanded into the sanitary code of 1875,[65] which, with its complex provisions, constitutes a whole body of law for the preservation of the public health. The Housing of the Working Classes Acts, which in effect began with the Labouring Classes Lodging House Act, 1851,[66] and attempted little more than to make possible and encourage the establishment by boroughs, and certain other places, of lodging-houses for the labouring classes, have developed into the Housing of the Working Classes Acts,[67] 1890–1900.[68] These enactments enjoin local authorities to clear unhealthy areas, and to close unhealthy dwelling-houses, or demolish them if unfit for human habitation, and empower local authorities to provide lodging-houses for the working-classes, and with a view to making such provision, to acquire land where necessary under the system of compulsory purchase.[69] The State, therefore, has indirectly gone a good way towards the provision of dwelling-houses for workmen; the housing of artisans has become in great measure a matter of public concern. If the Housing of the Working Classes Acts have in the main benefited artisans, something has of recent years been done towards meeting any wish for allotments[70] which may be cherished by country labourers, who cannot themselves afford to purchase or to obtain a lease of lands at the market rate, or who, as is possible, live in villages where no landlord is willing to sell or let allotments. The local authorities are now, under the

65. The Public Health Act, 1875 (38 & 39 Vict. c. 55). See for a list of a large number of separate Acts more or less referring to public health, Steph., *Comm.* iii. (14th ed.) p. 77, and note that the Acts there referred to, which extend from the Knackers Acts, 1786 and 1844 (26 Geo. III. c. 71; 7 & 8 Vict. c. 87), to the Factory and Workshop Act, 1901, are all administered by District Councils. It should never be forgotten that powers given to local authorities are, no less than powers possessed by the central government, in reality powers exercised by the State.

66. 14 & 15 Vict. c. 34.

67. 53 & 54 Vict. c. 70.

68. 63 & 64 Vict. c. 59.

69. See Housing of Working Classes Act, 1890, especially s. 57.

70. Allotments Acts, 1887–1890 (50 & 51 Vict. c. 48, and 53 & 54 Vict. c. 65).

Allotments Acts, empowered to obtain land, and, if necessary, under the system of compulsory purchase, which they are to relet to labourers.

The growth of modern collectivism has naturally coincided with the disposition to revive or to extend the socialistic element[71] which has always been latent in some of the older institutions of England, and notably in the English Poor Law. The strength of this tendency[72] will be best seen by a comparison or contrast between the ideas which produced and characterised the Poor Law reform of 1834, and the ideas which in 1905 have already to a certain extent changed the law, and to a still greater extent modified the administration of poor relief. The reformers of 1834 considered the existence of the Poor Law a great, though for the moment a necessary evil. They cut down its operation within limits as narrow as public opinion would then tolerate. They expected to put an end at some not very distant date to out-door relief. Nor can one doubt that many of them hoped that the Poor Law itself might at last be done away with. As late as 1869 the central authorities struggled to increase the strictness with which out-door relief was administered, and in 1871 Professor Fawcett, a fair representative of the economists of that day, still apparently advocated its abolition.[73] The reformers, moreover, specially relied on the use of two means for at any rate restricting the administration of poor relief. The one was the confining it in the very sternest manner to the relief of destitution; the aim of relief was in their eyes to avert starvation, not to bestow comfort; the second was the association of pauperism—a very different thing from mere poverty—with disgrace; hence the recipient of poor relief lost, because he was a pauper, his rights as an elector.[74] The tide of opinion has turned; the very desire to restrict out-door relief has, as regards popular sentiment, all but vanished. The idea of putting an end to poor relief altogether lies far out of the range of practical politics. Much has already

71. See *Report of Charity Organization Society on Relief of Distress due to Want of Employment*, Nov. 1904.

72. Which has been fostered by the provisions of the Local Government Act, 1894 (56 & 57 Vict. c. 73), s. 20, as to the election and qualification of poor-law guardians.

73. See Fawcett, *Pauperism*, pp. 26–35. In 1872 he hoped for the gradual abolition of the poor law itself. Fawcett, *Essays and Lectures*, pp. 83, 84.

74. See Steph., *Comm.* ii. (14th ed.) 295; and Representation of People Act, 1832, s. 36; Parliamentary and Municipal Registration Act, 1878, ss. 7, 12.

been done to diminish the discomfort and the discredit which may attach itself to pauperism. The Out-door Relief (Friendly Societies) Act, 1894,[75] authorised boards of guardians, when granting out-door relief, not to take into consideration any sum up to five shillings a week received by the applicant as member of a friendly society. The Out-door Relief (Friendly Societies) Act, 1904,[76] has made a course of action which was optional imperative. Nor is the anticipation unwarranted that other classes will, at no distant date, obtain the consideration or indulgence which is extended to members of friendly societies. Discredit, indeed, still attaches to the receipt of poor relief, yet Parliament has already done much to diminish the force of a sentiment which men of admitted wisdom have been accustomed to regard as a valuable, if not our chief, safeguard against the spread of pauperism; the receipt of out-door relief in the shape of medicine no longer disqualifies the recipient from exercising the functions of an elector.[77]

75. 57 & 58 Vict. c. 25.

76. 4 Edw. VII. c. 32. "In granting out-door relief to a member of any friendly society, the board of guardians shall not take into consideration any sum received from such friendly society as sick pay, except in so far as such sum shall exceed five shillings a week" (s. 1, sub. s. 2).

The effect of this enactment seems to be that, assuming ten shillings a week to be the sum adequate to save a man who has no property whatever from actual destitution, an applicant for relief who, as member of a friendly society, receives a pension of five shillings a week, will be entitled to receive by way of out-door relief ten shillings more, and thus receive five shillings beyond his strict needs. Nor is it easy to see how a board of guardians can now practically exercise the power, which the board still apparently possesses, of refusing to give out-door relief at all to a person entitled to sick pay from a friendly society. If so the Out-door Relief (Friendly Societies) Act, 1904, distinctly strikes at attempts to cut down out-door relief.

77. The Medical Relief Disqualification Removal Act, 1885. See Steph., *Comm.* ii. 296. Leading statesmen, whether they call themselves Conservatives or Liberals, are ready or eager to go still farther along the dangerous path on which Parliament has hesitatingly entered. The President of the Local Government Board is ready, by straining to the very utmost powers conferred upon him for another purpose under the Local Authorities (Expenses) Act, 1887 (50 & 51 Vict. c. 72), s. 3, to sanction expenditure by Borough Councils which is admittedly *ultra vires*, and thus create a sort of Borough Council common poor-fund, which may in effect give to the unemployed relief untrammelled by the restrictions imposed by the poor law (see *Report of Charity Organization Society*, 1904, p. 6); and Sir H. Campbell-Bannerman, as leader of the Opposition, has announced that he is "in favour of exemption

The general trend of legislation is often as clearly traceable in Bills laid before Parliament, which have not passed into law, as in statutes. From this point of view the Bills of 1904 are full of instruction. They discover the wishes of the electors. They reveal, for instance, the widespread desire for laws which make for the equalisation of advantages.[78] The methods proposed for the attainment of this end are various. One is the provision, at the expense of the tax-payers, of old age pensions, either for every applicant who has attained the age of sixty-five, or for any person of sixty-five who belongs to the indefinable class of the deserving poor. The creation of a system of old age pensions has been recommended, though not fully thought out, both by zealous philanthropists who pity the sufferings, and by politicians of undoubted humanity who possibly desire the votes, of the wage-earners. Enthusiasts, again, who have been impressed with the indisputable fact that poverty may exist in connection with merit, have propounded a scheme under which the Guardians of the Poor are to be authorised, and, no doubt, if the plan should receive the approbation of Parliament, will soon be enjoined, to provide the "necessitous deserving aged poor" with cottage homes where the inhabitants "will be treated with regard to food and other comforts with suitable consideration," or, in other words, will enjoy at least as much comfort as and perhaps more comfort than usually falls to the lot of the energetic working-man who, towards the close of his life, has out of his earnings and savings provided himself with a modest independence. All these plans, whatever their advantages, have some features in common. They all try to divest the receipt of relief from the rates of the discredit and the disabilities which have hitherto attached to pauperism;[79] they negative the idea that it is, as a rule, the duty of every citizen to provide for his own needs, not only in youth, but in old age; and

---

from disenfranchisement of the recipients of temporary poor law relief" (*Morning Post,* 1st December 1904, p. 9).

78. See p. 195, *ante.*

79. "No person admitted to a [cottage] home shall be considered a pauper, or be subject to any such disabilities as persons in receipt of parochial relief" (Cottage Homes Bill, 1904, sec. 7).

"A person whose name is on the pensioners' list shall not be deprived of any right to be registered as a parliamentary or county voter by reason only of the fact that he or she has been in receipt of poor law relief" (Old Age Pensions Bill, sec. 8).

that if age, as depriving a man of capacity to work, may be termed a disease, yet it is a malady so likely to occur as to create a special obligation to ensure against its occurrence. Would not the stern but successful reformers of 1834 have held that old age pensions and comfortable cottage homes, provided at the cost of the tax-payers, were little better than a decent but insidious form of out-door relief for the aged?[80]

Among Bills which aim at the equalisation of advantages may be numbered a proposal significant, rather than important, for the removal of every limit on the amount which may be raised from the rates for the support of free libraries, and also many Bills, as important as they are significant, which are intended to facilitate in various ways the acquisition of land, or of an interest in land, generally through the direct or indirect intervention of the State, by persons unable to acquire either land or a lease of land through freely made contracts with willing vendors. The Bills of 1904 also bring into light another characteristic of collectivism, namely, the favour with which persons who have in any degree adopted socialistic ideals look upon combined as contrasted with individual action.[81] Trade unionists, it is clear, urgently demand a revolution in the combination law. They claim, as regards trade disputes, the practical abolition of the law of conspiracy, the legalisation of so-called peaceful, which may nevertheless be oppressive, picketing, and the anomalous exemption of a trade union and its members from civil liability for damage sustained by any one through the action of any member of such trade union.[82] All these changes

---

80. Might they not have smiled grimly at the notion of a parliamentary enactment that a man supported by parish relief and provided at the expense of the parish with a comfortable cottage should not be "considered a pauper" (Cottage Homes Bill, sec. 7), and have suggested that citizens should be trained to dread the reality rather than to shun the name of pauperism? What would they have thought of the sentiment or the sentimentality which has induced the Local Government Board to sanction the suggestion that in registers of births a workhouse should be referred to by some name (*e.g.* Little Peddlington Hall), which might conceal the fact that a child there born was born in a workhouse and not in a private residence?

81. See p. 188, *ante.*

82. "An action shall not be brought against a trade union . . . for the recovery of damage sustained by any person or persons by reason of the action of a member or members of such trade union" (Trade Dispute Bill, 1904, sec. 3).

"An action shall not be brought against a trade union, or against any person or persons

suggest the conclusion that English artisans are keenly alive to the necessity for using the severest "moral pressure," or indeed pressure which can hardly by any possible expansion of language be fairly termed "moral," as a restraint upon the selfishness of any workman or employer who acts in opposition to the apparent interest of a body of wage-earners. But these proposed changes also suggest the conclusion that English artisans are blind to the dangers involved in such an extension of the right of association[83] as may seriously diminish the area of individual freedom. This disposition to rate low the value of personal liberty, and to rate high the interest of a class, is to a certain extent illustrated by the Aliens Immigration Bill, 1904. This measure is on the face of it intended to restrain the settlement in England of foreign paupers, and other undesirable immigrants, whose presence may add to the mass of English poverty. It has been brought before Parliament by the Government, and is supposed, possibly with truth, to be supported by a large body of working-men. No one can deny that arguments worth attention may be produced in favour of the Aliens Bill; but it is impossible for any candid observer to conceal from himself that the Bill harmonises with the wish to restrain any form of competition which may come into conflict with the immediate interest of a body of English wage-earners. However this may be, the Bill assuredly betrays a marked reaction against England's traditional policy of favouring or inviting the immigration of foreigners, and in some of its provisions shows an indifference to that respect for the personal freedom, even of an alien, which may be called the natural individualism of the common law.[84]

---

representing the members of a trade union, in his or their respective capacity" (Trade Dispute Bill, No. 2, sec. 3).

The latter proposal seems intended to exempt trade unions from all civil liabilities whatever.

If in the Trade Dispute Bills the term "trade union" is to bear the meaning given to it in the Trade Union, etc., Act, 1876 (39 & 40 Vict. c. 22), sec. 16, a combination of employers would apparently be, if the Bill should pass into law, as exempt from all civil liability as a combination of workmen. (Compare, however, the Trade Disputes Act, 1906, 6 Edw. VII. c. 47.) [Editor's note: The previous sentence was added in the second edition.]

83. See pp. 109–113, *ante*.

84. The Bills which aim at increased restrictions on the sale of liquor hardly need separate notice, for they represent only the conviction, which for years has been known to exist, that the traffic in drink involves so many evils that it ought to be kept within narrow limits, even

For our present purpose the Bills brought before the Imperial Parliament are hardly more instructive than the recent legislation of some self-governing English Colonies.[85] Compulsory arbitration in all disputes between employers and employed—that is, the authoritative regulation by the State of the relation between these two classes; a vast extension of the factory laws, involving, *inter alia,* the regulation by law of the hours of labour for every kind of wage-earner, including domestic servants, the employment by the State of the unemployed, the fixing by law of fair wages; the rigid enforcement of a liquor law, which may render sobriety compulsory; the exclusion from the country of all immigrants, even though they be British subjects, whose presence working-men do not desire; and other measures of the same kind—would appear to approve themselves to the citizens of Australia and New Zealand. The similarity between the legislation which has actually taken place in these Colonies and laws passed or desired in England is worth notice, for it throws considerable light on the natural tendencies of that latent socialism or collectivism, not yet embodied in any definite socialistic formulas, which has for the last thirty years and more been telling with ever-increasing force on the development of the law of England.

Our survey of the course of law and opinion from 1830 onwards suggests two reflections:

The difference between the legislation characteristic of the era of individualism and the legislation characteristic of the era of collectivism is, we perceive, essential and fundamental. The reason is that this dissimilarity (which every student must recognise, even when he cannot analyse it) rests upon and gives expression to different, if not absolutely inconsistent, ways

---

at the cost of what teachers, such as John Mill, considered a grave inroad on individual liberty. The only feature worth special remark is the proposal, based on precedents drawn from the laws of Canada and the United States, to place an anomalous and most extensive liability on any seller of drink for injuries done by the purchaser to a third person during a state of intoxication wholly or partially arising from the drink he has bought (see Liquor Seller's Liability Bill, 1904, s. 2). Under this Bill, if *X*, a licensed person, sells drink to *Y* for consumption on such person's premises, which wholly or in part causes *Y's* intoxication, *X* would be liable to *A* for any injury done to *A* by *Y* whilst thus intoxicated.

85. See W. P. Reeves, *State Experiments in Australia and New Zealand.*

of regarding the relation between man and the State. Benthamite Liberals have looked upon men mainly, and too exclusively, as separate persons, each of whom must by his own efforts work out his own happiness and well-being; and have held that the prosperity of a community—as, for example, of the English nation—means nothing more than the prosperity or welfare of the whole, or of the majority of its members. They have also assumed, and surely not without reason, that if a man's real interest be well understood, the true welfare of each citizen means the true welfare of the State. Hence Liberals have promoted, during the time when their influence was dominant, legislation which should increase each citizen's liberty, energy, and independence; which should teach him his true interest, and which should intensify his sense of his own individual responsibility for the results, whether as regards himself or his neighbours, of his own personal conduct. Collectivists, on the other hand, have looked upon men mainly, and too exclusively, not so much as isolated individuals, but as beings who by their very nature are citizens and parts of the great organism—the State—whereof they are members. Reformers, whose attention has thus been engrossed by the social side of human nature, have believed, or rather felt, that the happiness of each citizen depends upon the welfare of the nation, and have held that to ensure the welfare of the nation is the only way of promoting the happiness of each individual citizen. Hence collectivists have fostered legislation which should increase the force of each man's social and sympathetic feelings, and should intensify his sense of the responsibility of society or the State for the welfare or happiness of each individual citizen.

The force of collectivism is, we all instinctively feel, not spent; it is not, to all appearance, even on the decline. That legislation should, for the present and for an indefinite time to come, deviate farther and farther from the lines laid down by Bentham, and followed by the Liberals of 1830, need, however, cause no surprise. Public opinion is, we have seen, guided far less by the force of argument than by the stress of circumstances,[86] and the circumstances which have favoured the growth of collectivism still continue in existence, and exert their power over the beliefs and the feelings of the public. Laws again are, we have observed, among the most potent

---

86. See pp. 18–21, *ante.*

of the many causes which create legislative opinion; the legislation of collectivism has continued now for some twenty-five or thirty years, and has itself contributed to produce the moral and intellectual atmosphere in which socialistic ideas flourish and abound. So true is this that modern individualists are themselves generally on some points socialists. The inner logic of events leads, then, to the extension and the development of legislation which bears the impress of collectivism.[87]

87. On a movement which has not yet reached its close, it is impossible to pronounce anything like a final judgment. It may be allowable to conjecture that, if the progress of socialistic legislation be arrested, the check will be due, not so much to the influence of any thinker as to some patent fact which shall command public attention; such, for instance, as that increase in the weight of taxation which is apparently the usual, if not the invariable, concomitant of a socialistic policy.

LECTURE IX *The Debt of Collectivism to Benthamism*

THE PATENT OPPOSITION between the individualistic liberalism of 1830 and the democratic socialism of 1905 conceals the heavy debt owed by English collectivists to the utilitarian reformers. From Benthamism the socialists of to-day have inherited a legislative dogma, a legislative instrument, and a legislative tendency.

The dogma is the celebrated principle of utility.

In 1776[1] Bentham published his *Fragment on Government.* The shrewdness or the selfishness of Wedderburn[2] at once scented the revolutionary tendency of utilitarian reform.

"This principle of utility," he said, "is a dangerous principle." On this dictum Bentham has thus commented:

Saying so, he [Wedderburn] said that which, to a certain extent, is strictly true; a principle which lays down, as the only *right* and justifiable end of Government, the greatest happiness of the greatest number—how can it be denied to be a dangerous one? Dangerous it unquestionably is to every Government which has for its *actual* end or object the greatest happiness of a certain *one,* with or without the addition of some comparatively small number of others, whom it is a matter of pleasure or accommodation to him to admit, each of them, to a share in the concern on the footing of so many junior partners. *Dangerous* it therefore really was to the interest—the sinister interest—of all those functionaries, himself included, whose interest it was to maximise delay, vexation, and expense in judicial and other modes of

1. In the same year was published Adam Smith's *Wealth of Nations.*

2. Afterwards Lord Chancellor, under the title of Baron Loughborough, and created in 1801 Earl of Rosslyn.

procedure for the sake of the profit extractible out of the expense. In a Government which had for its end in view the greatest happiness of the greatest number, Alexander Wedderburn might have been Attorney-General and then Chancellor; but he would not have been Attorney-General with £15,000 a year, nor Chancellor, with a peerage with a veto upon all justice, with £25,000 a year, and with 500 sinecures at his disposal, under the name of Ecclesiastical Benefices, besides *et ceteras.*[3]

In 1905 we are less surprised at Bentham's retort, which betrays a youthful philosopher's enthusiastic faith in a favourite doctrine, than at Wedderburn's alarm, which seems to savour of needless panic. What is there, we ask, in the greatest happiness principle—a truism now accepted by conservatives no less than by democrats—that could disturb the equanimity of a shrewd man of the world well started on the path to high office? Yet Wedderburn, from his own point of view, formed a just estimate of the principle of utility. It was a principle big with revolution; it involved the abolition of every office or institution which could not be defended on the ground of calculable benefit to the public; it struck at the root of all the abuses, such as highly-paid sinecures, which in 1776 abounded in every branch of the civil and of the ecclesiastical establishment; it aimed a deadly blow, not only at the optimism of Blackstone, but also at the historical conservatism of Burke. It went, indeed, much farther than this, for, as in any State the poor and the needy always constitute the majority of the nation, the favourite dogma of Benthamism pointed to the conclusion—utterly foreign to the English statesmanship of the eighteenth century—that the whole aim of legislation should be to promote the happiness, not of the nobility or the gentry, or even of shopkeepers, but of artisans and other wage-earners.

The legislative instrument was the active use of parliamentary sovereignty.[4]

The omnipotence of Parliament, which Bentham learned from Blackstone, might well, considered as an abstract doctrine, command the acquiescent admiration of the commentator. But the omnipotence of Parliament—turned into a reality, and directed by bold reformers towards the

3. Bentham, *Principles of Morals and Legislation,* ch. i. p. 5 (n).

4. See p. 118, *ante.*

removal of all actual or apparent abuses—might well alarm, not only adventurers who found in public life a lucrative as well as an honourable profession, but also statesmen, such as Pitt or Wilberforce, uninfluenced by any sinister interest. Parliamentary sovereignty, in short, taught as a theory by Blackstone and treated as a reality by Bentham, was an instrument well adapted for the establishment of democratic despotism.

The legislative tendency was the constant extension and improvement of the mechanism of government.

The guides of English legislation during the era of individualism, by whatever party name they were known, accepted the fundamental ideas of Benthamism. The ultimate end, therefore, of these men was to promote legislation in accordance with the principle of utility;[5] but their immediate and practical object was the extension of individual liberty as the proper means for ensuring the greatest happiness of the greatest number. Their policy, however, was at every turn thwarted by the opposition or inertness of classes biassed by some sinister interest. Hence sincere believers in *laissez faire* found that for the attainment of their ends the improvement and the strengthening of governmental machinery was an absolute necessity. In this work they were seconded by practical men who, though utterly indifferent to any political theory, saw the need of administrative changes suited to meet the multifarious and complex requirements of a modern and industrial community. The formation of an effective police force for London (1829)—the rigorous and scientific administration of the Poor Law (1834) under the control of the central government—the creation of authorities for the enforcement of laws to promote the public health and the increasing application of a new system of centralisation,[6] the invention of Bentham

---

5. See p. 98, *ante.*

6. The English Government, even during the supremacy of reactionary toryism, did not attempt to build up a stronger administrative system. "The revolutionary movements of 1795 and of 1815–1820 were combated, not by departmental action, but by Parliamentary legislation. The suspension of the Habeas Corpus Act, the passing of the Libel Act, and of the 'Six Acts' of 1819, were severely coercive measures; but they contain no evidence of any attempt to give a continental character to administration. In so far as individual liberty was destroyed, it was destroyed by, and in pursuance of, Acts of Parliament."—Redlich and Hirst, *Local Government in England,* ii. p. 240.

On the other hand, there has been built up since 1832 a whole scheme of administrative

himself[7]—were favoured by Benthamites and promoted utilitarian reforms; but they were measures which in fact limited the area of individual freedom.

In 1830 the despotic[8] or authoritative element latent in utilitarianism was not noted by the statesmen of any party. The reformers of the day placed for the most part implicit faith in the dogma of *laissez faire,* and failed to perceive that there is in truth no necessary logical connection between it and that "greatest happiness principle," which may, with equal sincerity, be adopted either by believers in individual freedom, or by the advocates of paternal government. To the Liberals of 1830 the energy and freedom of individuals seemed so clearly the source from which must spring the cure of the diseases which afflicted English society, that they could hardly imag-

---

machinery. "The net result of the legislative activity which has characterised, though with different degrees of intensity, the period since 1832, has been the building up piecemeal of an administrative machine of great complexity, which stands in as constant need of repair, renewal, reconstruction, and adaptation to new requirements as the plant of a modern factory. The legislation required for this purpose is enough, and more than enough, to absorb the whole legislative time of the House of Commons; and the problem of finding the requisite time for this class of legislation increases in difficulty every year, and taxes to the utmost, if it does not baffle, the ingenuity of those who are responsible for the arrangement of Parliamentary business."—Ilbert, *Legislative Methods,* pp. 212, 213. See generally Redlich and Hirst, i. pp. 1–216.

7. "He [Bentham] attempts to solve anew the problem of the relations between local and central government. In his system the Legislator is omnipotent. His local 'field of service' is the State, his logical 'field of service' is the field of human action. . . . But the central Parliament and its organ, the Ministry, always preserve a supervisory control over local administration. Here, then, is formulated the principle, novel to the historic constitution of England, that there is no province or function of public administration in which a central government in its administrative as well as its legislative capacity is not entitled to interfere. The new principle of 'inspectability' is expressed on the one hand by the supervisory control of the Ministry, on the other by the subordination of the Local Headman. The Minister at the top controls the Headman at the bottom of the official ladder. The light at the centre radiates to the very circumference of the State. In the next chapter it will be shown how potent a force this new idea of central administrative control proved in the reformation of English local government."—Redlich and Hirst, i. pp. 95, 96; compare pp. 89, 106–108.

8. The true ground of Herbert Spencer's attack on utilitarianism is that the utilitarians, in the pursuit of the greatest happiness for the greatest number, often sacrificed the freedom of individuals to the real or supposed benefit of the State, *i.e.* of the majority of the citizens. See *The Man* v. *The State,* and *Social Statics.*

ine the possibility of a conflict between the true interest of the community and the universal as well as equal liberty of individual citizens.[9] The Tories of the day, on the other hand, were so impressed with the hostility of the utilitarian school to institutions (*e.g.* the Crown or the Church), the strength whereof depended on tradition, that they were blind to the authoritative aspect of Benthamism. And, oddly enough, the tendency of Benthamite teaching to extend the sphere of State intervention was increased by another characteristic which conciliated Whigs and moderate Liberals—that is, by the unlimited scorn entertained by every Benthamite for the social contract and for natural rights. This contempt was indeed a guarantee against sympathy with Jacobinical principles, but it deprived individual liberty of one of its safeguards. For the doctrine of innate rights, logically unsound though it be, places in theory a limit upon the despotism of the majority. This doctrine is no doubt a very feeble barrier against the inroads of popular tyranny; the Declaration of the Rights of Man did not save from death one among the thousands of innocent citizens dragged before the Revolutionary Tribunal; the American Declaration of Independence, with its proclamation of the inalienable rights of man, did not deliver a single negro from slavery. But these celebrated documents were after all a formal acknowledgment that sovereign power cannot convert might into right. They have assuredly affected public opinion. In France the Declaration of the Rights of Man has kept alive the conviction that a National Legislature ought not to possess unlimited authority. Some articles in the Constitution of the United States, inspired by the sentiment of the Declaration of Independence, have supported individual freedom; one of them has gone far to make the faith that the obligation of contracts is sacred, a part of the public morality of the American people, and does at this mo-

---

9. Benthamites, indeed, differed among themselves more deeply than they probably perceived, as to the relative importance of the principle of utility and the principle of non-interference with each man's freedom. Nominally, indeed, every utilitarian regarded utility as the standard by which to test the character or expediency of any course of action (see Mill, *On Liberty*, p. 24). But John Mill was so convinced of the value to be attached to individual spontaneity that he, in fact, treated the promotion of freedom as the test of utility; other utilitarians, *e.g.* Chadwick, were practically prepared to curtail individual freedom for the sake of attaining any object of immediate and obvious usefulness, *e.g.* good sanitary administration.

ment place a real obstacle in the way of socialistic legislation. The Liberals then of 1830 were themselves zealots for individual freedom, but they entertained beliefs which, though the men who held them knew it not, might well, under altered social conditions, foster the despotic authority of a democratic State. The effect actually produced by a system of thought does not depend on the intention of its originators; ideas which have once obtained general acceptance work out their own logical result under the control mainly of events. Somewhere between 1868 and 1900 three changes took place which brought into prominence the authoritative side of Benthamite liberalism. Faith in *laissez faire* suffered an eclipse; hence the principle of utility became an argument in favour, not of individual freedom, but of the absolutism of the State. Parliament under the progress of democracy became the representative, not of the middle classes, but of the whole body of householders; parliamentary sovereignty, therefore, came to mean, in the last resort, the unrestricted power of the wage-earners. English administrative mechanism was reformed and strengthened. The machinery was thus provided for the practical extension of the activity of the State; but, in accordance with the profound Spanish proverb, "the more there is of the more the less there is of the less," the greater the intervention of the Government the less becomes the freedom of each individual citizen. Benthamites, it was then seen, had forged the arms most needed by socialists. Thus English collectivists have inherited from their utilitarian predecessors a legislative doctrine, a legislative instrument, and a legislative tendency pre-eminently suited for the carrying out of socialistic experiments.

LECTURE X   *Counter-Currents and Cross-Currents of Legislative Opinion*

WE HAVE HITHERTO TRACED the connection between the development of English law and different dominant currents of opinion.[1] To complete our survey of the relation between law and opinion, we must now take into account the way in which the dominant legislative faith, and therefore the legislation, of a particular time may be counteracted or modified either by the existence of strong counter-currents or cross-currents of opinion,[2] or by the difference between parliamentary and judicial[3] legislation.

Concerning counter-currents little need here be said. The topic has been amply illustrated in the foregoing pages. The story of Benthamite liberalism is specially instructive; the increasing force of liberalism was long held in check by the survival of old toryism; the authority of liberalism, when it had become the legislative faith of the day, was diminished by the gradually rising current of collectivism.

To the effect produced by cross-currents of opinion which, as already noted,[4] deflect the action of the reigning legislative faith from its natural course, little attention has been directed in these lectures, yet the topic deserves careful consideration. The influence of such cross-currents, operating as it does in an indirect and subtle manner, often escapes notice,

---

1. See pp. 45–214, *ante*.

2. See pp. 27–30, *ante*.

3. See Lecture XI., *post*. Logically the results of this difference are merely an illustration of the effect produced by a particular cross-current of opinion, namely, the legislative opinion of the judges, but the distinctions between the legislative opinion of Parliament and the legislative opinion of the Courts, and the way in which these two kinds of opinion act and react upon one another, is so noteworthy as to deserve separate consideration.

4. See pp. 29, 30, *ante*.

and is always somewhat hard to appreciate. The easiest method whereby to render the whole matter intelligible is to trace out the way in which such a cross-current has told upon the growth of some particular part of the law. For this purpose no branch of the law of England better repays examination than the ecclesiastical legislation of the years which extend from the era of the Reform Act (1830–32) to the close of the nineteenth century; for this legislation is affected at every turn on the one hand by the liberalism of the time, which aims at the establishment of religious equality, *i.e.* at the abolition of all political or civil privileges or disabilities dependent upon religious belief, and on the other hand by the cross-current of clerical, or rather ecclesiastical, opinion, which desires to maintain the rights or privileges of the Established Church, and demands deference for the convictions or the sentiments of the clergy and of churchmen. To see that this is so, let us, in regard to matters which can be termed ecclesiastical, in a wide sense of that word, examine first the course—that is, both the current and the cross-current, of legislative opinion from 1830 to 1900, and next the legislation to which this course of opinion has in fact given rise.

A. The Course of Legislative Opinion

In 1832 the passing of the Reform Act seemed to prove that any institution, however venerable, might be called upon to show cause for its existence, and, in default of a popular verdict in its favour, would undergo drastic amendment or revolutionary destruction. In these circumstances no one among all the ancient institutions of the country was, to outward appearance, more open to attack, and less capable of defence, than the United Church of England and Ireland.[5]

The policy of the popular leaders, whether Whigs or Benthamites, was essentially secular and anti-clerical.[6] The Whigs had always been the cool

5. It is well to remember that the Established Church of England was in 1832 indissolubly united with the Irish Church Establishment.

6. The legislative opinion of the day since 1830, except in so far as it has been modified by the opinion of the clergy or of churchmen, has assuredly been anti-clerical, at any rate to this extent, that it has been opposed to the maintenance of Church privileges, as well as

friends, if not the foes, of the clergy, and had found their most constant adherents among Dissenters. The doctrines of Bentham clearly pointed towards Disestablishment. In 1832 popular feeling identified zeal for the Church with opposition to reform, and considered bishops and parsons the natural allies of boroughmongers and Tories. At the moment when the vast majority of the electors demanded parliamentary reform with passionate enthusiasm, no class was the object of more odium than the bench of Bishops. Proposals were once and again brought before Parliament to expel them from the House of Lords. Whatever, again, might be the other effects of the Reform Act, it assuredly gave new power to what was then termed the Dissenting interest; at the meeting of the first reformed Parliament it seemed for a moment possible that Dissenters might exercise political predominance,[7] and the rule of Nonconformists could mean nothing less than a revolution in the position of the Church. These things, it may be said, were merely the appearances of the moment, but any man of sense must have perceived that the Church Establishment, whilst open to the charges of sinecurism and the like, which might be brought against the civil administration of the time, exhibited two special weaknesses of its own which both provoked assault by and promised success to its assailants: The National Church was not the Church of the whole nation; the privileges of the Establishment were in many cases the patent grievances of the laity.

The National Church was not the Church of the whole nation.

Protestant Nonconformists whose ancestors had been thrust out of the Church by the legislation of 1662—Wesleyans who were originally ardent Churchmen, but had separated from the Church because its leaders had not known how either to control or to turn to good use the fervour or

---

to any law or institution which makes a man's civil or political rights dependent upon his religious belief. As far as the ecclesiastical legislation of the nineteenth century goes, one need not draw any marked distinction between the era of individualism and the era of collectivism, though the gradual rise of collectivism may have indirectly increased the influence of clerical opinion.

7. Whenever classes of citizens are for the first time admitted to political rights, their immediate influence is exaggerated. In 1832, at any rate, Tories and Radicals alike imagined that the ten-pound householders had obtained an amount of power far greater than they were really able to exert.

fanaticism of passionate religious conviction—the Roman Catholic gentry, who, at the end of the eighteenth century, formed the most conservative part of the whole community—Unitarians who till 1813 had not enjoyed the protection of the Toleration Act, and, under a sense of bitter oppression, had sympathised with French Revolutionists—philosophic sceptics, such as Bentham and James Mill, who contemned and distrusted every kind of ecclesiastical power—each and all stood, either openly or secretly, outside the pale, and hostile to the pretensions of the Established Church.

The privileges of the Establishment were, to large bodies of Englishmen, intolerable grievances.

The marriage laws, which forbade the celebration of marriage otherwise than in accordance with the rites of the Church of England, outraged the self-respect and in some cases offended the conscience of Nonconformists; the tithes, and, above all, the mode of their collection, were a hindrance to the proper cultivation of the land, and made the parson of the parish, in the eyes of farmers who had no objection to the doctrine of the Church, stand in the position of an odious and oppressive creditor.

In these circumstances observers of the most different characters and of opposite opinions felt assured that the Church was in danger. In 1833 Macaulay wrote that in case the House of Lords should venture on a vital matter to oppose the Ministry, he "would not give sixpence for a coronet or a penny for a mitre";[8] and Dr. Arnold was convinced, as is clearly shown by his pamphlet on the *Principles of Church Reform,*[9] that the Church Establishment was in extreme peril. In 1834 the author of the first of the *Tracts for the Times* anticipates for the Church and its leaders not only disestablishment and disendowment, but violent persecution. He proclaims to every clergyman throughout England that, "black event as it would be for the country, yet (as far as they [the Bishops] are concerned) we could not wish them a more blessed termination of their course than the spoiling of their goods, and martyrdom."[10] In this language there lurks a touch of irony, yet Newman was far too earnest a zealot to threaten perils which he knew to be unreal, and far too skilful a rhetorician to betray fears which

8. Trevelyan, *Life of Macaulay,* i. p. 303.
9. See Arnold, *Miscellaneous Works,* p. 259; Stanley, *Life of Arnold,* i. p. 336.
10. *Tracts for the Times,* No. 1, p. 1.

his audience would hold to be ridiculous. When he published his appeal, *Ad Clerum,* thousands of churchmen believed that the Church of England was threatened with spoliation, ruin, and persecution; and men of the calmest judgment assuredly anticipated, whether with regret or with satisfaction, a revolution in the position of the Established Church. Between 1830 and 1836, then, it was assuredly no unreasonable forecast that the future of the Church of England might be summed up in the formula, "either comprehension or disestablishment"; the Church must, men thought, either embrace within its limits the whole, or nearly the whole, of the nation, or cease to be the National Church. No one could at that time have believed that the ecclesiastical legislation of the nineteenth century would fail to touch the foundations of the Establishment, or would pay any deference to the convictions or to the sentiment of the clergy. The experience of more than seventy years has given the lie to reasonable anticipations. The country has, since 1832, been represented first by a middle class Parliament, and next by a more or less democratic Parliament, yet has not sanctioned either comprehension or disestablishment. In all ecclesiastical matters Englishmen have favoured a policy of conservatism combined with concession.[11] Conservatism has here meant deference for the convictions, sentiments, or prejudices of churchmen, whenever respect for ecclesiastical feeling did not cause palpable inconvenience to laymen, or was not inconsistent with obedience to the clearly expressed will of the nation. Concession has meant readiness to sacrifice the privileges or defy the principles dear to churchmen, whenever the maintenance thereof was inconsistent with the abolition of patent abuses, the removal of grievances, or the carrying out of reforms demanded by classes sufficiently powerful to represent the voice or to command the acquiescence of the country.

What have been the circumstances that have given rise to this unforeseen and apparently paradoxical policy of conservatism and concession? To put the same inquiry in another shape: What have been the conditions of opinion which, in the sphere of ecclesiastical legislation, have prevented the dominant liberalism of the day from acting with anything like its full force, and have in many instances rendered it subordinate to the strong cross-current of clerical or Church opinion?

11. See *Reign of Queen Victoria,* i., Religion and the Churches, by E. Hatch, pp. 364–393.

These circumstances or conditions were, speaking broadly, the absence of any definite programme of Church reform commanding popular support; and the unsuspected strength of the hold possessed by the Church of England on the affections of the nation.

The Whigs certainly failed to produce any clear scheme of ecclesiastical reform. By no two men are they more fairly represented than by Sydney Smith and Macaulay. Neither of them was a zealous churchman, neither of them entertained any respect for clerical opinion or prejudice, but neither of them advocated any scheme of ecclesiastical reform. If Sydney Smith had believed that any extensive change in the position of the Establishment was desirable, he would assuredly have spoken out his mind. He had shocked the religious world and, as he no doubt well knew, had ruined his chance of high preferment by his expressed distrust and dislike of English missionaries and the missionary spirit. He perceived the failings and hated the cant of zealots, and in no way recognised their virtues. Religious enthusiasm meant to him, as to most eighteenth-century reformers, nothing but intolerance and ignorance. Any change which might give freer play in the Church to religious fervour or fanaticism was hateful to him. Hence, as regards ecclesiastical affairs, he was simply a Tory, and was indeed more averse to amendments in the administration of the Established Church than were intelligent Conservatives. Inequalities in the incomes of bishops or of clergymen were, he argued, a benefit to the public; the offer of a few large prizes was the cheapest way of remunerating clerical success, and— a far more important consideration in Sydney Smith's eyes than economy—constituted the best means for tempting scholars and gentlemen to take orders, and for excluding ignorant enthusiasts from the ranks of the clergy. "Beware of enthusiasm and cant, and leave the Establishment as far as possible alone." Thus may be summed up the only ecclesiastical policy suggested by the most keen-sighted and the ablest exponent of Whig doctrine.[12] Macaulay was by temperament and training opposed to ecclesias-

---

12. In Ireland, indeed, Sydney Smith favoured, in common with most of the Whigs, the policy of concurrent endowment; he showed no wish to apply it to England. In this there was no inconsistency. The maintenance in Ireland of a Church hateful to the vast majority of the people was exactly the kind of wrong which Sydney Smith and the Whigs felt most keenly. Concurrent endowment, moreover, might possibly cool the fanaticism of the Roman

tical pretensions, and, in accordance with the historical traditions of the Whigs, might, one would have supposed, have favoured some scheme for the comprehension of orthodox Dissenters within the National Church, but his name as a statesman cannot be connected with any policy of this description. His celebrated review, *Gladstone on Church and State,* leads to the practical conclusions that the ecclesiastical should not be allowed to interfere with the civil power, and that every man should enjoy equal political and civil rights, irrespective of his religious or non-religious convictions. This was the last word of Whig ecclesiastical statesmanship. The Whig leaders indeed must, as practical politicians, have felt instinctively that the day for a scheme of comprehension was past.[13] Immediately after the Revolution of 1688 it had been found impossible to secure for Dissenters more than toleration. Since that date, the rise both of Unitarianism[14] and of Wesleyanism had changed the whole position of Noncon-

---

Catholic priests, and, as far as was compatible with justice, prolong the existence of the Protestant Establishment.

13. For the attitude of Lord Melbourne in 1834 see *Annual Register,* 1834, p. 199. "All attempts at a religious comprehension of the Dissenters, and they had been made by some of the greatest prelates that ever adorned the episcopal bench, had failed; but, at all events, the House might make a step towards the object by a general civil comprehension of the Dissenters, and by admitting them to the benefits to be derived from the public institutions of the country. He [Lord Melbourne] apprehended that the Universities were originally founded for the support of literature and science; but he agreed that it was most desirable that Church of England principles should prevail in their system of education, and he would reserve to them complete their right to teach the religion of the country. At the same time, however, though he would not rashly meddle with honest prejudices and well-founded feelings, he would admit Dissenters for the sake of general peace and union; and in doing so he would only be sanctioning that which the most distinguished members of these very institutions had declared might be safely effected."—*Ibid.*

14. One school of thinkers, who really stood apart from both the Whigs and the Tories of their time, desired to comprehend the majority of English Protestants within the limits of the Establishment. It consisted of the small, though remarkable, body of men of whom Dr. Arnold is the best representative. He and his followers took up a peculiar position which hopelessly deprived them of influence. To the Low Churchmen of the day their soundness on doctrines, which to Evangelicals were of vital import, was open to the gravest suspicion. Anglicans were thoroughly estranged from a school whose leader offered the most strenuous opposition to every form of sacerdotalism. Whigs and Radicals could not act with Arnold

formists and their relation to the Established Church, and had, though in different ways, indefinitely increased the obstacles to a policy of comprehension. The Whigs of 1832 possessed, then, no definite scheme of Church reform.

Nor did the Benthamites stand in a stronger position than the Whigs. The philosophic Radicals held all ecclesiastical establishments to be at best of dubious utility, and expected them to vanish away with the progress of enlightenment. In all matters regarding the Church they were utterly at sea. They were stone-blind to the real condition of opinion in England. James Mill in 1835 published a scheme of Church reform. This programme is the work of a hard-headed Scotchman who had enjoyed considerable experience of the world, had studied theology in order to become a minister of, and had for a short time been a preacher in, the Church of Scotland,[15] yet his scheme reads almost like a grim joke, and was certainly far less applicable to the actual state of England than the proposal, already put forward by some Dissenters, to sever the connection between Church and State. For James Mill propounded a plan which may fairly be described as a proposal for the transformation of the Church of England into a national Mechanics' Institute, devoted to the propagation of Utilitarian doctrine. The Establishment, as it then existed, did nothing, he held, but harm; the creeds, the sermons, the Sunday services, prayer itself, were either useless or noxious. But, after all, as things stood, some use, he hoped, might be found for the clergy. When converted to Benthamism they might become salutary teachers of utilitarianism.

> The work of the clergy would thus consist in supplying all possible inducements to good conduct. No general rules could be given for the work,

---

when they found that his honest insistence upon the formal recognition of Christianity, as the religion of the State, compelled him to withdraw from all connection with the London University. In truth he was hampered at every step by his theory of the identity of State and Church. His teaching, though by no means the same as, is historically connected with, the Broad Churchmanship of a later day represented by Dean Stanley. But neither Arnold's immediate disciples nor the Broad Churchmen produced much permanent effect on the legislation of the nineteenth century. They were unable to remove the Athanasian Creed from the Liturgy of the Church of England; they could not even relegate it, as it has been banished by the disestablished Church of Ireland, to an appendix to the Prayer-Book.

15. Bain, *James Mill*, pp. 22, 23.

but tests might be applied for results. Such would be—premiums for the minimum of crimes, of law-suits, of pauperism, of ill-educated children. The assembling of all the families on the Sunday, clean and well-dressed, has an ameliorating effect. Besides addresses of a purely moral kind, instruction in science and useful knowledge would be of great service. Even branches of political science might be introduced, such as political economy and the conditions of good government. Some of the elements of jurisprudence would be valuable—to teach the maxims of justice and the theory of protection of rights.

These would be the more serious occupations of the day of rest. There should also be social amusements of a mild character, such as to promote cheerfulness rather than profuse merriment. Sports involving bodily strength are not well adapted to promote brotherly feelings; their encouragement in antiquity had in view the urgency of war. Music and dancing would be important. It would be desirable to invent dances representing parental, filial, and fraternal affections, and to avoid such as slide into lasciviousness, which the author is always anxious to repress. Quiet and gentle motions, with an exhibition of grace, are what would be desired. To keep everything within the bounds of decency, the parishioners would elect a master and a mistress of ceremonies, and support their authority. A conjoint meal on Sunday would have the happiest effects, being a renewal of the *Agapai*—love feasts—of the early Christians; but with the exclusion of intoxicating liquors.[16]

This was the kind of reform advocated by the ablest among the Benthamites, whom his son, and doubtless other admiring pupils, mistook for a statesman. The publication of his programme in the *London Review* damaged the circulation of that periodical. To a modern critic it hopelessly ruins the reputation for statesmanship of the philosophic Radicals. It betrays their fundamental weakness. In ecclesiastical affairs they possessed neither insight not foresight; they did not understand the England in which they lived, they did not foresee the England of the immediate future. James Mill published his scheme of Church reform in 1835. In 1834 had appeared the first of the *Tracts for the Times,* which as regards the public opened the Oxford High Church movement.[17]

16. Bain, *James Mill,* pp. 387, 388.

17. Some authorities date it from Keble's sermon on National Apostasy, 1833. Coleridge, *Memoir of Keble,* p. 218. Incapacity for dealing with ecclesiastical questions characterised the

Although men of piety, and of public spirit, in all denominations, were profoundly aware of defects in the Establishment, and though many Dissenters felt certain privileges of the Church to be oppressive, the cause of Church reform did not at this time command popular support. James Mill's proposals were no more acceptable to Dissenting ministers than to clergymen. The demand for Disestablishment, though formulated at least as early as 1834, did not even among Nonconformists obtain any wide favour. The Established Church, if not highly esteemed, was not hated either by Whigs or by Radicals. Dr. Arnold, who in 1832 had believed that Disestablishment and Disendowment were immediately at hand, was prepared in 1840 to acknowledge his error.[18] Englishmen, after their manner,

---

philosophic liberalism of the eighteenth century. To this defect Quinet ascribes the mistakes and failures of revolutionary statesmanship in all matters of Church policy. [Editor's note: The rest of this footnote was added in the second edition.] An idea was certainly current at the end of the eighteenth and the beginning of the nineteenth century that religious differences would become politically unimportant. "Let us," writes Burke, in 1792, "form a supposition (no foolish or ungrounded supposition) that in an age when men are infinitely more disposed to heat themselves with political than religious controversies, the former should entirely prevail, as we see that in some places they have prevailed, over the latter; and that the Catholics of Ireland, from the courtship paid them on the one hand, and the high tone of refusal on the other, should, in order to enter into all the rights of subjects, all become Protestant dissenters, and as the others do, take all your oaths. They would all obtain their civil objects; and the change, for any thing I know to the contrary (in the dark as I am about the Protestant dissenting tenets), might be of use to the health of their souls. But, what security our constitution in Church or State could derive from the event I cannot possibly discern. Depend upon it, it is as true as nature is true, that if you force them out of the religion of habit, education, or opinion, it is not to yours they will ever go. Shaken in their minds, they will go to that where the dogmas are fewest; where they are the most uncertain; where they lead them the least to a consideration of what they have abandoned. They will go to that uniformly democratic system to whose first movements they owed their emancipation."—M. Arnold, *Edmund Burke on Irish Affairs*, Letter to Sir H. Langrishe, M.P., pp. 270, 271.

18. The "pamphlet [on Church Reform] was written on the supposition—not implied, but expressed repeatedly—that the Church Establishment was in extreme danger. . . . I mistook, undoubtedly, both the strength and intenseness of the movement, and the weakness of the party opposed to it; but I do not think that I was singular in my error—many persisted in it; Lord Stanley, for example, even in 1834, and the subsequent years—many even hold it

wished to amend the obvious faults of an existing institution, and were eager to get rid of immediate and pressing grievances, but cared nothing for the assertion of general principles.

Even in 1832 the Church, though suffering from transitory unpopularity, possessed a source of untold strength in its recognition as the Church of the nation.

The Bishops were the object of violent attack, but they were reviled, not because they were prelates, but because they were Tories. Had they seen their way to advocate parliamentary reform, the episcopal bench would have become the most popular part of the House of Lords. The Church Establishment was full of abuses, but these defects did not excite indignation among the mass of the people. The easygoing parsons of the old school were not, except when they pressed too hard for tithes, disliked by their parishioners. Lax discharge of clerical duty by a rector or vicar, who might be described as a squire who wore a white tie, excited little attention and less censure. The new fervour and the moral severity of an Evangelical clergyman occasionally aroused opposition.[19] But moral worth always with Englishmen gains respect, and the religious energy of the Evangelicals, after all, gave increased dignity and weight to the clergy. Low Church doctrine, moreover, combined with the prevalent dread of French infidelity, and with the traditional fear of Popery, created a bond of sympathy between the most religious of the clergy and the most religious among orthodox Dissenters. At no time since 1662 has there been, it may be conjectured, more community of feeling between the clergy of the Established Church and Nonconformist ministers than during the last quarter of the eighteenth and the first quarter of the nineteenth century. At that period Evangelical clergymen, occasionally at any rate, preached in Dissenting chapels; community of religious conviction nearly, it seems, broke down the barriers which divided members of the Church from Dissenters.[20] However this

---

still, when experience has proved its fallacy."—Letter of Arnold in 1840, Stanley, *Life of Arnold,* i. (5th ed.), p. 336.

19. See *Venn Family Annals,* p. 187.

20. Note the friendly relations between George Butt, incumbent of Kidderminster, and the Dissenting ministers of the town, as described in the biography of Butt's daughter, the well-known Mrs. Sherwood. The whole tone of her stories implies that community of reli-

may be, the Established Church had been at no time during the eighteenth century unpopular with the body of the people. It was the High Church-manship of Sacheverell which in 1710 made him the hero both of the gentry and of the mob. In 1791 the people of Birmingham were as ready to destroy Dissenting chapels, and to burn down the houses of Priestley and other democrats who toasted the sovereignty of the people as to shout "Church and King for ever." In 1794 the villagers of Lavenham proved their loyalty to the Church by the attempt to destroy the home of Isaac Taylor, the most estimable and religious of independent ministers.

"The Revolution in France," writes his daughter Mrs. Gilbert,[21]

> had [in 1794] produced, in England, universal ferment, and with it, fear. Parties in every nook and corner of the country bristled into enmity, and the Dissenters, always regarded as the friends of liberty, fell under the fury of toryism, exploding from the corrupt under-masses of what, in many places, was an all but heathen population. "No Press, no Press," meaning no Pres-byterians, was the watchword of even our quiet town. Troops of ill-disposed, disorderly people often paraded the streets with this hue-and-cry, halting, especially, at the houses of known and leading Dissenters. On one occasion, as has been related, both in my sister's *Life* and in my brother's *Recollections,* our house was only saved from wreck by the appearance of our clerical neigh-bour, Mr. Cooke, at his door, with a request to the vagabond concourse to pass on, but the credit of which interference he entirely disclaimed to my father when he went to thank him the next day, coolly giving as his reason

---

gious convictions obliterated in her mind any marked distinction between members of the Church of England and Nonconformists. Note, too, the respect felt by members of the Church of England for Robert Hall. The action of Henry Venn of Huddersfield is also instructive. "In one case Mr. Venn certainly gave very definite assistance to the establishment of a Dissenting congregation, but this was somewhat early in his career [1771], and his son assures us that he afterwards strongly regretted the step he had taken."—*Venn Family Annals,* p. 95. [Editor's note: The rest of this footnote was added in the second edition.]

"We do not differ from our brethren in the Establishment in essentials: we are not of two distinct religions: while we have conscientious objections to some things enjoined in their public service. We profess the same doctrines which they profess; . . . we have the same rule of life; and maintain, equally with them, the necessity of that 'holiness, without which none shall see the Lord.'"—Robert Hall, 1831, *Works,* v. p. 317, cited Henson, *Religion in the Schools,* p. 104.

21. Better known as Anne Taylor.

that Mrs. Cooke's sister was unwell at the time, and the disturbance might have been injurious to her.[22]

The Established Church, in short, though not co-extensive with the people of England, was, even in 1832, felt to be the National Church in a sense in which no other religious body could claim to be the representative of the nation.

If the clergy were, during the contest over the Reform Bill, regarded with suspicion as Tories, neither then nor at any other time since the Restoration has Dissent commanded any general popularity whatever. During the eighteenth century Dissenters suffered under the tradition of Puritanic severity and hypocrisy. In 1832 Dissent was connected in public opinion with vulgarity and fanaticism. Novels, it has been well said, never lie; they always reflect the features of the time in which they were written. Now it is easy enough to find in the literature of English fiction more or less favourable pictures of the clergy. The Vicar of Wakefield has been laughed at and loved by one generation of Englishmen after another. Miss Austen's young clergymen would not satisfy Miss Yonge's ideal of clerical zeal; but they are well-meaning, kindly young fellows, who no doubt were admired by Miss Austen's heroines and Miss Austen's readers. They certainly were not persons at all likely to excite any hostility among good-natured Englishmen. Modern novels are almost without exception friendly in their tone towards the Established Church, and teem with clerical heroes. Contrast the treatment—in the main the grossly unfair treatment—which Dissenting ministers have till fifty or sixty years ago received at the hands of novel-writers. Warren's[23] *Ten Thousand a Year* tells us how Dissenters were regarded by a vulgar but very effective Tory satirist of 1839. The meanest character in a novel which abounds with vulgar characters vulgarly caricatured, is a Dissenter who ends his career as an agitator against Church rates, whilst the gentleman-like virtues of the Tory rector are made the object of unctuous admiration. The Shepherd of the *Pickwick Papers* and the Chadband

---

22. *Autobiography, etc., of Mrs. Gilbert*, vol. i. pp. 78, 79.

23. The novelist was brought up in an atmosphere of devout and very strict Methodism. He was the son of Dr. Samuel Warren, who became a highly influential Wesleyan minister and preacher, but who later in life (1838) was admitted to orders in the Church of England.

of *Bleak House* are caricatures of Dissenting vulgarity and cant drawn by a man of genius who began life as a Benthamite Liberal, who at no period of his career believed himself to be a Tory, and who was the most widely read novelist of his day.[24]

The Church Establishment, further, if in 1832 it was strong both in its own inherent strength and in the weakness of its opponents, assuredly obtained, for some time at any rate, a great increase of power from the High Church movement. With the religious side of this movement these lectures have no concern; it must here be regarded simply as a current of opinion which enhanced the political authority of the Established Church. It was from this point of view a most successful effort to impress upon Churchmen, and especially upon clergymen, the belief that the very existence of the Established Church was in peril, to inspire clerical convictions with new life, and to place Church opinion in direct opposition to the liberalism which undermined the basis of ecclesiastical authority. Newman's appeal, *Ad Clerum*—the first of the *Tracts for the Times*—contains the gist of the whole matter. The clergy are warned that they may any day be deprived of the advantages which accrue to them from their connection with the State; they cannot rely upon their wealth or upon the dignity of their position. If they are not to sink to the level of Dissenting ministers, they must trust in some source of power which the State cannot touch. They must remember that they, and they only, are in England the representatives of the Apostles; they must magnify their office and glory in their special authority.

"Therefore, my dear Brethren," writes Newman,

> act up to your professions. Let it not be said that you have neglected a gift; for if you have the Spirit of the Apostles on you, surely this *is* a great gift. "Stir up the gift of God which is in you." Make much of it. Show your value of it. Keep it before your minds as an honourable badge, far higher than that secular respectability, or cultivation, or polish, or learning, or rank, which

24. It may be doubted whether in a single novel of high repute published before 1850 there will be found a favourable picture of an English Dissenting minister. This statement has, of course, no application to pictures of Presbyterian ministers, or of Presbyterianism by Scottish writers.

gives you a hearing with the many. Tell *them* of your gift. The times will soon drive you to do this, if you mean to be still anything. But wait not for the times. Do not be compelled, by the world's forsaking you, to recur as if unwillingly to the high source of your authority. Speak out now, before you are forced, both as glorying in your privilege, and to ensure your rightful honour from your people. A notion has gone abroad, that they can take away your power. They think they have given and can take it away. They think it lies in the Church property, and they know that they have politically the power to confiscate that property. They have been deluded into a notion that present palpable usefulness, produceable results, acceptableness to your flocks, that these and such like are the tests of your Divine commission. Enlighten them in this matter. Exalt our Holy Fathers, the Bishops, as the Representatives of the Apostles, and the Angels of the Churches; and magnify your office, as being ordained by them to take part in their Ministry.[25]

To imagine that Newman's appeal aimed at a political, rather than a religious, object would be the height of unfairness, no less than of absurdity; but his manifesto, and the writings and the action of the Tractarian leaders, had assuredly, in the long-run, a most important political result. The High Church movement reinvigorated the faith of the clergy in their own high authority; it disciplined them for political no less than for ecclesiastical conflicts. If youthful Radicals, such as John Sterling, could ask whether the Church had not in every parish its black dragoon, we may feel well assured that these isolated soldiers became for the moment tenfold more powerful when brigaded into regiments and trained to fight as defenders of the Church. Newman and his allies created such a Church party as had not existed in England since the days of the Stuarts. This was an achievement for which the Evangelicals were not qualified. Their leaders exercised great influence, they in the main supported the Tory governments of the day. But the authority of the Evangelical clergy depended upon their doctrine and upon their zeal, not upon their clerical character. They were many of them in close sympathy with Dissenters. The Evangelicals were, at the time when they were most powerful in the religious world of England, guided at least as much by laymen as by clergymen. The so-called Clapham sect consisted to a great extent of men who were not in orders.

---

25. *Tracts for the Times,* vol. i. 1833–34, No. 1, pp. 3, 4.

The authority of Wilberforce was as great as the authority of Simeon. The Evangelicals were indeed churchmen, but since their strength did not lie in their churchmanship, it was impossible for them to form an ecclesiastical party such as has been the outcome of the High Church movement. The High Churchmen of 1834 were the leaders—in many cases, no doubt, unconsciously—of an assault from the side of the Church upon individualism,[26] and represented the intellectual and moral reaction against the reasonableness or the rationalism of the eighteenth century. Thus the course of events and of opinion since 1834 has assuredly, from some points of view, strengthened the position of the Established Church. The expansion, or transformation, of the High Churchmanship, which was the peculiar creed of a Church party, into the Anglicanism which at this moment apparently characterises the general body of the clergy, and may be described as the faith of the modern Church of England, has welded the clergy and their adherents into a homogeneous body which can exert considerable political power in defence of the interests or the convictions of churchmen. The same change has also more or less dissociated zealous churchmanship from Tory principles. The advance of democracy has transferred political predominance from the ten-pound householders, among whom lay the strength of the Dissenting interest, to the working classes, who, so far at any rate as they are represented by the artisans, are seemingly indifferent to the religious questions which divide High Churchmen from Low Churchmen, or Churchmen from Dissenters. The body of wage-earners may not read the reports of a Church congress, but there is no reason to suppose that they subscribe largely to the funds of the Liberation Society. Indifference tells in favour of the Established Church as of other established institutions. Opposition, lastly, to individualism constitutes a genuine, if as yet unrecognised, bond between clericalism and collectivism. No doubt there is another side to the picture. The changes of ecclesiastical opinion since 1834 have, in some respects, widened the separation between the convictions of the clergy and the convictions of the laity. All that need here be insisted upon is that, from some points of view, the political, and therefore the legislative power of the Established Church has been increased; in

26. See Lect. XII. pp. 284–290, *post*.

any case it has been for seventy years and more a power which every politician has been compelled to take into account.[27]

Since 1832 not an Act of Parliament directly or indirectly affecting the Church has been passed which does not bear traces of the influence exerted by ecclesiastical opinion.

From this date onwards the conflict between the dominant liberalism of the day and clerical or ecclesiastical opinion made the political position a strange one. The Established Church, as the Whigs soon found, was not the weakest, but one among the strongest of existing institutions. The attempt to deal, in the most moderate manner, with the patent defects of the Church Establishment in Ireland shattered the Reform Ministry. Within two years after the passing of the Reform Act the Whig Premier gave a pledge not to sanction attacks upon the Church. To open English universities to Dissenters was an impossibility; to provide Dissenters with anything like a real university of their own overtasked the power of the Ministry. The election of 1834 showed that the tide of public opinion no longer flowed strongly in favour of reform, but it also showed that the nation demanded the removal of those defects of the Church Establishment which were condemned by all serious churchmen and all intelligent Conservatives. For this work Peel was as ready as any Whig Premier. The creation of the Ecclesiastical Commission and all the reforms it involved were made possible because in this matter the Whig Ministry of 1836 was supported by the Bishops and by the Conservative Opposition.

Gradually the necessary, or at any rate the easiest, line of action became clear. The fundamentals of the Establishment must be left untouched; patent abuses which shocked the dominant opinion of the day, or grievances which irritated powerful classes, must be removed, but even the most salutary reforms might be long delayed and tempered or curtailed out of deference to the principles or the sentiment of Churchmen. Here we have

27. Political dissent or the development among Nonconformists of distinct opposition to all connection between Church and State on any terms whatever dates, it is said, from 1834. The movement for Disestablishment has combined with the High Church movement of 1835 to prevent fundamental alterations in the position or the doctrine of the Establishment. In 1832 the Church forbade Disestablishment. Political dissent, as represented by Mr. Miall and the *Nonconformist* newspaper, has negatived all idea of comprehension.

the policy of conservatism combined with concession which has coloured the whole of modern ecclesiastical legislation.

B. *The Actual Course of Ecclesiastical Legislation*

Note first its essential conservatism. Parliament has in no way altered the doctrine or extended the boundaries of the Church of England.[28] Nonconformists who stood outside the National Church in 1832 have not been brought within its limits.

Note next the extent of the concessions gradually made to the permanent demand for reform, and note, at the same time, that each concession to liberalism has been tempered by deference for ecclesiastical opinion.

The demand for reform took two shapes. It was either a demand for the amendment of abuses within the Established Church, *i.e.* for internal reform, or a demand for the removal of grievances connected with the Establishment, but which were mainly felt by persons not belonging to the Established Church, *i.e.* for external reform.

As to internal reform. Abuses which shocked even zealous Churchmen were in 1835 made patent to the whole nation by the Report of the Commissioners appointed to inquire into the financial condition of the Establishment. The state of things thus revealed has been well described by a judicious writer.

---

28. In 1791 Bishop Watson wrote to the Duke of Grafton: "In England we certainly want a reform, both in the civil and ecclesiastical part of our constitution. Men's minds, however, I think, are not yet generally prepared for admitting its necessity. A reformer of Luther's temper and talents would, in five years, persuade the people to compel the Parliament to abolish tithes, to extinguish pluralities, to enforce residence, to confine episcopacy to the overseeing of dioceses, to expunge the Athanasian Creed from our Liturgy, to free Dissenters from Test Acts, and the ministers of the establishment from subscription to human articles of faith."—Watson's *Memoirs*, p. 256, and see Bain, *James Mill*, p. 381. More than a century has passed since Watson wrote these words. Observe how incompletely his anticipation of impending changes has been fulfilled. Tithes are still paid, the Athanasian Creed still remains part of our Liturgy, ministers of the Church are not freed from subscription to human articles of faith.

The income of the Episcopate was found sufficient to provide, on an average, £6000 a year to each see. But how was this distributed? So as to give over £19,000 a year apiece to the Archbishop of Canterbury and the Bishop of Durham; over £11 000 a year to the Archbishop of York, and to each of the Bishops of London, Winchester, and Ely; while Rochester had to put up with less than £1500, and Llandaff with but £900 a year. The revenues of the cathedrals and collegiate churches were on such a scale that the Commissioners had no hesitation in reporting that the objects of those institutions might be fully secured and continued, and their efficiency maintained, consistently with a considerable reduction of their revenues, a portion of which should be appropriated towards making a better provision for the cure of souls. The deficiency of church accommodation in the big towns, and the dearth of clergy, caused almost a denial of religious instruction to the population of many parishes, so far, at least, as the State Church was concerned. In four parishes of London and the suburbs, containing over 160,000 persons, there was church accommodation for little over 8000, while in the same district there were but eleven clergymen; and this notwithstanding all that had been done by private generosity and by Act of Parliament to increase the number of churches and chapels and to augment benefices throughout the kingdom. In many parishes the income was too small to support a clergyman, so that the work was often done by the incumbent of another parish, thus giving rise to another evil, that of non-residence and the holding of a plurality of livings by one clergyman. Nearly 300 livings were found to be of less value than £50 a year, rather more than 2000 less than £100, and about 3500 less than £150, and in many of these incumbencies there was no house for the incumbent. At the other end of the scale were nearly 200 livings enjoying an income exceeding £1000 a year, the most valuable being that of Doddington, in the diocese of Ely, where, owing to the reclamation of fen land, the tithe had enormously increased.[29]

Add to this that the means of enforcing discipline upon the clergy, and especially of removing from the cure of souls men obviously unfit to discharge clerical duty, were wanting, or at any rate were grossly inadequate. Non-residence, sinecurism, and pluralism had at the same time, in part at any rate from changes in circumstances for which no man was morally responsible, come to pervade the whole Church Establishment—and this

29. Elliot, *The State and the Church* (2nd edition), pp. 104, 105.

state of things existed at a time when, for at least fifty years, the standard of clerical duty had been gradually rising at least as much among the clergy as among the laity of England. The need for reform was urgent; it was met by several measures.

Of these the chief were the Ecclesiastical Commissioners Acts, 1836 and 1840.[30] This legislation,[31] if we dismiss from our view all minor details, is marked by two leading features:

1. It is founded on the principle, then unknown to English law, that the property of bishops and chapters ought to be considered the property of the Church as a sort of quasi-corporation, and ought to be employed for the benefit of the Church as a whole.[32] This principle was in 1836 a novelty. Historically, the Church of England has never been a corporation, nor has it ever in strictness been the owner of any property;[33] the so-called wealth of the Church has been the wealth of bishops, deans, chapters, and other ecclesiastical corporations, of which the Church as an establishment is composed.

2. It gives effect to this new principle by the creation of a new and perpetual corporation, namely, the Ecclesiastical Commissioners for England. The functions of this corporation were to hold as trustee for the Church at large funds derived from the surplus[34] revenue of bishops and chapters, and, in accordance with powers given by Act of Parliament, to carry out various necessary reforms. Of these reforms the earliest was the provision of more or less fixed, though not always equal, incomes for bishops; combined with such an equalisation of episcopal incomes as might provide for most bishops a yearly income of from £4000 to £5000.

---

30. *I.e.* 6 & 7 Will. IV. c. 77, which relates to bishoprics, and 3 & 4 Vict. c. 113, which relates to chapters. See also Elliot, *State and Church* (2nd ed.), c. xi. and Appendix, Note II., *post*, Ecclesiastical Commission.

31. In which should be included the Ecclesiastical Commissioners Acts, 1841–1885.

32. It is hardly necessary to state that in the Acts of 1836 and 1840, as indeed in all the Ecclesiastical Commissioners Acts, the vested interests of individuals were carefully respected.

33. Elliot (2nd ed.), pp. 79, 108.

34. *I.e.* that part of the revenue of any bishop or chapter which in the opinion of Parliament exceeded the amount necessary or suitable for the performance of his or its duties.

This legislation has produced immense results. It has fixed the incomes of archbishops and bishops; it has, while making due allowance for the greater dignity and importance, and for the peculiar circumstances of certain sees, *e.g.* the archbishopric of Canterbury, and the see of London, more or less equalised the incomes of other bishops; it has suppressed sinecures and non-residentiary offices in cathedrals, as well as reduced the number of residentiary canons; it has settled the maximum incomes for deans and canons; it has transferred the surplus estates and revenues resulting from all these transactions to the Commissioners to be applied by them to the augmentation of poor benefices, to the endowment of new ones, and otherwise towards making increased provision for the cure of souls in places where it is most needed.

This legislation has, in truth, as regards the financial position of the Church of England, amounted to a revolution. But this revolution has—and this is the point which specially deserves our notice—been marked by tender consideration for the conservatism and the fears of Church people. Of this let two examples suffice.

The Ecclesiastical Commission, it was feared, might as originally constituted[35] become a mere department of the civil Government. This fear, though natural, was not reasonable. A board consisting of thirteen persons, all of whom were of necessity churchmen, and five of whom were bishops, could not, even though it did contain high officials such as the Lord Chancellor and the First Lord of the Treasury, who would always form part of the Cabinet, come under the control of the Government for the time being. But attention was paid to the nervousness of Churchmen. In 1840 the constitution of the Commission was modified, so that all bishops became

---

35. "The original composition of the corporation under the Act of 1836 seemed almost to contemplate its becoming a department of the State, so closely were its members connected with the Government of the day. The First Lord of the Treasury, the Lord Chancellor, a Secretary of State, the Lord President of the Council, and the Chancellor of the Exchequer, with the Archbishops and the Bishops of London, Lincoln, and Gloucester, with three distinguished laymen named in the Act, formed the original Ecclesiastical Commission, and provision was made that in supplying vacancies the proportion of laymen to bishops should be preserved, and that the former should of necessity be members of the Church of England."—Elliot, *The State and the Church* (2nd ed.), pp. 106, 107.

ex officio Commissioners. The Commission has not become, and is not likely to become, a Government office.

Bishops and other ecclesiastical dignitaries were in danger, it was fancied, of sinking into mere stipendiaries, receiving from the State fixed incomes, which might any day be diminished or cut off by Parliament, and such dignitaries, it was feared, might at least lose the consideration which in England attaches to the ownership of large estates. These fears were not unnatural to a generation which could recollect the spoliation of the Church of France. But the complex provisions of the Ecclesiastical Commissioners Acts as to the mode of dealing, *e.g.* with episcopal property, betray the painful anxiety of Parliament that no bishop should lose the dignified position of a landowner. The Ecclesiastical Commissioners Act of 1836 in effect enacts that a bishop should pay the surplus revenue of his see to the Ecclesiastical Commissioners, but should retain the estates from which his revenue is derived. The ideal aimed at by the reformers of 1836, in short, was not to deprive the bishops of their estates, but that each bishop should be endowed with sufficient property vested in himself in his corporate capacity to produce what was considered an adequate income.

This idea could not always be carried out. Thus the poorer bishops, whose incomes were increased, received incomes payable out of funds in the hands of the Commissioners, who were, however, empowered to make the necessary augmentations by the transfer of property from one bishop to another. In 1860 it was desirable for the benefit of the Church to get rid of the system of leases for lives. With this end the estates of all the Bishops were vested in the Commissioners, but the Ecclesiastical Commissioners were bound in place thereof to put the Bishops in possession of estates freed from the peculiar leasehold tenure, or to pay them fixed incomes until such re-endowment had taken place.[36]

The fears of churchmen have turned out absolutely groundless. Not one penny of Church revenues has ever been devoted to any secular purpose. The dignitaries of the Church have assuredly not been transformed into part of the civil service. Under the management of the Commissioners the aggregate wealth of the Church has year by year increased, and its riches

36. This re-endowment has, in fact, been effected.

have been employed for the benefit of the Church.[37] With this great reform must be connected the enactments by which non-residence and pluralism[38] on the part of the clergy have been all but brought to an end, and the amendments of legal procedure[39] which have made it possible to remove from benefices clergymen whose lives bring discredit on the Church.

Nothing, indeed, is more noteworthy than the rapidity with which the internal reform of the Establishment,[40] as carried out bit by bit throughout the nineteenth century, has produced its full effect. Pluralism, the non-residence of the clergy, the neglect of clerical duties, the dependence of the Bishops on the Government of the day, the scandals or abuses which shortly before the era of reform were denounced and exaggerated by the authors of the Black Book, became by the middle of the nineteenth century utterly foreign to the spirit and the habits of the Church. The Church Establishment of 1850 was in all these matters not the Establishment of 1800, or even of 1832, but the Church Establishment of 1905. The rapidity of this change becomes apparent when we remember that the first Ecclesiastical Commissioners Act dates from 1836, and that therefore some fourteen years were sufficient to abolish, not, indeed, all ecclesiastical abuses, but the condition of public sentiment under which these abuses flourished. It is, indeed, a fair presumption that the Evangelical movement which had long preceded, and the High Church movement which followed 1834, both contributed to produce a state of religious and moral feeling among the laity and the clergy which gave effectiveness to legislative reform. Still the reform itself must have done much to stimulate the development of a sound public spirit.[41]

---

37. Jealousy of the Commission has died away. By agreement with each bishop the Commissioners have undertaken the management of episcopal estates.

38. Pluralities Act, 1838, 1 & 2 Vict. c. 106; 1850, 13 & 14 Vict. c. 98; 1885, 48 & 49 Vict. c. 54.

39. Privy Council Appeals Act, 1832, 2 & 3 Will. 4, c. 92; the Judicial Committee Act, 1833, 3 & 4 Will. 4, c. 41; the Church Discipline Act, 1840, 3 & 4 Vict. c. 86, with which read the Public Worship Regulation Act, 1874, 37 & 38 Vict. c. 85.

40. See Appendix, Note II., Ecclesiastical Commission.

41. Bishop Watson was a man of some liberality. He could denounce pluralism (see p. 238, *ante*), and, according to a recent biographer, kept in view the interests of practical religion. He held, including his bishopric, and received the emoluments of, four ecclesiastical

As to external reform. From 1832 onwards the tendency of legislation has been to make the political and civil rights of Englishmen independent in the main, not only of their churchmanship but of their religious belief. But English lawmakers, whilst showing little respect for ecclesiastical dogmas, and whilst attending very little to abstract principles of any kind, have been guided in the main by ideas of immediate expediency, or, to put the matter more plainly, by the wish to remove the grievances of any class strong or organised enough to make its wishes effectively heard in Parliament. By 1854 the political disabilities of Nonconformists and Roman Catholics were for the most part, though not entirely, abolished. Restrictions on the worship of Nonconformists and hindrances to bequests for the educational or religious purposes of Nonconformists have been removed from the Statutebook.[42] Not till late in the nineteenth century, when one Act after another had been passed to meet the conscientious difficulties of special classes of persons who scrupled to take an oath, was the broad principle established by law[43] that no man, even though he were an avowed atheist, ought to suffer any civil or political disadvantage from unwillingness or disability to take an oath. Jews, after a long struggle, were admitted in 1844 to mu-

----

offices. He systematically neglected the duties attaching to all of them. "He lived [for some years before his death, in 1815] in his pleasant country house at Windermere, never visiting his diocese, and, according to De Quincey, talking Socinianism at his table."—L. Stephen, *English Utilitarians*, i. p. 39. In 1850 Bishop Watson was an impossibility. It was the age of Bishop Proudie.

42. The Nonconformists Chapels Act, 1844, 7 & 8 Vict. c. 45, established a sort of Statute of Limitations enabling congregations of Dissenters to retain chapels and endowments to which they had by usage acquired a moral right, but to which, under the trust deeds of an earlier age, they had, through changes in the doctrine held by particular congregations, lost their legal right. The Act mainly benefited Unitarians: it did not touch the rights of the Established Church, and may have passed the more easily because by 1844 many of the Anglican clergy were indifferent to the distinction between so-called orthodox and unorthodox forms of dissent.

43. Oaths Act, 1888, 51 & 52 Vict. c. 46. It was possible, certainly till 1869 (32 & 33 Vict. c. 68), and perhaps till 1888, that an honest atheist might have been unable, on account of his inability to take an oath, to maintain with success an action, *e.g.* for the recovery of a debt. See Stephen, *Comm.* iii. 598, 599.

nicipal offices, and in 1859 to a seat in Parliament.[44] These are but a few examples of the concessions made to the demand of dominant liberalism for the extension of religious and civil equality, and even more of the way in which these concessions were curtailed or delayed, often for years, by deference, partly indeed to the general conservatism, but mainly to the ecclesiastical convictions or sentiment of the time.

The system, however, of combined concession and conservatism can be made intelligible only by studying concrete illustrations of the way in which it worked. Let us examine, therefore, though in the barest outline, the legislation by which Parliament has in several instances removed palpable grievances connected with the position or privileges of the Church, or supported by ecclesiastical opinion.

In 1832 a valid marriage could not be celebrated[45] otherwise than in the parish church, and in accordance with the rites of the Church of England. This state of things was resented by Nonconformists (under which term may for the present purpose be included Roman Catholics), and especially by Unitarians, who were compelled to take part in a service containing a distinctly Trinitarian formula.[46] After 1832 concession to the wishes of Dissenters became a necessity. The Marriage Act, 1836, 6 & 7 Will. IV. c. 85, taken together with the Births and Deaths Registration Act, 1836, 6 & 7 Will. IV. c. 86, removed a grievance, and also introduced a substantial reform. It allowed the celebration of marriages in three different ways: (1) As heretofore, in the parish church in accordance with the rites of the Church of England; (2) Without any religious ceremony, but in the presence of a registrar; (3) In a Nonconformist place of worship duly registered, according to such forms and ceremonies as the parties might see fit to adopt. The public was also benefited by arrangements which were intended to secure the registration at a central office of every marriage wherever celebrated. The Marriage Act of 1836 was disliked by the clergy, even though

44. And that at first in a curiously indirect manner.

45. Except in the case of Jews and Quakers.

46. The grievance was felt the more bitterly because it was in reality recent. Prior to the Marriage Act, 1753, 26 Geo. II. c. 33 (which had been re-enacted with some amendments in 1823, 4 Geo. IV. c. 76), the marriages of Nonconformists celebrated in Dissenting chapels and not in accordance with the rites of the Church of England, had, it is said, been treated as valid.

a Conservative statesman, such as Peel, accepted whilst attempting to limit the effect of a necessary change. But the Act was deeply marked by deference to Church feeling. The State did not institute any general system of civil marriage. Church marriages were hardly affected by the new law. Marriage in a Nonconformist chapel was not put on the same footing as a marriage in a church. The one derived its validity from the presence of the registrar, the other from celebration by the clergyman.[47] Thus a practical grievance was removed, but a sentimental grievance was kept alive. As time went on Nonconformists claimed the removal of what they deemed a badge of inferiority. If politicians could have looked only to the interest of the public, this grievance might easily have been remedied, and the proper registration of marriages been secured by requiring the presence of a registrar at every marriage, whether solemnised in church or in chapel. This simple course was not taken; it was opposed to the sentiment of the clergy, and no politician could overlook the force of ecclesiastical opinion. In 1898 the grievance of the Nonconformists was, after a lapse of sixty-two years, completely removed; but this removal was achieved by dispensing with the presence of a registrar at a marriage in a registered Nonconformist chapel.[48] This method of reform satisfied Nonconformists, and gave no offence to Churchmen. It had but one defect: it somewhat diminished the security for the registration of marriages. To the deference, then, yielded to ecclesiastical opinion was sacrificed in 1836 the completeness of a necessary reform, and sixty years later, in 1898, the public interest in the due registration of marriages.

The Divorce Act of 1857[49] was a triumph of individualistic liberalism and of common justice. It did away with the iniquity of a law which theoretically prohibited divorce, but in reality conceded to the rich a right denied to the poor. In the face of strenuous ecclesiastical opposition, headed by Mr. Gladstone, divorce was legalised, and divorced persons were left ab-

47. The fees moreover payable to the registrar were heavier than the fees payable on a marriage in the parish church. This, it is said, imposed a tax or fine upon persons often very poor, who were not married in church (Lilly and Wallis, *Manual of Law specially affecting Catholics*, pp. 54–57).

48. The Marriage Act, 1898, 61 & 62 Vict. c. 58.

49. The Matrimonial Causes Act, 1857, 20 & 21 Vict. c. 85.

solutely free to marry. But here, again, regard was paid to clerical feeling. A clergyman of the Church of England is, after all, an official of the National Church; but under the Divorce Act he is allowed to decline to solemnise the marriage of any person whose former marriage has been dissolved on the ground of his or her adultery.[50] Thus a clergyman, while acting as an official of the State, is virtually allowed to pronounce immoral a marriage permitted by the morality of the State.

In 1832 the burial law involved a grievance to Dissenters. A man was entitled to be buried in the parish churchyard which contained, it might be, the tombs of all his friends and relatives, but any funeral in a churchyard was of necessity accompanied by the burial service of the Church of England, performed by a clergyman. There might well be Dissenters who either desired some other service, or on grounds of conscience or feeling objected to the burial service of the Church of England. At last in 1880, the Burial Laws Amendment Act[51] made to any one who, for any reason, objected to the use of the Church burial service, the concession that any person entitled to burial in a particular churchyard might be buried there without the Church service, or with such religious service, if professedly Christian, as the person responsible for the funeral might think fit. Note, however, that no address which is not part of a religious service can be delivered in a churchyard. The concession, in short, made to the sentiment of persons not members of the Church of England has been restricted within the very narrowest limits compatible with the removal of a practical grievance.

In 1832 a system of religious tests still closed the national universities— in the case of Oxford wholly, in the case of Cambridge all but wholly—to any person who was not an avowed member of the Church of England.[52]

---

50. *Ibid.* c. 55, 57, 58.

51. 43 & 44 Vict. c. 41.

52. At Oxford a young man, or, as in the case of Bentham, a mere boy, was required at matriculation to subscribe the Thirty-nine Articles of the Church of England. Subscription was again required before taking the degree of B.A., and lastly before taking the degree of M.A. At Cambridge in 1832, no subscription of religious belief was, or (it is conceived) ever had been required at matriculation. If accepted by the college authorities students of any belief could come into residence, reside their full time, and enter for the degree examination.

In every college church services were daily performed, and the attendance thereat of undergraduates was required. Any religious education given was education in the doctrines of the Church of England. The national universities were no places for Nonconformists of any class, and practically few Nonconformists, indeed, studied even at Cambridge till, at any rate, after the middle of the nineteenth century.[53]

The era of reform did not bring with it the admission of the nation to the national places of learning. The passing through the House of Commons in 1834 of a Bill abolishing university tests, showed what was the wish of Dissenters, and proved that it was sanctioned by the liberalism of the day. The rejection of the Bill by the House of Lords, without any effective protest on the part of the nation, showed how great was the strength of the Church. The attempt, which was only in part successful, to provide in London something like a university open to men of all creeds, probably diverted the pressure of Dissenters for admission to Oxford and Cambridge.[54]

Their names would appear in the order of merit in the Tripos, but they could not actually obtain the degree without declaring themselves *bona fide* members of the Church of England. But whilst the University of Cambridge did not exclude Nonconformists from anything but the degree, they were practically all but excluded from the colleges. The masters and tutors would in most cases have either directly refused admission to a Nonconformist, or if he had been admitted, would probably have forced him to attend the college chapel.

At Oxford, in short, Nonconformists were excluded by the rules of the university, at Cambridge they were virtually excluded by the rules of the colleges. All but a very few Dissenters were, till late in the nineteenth century, excluded both by the atmosphere of the place and by the conduct of the college authorities. See Appendix, Note III., University Tests.

53. Early in the nineteenth century a popular writer could describe our universities with gross technical inaccuracy, but with much substantial truth, as academies for the education of ministers of the Church of England.

54. Policy or accident favoured the opposition, supported in the main by the opinion of Churchmen, to a necessary reform. The London University never became, in a strict sense, a university at all. University College provided a place of liberal education for Dissenters, just as King's College provided in London a place of liberal education for Churchmen. The London University itself became at last nothing but an examining body. The result was that, while the agitation for the abolition of tests at the national universities was checked and weakened, the foundation in London of a really national university open to every class of the nation was prevented.

At last in 1854[55]—twenty-two years after the passing of the Reform Act— the demand for university reform, at any rate at Oxford,[56] could no longer be resisted. Parliament grudgingly opened or set slightly ajar the gates of the university, so as to make possible the entrance of persons not members of the Church of England. In principle this change was important. It alarmed zealous Churchmen. An eminent divine declared from the pulpit of St. Mary's, that on the admission of a Nonconformist within its pre- cincts, "Oxford would be Oxford no longer." In practice the change was insignificant. At both universities every Nonconformist was excluded from most of the emoluments and posts of dignity which were the important reward of success at the university. No one but an avowed member of the Church of England could at Oxford become, or at Cambridge enjoy the full privileges of, an M.A. At last in 1871—thirty-nine years after the passing of the Reform Act and three years after the introduction of household suffrage—Parliament abolished the tests[57] which kept large bodies of En- glishmen away from Oxford and Cambridge. The national universities have at length become the universities of the nation. The length of time, the slowness of the process, the greatness of the efforts needed for the attain- ment of this result—and this during a period when liberalism was the dominant opinion of the day—gives us some measure of the force exerted by the opposing current of ecclesiastical opinion.

Concession is still balanced by conservatism. At Oxford no Noncon- formist has access to the university pulpit; the services in the college chapels are the services of the Church of England; the degrees in divinity, the right to examine in the school of theology, the divinity professorships, the head- ship of one college,[58] are all the monopoly of the Established Church. The

55. The Oxford University Act, 1854, 17 & 18 Vict. c. 81.

56. At Cambridge the Cambridge University Act, 1856, 19 & 20 Vict. c. 88, threw open to Nonconformists all ordinary bachelors' degrees, all endowments tenable by undergraduates, and the nominal title of M.A.; but under that Act Nonconformist M.A.'s were still kept out of the senate and the parliamentary constituency. See Sir George Young, *University Tests*, p. 53, and Appendix, Note III. *post.*

57. Universities Tests Act, 1871, 34 Vict. c. 26, and College Charter Act, 1871, 34 & 35 Vict. c. 63.

58. The Deanery of Christ Church.

state of things at Cambridge[59] is in substance, though not always in form, pretty much the same as at Oxford. The national universities have been restored to the nation, but the Church still occupies there a position of pre-eminence and predominance.[60]

In 1832 nothing brought more unpopularity upon the Church than tithes and Church rates. An attack upon them gave hopes of success, and there were agitators or reformers ready to conduct the assault. It has been crowned with very little success. Tithes still exist, but a change in the mode of their collection and in their incidence under the Tithe Acts, 1836–1891,[61] has gone far to free the Church from unpopularity. Church rates have, after a long controversy extending over thirty-four years, been in a sense abolished, but the very title of the enactment, the Compulsory Church Rate Abolition Act, 1868,[62] reminds us that the Establishment, if in this matter defeated, has been allowed to retreat with honour. The Act abolishes, not the right to Church rates, but the means of compelling the payment thereof.[63] This method of abolition, characteristic as it is of English love of compromise, whilst it saved the dignity, also promoted to a slight extent the pecuniary interest of the Established Church. A rate which may be imposed but which cannot be exacted, may sometimes be in practice paid, at any rate by Churchmen.[64]

---

59. As at Oxford, the university pulpit is closed to every Nonconformist minister, and the services in the colleges are the services of the Church of England. An avowed or conscientious Nonconformist cannot become a Doctor of Divinity. The theological professorships are, with one exception, or possibly two exceptions, not open to any but Churchmen. No layman has, in fact, ever been elected a theological professor.

Compare Henry Sidgwick's statement in 1898 as to the extent to which theological teaching was at Cambridge left in the hands of the Church of England by the Universities Tests Act, 1871.—H. Sidgwick, A Memoir, p. 564.

60. The law does not forbid the foundation in the universities of denominational colleges, such e.g. as Hertford College. See R. v. Hertford College (1877), 2 Q.B.D. 590; (1878) 3 Q.B.D. (C.A.) 693.

61. 6 & 7 Will. IV. c. 71 to 54 & 55 Vict. c. 8.

62. 31 & 32 Vict. c. 109.

63. Though this is so as to newly imposed Church rates, the Act of 1868 "contained provisions preserving the old system in certain specified instances, generally of only local application." See Elliot, State and Church, 2nd ed. p. 43 (n.).

64. In 1834 the Whig ministry offered the Church a considerable pecuniary compensation

These examples, whereof the number might easily be increased,[65] suffi-ciently illustrate and confirm the statement that in all legislation affecting the Church, the dominant current of liberal opinion has been modified by the strong cross-current of ecclesiastical conviction. The whole view, how-ever, taken in this lecture of the policy of conservatism and concession is open to two objections. The one is grounded on certain attempts to widen the foundations of the Church, the other on the disestablishment of the Irish Church.

As to attempts to widen the foundation of the Church. It cannot be denied that during the last seventy-five years nothing has been done to further the policy of comprehension, or to bring again within the Church any large body of Dissenters, but the doctrine of the Church has, it may be argued, been affected by legislation, whether judicial or parliamentary, which tells upon subscription to the Articles, or otherwise affects the status of clergy-men.

The decisions of the Privy Council have, it is constantly alleged, made for comprehension of a particular kind. The judgment in the Gorham case[66] has enabled Evangelical clergymen to remain with a quiet conscience ministers of the Church of England. The Bennet case[67] has averted the possible secession of High Church clergymen. A series of cases[68] more or less connected with the publication in 1861 of *Essays and Reviews* have, it is supposed, established the right of clergymen to criticise with consider-able freedom the doctrines of the Church and the contents of the Bible, and yet, as Broad Churchmen, to retain the position of clergymen of the Church of England. But even if it be granted that this is so, the judgments of the Privy Council have after all done little more than maintain the *status quo.* Clergymen of the Church of England, in common with the whole

---

for the abolition of Church rates (*Annual Register,* 1834, pp. 207, 213). Both the offer and the refusal show a recognition of the strength still possessed by the Establishment.

65. *E.g.* by an examination of the policy pursued and the Acts passed with regard to the elementary education of the people of England.

66. See *Gorham* v. *Bishop of Exeter,* heard and determined in the Privy Council (8th March 1850). E. F. Moore.

67. *Sheppard* v. *Bennet* (No. 2) (1871), L.R. 4, P.C. 371.

68. E.g. *Williams* v. *Bishop of Salisbury,* and *Wilson* v. *Fendall* (1864); *Brodrick* v. *Fremantle,* Ecc. Cas. 247.

body of Churchmen, have always been divided into Low Churchmen, High Churchmen, and Broad Churchmen or Latitudinarians. As far, therefore, as the judgments of the Courts go, they have introduced little change and have always left things to stand as they have been for generations.[69]

The Clerical Subscription Act, 1865,[70] has undoubtedly to a slight degree relaxed the terms on which an Anglican clergyman is required to signify his belief in the articles and formulas of the Church of England, whilst the Clerical Disabilities Act, 1870,[71] which is constantly, though quite errone-ously, described as an Act abolishing the indelibility of Orders, has enabled a clergyman to resume the rights and liabilities of a layman. These statutes, which deserve the careful attention of anyone engaged in examining the theological tendencies in England of the nineteenth century, do most un-doubtedly show the existence between 1860 and 1870 of a peculiar condition of public sentiment. The two Acts cited above, together with several judg-ments of the Privy Council, bear witness to the existence and to the tem-porary influence of the Broad Church movement. They were acts of relief for Broad Church or Latitudinarian clergymen, they enable a man of sen-sitive conscience to take orders, even though he does not assent to every one of the Thirty-nine Articles, and make him feel with reason that his position as a clergyman is made the easier because he is allowed, as far as the State is concerned, to resume at any moment the status of a layman.

69. It is, of course, indisputable that at any rate during the last fifty years and more public opinion has changed, though the extent of the change is liable to be a good deal exaggerated, as to the moral obligations incurred by subscription to the Articles. The circumstance which raises a suspicion that the change in public opinion may be less than is generally supposed, is the very slight effect produced thereby on legislation. Throughout the nineteenth century many have been the Churchmen, whether clerics or laymen, who have objected to the re-tention in the Church services of the Athanasian creed, but the efforts for its removal from the services by legislation have been few and entirely unsuccessful. It is further noteworthy that clergymen and others, who maintain that subscription or declaration of assent to the doctrine of the Church of England leaves almost unlimited freedom of dissent from that doctrine, do not make any serious attempt to obtain a legislative declaration of the soundness of an opinion on which both legally, and in a certain sense morally, depends the whole position of a clergyman of the Church of England.

70. 28 & 29 Vict. c. 122.

71. 33 & 34 Vict. c. 91.

But the legislation which bears witness to the influence of the Broad Church movement has neither in reality affected the doctrine of the Church, nor even tended towards the admission of Dissenters.[72]

As to the Irish Church Act, 1869.[73] This enactment tended, it is alleged, towards the disestablishment of the Church of England, and the tendency becomes the more manifest when we remember that the so-called Church of England was, between 1800 and 1869, simply a part of the United Church of England and Ireland, which in the eye of the law constituted one ecclesiastical establishment. It may, therefore, be alleged, with technical truth, that the Legislature did in 1869 actually disestablish part of the National Church. Nor can it be denied that the legislation of 1869 was supported by Dissenters who desired disestablishment no less in England than in Ireland. Yet appearances are here delusive. The Act of 1869 did not touch the foundations of the Church of England. It was carried in reality owing to circumstances peculiar to Ireland. The Irish Church Establishment had been for more than half a century attacked by Whigs no less than by Radicals. An institution which had been morally undermined for generations was easily overthrown by a statesman whose genius enabled him to unite for the assault upon it Whigs and Radicals, Nonconformists and High Churchmen. The Irish Establishment fell mainly because Englishmen believed rightly enough that the maintenance thereof was unjust, and thought, erroneously as the event proved, that it was the grievance which mainly fostered Irish discontent, and partly because High Churchmen felt no sympathy with a Church which was the stronghold of Protestantism. One thing, at any rate, the Act of 1869 places past dispute; the Evangelicals, who were the natural allies of the Protestant Churchmen of Ireland, had by that date ceased to control the religious opinion of England. Yet even the policy of 1869 illustrates the legislative power of clerical convictions. The terms of

---

72. In nothing is the influence of Church opinion more marked than in the language of the Clerical Disabilities Act, 1870, 33 & 34 Vict. c. 91. This statute, which enables a clergyman to resume all the rights and duties of a layman, and to free himself, as far as the State is concerned, from the liabilities, whilst giving up the rights, of a clergyman of the Church of England, contains no expression which either affirms or denies the indelibility of orders.

73. 32 & 33 Vict. c. 42.

disestablishment were singularly favourable to the Church. It retained all the ecclesiastical edifices which it possessed in 1868; it was not in effect deprived of all pecuniary resources. Nor is it irrelevant to remark that the Irish Church Act of 1869 renders it all but impossible for the Church, although disestablished, to form without the aid of Parliament a body which might include the Protestant Dissenters of Ireland. Here, as elsewhere, is apparent the influence of ecclesiastical, and indeed, of High Church opinion.

The very instances, therefore, which appear at first sight inconsistent with the policy of conservatism and concession, lose, when carefully examined, this appearance of inconsistency. They do more than this; they illustrate in the most marked manner that dependence of legislation upon opinion which is the theme of these Lectures: in the slight relaxation of the terms of clerical subscription, and in the disestablishment of the Church of Ireland in 1869, is to be found the conclusive proof, that any deviations from the ordinary course of legislation correspond at bottom with some peculiar, it may be transitory, fluctuation in public sentiment. The ecclesiastical legislation of the last seventy-five years leads to this result. It has been continuously affected by the dominant liberalism of the day which has told in favour of religious, no less than of civil equality. It has been modified by that cross-current (in this instance a very powerful one) of ecclesiastical opinion which has enforced respect for the convictions of Churchmen and the interest of the Established Church. But the action of this cross-current itself has been complicated by subtle modifications of ecclesiastical opinion. In no department of English law is more clearly visible to the intelligent investigator the close relation between the legislation and the opinion of a particular era.

Our survey of ecclesiastical legislation suggests both an observation and a question.

The observation is this: The policy, as regards Church affairs, of concession combined with conservatism, is merely one marked instance of that perpetual compromise between the spirit of innovation and the spirit of conservatism, which is the essential characteristic of English legislation and of English public life.

The inquiry is: Whether the merits of this system of compromise are or are not overbalanced by its defects?

Compromise involving great deference to clerical sentiment has averted the intense bitterness which, in foreign countries, and notably in France, has accompanied ecclesiastical legislation. The position of the Church of England has throughout the nineteenth century been gradually shifted rather than violently altered. The grievances which in 1828 excited the hostility of Nonconformists have been immensely diminished, yet the sentiment even of the clergy has not been embittered by a revolution every step of which they and zealous Churchmen have opposed; and whilst, in some respects, the wealth, the influence, and the popularity of the Church have been increased, the profound discord which arises from the identification of political with theological or anti-theological differences, and amounts in some countries to a condition of moral civil war, has been all but entirely averted. These are the virtues of compromise.

In the field, however, of ecclesiastical legislation the vices of compromise are as marked as its merits. Controversies, which are deprived of some of their heat, are allowed to smoulder on for generations, and are never extinguished. Thus national education has been for more than fifty years the field of battle between Church and Dissent, each settlement has been the basis of renewed dispute, and even now controversy is not closed, simply because the law has never established any definite principle. One change in the marriage law after another has failed to rest the whole matter on any satisfactory foundation. Our law of divorce enables a clergyman of the Church of England to cast a slur upon a marriage fully sanctioned by the law of the State. The piecemeal legislation engendered by the desire for compromise, and the spirit which this piecemeal legislation produces, are no small evils. "The time to do justice," it has been well said, "is now." To do justice bit by bit is in reality nothing else than to tolerate injustice for years. The long line of Oaths Acts is a monument to English pertinacity in the path of reform, but it is also a record—not at all a solitary one—of English indifference to the complete discharge of public duty.

Moralists or historians must weigh the merits against the faults of legislative compromise. Persons engaged in the study of legislative opinion will take a possibly fairer view of this subject, if they consider that the spirit of compromise in ecclesiastical no less than in civil legislation is in reality nothing but the evidence of the accuracy with which the English legislature reflects the ebb and flow, the weakness and the strength, the action and the counter-action of every current of public feeling or conviction strong enough to arrest the attention of Parliament.[74]

74. If anyone looks at politics from the somewhat abstract point of view suggested by these Lectures he will find a peculiar interest in the career of Gladstone. Such an observer will note that Gladstone from peculiarities of character and education was able to unite, whether consistently or not, the sentiment of liberalism with the ecclesiastical sentiment belonging to a High Churchman. In the sphere of economics, and even of politics, he to a great extent accepted the doctrines of Benthamite individualism as represented by the Manchester school. In the ecclesiastical sphere he accepted, it would seem, High Church principles as represented by Archdeacon Manning, until the archdeacon was transformed into a Roman Catholic ecclesiastic. This singular combination of sentiments or principles, which are rarely united in the mind of one man, contributed greatly to Gladstone's influence. The capacity for honestly sharing the varying, and even the inconsistent, sentiments of his age augments the influence of a statesman.

Judicial Legislation

MY PURPOSE IN THIS LECTURE IS, first, the description of the special characteristics of judicial legislation[1] as regards its relation to public opinion; and, next, the illustration, by a particular example—namely, the changes in the law as to married women's property—of the way in which judge-made law may determine the course and character of parliamentary legislation.

*I. The Special Characteristics of Judicial Legislation in Relation
to Public Opinion*

As all lawyers are aware, a large part and, as many would add, the best part of the law of England is judge-made law—that is to say, consists of rules[2] to be collected from the judgments of the Courts. This portion of the law has not been created by Act of Parliament, and is not recorded in the statute-book. It is the work of the Courts; it is recorded in the Reports; it

---

1. See Ilbert, *Legislative Methods,* pp. 6–8; Pollock, *Essays in Jurisprudence and Ethics,* p. 237; Pollock, *First Book of Jurisprudence* (2nd ed.), Pt. II. ch. vi.

2. These rules will assuredly be enforced by the Courts, and are therefore laws. True indeed it is that the function of an English Court is primarily to decide in accordance with legal principles any particular case which comes before it. It is the interpreter, not the maker of a law. As, however, "it may with equal verbal correctness be affirmed in one sense, and denied in another, that interpretation (whether performed by judges or by text-writers) makes new law" (*First Book of Jurisprudence* (2nd ed.), p. 236), the question whether we ought to use such expressions as judge-made law or judicial legislation is, for the purpose of these Lectures, of no real consequence. See Appendix, Note IV., Judge-made Law.

is, in short, the fruit of judicial legislation. The amount of such judge-made law is in England far more extensive than a student easily realises. Nine-tenths, at least, of the law of contract, and the whole, or nearly the whole, of the law of torts are not to be discovered in any volume of the statutes. Many Acts of Parliament, again, such as the Sale of Goods Act, 1893, or the Bills of Exchange Act, 1882, are little else than the reproduction in a statutory shape of rules originally established by the Courts. Judge-made law has in such cases passed into statute law. Then, too, many statutory enactments, *e.g.* the fourth section of the Statute of Frauds, though they originally introduced some new rule or principle into the law of England, have been the subject of so much judicial interpretation as to derive nearly all their real significance from the sense put upon them by the Courts.[3] Nor let anyone imagine that judicial legislation is a kind of law-making which belongs wholly to the past, and which has been put an end to by the annual meeting and by the legislative activity of modern Parliaments. No doubt the law-making function of the Courts has been to a certain extent curtailed by the development of parliamentary authority. Throughout the whole of the nineteenth century, however, it has remained, and indeed continues to the present day, in operation. New combinations of circumstances—that is, new cases—constantly call for the application, which means in truth the extension of old principles; or, it may be, even for the thinking out of some new principle, in harmony with the general spirit of the law, fitted to meet the novel requirements of the time. Hence whole branches not of ancient but of very modern law have been built up, developed, or created by the action of the Courts. The whole body of rules, with regard to the conflict of laws (or, in other words, for the decision of cases which contain some foreign element),[4] has come into existence during the last hundred and twenty, and, as regards by far the greater part of it, well within the last eighty, or even seventy years. But the whole of this

---

3. It is certain that no man could understand the full and true effect of either the fourth or the seventeenth section of the Statute of Frauds (which now is the fourth section of the Sale of Goods Act, 1893), without studying the vast number of cases interpreting these enactments. See *Law Quarterly Review* (i. p. 1) for an expression in words by Sir J. F. Stephen and Sir F. Pollock of the full import of the Statute of Frauds, s. 17.

4. Dicey, *Conflict of Laws,* p. 1.

complex department of law has neither been formed nor even greatly modified by Parliament. It is the product of an elaborate and lengthy process
of judicial law-making.

The Courts or the judges, when acting as legislators, are of course influenced by the beliefs and feelings of their time, and are guided to a considerable extent by the dominant current of public opinion; Eldon and Kenyon belonged to the era of old toryism as distinctly as Denman, Campbell,
Erle, and Bramwell belonged to the age of Benthamite liberalism. But
whilst our tribunals, or the judges of whom they are composed, are swayed
by the prevailing beliefs of a particular time, they are also guided by professional opinions and ways of thinking which are, to a certain extent,
independent of and possibly opposed to the general tone of public opinion.
The judges are the heads of the legal profession. They have acquired the
intellectual and moral tone of English lawyers. They are men advanced in
life. They are for the most part persons of a conservative disposition. They
are in no way dependent for their emoluments, dignity, or reputation upon
the favour of the electors, or even of Ministers who represent in the long
run the wishes of the electorate.[5] They are more likely to be biassed by
professional habits and feeling than by the popular sentiment of the hour.
Hence judicial legislation will be often marked by certain characteristics
rarely to be found in Acts of Parliament.

First. Judicial legislation aims to a far greater extent than do enactments
passed by Parliament, at the maintenance of the logic or the symmetry of
the law. The main employment of a Court is the application of well-known
legal principles to the solution of given cases, and the deduction from these
principles of their fair logical result. Men trained in and for this kind of
employment acquire a logical conscience; they come to care greatly—in
some cases excessively—for consistency. A Court, even when it really leg-
islates, does so indirectly. Its immediate object is to apply a given principle
to a particular case, or to determine under which of two or more principles

5. Till quite recently judges not only were, as they still are, irremovable by any Ministry,
however powerful, but had also little to hope for from the Government by way of promotion.
The system created by the Judicature Acts has, with its many merits, the unintended defect
that it makes the promotion of a judge, *e.g.* to a seat in the Court of Appeal, dependent on
the goodwill of the Chancellor or the Prime Minister.

a particular case really falls. The duty of a Court, in short, is not to remedy a particular grievance, but to determine whether an alleged grievance is one for which the law supplies a remedy. Hence the further result that Courts are affected, as Parliament never is, by the ideas and theories of writers on law. A Court, when called upon to decide cases which present some legal difficulty, is often engaged—unconsciously it may be—in the search for principles. If an author of ingenuity has reduced some branch of the law to a consistent scheme of logically coherent rules, he supplies exactly the principles of which a Court is in need. Hence the development of English law has depended, more than many students perceive, on the writings of the authors who have produced the best text-books. Some eighty years ago Serjeant Stephen published a *Treatise on the Principles of Pleading,* which transformed the maxims of art followed by skilful pleaders into the principles of a logically consistent system. His book told almost immediately upon the whole course of procedure in a civil action. Story's *Conflict of Laws,* which appeared in 1834, though the work of an American lawyer, forthwith systematised, one might almost say created, a whole branch of the law of England.[6] The law of damages has, it is said, come into existence through the writings of a well-known English and a well-known American author.

Secondly. Judicial legislation aims rather at securing the certainty than at amending the deficiencies of the law. The natural tendency of a well-trained judge is to feel that a rule which is certain and fixed, even though it be not the best rule conceivable, promotes justice more than good laws which are liable to change or modification. This is the true and valid defence for reverence for precedent. A satirist has suggested[7] that the reso-

---

6. My learned friend Mr. Westlake's *Private International Law* was published in 1858. It introduced English lawyers to the theories of Savigny on the conflict of laws, and showed the applicability of Savigny's doctrines to questions which came before the English Courts. The influence of Mr. Westlake's work is traceable in whole lines of cases decided during the last forty-six years.

7. "It is a maxim," says Gulliver, "among [our] lawyers, that whatever has been done before may legally be done again, and therefore they take special care to record all the decisions formerly made against common justice and the general reason of mankind. These, under the name of precedents, they produced as authorities to justify the most iniquitous

lution to follow precedents is the same thing as the determination that, when once you have decided a question wrongly, you will go on deciding it wrongly ever after, and there are instances enough to be found in the Reports where a decision of very dubious soundness has been systematically followed, and has led to a misdevelopment of the law.[8] But the best answer to the contempt thrown on precedent may be given in the language of one of the most eminent among our judges.

> Our common law system consists in the applying to new combinations of circumstances those rules of law which we derive from legal principles and judicial precedents; and for the sake of attaining uniformity, consistency, and certainty, we must apply those rules, where they are not plainly unreasonable and inconvenient, to all cases which arise; and we are not at liberty to reject them, and to abandon all analogy to them, in those to which they have not yet been judicially applied, because we think that the rules are not as convenient and reasonable as we ourselves could have devised. It appears to me to be of great importance to keep this principle of decision steadily in view, not merely for the determination of the particular case, but for the interests of law as a science.[9]

And this view is substantially sound. Respect for precedent is the necessary foundation of judge-made law. If Parliament changes the law the action of Parliament is known to every man, and Parliament tries in general to respect acquired rights. If the Courts were to apply to the decision of substantially the same case one principle to-day, and another principle to-morrow, men would lose rights which they already possessed; a law which was not certain would in reality be no law at all. Judicial legislation, then, is a form of law-making which aims at and tends towards the maintenance of a fixed legal system.

Thirdly. The ideas of expediency or policy accepted by the Courts may differ considerably from the ideas which, at a given time, having acquired

---

opinions, and the judges never fail of directing accordingly."—Swift, *Works,* xi., edited by Sir Walter Scott (2nd ed.), p. 318.

8. See *R.* v. *Millis* (1844), 10 Cl. & F. 534; *Beamish* v. *Beamish* (1861), 9 H.L.C. 274.

9. Per Parke, J., *Mirehouse* v. *Rennell* (1833), 1 Cl. & F., pp. 527, 546; 36 R.R. p. 180, cited Pollock, *First Book of Jurisprudence* (2nd ed.), p. 339.

predominant influence among the general public, guide parliamentary legislation.

It is quite possible that judicial conceptions of utility or of the public interest may sometimes rise above the ideas prevalent at a particular era. It is clear that the system of trusts, invented and worked out by the Courts of Equity, has stood the test of time, just because it gave effect to ideas unknown to the common law, and at one period hardly appreciated by ordinary Englishmen. In the field of commercial law Lord Mansfield carried out ideas which, though in harmony with the best opinion of the time, could hardly have been, during the era of old toryism, embodied in Acts of Parliament. Even at the present day the Courts maintain, or attempt to maintain, rules as to the duty of an agent towards his employer which are admitted by every conscientious man to be morally sound, but which are violated every day by tradesmen, merchants, and professional men, who make no scruple at giving or accepting secret commissions; and these rules Parliament hesitates or refuses to enforce by statute. Here, at any rate, the morality of the Courts is higher than the morality of traders or of politicians. But it has of course often happened that the ideas entertained by the judges have fallen below the highest and most enlightened public opinion of a particular time. The Courts struggled desperately to maintain the laws against regrating and forestalling when they were condemned by economists and all but abolished by Parliament.[10] It is at least arguable that the Courts restricted within too narrow limits the operation as regards wagers of the Gaming Act, 1845, and missed an opportunity of freeing our tribunals altogether from the necessity of dealing at all with wagering contracts. There are certainly judicious lawyers who have thought that, if the Common Law Courts had given more complete effect to certain provisions of the Common Law Procedure Act, 1854, part of the reforms introduced by the Judicature Act, 1873, might have been anticipated by nearly twenty years. However this may be, we may, at any rate as regards the nineteenth

---

10. Namely by 12 Geo. III. c. 71. "Notwithstanding the broad terms and the obvious intent of the repealing Act of 12 Geo. III., the Courts, under the lead of Lord Kenyon, continued to hold that regrating, forestalling, and engrossing, were offences at the common law" (Eddy, *On Combinations,* i. s. 54), and maintained that doctrine until it was definitely abolished by Parliament in 1844, 7 & 8 Vict. c. 24; Eddy, s. 58.

century, lay it down as a rule that judge-made law has, owing to the training and age of our judges, tended at any given moment to represent the convictions of an earlier era than the ideas represented by parliamentary legislation. If a statute, as already stated,[11] is apt to reproduce the public opinion not so much of to-day as of yesterday, judge-made law occasionally represents the opinion of the day before yesterday. But with this statement must be coupled the reflection, that beliefs are not necessarily erroneous because they are out of date; there are such things as ancient truths as well as ancient prejudices. For the purpose of these lectures, however, the essential matter to bear in mind is neither the merit nor the demerit of judge-made laws, but the fact that judicial legislation may be the result of considerations different from the ideas which influence Parliament. The legislative action of the Courts represents in truth a peculiar cross-current of opinion, which may in more ways than one modify the effect of that predominant opinion of the day which naturally finds expression in a representative assembly such as the House of Commons. Thus ideas derived from the Courts (which, be it added, may tell upon public opinion itself) may promote or delay the progress—may mould the form or even deeply affect the substantial character of parliamentary legislation.[12]

11. See p. 24, *ante.*

12. If one may be allowed to apply the terms of logic to law, one is tempted to assert that judicial legislation proceeds by a process of induction, whilst parliamentary legislation proceeds, or may proceed, by a process of deduction. This contrast contains an element of truth. Courts when deciding particular cases arrive gradually and half unconsciously at some general principle applicable to all cases of a given class; a general principle is the *terminus ad quem,* though it is theoretically treated as the *terminus a quo,* of judicial legislation; Parliament, on the other hand, certainly may lay down a general principle, and may embody in an Act the consequences flowing from it; but the suggested contrast, unless its limits be very carefully kept in mind, is apt to be delusive. The Courts no doubt do not begin by laying down a general principle, but then a great deal of their best work consists in drawing out the conclusions deducible from well-established principles, and has therefore a deductive character. Parliament, on the other hand, may legislate by establishing a broad and general principle and enacting the consequences which flow from it, and thus may pursue a strictly deductive method; but this course is one rarely taken by Parliament (see pp. 30–35, *ante*). It begins a course of legislation generally by some Act meant to meet a particular want or grievance. Far more important in matter of method is the similarity than the contrast between judicial and parliamentary legislation in England. In the vast majority of instances

II. The Effect of Judge-made Law on Parliamentary Legislation

This topic is well illustrated by considering, though in the merest outline, the history, during the nineteenth century, of the law as to the property of married women.

In 1800, and indeed up to 1870, the property rights of a married woman were mainly determined by rules contained in two bodies of judge-made law, namely, the Common Law, and Equity.

As to the Common Law. A married woman's position in regard to her property was the natural result, worked out by successive generations of lawyers with logical thoroughness, of the principle that, in the words of Blackstone, "by marriage, the husband and wife are one person in law: that is, the very being or legal existence of the woman is suspended during the marriage, or at least is incorporated and consolidated into that of the husband."[13]

If, for the sake of clearness, we omit all limitations and exceptions, many of which are for the purpose of these Lectures unimportant, the result at common law of this merger of a wife's legal status in that of her husband may be thus broadly stated. Marriage was an assignment of a wife's property rights to her husband at any rate during coverture. Much of her property, whether possessed by her at or coming to her after her marriage, either became absolutely his own, or during coverture might, if he chose,

---

they each start with the effort to meet some narrow or particular want or grievance. They each of them arrive only slowly and with great effort at some general principle; they are each much governed by precedent; they each, therefore, may in a sense be said to employ the inductive method. But here the advantage lies wholly with the Courts. The Courts of necessity deal with particular cases, but, as one case after another of a similar kind comes before them, they certainly attempt to elicit and determine the general principle on which the decision of all such cases should depend. They attempt to reach logically, and generally succeed in reaching, some general and reasonable rule of decision. Parliament in most instances pays little regard to any general principle whatever, but attempts to meet in the easiest and most off-hand manner some particular grievance or want. Parliament is guided not by considerations of logic, but by the pressure which powerful bodies can bring to bear upon its action. Ordinary parliamentary legislation then can at best be called only tentative. Even ordinary judicial legislation is logical, the best judicial legislation is scientific.

13. *Comm.* i. p. 441.

be made absolutely his own, so that even if his wife survived him it went to his representatives.

This statement is, from a technical point of view, as every lawyer will perceive, lacking in precision, or even in strict accuracy, but it conveys to a student, more clearly than can otherwise be expressed in a few words, the real effect between 1800 and 1870 of the common law[14] (in so far as it was not controlled by the rules of equity) on the position of a married woman in regard to her property. The statement lacks precision, because at common law the effect of marriage on a woman's property varied with the nature of the property;[15] the interest which a husband acquired in his

---

14. Affected occasionally by an old statute, such as the Wills Act, 1542 (34 & 35 Hen. VIII. c. 5), s. 14.

15. *Outline of effect of marriage at common law as assignment of wife's (W's) property to husband (H).*

(A) *W's* personal property.

I. Goods, *e.g.* money and furniture in actual possession of *W* became the absolute property of *H.*

II. W's *choses in action* (*e.g.* debts due to *W*) became *H's* if he recovered them by law, or reduced them into possession during coverture, but not otherwise.

III. *W's* chattels real (leaseholds) did not become *H's* property, but he might, during coverture, dispose of them (give them away or sell them) at his pleasure, and, if he sold them, the proceeds of the sale were his property.

On the death of *W* before *H* all her personal property, if it had not already absolutely become his, passed to *H.*

On the death of *H* before *W,* her *choses in action* if not reduced into possession, and her leaseholds, if not disposed of by *H,* remained *W's.*

(B) *W's* freehold estate.

Any freehold estate of which *W* was seised vested in *W* and *H* during coverture, but was during coverture under his sole management and control.

On the death of *W* before *H* her freehold estate went at once to her heir, unless *H* was entitled, through the birth of a child of the marriage, to an interest therein for life by the curtesy of England.

On the death of *H* before *W, W's* freehold estate remained her own.

N.B.—(1) These rules apply to property coming to *W* during coverture as well as to property possessed by her at the time of marriage.

(2) *H* was entitled during coverture to the whole of *W's* income from whatever source it came, *e.g.* if it were rent from her leasehold or freehold property, or if it were her own earnings. The income, when paid to her or to *H,* was his, whilst still unpaid it was a *chose*

wife's freeholds differed from the interest which he acquired in her lease-holds; of the goods and chattels again which were at the time of marriage in, or after marriage came into, the possession of his wife, he acquired an interest different from his rights over her *choses in action*, such as debts due to her, *e.g.* on a bond, or as money deposited at her bankers. The statement, however, is substantially true, because a husband on marriage became for most purposes the almost absolute master of his wife's property. The whole of her income, from whatever source it came (even if it were the earnings of her own work or professional skill), belonged to her husband. Then, too, a married woman, because her personality was merged in that of her husband, had no contractual capacity, *i.e.* she could not bind herself by a contract. Her testamentary capacity was extremely limited; she could not make a devise of her freehold property, and such testamentary power as she possessed with regard to personal property could be exercised only with the consent of her husband, and this consent, when given, might be at any time revoked. If she died intestate the whole of her personal estate either remained her husband's or became his on her death. The way in which the rules of the common law might, occasionally at any rate, deprive a rich woman of the whole of her wealth may be seen by the following illustration. A lady is possessed of a large fortune; it consists of household furniture, pictures, a large sum in money and bank notes, as well as £10,000 deposited at her bankers, of leasehold estates in London, and of freehold estates in the country. She is induced, in 1850, to marry, without having made any settlement whatever, an adventurer, such as the Barry Lyndon of fiction, or the Mr. Bowes of historical reality, who supplied, it is said, the original for Thackeray's picture of Barry Lyndon's married life. He at once becomes the actual owner of all the goods and money in the possession of his wife. He can, by taking the proper steps, with or without her consent, obtain possession for his own use of the money at her bankers, and exact payment to himself of every debt due to her. He can sell her leaseholds and put the proceeds in his own pocket. Her freehold estate, indeed, he cannot sell out and out, but he can charge it to the extent of his own interest therein at any rate during coverture,

---

in action which he might reduce into possession. See Blackstone, *Comm.* ii. 433–435; Stephen, *Comm.* ii. (14th ed.), 308–314.

and if under the curtesy of England he acquires a life interest in the freehold estate after the death of his wife, he can charge the estate for the term of his natural life. In any case he can spend as he pleases the whole of his wife's income. He turns out a confirmed gambler. In the course of a few years he has got rid of the whole of his wife's property, except the freehold estate, but though it has not been sold, he has charged it with the payment of all his debts up to the very utmost of his power. If he outlives his wife she will never receive a penny of rent from the estate. He and his wife are in truth penniless; she earns, however, £1000 a year as a musician or an actress. This is a piece of rare good luck—for her husband. He is master of the money she earns. Let him allow her enough, say £200 a year, to induce her to exert her talents, and he may live in idleness and modest comfort on the remaining £800. Under this state of things, which up to 1870 was possible, though, of course, not common, it is surely substantially true to say that marriage transferred the property of a wife to her husband. Blackstone, indeed, though he knew the common law well enough, tells us that, "even the disabilities which the wife lies under, are for the most part intended for her protection and benefit. So great a favourite is the female sex of the laws of England."[16] But this splendid optimism of 1765 is too much for even the complacent toryism of 1809, and at that date, Christian, an editor of Blackstone's *Commentaries*, feels bound to deny that the law of England has shown any special partiality to women, and protests that he is not so much in love with his subject "as to be inclined to leave it in possession of a glory which it may not justly deserve."[17]

As to Equity.[18] In 1800 the Court of Chancery had been engaged for centuries in the endeavour to make it possible for a married woman to hold property independently of her husband, and to exert over this property the rights which could be exercised by a man or an unmarried woman. Let it, however, be noted, that the aim of the Court of Chancery had throughout been not so much to increase the property rights of married women generally, as to enable a person (*e.g.* a father) who gave to, or settled

---

16. Blackstone, *Comm.* i. p. 445.

17. See Christian's edition of Blackstone's *Commentaries*, i. p. 445, note 23.

18. Stephen, *Comm.* ii. 319–321; Ashburner, *Principles of Equity*, 231–244; Lush, *Law of Husband and Wife*, ch. v.

property on a woman, to ensure that she, even though married, should possess it as her own, and be able to deal with it separately from, and independently of, her husband, who, be it added, was, in the view of equity lawyers, the "enemy" against whose exorbitant common-law rights the Court of Chancery waged constant war. By the early part of the nineteenth century, and certainly before any of the Married Women's Property Acts, 1870–1893, came into operation, the Court of Chancery had completely achieved its object. A long course of judicial legislation had at last given to a woman, over property settled for her separate use, nearly all the rights, and a good deal more than the protection, possessed in respect of any property by a man or a *feme sole.* This success was achieved, after the manner of the best judge-made law, by the systematic and ingenious development of one simple principle—namely, the principle that, even though a person might not be able to hold property of his own, it might be held for his benefit by a trustee whose sole duty it was to carry out the terms of the trust. Hence, as regards the property of married women, the following results, which were attained only by degrees.

Property given to a trustee for the separate use of a woman, whether before or after marriage, is her separate property—that is, it is property which does not in any way belong to the husband. At common law indeed it is the property of the trustee, but it is property which he is bound in equity to deal with according to the terms of the trust, and therefore in accordance with the wishes or directions of the woman. Here we have constituted the "separate property" or the "separate estate" of a married woman.

If, as might happen, property was given to or settled upon a woman for her separate use, but no trustee were appointed, then the Court of Chancery further established that the husband himself, just because he was at common law the legal owner of the property, must hold it as trustee for his wife. It was still her separate property, and he was bound to deal with it in accordance with the terms of the trust, *i.e.* as property settled[19] upon

---

19. It will be convenient in the rest of this Lecture to treat the separate property of a married woman, whenever the contrary is not stated, as coming to her under a marriage settlement, but of course it might come to her in other ways. It might be bestowed upon her as a gift or left to her by will for her separate use.

or given to her for her separate use.[20] The Court of Chancery having thus created separate property for a married woman, by degrees worked out to its full result the idea that a trustee must deal with the property of a married woman in accordance with her directions. Thus the Court gave her the power to give away or sell her separate property, as also to leave it to whomsoever she wished by will, and further enabled her to charge it with her contracts. With regard to such property, in short, equity at last gave her, though in a round-about way, nearly all the rights of a single woman. But equity lawyers came to perceive, somewhere towards the beginning of the nineteenth century, that though they had achieved all this, they had not given quite sufficient protection to the settled property of a married woman. Her very possession of the power to deal freely with her separate property might thwart the object for which that separate property had been created; for it might enable a husband to get her property into his hands. Who could guarantee that Barry Lyndon might not persuade or compel his wife to make her separate property chargeable for his debts, or to sell it and give him the proceeds? This one weak point in the defences which equity had thrown up against the attacks of the enemy was rendered unassailable by the astuteness, as it is said, of Lord Thurlow. He invented the provision, constantly since his time introduced into marriage settlements or wills, which is known as the restraint on anticipation. This clause, if it forms part of the document settling property upon a woman for her separate use, makes it impossible for her during coverture either to alienate the property or to charge it with her debts. Whilst she is married she cannot, in short, in any way anticipate her income, though in every other respect she may deal with the property as her own. She may, for example, bequeath or devise her property by will, since the bequest or devise will have no operation till marriage has come to an end. But this restraint, or fetter, operates only during coverture. It in no way touches the property rights either of a spinster or of a widow. The final result, then, of the judicial

---

20. So completely was a wife's separate property her own that even after it was paid over to her, say, by a trustee under her marriage settlement, it was still in equity, during her life, her property, and not that of her husband. See *Herbert* v. *Herbert* (1692), 1 Eq. Ca. Ab. 661; *Bird* v. *Pegrum* (1853), 13 C.B. 639; *Duncan* v. *Cashin* (1875), L.R. 10 C.P. 554; *Butler* v. *Cumpston* (1868), L.R. 7 Eq. 16, 24.

legislation carried through by the Court of Chancery was this. A married woman could possess separate property over which her husband had no control whatever. She could, if it was not subject to a restraint on anticipation, dispose of it with perfect freedom. If it was subject to such restraint, she was during coverture unable to exercise the full rights of an owner, but in compensation she was absolutely guarded against the possible exactions or persuasions of her husband, and received a kind of protection which the law of England does not provide for any other person except a married woman.

It is often said, even by eminent lawyers, that a married woman was in respect of her separate property made in equity a *feme sole.*[21] But this statement, though broadly speaking true, is not accurate, and conceals from view the fact (which is of importance to a student who wishes to understand the way in which equity has told upon the form and substance of the Married Women's Property Acts, 1870–1893) that the process of judicial legislation which gave to a married woman a separate estate, led to some very singular results. Three examples will make plain my meaning.

21. "When the Courts of equity established the doctrine of the separate use of a married woman, and applied it to both real and personal estate, it became necessary to give the married woman, with respect to such separate property, an independent personal *status,* and to make her in equity a *feme sole.* It is of the essence of the separate use, that the married woman shall be independent of, and free from the control and interference of her husband. With respect to separate property, the *feme covert* is, by the form of trust, released and freed from the fetters and disability of coverture, and invested with the rights and powers of a person who is *sui juris.* To every estate and interest held by a person who is *sui juris,* the common law attaches a right of alienation, and accordingly the right of a *feme covert* to dispose of her separate estate was recognised and admitted from the beginning, until Lord Thurlow devised the clause against anticipation (*Parkes* v. *White,* 11 Ves. 209, 221). But it would be contrary to the whole principle of the doctrine of separate use, to require the consent or concurrence of the husband in the act or instrument by which the wife's separate estate is dealt with or disposed of. That would be to make her subject to his control and interference. The whole matter lies between a married woman and her trustees; and the true theory of her alienation is, that any instrument, be it deed or writing, when signed by her, operates as a direction to the trustees to convey or hold the estate according to the new trust which is created by such direction. This is sufficient to convey the *feme covert's* equitable interest. When the trust thus created is clothed by the trustees with the legal estate, the alienation is complete both at law and in equity."—*Taylor* v. *Meads* (1865), 34 L.J. Ch. 203, 207, per Westbury, L.C.

First. The restraint on anticipation which to-day, no less than before 1870, is constantly to be found in marriage settlements, has (as already pointed out) given to a married woman a strictly anomalous kind of protection.

Secondly. Equity, whilst conferring upon a married woman the power to dispose of her separate property by will, gave her no testamentary capacity with respect to any property which was not in technical strictness separate property. Take the following case: *W* was possessed of separate property. By her will made in 1850, she left, without her husband's knowledge, the whole of her property of every description to *T.* In 1855 *H,* her husband, died and bequeathed £10,000 to *W. W* died in 1869, leaving her will unchanged. The property which had been her separate property in 1850 passed to *T,*[22] but the £10,000 did not pass to *T.*[23] It would not pass at common law—it would not pass according to the rules of equity—for the simple reason that as it came to *W* after her husband's death, it never was her separate property.

Thirdly. Equity never in strictness gave a married woman contractual capacity; it never gave her power to make during coverture a contract which bound herself personally. What it did do was this: it gave her power to make a contract, *e.g.* incur a debt, on the credit of separate property which belonged to her at the time when the debt was incurred, and it rendered such separate property liable to satisfy the debt. Hence two curious consequences. The contract of a married woman, in the first place, even though intended to bind[24] her separate property, did not in equity bind any property of which she was not possessed at the moment when she made the contract, *e.g.* incurred a debt.[25] The contract of a married woman, in the second place, if made when she possessed no separate prop-

22. *Taylor* v. *Meads* (1865), 34 L.J. Ch. 203.
23. *Willock* v. *Noble* (1875), L.R., 7 H.L. 580.
24. The contract of a married woman is said, even in Acts of Parliament, to "bind" her separate estate, but it did not in equity, nor does it now under the Married Women's Property Acts, bind her separate property in the sense of being a charge on such property. As far as the separate property of a married woman was, or is bound for the payment, *e.g.* of her debts, it was or is liable to satisfy them in the sense in which the whole property of a man is liable to satisfy his debts.
25. *Pike* v. *Fitzgibbon* (1881), 17 Ch.D. (C.A.) 454.

erty, in no way bound any separate property, or indeed any property whatever of which she might subsequently become possessed.[26] W, a married
woman, on the 1st January 1860, borrows £1000 from A on the credit of
her separate property, which is worth £500. A week afterwards W acquires,
under her father's will, separate property amounting to £10,000. The £500
she has meanwhile spent, the £10,000 is not chargeable with her debt to
A. Let us suppose a case of exactly the same circumstances except that
when W borrows the £1000 from A she is not possessed of any separate
property whatever, but tells A that she expects that her father will leave her
a legacy and that she will pay for the loan out of it. She does, as in the
former case, acquire a week after the loan is made £10,000 under her
father's will, and acquires it as separate property. It is not in equity chargeable with the debt to A.[27]

In spite, however, of these anomalies, there would have been little to
complain of in the law, with regard to the property of married women, if
the Court of Chancery had been able to supersede the common[28] law and
to extend to all women on their marriage the protection which the rules
of equity provided for any woman whose property was the subject of a
marriage settlement. But the way in which equity was developed as a body
of rules, which in theory followed and supplemented the common law,
made such a thorough-going reform, as would have been involved in the
superseding of the common law, an impossibility. As regards a married
woman's property the two systems of common law and of equity coexisted
side by side unconfused and unmingled till the reform introduced by the
Married Women's Property Acts. Hence was created in practice a singular

---

26. *Palliser* v. *Gurney* (1887), 19 Q.B.D. 519. Both these results seem to follow logically
from the view that when a woman's engagement bound her separate estate, she did nothing
more than agree to direct her trustee to pay what was due under the contract out of her
separate estate.

27. In neither case, of course, will the property be chargeable at common law, since W at
common law would be, as a married woman, incapable of binding herself by a contract. See
In re Shakespear (1885), 30 Ch.D. 169.

28. This might conceivably have been achieved if the Court of Chancery could have
established the principle that on any marriage taking place there was presumably a contract
between the intended husband and wife—that the wife's present and future property should
be her separate property, held for her separate use by her husband as trustee.

and probably unforeseen inequality between the position of the rich and the position of the poor. A woman who married with a marriage settlement—that is, speaking broadly, almost every woman who belonged to the wealthy classes—retained as her own any property which she possessed at the time of marriage, or which came to her, or was acquired by her during coverture. She was also, more generally than not, amply protected by the restraint on anticipation against both her own weakness and her husband's extravagance or rapacity. A woman, on the other hand, who married without a marriage settlement—that is, speaking broadly, every woman belonging to the less wealthy or the poorer classes—was by her marriage deprived of the whole of her income, and in all probability of the whole of her property. The earnings acquired by her own labour were not her own, but belonged to her husband. There came, therefore, to be not in theory but in fact one law for the rich and another for the poor. The daughters of the rich enjoyed, for the most part, the considerate protection of equity, the daughters of the poor suffered under the severity and injustice of the common law.[29]

This condition of things could not last for ever. It was terminated by parliamentary legislation during the last third of the nineteenth century (1870–1893). The point which for our purpose deserves notice is that the rules of equity—that is, a body of judge-made law—determined to a great extent the date, the method, and the nature of the reform carried through by Parliament.

Not till 1870 did Parliament make any systematic attempt to place the law governing the property of married women on a just foundation. What was it which delayed till well-nigh the end of the Benthamite era a reform which must, one would have thought, have approved itself to every Liberal? The answer is to be found in the existence under the rules of equity of a married woman's separate property. The barbarism of the common law did not, as a rule, press heavily either upon the rich who derived political power from their wealth and position, or upon the labouring poor who

29. This state of things recalls the injustice which up to 1857 marked the law of divorce. The rights of the rich and of the poor were theoretically equal, but in practice divorce was obtainable by a rich man or rich woman when it was not obtainable by any poor man or poor woman. See p. 246, *ante.*

had at last obtained much of the political power due to numbers. The daughters of the wealthy were, when married, protected under the rules of equity in the enjoyment of their separate property. The daughters of working men possessed little property of their own. The one class was protected, the other would, it seemed, gain little from protection. A rich woman indeed here or there who married without having the prudence to obtain the protection of a marriage settlement, or a woman of the poorer classes who was capable of earning a good income by the use of her talents, might suffer grievous wrong from the right of her husband to lay hands upon her property or her earnings, but, after all, the class which suffered from the severity of the common law was small, and injustice, however grievous, which touches only a small class commands in general but little attention. Changes in the law, moreover, which affect family life always offend the natural conservatism of ordinary citizens. It is easy, then, to see that the rules of equity by mitigating the harshness of the common law did for a certain time postpone a necessary reform. It is harder to understand why an amendment of the law which had been deferred so long should, in 1870, have become more or less of a necessity. To answer this inquiry we must look to the circumstances of the time and the general current of public opinion. The Parliament of 1870 had been elected under the then recent Reform Acts. It was inspired by the hopes and endowed with the vigour which have generally been the immediate, though by no means always the permanent, result of an advance towards democracy. The power at common law of a husband to appropriate his wife's property and earnings was in reality indefensible. But though the theoretical injustice of the law was no greater, the wrong actually wrought thereby was far more extensive, and far more visible to the public in 1870 than in 1832. In 1870 the women, even among the wage-earners, who could earn good wages by their own labour, must have been far more numerous than they were forty years earlier. What is certain is that the number of women belonging to the middle class, who could as teachers, musicians, actresses, or authoresses, gain large emoluments by their professional skill had, since the beginning of the nineteenth century, greatly increased, and that this body of accomplished women had obtained the means of making known to the public through the press every case of injustice done to any one of them. How great was the effect of their complaints is proved by the fact that the earliest Married Women's Prop-

Judicial Legislation / 275

erty Act aims at little else than securing to a married woman the possession of her own earnings and savings. Much must also be attributed to the influence of one man. John Mill was between 1860 and 1870 at the height of his power. His authority among the educated youth of England was greater than may appear credible to the present generation. His work *On Liberty* was to the younger body of Liberal statesmen a political manual. To no cause was he more ardently devoted than to the emancipation of women. He wished to give them the full privileges of citizenship, and of course favoured the abolition of any law which interfered with their property rights. At the same time many Conservatives who could not support the admission of women to all the political rights of men, desired to give every woman the control over her own property. The Divorce Act, lastly, of 1857 had given to a wife deserted by her husband,[30] and also to a wife judicially separated from her husband, nearly the property rights of a *feme sole*,[31] and had set a precedent which told strongly on legislative opinion.

When at last reform became a necessity, the method thereof was determined almost wholly by the existence of the rules of equity.

In 1870 two different methods of removing the injustice suffered by married women were open to reformers. The one and apparently the simpler mode of proceeding was to enact in one form or another that a married woman should, as regards her property and rights or liabilities connected with property, stand on the same footing as an unmarried woman.[32]

---

30. "If any . . . order of protection be made, the wife shall, during the continuance thereof, be and be deemed to have been, during such desertion of her, in the like position in all respects, with regard to property and contracts, and suing and being sued, as she would be under this Act if she obtained a decree of judicial separation."—Matrimonial Causes Act, 1857 (20 & 21 Vict. c. 85), s. 21.

31. "In every case of a judicial separation the wife shall, whilst so separated, be considered as a *feme sole* for the purposes of contract, and wrongs and injuries, and suing and being sued in any civil proceeding."—*Ibid.* s. 26.

32. Compare the Indian Succession Act, s. 4. "No person shall, by marriage, acquire any interest in the property of the person whom he or she marries, nor become incapable of doing any act in respect of his or her own property, which he or she could have done if unmarried."—See Ilbert, *Legislative Methods*, p. 152.

It would have been possible to place husband and wife, as under French law, in something like the position of partners as regards each other's property. An innovation, however, of

This course of proceeding lay ready to hand and was in appearance at any rate easy. It had, as we have seen, been followed in the Divorce Act of 1857. But the direct and simple plan of giving to a married woman the same property rights as those of a *feme sole* was not adopted by the authors of the Married Women's Property Acts. The other, but the less obvious method was to make the property of a married woman, or some part thereof, during coverture, her "separate property" in the technical sense which that term had acquired in the Courts of Equity, and thus to secure for all married women, as to some part at any rate of their property, the rights which the Court of Chancery had secured for those women who enjoyed the advantage of a marriage settlement.[33] This was the policy actually pursued by Parliament and embodied in the Married Women's Property Acts, 1870–1893. The adoption of this method excites surprise. It was open to obvious objections. It made it necessary to pass statutes of a complicated and artificial character. It precluded the possibility of defining the position of a married woman in regard to her property in language which could be easily understood by laymen. The Married Women's Property Acts have, as a matter of fact, perplexed not only lawyers, but even judges, who, while accustomed to the rules of the common law, were unfamiliar with the principles of equity, and have raised a whole host of nice and thorny questions as to the precise rights and liabilities of married women. And these objections to the method of reform adopted by the Legislature must have been obvious to many reformers, though they may not have been understood by most of the members of Parliament who in 1870 voted for the first Married Women's Property Act.

Still the course of legislation actually pursued may well have commended itself on at least two grounds to practical reformers. The one was that, while many members of Parliament dreaded a revolution in the law affecting family life, their fears were dispelled by the assertion that the proposed change did no more than give to every married woman nearly the same rights as every English gentleman had for generations past secured under a marriage settlement for his daughter on her marriage. The other

this kind would have been radically opposed to English habits. It has not, as far as my knowledge goes, been advocated either in or out of Parliament.

33. But of a settlement which did not contain a restraint on anticipation. See p. 269, *ante*.

was that members of Parliament belonging as they did to the wealthier classes of the community were, though ready to save hard-working women from injustice, determined not to sacrifice the defences by which the Court of Chancery had protected the fortunes of well-to-do women against the attacks of their husbands. Now to enact off-hand that a married woman should, as regards her property, stand in the position of a *feme sole* might shake the validity of that restraint on anticipation which most English gentlemen thought and still think necessary for the protection of a married woman against her own weakness or the moral authority of her husband; but to make every married woman's possessions her separate property was clearly quite compatible with maintaining the useful though anomalous restraint on anticipation. Whatever in any case may have been the grounds on which Parliament acted, it is certain that the legislative policy embodied in the successive Married Women's Property Acts is based upon the principles of equity with regard to the "separate estate" of a married woman.[34]

The closeness in this instance of the connection between a whole line of Acts and the rules of equity, or in other words, a body of already existing judge-made law, becomes apparent if we follow in the very most general way, without attempting to go into details, the course of parliamentary enactment from 1870–1893.

The Married Women's Property Act, 1870, though most important as fixing the method of reform and as an acknowledgment of the right of every married woman to hold property as her separate estate, was a merely tentative enactment which went very little way towards removing the grievances of which women had a right to complain, and rested on no clear principle. It secured to a woman as her separate property the earnings during coverture of her own labour,[35] and also certain investments. The Act no doubt gave her some other advantages, and especially the right to the income of real estate which might descend upon her during marriage. The utter indifference, however, of Parliament to any fixed principle of

34. "It was this equitable principle of the wife's separate estate which formed the model of the legal separate estate created by the Married Women's Property Acts, 1870 and 1882."— Stephen, *Comm.* ii. (14th ed.), p. 319.

35. 33 & 34 Vict. c. 93, s. 1.

fairness may be seen in one provision of the Act,[36] of which the effect was as follows: If *A*, a widower, having an only child who is a married woman, left her all his personal property worth £10,000 by will, the whole of it (except possibly £200 in money) went to her husband, but if *A* died intestate she had it all for her separate use.[37] The Married Women's Property Act, 1874,[38] is simply an attempt, which did not completely attain its end, to correct an absurd blunder by which Parliament had in 1870 entirely freed a husband from liability for his wife's ante-nuptial debts, whilst allowing him still to obtain by marriage the greater part of his wife's property. The Married Women's Property Act, 1882,[39] brought, or tried to bring, the course of reform, commenced in 1870, to its logical and legitimate conclusion. The statute, if we omit many details, and look at it as a whole, embodies two principles. The whole property, in the first place, of a married woman, whether it is hers at marriage or comes to her after marriage, is made her separate property, and as such separate property is (except as may be otherwise provided by the Act)[40] subject to the incidents which the Court of Chancery had already attached to the separate property of a married woman; the Act, as it were, provides every woman on her marriage with a settlement. Marriage settlements, in the second place, are left untouched by the Act,[41] and the protection which a married woman may derive from the restraint on anticipation if imposed upon her property by, *e.g.* a marriage settlement, is in no way diminished. Assuming that the method of reform adopted by Parliament from 1870 onwards was the right one, there is little to be said either against the Act of 1882, at any rate as regards the principles on which it was founded, or against the construction put upon it by the judges who, rightly (it is submitted), treated the legal separate property created by the Act as having the character of separate property created by the rules of equity. The plan, however, of making a married woman's property her separate property, instead of placing her in

36. 33 & 34 Vict. c. 93, s. 7.
37. *In re Voss* (1880), 13 Ch.D. 504.
38. 37 & 38 Vict. c. 50.
39. 45 & 46 Vict. c. 75.
40. See generally 45 & 46 Vict. c. 75, s. 1, and note sub-ss. (3), (4).
41. *Ibid.* s. 19.

the position of a *feme sole,* led to curious results which may have been quite unforeseen by members of Parliament. A married woman, for instance, did not under the Act acquire true contractual capacity; a contract made by her after 1882 still binds not herself but her separate property.[42] Hence, when a married woman at the time of entering into a contract, *e.g.* incurring a debt, was possessed of no separate property, any separate property which she might afterwards acquire was not, until after the passing of the Married Women's Property Act, 1893, liable to satisfy the debt.[43] The effect of the restraint on anticipation remained in full force. Contractual liabilities incurred by a married woman could not under the Act of 1882, and cannot now, be satisfied out of property subject to such restraint, even after the restraint had ceased to operate, *e.g.* by the death of her husband.[44] A married woman did not, moreover, under the Act of 1882 acquire full testamentary capacity. A will made by her during coverture, though purporting to deal with the whole of her property, did not at her death, if occurring after the death of her husband, pass property, *e.g.* left to her by his will, which had never been her "separate property" in the technical sense of the term.[45] The Married Women's Property Act, 1893,[46] has removed some of the anomalies arising from defects in the Married Women's Property Act, 1882, and the policy of the Act of 1882 has received pretty nearly its full development. All the property of a married woman is her separate property; she may, except in so far as her power is limited by the restraint on anticipation, deal with it as she pleases. She has (subject always to this possible restraint) full contractual and full testamentary capacity. Marriage settlements, however, and above all the restraint on anticipation,

42. She does not incur a personal liability. Hence there is no power under the Debtors Act, 1869, to commit a married woman for default in paying a sum of money for which judgment has been recovered against her under the Married Women's Property Act, 1882.— *Draycott* v. *Harrison* (1886), 17 Q.B.D. 147.

43. *Palliser* v. *Gurney* (1887), 19 Q.B.D. 519. Nor indeed was any property which might afterwards come to her as a widow, and was therefore not "separate property" at all.

44. *Barnett* v. *Howard* [1900], 2 Q.B. (C.A.) 784.

45. Compare *Willock* v. *Noble* (1875), L.R. 7 H.L. 580; *In re Price* (1885), 28 Ch.D. 709; *In re Cuno* (1889), 43 Ch.D. (C.A.), 12; and Lush, *Law of Husband and Wife* (2nd ed.), pp. 138–140.

46. 56 & 57 Vict. c. 63.

remain untouched by the Married Women's Property Acts. The policy of Parliament has by means of hesitating and awkward legislation been at last carried out. But this parliamentary policy is in reality little else than the extension to the property of women who marry without a marriage settlement, of the rules established in equity with regard to the rights of a married woman over property settled upon her or given to her for her separate use.[47]

The rules of equity, however, have done much more than delay for a certain period the complete reform of the law governing the property of married women, or than fix the method in accordance with which that reform should be carried out. They have told upon the whole public opinion of England as to the property rights which a married woman ought to possess. We shall see that this is so if we search for the answer to an inquiry which must surely perplex anyone who turns his thoughts towards the modern development of the law of England. How are we to account for the fact that whilst till the end of 1869 a married woman possessed at common law hardly any property rights whatever—and many were the women who fell under the operation of the common law—yet the Parliament of England within thirteen years from that date, i.e. in 1882, gave to every married woman more complete and independent control of her property than is possessed by the married women of France or of Scotland? Under French law husband and wife are in general, as regards their common property, members of a sort of partnership, but the husband is the predominant partner and has complete control of the partnership, capital,

---

47. The Married Women's Property Acts, 1882–1893 (the Acts of 1870 and 1874 are repealed), are so drawn as still to leave some important points unsettled. What, for example, is the effect of the proviso contained in the Married Women's Property Act, 1893, s. 1? Does it exempt the separate property of a married woman subject to restraint on anticipation, from liability to satisfy a contract made by her during coverture, even though such restraint has by the death of her husband ceased to operate? The Court of Appeal has answered this inquiry in the affirmative—*Barnett* v. *Howard* [1900], 2 Q.B. (C.A.), 784; *Brown* v. *Dimbleby* [1904], 1 K.B. (C.A.), 28; *Birmingham Excelsior Society* v. *Lane* [1904], 1 K.B. (C.A.), 35; Lush, *Husband and Wife* (2nd ed.), pp. 314, 315. But some lawyers of eminence find the decisions of the Court of Appeal difficult to reconcile with *Hood Barrs* v. *Heriot* [1896], A. C., 174; *Whiteley* v. *Edwards* [1896], 2 Q.B. (C.A.), 48. See Pollock, *Principles of Contract* (8th ed.), pp. 90–95.

and revenues.[48] Under Scottish law a wife cannot part with her property without her husband's consent.[49] In England a wife's property has been, since 1882, truly her own; her husband cannot touch it. If she wishes to sell it or give it away, she need not ask for his consent. The answer to our inquiry is to be found in the rules of equity. Long before 1870 Chancery had habituated English gentlemen to the idea that a married woman of wealth ought to hold and dispose of her property at her own will, and with absolute freedom from the control of her husband. The change introduced by the Married Women's Property Acts, 1870–1893, was no sudden revolution: it was the tardy recognition of the justice of arrangements which, as regards the gentry of England, had existed for generations. The reform effected by the Married Women's Property Acts is simply one more application of the principle insisted upon by the historians of English law,[50] that in England the law for the great men has a tendency to become the law for all men. The rules of equity, framed for the daughters of the rich, have at last been extended to the daughters of the poor.

What are the respective merits and defects of judicial and of parliamentary legislation?

This is an inquiry naturally raised, and to a considerable extent answered, by the history of the law as to the property of married women.

Judicial legislation, extending over more than two centuries, worked out an extraordinary and within certain limits a most effective reform which was logical, systematic, and effectual, just because it was the application to actual and varying circumstances of a clear and simple principle. But judicial legislation here, as elsewhere, exhibited its inherent defects. The progress, in the first place, of reform was slow; the nineteenth century had already opened before the restraint on anticipation, which at last gave effectual protection to the property of a married woman, became a firmly established part of the law of England. A time, in the second place, inevitably arrived when judicial legislation had reached its final limits, and the

48. *Code Civil*, art. 1421.

49. Bell, *Principles of the Law of Scotland* (10th ed.), s. 1560 D. But a wife can dispose of accrued income of her estate.

50. Pollock and Maitland, *History of English Law*, i. p. 203.

reform accomplished by the Court of Chancery was thus marked by incompleteness. Before 1870 judicial legislation, it was clear, could do no more than had been already achieved to secure for married women their full property rights; and this necessary arrest of judicial power was the more to be lamented, because the operation of the common law combined with the modification thereof introduced by the Court of Chancery, had in fact established one law for the daughters of the rich, and another, but far less just law, for the daughters of the poor.

Parliamentary legislation from the time when it began to operate produced its effect with great rapidity. For within twelve years (1870–1882), or at most twenty-three years (1870–1893), Parliament reformed the law as to married women's property, and thus revolutionised an important part of the family law of England; and neither twelve nor twenty-three years can be considered as more than a moment in the history of a nation. Add too that the reform carried out by Parliament was, when once accomplished, thorough-going, and can at any moment, if it needs extension, be carried further under the authority of a sovereign legislature. The Court of Chancery, it may be said, took centuries to work out incompletely a reform which Parliament at last carried out with more or less completeness in little less than a quarter of a century; but in fairness we must remember that parliamentary reformers borrowed the ideas on which they acted from the Courts of Equity, and that during the centuries when the Court of Chancery was gradually but systematically removing for the benefit of married women the injustice of the common law, Parliament did little or nothing to save any woman from rules under which marriage might and sometimes did deprive her of the whole of her property.

The four Married Women's Property Acts are, further, a record of the hesitation and the dulness of members of Parliament. Want of support by popular opinion probably made it necessary to proceed step by step, but it is difficult to believe that enlightened reformers who had understood the actual state of the law could not in 1870 have gone much further than they did towards establishing the principles now embodied in the Married Women's Property Acts, 1882–1893. It is in any case certain that the necessity for the Married Women's Property Act, 1874, was caused by a gross blunder or oversight on the part of the Legislature, and that the Married Women's Property Act, 1893, proves that Parliament, whilst wishing in 1882 to put the law on a sound basis, had not understood how to attain its object. The plain truth is that Parliament tried, whether wisely or not, to reform the law in accordance with ideas borrowed from equity, and some even of the lawyers by whom Parliament was guided did not fully understand the principles of equity which they meant to follow. Hence recurring blunders which one may hope, though without any great confidence, have been at last corrected. Parliamentary legislation, in short, if it is sometimes rapid and thorough-going, exhibits in this instance, as in others, characteristic faults. It is the work of legislators who are much influenced by the immediate opinion of the moment, who make laws with little regard either to general principles or to logical consistency, and who are deficient in the skill and knowledge of experts.

For our own purpose, however, the most important matter to note is after all neither the merits nor the defects of the Married Women's Property Acts, but the evidence which they give of the way in which judicial may tell upon parliamentary legislation. Nor ought the care devoted to the examination of the connection between judge-made law and Acts of Parliament in the case of the Married Women's Property Acts to lead any student to suppose that the same connection is not traceable in many other departments of law. It may be illustrated by the laws governing the right of association,[51] by the law with reference to an employer's liability for damage done by the negligence of his servants,[52] or by provisions of the Judicature Acts which substitute rules of equity for the rules of common law. In studying the development of the law we must allow at every turn for the effect exercised by the cross-current of judicial opinion which may sometimes stimulate, which may often retard, and which constantly moulds or affects, the action of that general legislative opinion which tells immediately on the course of parliamentary legislation.

51. See pp. 68–74, 136–143, 189–193, *ante*.
52. See pp. 198–201, *ante*.

Relation between Legislative Opinion and General Public Opinion

LAW-MAKING OPINION is merely one part of the whole body of ideas and beliefs which prevail at a given time. We therefore naturally expect, first, that alterations in the opinion which governs the province of legislation will reappear in other spheres of thought and action and be traceable in the lives of individuals, and, next, that the changes of legislative opinion will turn out to be the result of the general tendencies of English or indeed of European thought during a particular age. This lecture is an attempt to show that these anticipations hold good in a very special manner of that transition from individualistic liberalism to unsystematic collectivism or socialism, which has characterised the development of English law during the later part of the nineteenth century.

I. As to analogous changes of opinion in different spheres and also in the lives of individuals.

Let us here consider rather more fully a matter several times touched upon in the foregoing lectures, namely, the relation between legislative and theological opinion.

The partial coincidence in point of time between the reign of Benthamism in the field of legislation and of Evangelicalism in the religious world is obvious. The influence of each was on the increase from the beginning of the nineteenth century, and reached its height about 1834–35. From that date until about 1860 utilitarian philosophy and Evangelical theology were each dominant in England. By 1870, however, it was manifest that Benthamism and Evangelicalism had each lost much of their hold upon Englishmen. This decline of authority, when once it became noticeable, was rapid. In the England of to-day the very names of Benthamites and of Evangelicals are forgotten. Their watchwords are out of date. Many ideas, it is true, which we really owe to Bentham and his followers, or to Simeon and his predecessors, exert more power than would be suspected from the current language of the time. But as living movements Benthamism and Evangelicalism are things of the past. Have they no real inter-connection or similarity? To this question many critics will reply with a decided negative. It appears at first sight a hopeless paradox to contend that the doctrines of Jeremy Bentham and James Mill had any affinity with the faith of Simeon, of Wilberforce, and of Zachary Macaulay. The political reformers were Radicals, or, in the language of their day, democrats; they were certainly freethinkers, and must sometimes in the eyes of Evangelicals have appeared infidels, if not atheists; they assuredly attached no value to any theological creed whatever; their only conception of church reform[1] was to make the Church of England a fit instrument for the propagation of utilitarian morality. The Evangelical leaders, on the other hand, were Tories; they were men of ardent personal piety; to Bentham and his followers they must have seemed bigots; their efforts were directed to the revival, throughout the nation, of religious fervour. The only kind of church reform which enlisted their sympathy was the removal of all abuses, such as pluralism, which hindered the Church of England from being the effective preacher of what they held to be saving truth. Evangelicalism, in short, with its gaze constantly directed towards the happiness or terrors of a future life, might well be considered the direct antithesis of utilitarianism, which looked exclusively to the promotion in this world of the greatest happiness of the greatest number. The difference is nothing else than the gulf which severs religion from secularism. Yet as we can now see, Benthamism and Evangelicalism represented the development in widely different spheres of the same fundamental principle, namely, the principle of individualism.[2]

1. See pp. 228–229, *ante.*

2. "The Evangelical movement," writes Dr. Dale, "had its characteristic ἦθος or spirit, as well as its characteristic creed; and this ἦθος or spirit it is not hard to discover. Its supreme care in the days of its strength was not for any ideal of ecclesiastical polity; it contributed to

The appeal of the Evangelicals to personal religion corresponds with the appeal of Benthamite Liberals to individual energy. Indifference to the authority of the Church is the counterpart of indifference to the authoritative teaching or guidance of the State or of society. A low estimate of ecclesiastical tradition, aversion to, and incapacity for inquiries into the growth or development of religion, the stern condemnation of even the slightest endeavour to apply to the Bible the principles of historical criticism, bear a close resemblance to Bentham's contempt for legal antiquarianism, and to James Mill's absolute blindness to the force of the historical objections brought by Macaulay against the logical dogmatism embodied in Mill's essay on government. Evangelicals and Benthamites alike were incapable of applying the historical method, and neither recognised its value nor foresaw its influence.[3] The theology, again, which insisted upon personal responsibility, and treated each man as himself bound to work out his own salvation,[4] had an obvious affinity to the political philosophy

---

the extinction among Congregationalists, and, I think, among Baptists and Presbyterians, of that solicitude for an ideal Church organisation which had so large a place in the original revolt of the Nonconformists against the Elizabethan settlement of the English Church. Nor were the Evangelical clergy zealous supporters of Episcopacy; their imagination was not touched by that great—though, as we believe false—conception of the Church which fired the passion of the leaders of the Tractarian Revival—a Church whose living ministers can claim to inherit, by unbroken succession, awful powers and prerogatives attributed to the original apostles. The Evangelical movement encouraged what is called an undenominational temper. It emphasised the vital importance of the Evangelical creed, but it regarded almost with indifference all forms of Church polity that were not in apparent and irreconcilable antagonism to that creed. It demanded as the basis of fellowship a common religious life and common religious beliefs, but was satisfied with fellowship of an accidental and precarious kind. It cared nothing for the idea of the Church as the august society of saints. It was the ally of individualism."—R. W. Dale, *The Old Evangelicalism and the New,* pp. 16, 17.

3. Note the account of Thomas Scott's theology given about the middle of the nineteenth century by a sympathetic critic. It is clear that while Scott's autobiography, published under the title of *The Force of Truth,* will retain a permanent place in religious literature as a record of personal experience, his mode of reasoning must be utterly unconvincing to a thinker of to-day. It is as much out of date as the argument of James Mill's *Government.* It could not now be written by a man of anything like Scott's intellectual power. See Sir J. Stephen, *Ecclesiastical Biography,* ii. p. 121, and following.

4. When Wesley refused, though earnestly requested by his father, to leave Oxford, he

which regards men almost exclusively as separate individuals, and made it the aim of law to secure for every person freedom to work out his own happiness.

Nor from one point of view was Evangelical teaching opposed to the fundamental dogma of Benthamism. Paley's *Principles of Moral and Political Philosophy*, of which the publication[5] preceded by four years the appearance of Bentham's treatise on the *Principles of Morals and Legislation*,[6] was the extension of the greatest-happiness principle to the sphere of religion, and Paley was accepted by the religious world of England as the philosophic theologian of the age. Nor need this excite surprise. The preachers who, whether within or without the limits of the Church of England, aroused the consciences of Englishmen to a sense of religious and moral duty by appeals to the dread of hell-fire in the next world, and the thinkers who pressed upon Englishmen the necessity and wisdom of promoting in this world, in so far as law could accomplish the end, the greatest happiness of the greatest number, relied alike, in theory at least, upon the principle of utility, which bade every man to strive for the attainment, whether in this world or in any other, of the greatest possible happiness. Practically both the preachers and the philosophers appealed to much nobler feelings than the mere desire to avoid pain or to enjoy pleasure. Evangelical teachers and philosophic Radicals urged their disciples, though in very different ways, to lead better and nobler lives; they appealed, as regards matters of national concern, to the public spirit and to the humanity of Englishmen; they excited among all whom they could influence the hatred of palpable injustice, and felt themselves, and kindled among others, a special abhorrence for that kind of oppression which manifestly increased human suffering. Wesley on his death-bed wrote to encourage Wilberforce

---

wrote: "'The question is not whether I could do more good to others there, than here; but whether I could do more good to myself, seeing wherever I can be most holy myself, there I can most promote holiness in others'" (cited Lecky, *History of England*, ii. p. 554, from Tyerman's *Wesley*, i. p. 96). "'My chief motive,' he wrote, when starting for Georgia, 'is the hope of saving my own soul. I hope to learn the true sense of the Gospel of Christ by preaching it to the heathen'" (cited Lecky, *History of England*, ii. p. 554, from Tyerman's *Wesley*, i. p. 115).

5. 1785.

6. The first edition of this book was printed in the year 1780, and first published in 1789.

in his "glorious enterprise, in opposing that execrable villany [the slave trade] which is the scandal of religion, of England, and of human nature,"[7] whilst Bentham in a later year wrote to express his sympathy with the exertions of Wilberforce "in behalf of the race of innocents, whose lot it has hitherto been to be made the subject-matter of depredation, for the purpose of being treated worse than the authors of such crimes are treated for those crimes in other places."[8] It is indeed a coincidence that one can thus link together the names of Wesley and Bentham; but it is no mere coincidence.

This community of feeling[9] points to the humanitarianism which, during the latter part of the eighteenth and the first half of the nineteenth century, was in England the noblest trait alike of religious and of philosophic reformers. In minor, though significant, characteristics the moral tone of Benthamism is akin to Evangelicalism. Bentham, says J. S. Mill,

> both wrote and felt as if the moral standard ought not only to be paramount (which it ought), but to be alone; as if it ought to be the sole master of all our actions, and even of all our sentiments; as if either to admire or like, or despise or dislike a person for any action which neither does good nor harm, or which does not do a good or a harm proportioned to the sentiment entertained, were an injustice and a prejudice. He carried this so far, that there were certain phrases which, being expressive of what he considered to be this groundless liking or aversion, he could not bear to hear pronounced in his presence. Among these phrases were those of *good* and *bad taste*. He thought it an insolent piece of dogmatism in one person to praise or condemn another in a matter of taste: as if men's likings and dislikings, on things in themselves indifferent, were not full of the most important inferences as to every point of their character; as if a person's tastes did not show him to be wise or a fool, cultivated or ignorant, gentle or rough, sensitive or callous, generous or sordid, benevolent or selfish, conscientious or depraved.[10]

7. Stephen, *Essays in Ecclesiastical Biography*, ii. p. 282.

8. *Ibid.* p. 283. As to the relation between Wilberforce and Bentham see article by Burton, *Westminster Review*, xxxvii. (1842).

9. Robert Hall, the most eloquent preacher of his day, was deeply respected and greatly admired by Evangelicals. He condemned the absence of religion in the writings of Miss Edgeworth, and had no sympathy with the theological scepticism of Bentham, but he nevertheless avowed his intense admiration for Bentham as a legislative reformer.

10. J. S. Mill, *Dissertations and Discussions,* i. p. 388.

May not this failing of Bentham, with some plausibility at least, be charged against the religious world of which Simeon was the hero and the saint?[11] Evangelicals assuredly did not exaggerate the value of the aesthetic side of human nature, and the High Church movement, looked at from one side, was a revolt against that underestimate of taste which was common to the philanthropy and to the religion of 1834. Nor is the abhorrence of ardent utilitarians for declamation, sentiment, or vague generalities[12] altogether unlike the distaste which may be observed in some of the ablest and best of Evangelical teachers for anything indefinite, vague, or mystical.[13] However this may be, it can hardly be doubted that Benthamism and Evangelicalism each represent different forms of individualism, and to this owe much of their power.[14]

Hence the Church movements, which from one side or another have attacked and undermined the power of Evangelicalism have, as the assailants of individualism, been in the social or political sphere the conscious or unconscious allies of collectivism. Any movement which emphasises the importance of the Church as a society of Christians must, in the long run, direct men's thoughts towards the importance of the State as the great political and moral organism of which individual citizens are members. This is true of teachers whom no one would dream of placing among High Churchmen.

Dr. Arnold and F. D. Maurice each brought into prominence the idea of a Christian's position as a member of the Church. Dr. Arnold carried this idea so far as to advocate a fusion between Church and State which should exclude from citizenship any man avowedly not a Christian, and Arnold, as we have seen, stood apart from the Liberals of his day by his denunciation of *laissez faire* and his opposition to the whole view of life

---

11. "This is one of the peculiarities of the English mind; the Puritan and the Benthamite have an immense part of their nature in common; and thus the Christianity of the Puritan is coarse and fanatical;—he cannot relish what there is in it of beautiful, or delicate, or ideal."—Arnold, *Life,* ii. p. 53.

12. Mill, *Autobiography,* p. 111.

13. See *Venn Family Annals,* p. 74.

14. They both appealed to the strength, though also to the weaknesses, of the middle class. This explains how it happened that they each reached the height of their power at the time when, under the reformed Parliament of 1832, the middle classes guided the public life of England.

and society represented by Benthamism. Maurice was so profoundly impressed with the evils of unrestricted competition that, at a time when socialists were decried throughout England, he and his disciples preached the doctrine, if they did not create the name, of Christian socialism.

The High Church movement of 1834 was at its origin guided by Tories who supported authority in the State as well as in the Church. These leaders were occupied almost exclusively with questions of dogma or of church discipline. They took little interest in, and showed small sympathy with, the humanitarianism which commanded the ardent support of Evangelicals.[15] Between 1830 and 1840 it might well seem that the Oxford movement would not tell upon the course of social reforms, but, as the century wore on, it became apparent that the new prominence given to the idea of churchmanship would directly, and still more indirectly, affect the course of philanthropic efforts. It may without unfairness be asserted, that partly under the influence of the High Church movement, zeal for the promotion of that personal humanitarianism—if the expression may be allowed— which meant so much to the reformers (whether Benthamites or Evangelicals) of an earlier generation has declined, but, on the other hand, men and especially ecclesiastics, anxious to promote the physical, as well as the moral welfare of the people, have of recent years exhibited towards the socialism of the wage-earners a sympathy as unknown to Bentham as to Wilberforce. This difference is one easier to perceive than to define. It is a change of moral attitude which is very closely connected with the reaction against individualism, and if stimulated by the High Church movement, is not confined to teachers of any one school or creed. Westcott,[16] an Anglican

15. Hurrell Froude excited the sympathetic admiration of the early Tractarians; his *Remains* were published in 1837, under the editorship of James Mozley, and with a preface by Newman; they were not afraid to publish without censure the following report of his feelings: "I have felt it a kind of duty to maintain in my mind an habitual hostility to the niggers, and to chuckle over the failures of the new system, as if these poor wretches concentrated in themselves all the Whiggery, dissent, cant, and abomination that have been ranged on their side." ... "I am ashamed I cannot get over my prejudices against the niggers." ... "Every one I meet seems to me like an incarnation of the whole Anti-Slavery Society, and Fowell Buxton at their head."—Sir J. Stephen, *Essays in Ecclesiastical Biography*, ii. pp. 188, 189.

16. *Life and Letters of B. Foss Westcott*, ii. p. 115.

bishop, and Manning, an English cardinal,[17] have each composed, or attempted to compose, conflicts between the parties to a strike, and have been actuated therein by admitted sympathy with wage-earners. Nor is it a far-fetched idea that in certain circles, at least, the attacks made by Professor T. H. Green and other impressive teachers on the assumptions of utilitarianism and individualism may have facilitated the combination, not unnatural in itself, of church doctrine with socialistic sympathies.[18] The attack on individualism, then, in any sphere means the promotion of a state of public feeling which fosters the growth of collectivism in the province of law.

Politics are not the same thing as law, but in modern England any revolution in political ideas is certain to correspond with alterations in legislative opinion. If then we take care not to confound the accidental division of parties with essential differences of political faith,[19] we discover a change in the world of politics which closely resembles, if it be not rather a part of, the transition, with which these lectures have been occupied, from individualism to collectivism. One example of this change in political opinion is to be found in the altered attitude of the public towards peace and economy. During the era of Benthamism "peace and retrenchment" were the watchwords of all serious statesmen.[20] This formula has now fallen out of remembrance. The point to be noted is that this fact is significant of a very profound revolution in political belief. The demand for peace abroad and economy at home stood in very close connection with the passion for individual freedom of action which was a leading characteristic of Benthamite liberalism. Peace ought to mean light, and war certainly does mean heavy taxation, but heavy taxation whether justifiable, as it often

---

17. See *Dict. National Biography*, xxxvi. pp. 66, 67. "On occasion of the strike of the London dock labourers in August 1889 [Manning] warmly espoused their cause, and materially contributed to bring about an adjustment of the dispute."—*Ibid.*

18. For the inclination of the Church party in France to favour a certain kind of socialism, see Pic, *Traité Élémentaire de Législation Industrielle*, ss. 354, 355.

19. See p. 126, *ante.*

20. Compare for the tone of English public life from 1830–1850, Martineau's *History of the Thirty Years' Peace*, and Walpole's *History of England*, published 1878–1886, which embodies the sentiment of the era of reform, though the book is written rather from the Whig than from the Radical point of view.

is, or not, always must be a curtailment of each citizen's power to employ his property in the way he himself chooses. It is an interference, though in many cases a quite justifiable interference, with his liberty. The augmentation, moreover, of the public revenue by means of taxation is not only a diminution of each taxpayer's private income and of his power within a certain sphere to do as he likes, but also an increase in the resources and the power of the State; but to curtail the free action of individuals, and to increase the authority of the Government, was to pursue a policy opposed to the doctrine, and still more to the sentiment of Benthamite Liberals. Indifference to the mere lightening of taxation, as an end absolutely desirable in itself, is assuredly characteristic of a state of opinion under which men expect far more benefit for the mass of the people from the extension of the power of the State than from the energy of individual action. No doubt collectivists may hold that the proceeds of heavy taxes are wasted or are spent on the effort to attain objects in themselves undesirable; but the mere transference of the wealth of individuals to the coffers of the State cannot appear to a collectivist,[21] as it did to the individualistic Radicals of 1830, to be in itself a gigantic evil. We may put side by side with the decline of the economic radicalism represented in the last generation by Joseph Hume,[22] both the growth of imperialism, and the discredit which has fallen upon the colonial policy of *laissez faire* connected with the name of Cobden. For imperialism, whatever its merits and demerits, bears witness to a new-born sense among Englishmen of their

21. A sagacious collectivist may, indeed, look to some system of taxation as the best means for achieving that gradual transfer to the community of the wealth of individuals which, though it involves an immense inroad on personal freedom, might realise the ideals of socialism.

22. No politician was a more typical representative of his time than Joseph Hume. He was a utilitarian of a narrow type; he devoted the whole of his energy to the keeping down or paring down of public expenditure. Even at the period of his greatest influence (1820–1850) his passion for economy met with as much derision as admiration. Still in his day, though he was never a popular hero, he commanded some real and more nominal support. He has left no successor; no member of Parliament has taken up Hume's work. Could a politician who avowedly wished to follow in Hume's steps now obtain a seat in the House of Commons?

membership in a great imperial State. From whichever side the matter be looked at, the changes of political show a close correspondence with the alterations of legislative opinion.

Political economy and jurisprudence were between 1830 and 1850 little more than branches of utilitarianism.

The dismal science denounced by Carlyle seemed to him and his disciples simply the extreme expression of a philosophy which in their eyes was based on selfishness. The notion, indeed, that enthusiastic philanthropists were guided by nothing but the dictates of self-interest, now needs no confutation. What is worth attention is that Malthus, Senior, and McCulloch, and the so-called orthodox economists, were in popular imagination, and not without reason, identified with the philosophic Radicals; whilst the dogmas of political economy were considered to be articles of the utilitarian creed. The economists were in truth strenuous individualists. A statement somewhere to be found in Bagehot's works, that every treatise on political economy which he read in his youth began with the supposition that two men were cast on an uninhabited island, means, in reality, that economical doctrines were then inferences drawn from the way in which the supposed "economical man" would act, if he and others were left each of them free to pursue his own interest. Economics were based on individualism. Whatever may be the soundness of deductions drawn from the possible conduct of imagined human beings placed, for the sake of argument, in an imaginary state of freedom, two things are pretty clear: the one (which has already been dwelt upon), that the habit of regarding men as isolated individuals was characteristic of the period of Benthamism; the other, that this mode of considering human beings apart from their relation to society has, in economics as elsewhere, gone more or less out of fashion. In economics, as in other spheres of thought, our tendency now is to regard human beings as members of society or persons who are by nature citizens.

Jurisprudence was in the hands of Austin, as of James Mill and of Bentham, the application to existing legal conceptions of that analysis of current ideas to which Benthamites devoted their powers. The object of Austin's *Province of Jurisprudence Determined* is simply to analyse with accuracy "law," "sovereignty," "obligation," and other legal expressions, which ordinary Englishmen in a vague way understand, but to which until aided by careful definition they attach no very precise meaning.[23] This analytical method, which was pursued by the Benthamites in every department of thought, and which characterises their ethical and economical speculations no less than their jurisprudence, has no connection with historical inquiry or research, which it practically discourages or excludes. Austin's *Province of Jurisprudence Determined* was published in 1832. It belongs in its whole tendency to the era of the Reform Act. It is a work of rare power, but when first published did not obtain any wide notice. The second edition appeared, after the author's death, in 1861,[24] and then assuredly affected the thoughts of many readers. But by one of the curious paradoxes of which history is full, Austin's work produced its greatest effect just at the time when the power of the school to which he belonged was passing away. The second edition of his *Jurisprudence* was, by the date of its publication, placed in curious juxtaposition with another celebrated book which also appeared in 1861, and brought into fashion among Englishmen a new spirit of legal speculation. In Maine's *Ancient Law: its Connection with the Early History of Society and its Relation to Modern Ideas*—the full title of the book is very significant—you can still indeed trace the deep respect felt by him and his generation for Bentham. We may even doubt whether he distinctly realised the breach between his own theories and Benthamite doctrine.[25] But though Maine may have looked from a legislative point of view with favour on the principle of utility, his *Ancient Law* and his other works have

23. Jurisprudence was also in the minds of Benthamites most intimately connected with the doctrine of utility. This fact explains a peculiarity which often perplexes readers of Austin's *Jurisprudence*. The whole line of his general argument is illogically broken by an interesting but long and irrelevant disquisition on the principle of utility. See Austin, *Jurisprudence*, Lects. III. and IV.

24. In this edition the greater part of his lectures appeared not for the second but for the first time. [Editor's note: This footnote was added in the second edition.]

25. See Maine, *Early History of Institutions*, Lect. xii. p. 342. It is difficult, for example, to say whether Maine does or does not accept Austin's analysis of sovereignty as sound, if it be taken as an account of the fully developed idea of sovereignty, as it exists in a modern civilised state such as England; but it is quite clear that he attaches an importance to the historical growth of conceptions, such as sovereignty or law, which was unknown to Austin, and to the school of Bentham.

no more to do with utilitarianism than with any other ethical theory. Under his guidance we pass from the analysis to the history of legal ideas. We are introduced to the historical method.

Let us now turn from alterations of view in different departments of thought to similar revolutions of beliefs recorded in the lives of known leaders of public opinion.

This mode of looking at our subject has one great advantage: it affords protection against that fallacy of abstraction which consists in the delusion that abstract terms, such as optimism, individualism, Benthamism, collectivism, and the like, afford the explanation of facts, of which they are no more than the summary, and therefore always imperfect statement. Public opinion itself is, after all, a mere abstraction; it is not a power which has any independent existence; it is simply a general term for the beliefs held by a number of individual human beings. If we are not to become the dupes of abstract conceptions, we must individualise them and fix our attention upon the thoughts and beliefs of men who have lived and worked, and whose ideas are known to us through their conduct, their writings, or their biographies. We had far better think about Blackstone than about Blackstonianism, about Bentham or the two Mills than about Benthamism, about Sadler and Lord Shaftesbury than about the undeveloped socialism of the factory movement. The change, at any rate, from individualism to collectivism is best exemplified and explained by the lives of such leaders of thought or action. My meaning is well illustrated by the careers of Harriet Martineau, of Charles Dickens, and of John Mill. They all of them began life well imbued with the liberalism of their day. Before their lives came to an end, they had each of them deviated, more than they themselves probably perceived, from the creed of their youth, and had gone a good way along the path which led from the individualism of their early years towards the socialism of 1900.

Harriet Martineau (1802–1876) was not in a technical sense a disciple of Bentham, but when she first came before the public she was the incarnation of the liberalism of 1832–1834. To her the Reform Act was the new birth of the nation; she belonged to the generation of Liberals who, to use her own words, "saw in the parliamentary reform of Lord Grey a noble beginning of a great work which it might take centuries to perfect, and in every stage of which the national mind would renew its strength and gain fresh virtue and wisdom." The Municipal Corporations Act, the reform of the Poor Law, the founding of Mechanics' Institutes, the cheapening of books and newspapers, the diffusion of useful knowledge, and, above all, the education of the common people in the tenets of sound political economy and Malthusianism, would, she firmly believed, regenerate the world. When all but daunted by the difficulty of finding, in 1831, a publisher for her *Stories in Illustration of Political Economy,* she kept up her courage by repeating to herself, "the people wanted the book, and they should have it." For to her and to the Liberals of the day these tales were no mere stories; they were the popularisation of a saving faith.

> The "tales" are now an unreadable mixture of fiction, founded on rapid cramming, with raw masses of the dismal science. They certainly show the true journalist's talent of turning hasty acquisitions to account. But they are chiefly remarkable as illustrations of the contemporary state of mind, when the Society for the Diffusion of Useful Knowledge testified to a sudden desire for popularising knowledge, and when the political economists of the school of Malthus, Ricardo, and James Mill were beginning to have an influence upon legislation. A revelation of their doctrine in the shape of fiction instead of dry treatises just met the popular mood. The "stern Benthamites," she says, thanked her as a faithful expositor of their doctrines.[26]

Thus writes in 1893 the not unfriendly and the ablest critic of utilitarianism: he describes with admirable clearness the way in which students of to-day must of necessity regard the didactic fiction of our authoress, and brings at the same time into the most vivid light the difference or the opposition between the sentiment of 1832 and the sentiment prevalent towards the end of the nineteenth century. He reminds us that Harriet Martineau began her career as the expositor and prophetess of the sternest Benthamism, and especially of its economic creed. She was, moreover, by nature a person of singular intellectual tenacity. To her mind has been applied the description, "wax to receive, and marble to retain." If ever there lived a teacher of whom we might have expected unswerving faith in the creed of her youth, by the preaching whereof she had gained her fame, it was Harriet Martineau. Yet

---

26. Martineau, *Dictionary of National Biography,* vol. xxxvi. pp. 310, 311, article by Leslie Stephen.

her *History of the Thirty Years' Peace,* published in 1849, shows that, before the nineteenth century was half over, conceptions had intruded themselves upon her thoughts which were hardly reconcilable with the Benthamite individualism and the political economy of 1832. Whilst, for example, she on the whole still condemns the principles of the Factory Acts, she recognises with mixed sadness and perplexity that

> the tremendous labour question remains absolutely untouched—the question whether the toil of a life is not to provide a sufficiency of bread. No thoughtful man can for a moment suppose that this question can be put aside. No man with a head and a heart can suppose that any considerable class of a nation will submit for ever to toil incessantly for bare necessaries—without comfort, ease, or luxury, now—without prospect for their children, and without a hope for their own old age. A social idea or system which compels such a state of things as this, must be, in so far, worn out. In ours, it is clear that some renovation is wanted, and must be found.[27]

Have we not here a confession that, whilst old toryism was dead, philosophic radicalism had proved in her judgment inadequate to ensure the welfare of the nation? One fact points with even more certainty towards a subtle and noteworthy change of fundamental feeling or conviction. The writer whose fictitious but faithful and pragmatical exposition of economical truth had in 1832 delighted the most rigid of the Benthamites, published in 1853 an English rendering of Comte's *Philosophie Positive;* but Auguste Comte was assuredly a severe critic[28] or formidable assailant of the economical doctrine whereof Harriet Martineau had been the preacher.

Charles Dickens (1812–1870) was not, and hardly affected to be, a systematic thinker. Happily for his own reputation and for his effect on the world, he placed his trust not in any scheme of doctrine, but in his sense of humour, in his amazing power of observation, and in his insight into character. But, just because he was no systematiser, he reflected with the greater rapidity and truth the varying sentiment of the age in which he lived. The ideas with which Dickens started in life have been traced by an acute critic to Bentham. "It does not seem to me," writes Maine,

27. Martineau, *Thirty Years' Peace,* iv. (ed. 1878), p. 454. This is part of a passage which should be read as a whole.

28. See Comte, *Cours de Philosophie Positive,* iv. Leçon 47, and pp. 263–286.

a fantastic assertion that the ideas of one of the great novelists of the last generation may be traced to Bentham. . . .

Dickens, who spent his early manhood among the politicians of 1832 trained in Bentham's school, hardly ever wrote a novel without attacking an abuse. The procedure of the Court of Chancery and of the Ecclesiastical Courts, the delays of the Public Offices, the costliness of divorce, the state of the dwellings of the poor, and the condition of the cheap schools in the North of England, furnished him with what he seemed to consider, in all sincerity, the true moral of a series of fictions.[29]

And if in this estimate there is to be found a touch of paradox, it contains a far greater amount of substantial and important truth. Dickens, in 1846, seemed to himself and his friends a Radical of the Radicals; he was in that year appointed the first editor of the *Daily News,* and the *Daily News* was established to advocate radicalism, and radicalism as understood by Cobden and Bright; yet in 1854 Dickens published *Hard Times.* This tale is from beginning to end a crude satire on what Dickens supposed to be the doctrines of the political economists. Consider the opening words of the novel:

"Now, what I want," says Mr. Gradgrind,

is Facts. Teach these boys and girls nothing but Facts. Facts alone are wanted in life. Plant nothing else, and root out everything else. You can only form the minds of reasoning animals upon Facts: nothing else will ever be of any service to them. This is the principle on which I bring up my own children, and this is the principle on which I bring up these children. Stick to Facts, sir![30]

And Gradgrind is the honest though narrow-minded disciple of Malthus and McCulloch. This gross caricature of an economist's confession of faith strikes the key-note of the whole book. Dickens in 1846 was the editor of the organ of the Manchester school. In 1854 he has become the satirist and the censor of political economy and utilitarianism, and by this conversion earned for himself the vehement eulogy of John Ruskin.

The essential value and truth of Dickens's writings have been unwisely lost sight of by many thoughtful persons, merely because he presents his truth

29. Maine, *Popular Government,* p. 153.
30. Dickens, *Hard Times,* p. 1.

with some colour of caricature. Unwisely, because Dickens's caricature, though often gross, is never mistaken. Allowing for his manner of telling them, the things he tells us are always true. I wish that he could think it right to limit his brilliant exaggeration to works written only for public amusement; and when he takes up a subject of high national importance, such as that which he handled in *Hard Times,* that he would use severer and more accurate analysis. The usefulness of that work (to my mind, in several respects, the greatest he has written) is with many persons seriously diminished because Mr. Bounderby is a dramatic monster, instead of a characteristic example of a worldly master; and Stephen Blackpool a dramatic perfection, instead of a characteristic example of an honest workman. But let us not lose the use of Dickens's wit and insight, because he chooses to speak in a circle of stage fire. He is entirely right in his main drift and purpose in every book he has written; and all of them, but especially *Hard Times,* should be studied with close and earnest care by persons interested in social questions. They will find much that is partial, and, because partial, apparently unjust; but if they examine all the evidence on the other side, which Dickens seems to overlook, it will appear, after all their trouble, that his view was the finally right one, grossly and sharply told.[31]

The literary value of the criticism which ranks *Hard Times* among the greatest of Dickens's novels may be open to doubt, but Ruskin's admiration assuredly bears witness to the changed attitude of a novelist who in early life had been indoctrinated with Benthamism. The alteration was, we take it, unconscious. The change thereby gains additional impressiveness as the record and even the anticipation of a revolution in the course of public opinion. Nor is the importance of this record diminished when one observes that in *Hard Times* an unmeasured attack on the economics and on the morality of individualism is accompanied by a vehement demand for freedom of divorce. Legislation which treats marriage mainly as a contract between husband and wife, and therefore dissolvable if it ceases to conduce to their happiness, harmonises with individualistic ideas; whether it will be found equally in harmony with the conviction that citizens are to be regarded primarily as parts of a social organism admits of discussion. The whole tone of *Hard Times* at any rate suggests that in 1854 Charles Dickens,

31. Ruskin, *Unto This Last* (2nd ed. 1877), pp. 14, 15 (*n.*), published 1860.

with the sensitiveness of genius[32] to the changes in the moral atmosphere of his age, combined beliefs which belonged to the still dominant Benthamism of the day, with sentiments appropriate to the approaching collectivism of the then coming time.

John Mill (1806–1873) was at the time of his death the acknowledged representative of utilitarianism. Indeed if we read between the lines of the *Autobiography,* we may conjecture that James Mill formed the deliberate design of so educating his son John that he might become the adherent, the defender, and the propagator of the philosophical, moral, political, and social creed to which James Mill was himself devoted. The father's labours were crowned with a success which has rarely fallen to an educationalist. He developed in his son an unrivalled capacity for logical controversy and for the lucid statement of argument;[33] he indelibly impressed on John's mind faith in the fundamentals of the utilitarian creed, whilst inspiring him with the noble conviction that the propagation of truth and the service of mankind were the only worthy objects of ambition. He, lastly, left to his son and disciple a freedom of mind which fitted John Mill to think for himself, and thus to become not only a soldier, but a general, in the army of philosophic Radicals.

In Mill's early manhood, however, the influences of the reaction of the nineteenth century against the eighteenth came streaming in upon him.[34] The more rigid members of the utilitarian sect feared or lamented a defection from the true faith. Place, like Mrs. Grote and the other sectarian Benthamites, was grievously disappointed at a certain tendency in John Mill's writings. "I think John Mill," Place wrote in 1838, "has made great progress in becoming a German metaphysical mystic,"[35] whilst in 1837 Mrs. Grote called him, in a letter to Place, "that wayward intellectual deity."

---

32. In 1857 Dickens satirised in *Little Dorrit* the inefficiency of Government offices, *i.e.* attacked the action of the State as compared with that of individuals, and rendered his satire memorable by the invention of the term "circumlocution office."

33. Critics who perceive that this was the one object of James Mill's educational efforts will regard with comprehension, if not with sympathy, his harsh and also absurd indignation when John, as a mere child, stated that something might be true in theory but not in fact. The least blunder in the boy's logic threatened James Mill's design with total failure.

34. *Autobiography,* p. 161.

35. Wallas, *Life of Francis Place,* p. 91.

Neither the Westminster breeches-maker nor the sharp-tongued wife of George Grote were, it is true, discriminating critics, but Carlyle, with his keen insight into character, conjectured from some of Mill's writings that he was a mystic. In plain fact Mill was between 1830 and 1840 deeply moved by the changing sentiment of the age. He conceived that the dogmas in which he had been educated represented but half the truth. He would willingly have taken to himself Goethe's device of many-sidedness—a motto which, whatever its worth, was not applicable either to Bentham or to his followers. But when on his death-bed in 1873 Mill, according to current report, consoled some friend with the reflection, "I have done my work," he said what was palpably true, and meant, we may conjecture, that he had throughout his career remained the honest and the powerful defender and exponent of the truths handed down to him by his teachers. It is certain that to the end of his life Mill was and would have described himself as a utilitarian. Yet the true peculiarity of John Mill's position is that while to his dying day he defended principles derived from his father and from Bentham, he had to a great extent imbibed the sentiment, the sympathies, and the ideals of the later nineteenth century. The labour of his life was the reconciliation of inherited beliefs, from which he never departed, with moral and intellectual ideas and sympathies which, belonging to himself and to his time, were foreign, if not opposed, to the doctrines of his school. This double aspect of Mill's work can be discerned in his writings.

His earliest literary task (1825) was the editing, which meant in fact the re-writing, of Bentham's *Rationale of Judicial Evidence*.[36] Towards the close of his life (1869) he re-edited James Mill's *Analysis of the Phenomena of the Human Mind*. In 1843 his *System of Logic* provided, for more than one generation of Englishmen, the logical foundation of Benthamism. This book, of which the last edition appeared in 1884, carried forward the traditional teaching of English philosophers on the lines originally laid down by Locke, whilst in 1861 the *Examination of Sir William Hamilton's Philosophy* constituted Mill's final reply to one whom he regarded as the chief representative of the intuitionists. His *Principles of Political Economy*—first published in 1848, and continually republished till 1865—was built on the foundations of Ricardo and of Malthus. In 1859 appeared his treatise *On*

---

36. *Autobiography,* pp. 114–116.

302 / *Lecture XII*

Liberty; it gives utterance to the essentially individualistic idea of freedom. It is in style the most perfect, as it was in respect of influence the most effective of Mill's writings. It revived the languishing enthusiasm of utilitarianism. It carried the crusade for liberty a stage farther than it had reached under the guidance of the older philosophic Radicals. They and the generation which followed their teaching had practically enforced the removal of almost all the checks placed by law on freedom of opinion. He went a step beyond this, and proclaimed a moral crusade against the bondage which, as he taught, social conventions imposed not only on freedom of opinion, but on freedom of conduct and on the free development of character.

Laissez faire, under Mill's treatment, became for the youth of 1860 a warcry urging on an assault upon a peculiarly insidious and, therefore, a specially dangerous form of oppression, and upon that tyranny of opinion which may exist as easily under the sovereignty of a democracy as under the despotism of a king. The appeal told immediately on the public to whom it was addressed; nor have its results been transient. It anticipated and fostered that absolute freedom of discussion[37] as regards matters of politics, of religion, or of morality, which in England has marked the last quarter of the nineteenth century. Mill's *Utilitarianism* (1863) afforded a popular apology for the greatest-happiness principle taught by Bentham, whilst his *Representative Government* (1861) is, from one point of view, a restatement of the arguments in favour of democracy. So far John Mill is the Benthamite apologist. His short parliamentary career is consistent with this position. He never conservatised, as did many of the men who in their youth had been philosophic Radicals. To him Tories always remained the "stupid party." He told working men of their own faults with a manly freedom which excited the respect and applause of an audience of artisans, but he sympathised with every attempt to open the parliamentary suffrage to wage-earners, and, in rigid consistency with Benthamite doctrine, was specially eager to confer full political rights upon women.

Mill, however, though he always remained the representative of Benthamism, had before the end of his life deviated a great way from the teaching of the earlier utilitarians.

37. See p. 307, *post*.

In 1838 he published his article on Bentham, and followed it up in 1840 with an article on Coleridge. They are clearly meant each to be the complement of the other. He placed both philosophers side by side as the two great seminal minds of England in their age.[38] This of itself marks an extraordinary departure from the standard of criticism maintained among the school of Bentham. We may be certain that James Mill never wasted a compliment upon Coleridge, or upon Coleridge's philosophy. It is easy to discover an analogous change in John Mill's political creed. He remained indeed to his dying day a democrat. But his belief in democracy was very different in spirit from the confident democratic faith of his father. It was limited by the dread, inspired by Tocqueville, of the tyranny of the majority, and also by childlike trust in Hare's mechanical device for the representation of minorities. The democrat who holds that the majority ought to rule, but that wisdom is to be found mainly in minorities, and that every possible means ought to be adopted to prevent the ignorant majority from abusing its power, has retreated a good way from the clear, the confident, and the dogmatic Radicalism of 1830.

Mill's *Liberty* should be read together with his *Utilitarianism* and his *Subjection of Women*. It no doubt rekindled enthusiasm for one side of the Benthamite creed, but it emphasised ideas, and still more sentiments, alien to the convictions of John Mill's teachers.[39] An unskilful eulogist sometimes plays the part of a severe censor. Charles Kingsley wrote to Mill that the perusal of his *Liberty* "affected me in making me a clearer-headed, braver-minded man on the spot."[40] Such praise must, one thinks, have suggested to Mill himself the conviction, or possibly the fear, that he had achieved success by just that kind of appeal to emotion or to moral rhetoric which would have excited derision among the philosophic Radicals of his youth.

This tendency to address himself to the instinctive feelings of his readers is well illustrated by the one passage in the grave *Examination of Sir William*

38. *Dissertations*, i. p. 331. Both articles were published after the death of James Mill.

39. Sir J. F. Stephen's *Liberty, Equality, and Fraternity* is a strenuous assault on the fundamental ideas of the treatise, *On Liberty*, but this forcible attack is little more than a vehement criticism of Mill from the point of view of the older utilitarians, and certainly shows that Mill had diverged considerably from Bentham. See Leslie Stephen, *English Utilitarians*, iii. p. 244.

40. *Life of Kingsley*, ii. p. 88.

Hamilton's Philosophy which gained the attention and the sympathy of the general public. "I will call," he wrote, "no being good, who is not what I mean when I apply that epithet to my fellow-creatures; and if such a being can sentence me to hell for not so calling him, to hell I will go."[41] These expressions excited the enthusiastic approval of thousands of young men who in 1865 revered Mill as their philosopher and guide. They elicited the sympathy of teachers so much opposed to utilitarianism as Maurice and James Martineau, but are we sure that James Mill might not have read his son's defiance of an unmoral deity with very dubious approval? Is it certain that he might not, with Mansel, have been amazed "at this extraordinary outburst of rhetoric"?[42]

With Mill's theology we need not concern ourselves except to note that the *Three Essays on Religion* are marked by the same transition from one school of thought or feeling to another which is traceable in his other writings. More to our purpose is the gradual change discoverable in his economical and social opinions. He built his economical views upon the foundations of Ricardo and Malthus, but Malthusian principles appeared to him not as a barrier to progress, but as showing the conditions by which progress could be achieved. "If he appears to the modern socialist as a follower of Ricardo, he would have been regarded by Ricardo's disciples as a socialist."[43] Mill, it appears, says the same writer, "was [in the latter part of his life] well on the way to State Socialism."[44] "In [Mill's] case," writes

41. *Examination*, p. 129.

42. *English Utilitarians*, iii. p. 430.

43. John Mill, *Dict. of Nat. Biog.* xxxvii. p. 398.

44. *English Utilitarians*, iii. p. 230. "Sir Louis Mallet reports a conversation with him only a few days before his death, in which Cobden said with peculiar earnestness: 'I believe that the harm which Mill has done to the world by the passage in his book on *Political Economy* in which he favours the principle of Protection in young communities has outweighed all the good which may have been caused by his other writings.'" "Quoted in a letter of Sir Louis Mallet, given in the Appendix to Mr. Gowing's admirable *Life of Richard Cobden* (Cassell & Co.)." See Armitage Smith, *The Free Trade Movement and its Results* (1898 ed.), p. 153.

Cobden's remark is a recognition of Mill's tendency to qualify by concessions (of which he hardly perceived the full effect) the rigidity of the economic doctrine professed by his early teachers. [Editor's note: In the first edition, Dicey attributed this dictum to John Bright.]

Henry Sidgwick, whose profound knowledge and absolute impartiality cannot be questioned,

> we have the remarkable phenomenon that the author of the book which became, for nearly a generation, by far the most popular and influential text-book of Political Economy in England, was actually—at any rate when he revised the third and later editions—completely Socialistic in his ideal of ultimate social improvement. "I look forward," he tells us, in his *Autobiography,* "to a time when the rule that they who do not work shall not eat will be applied not to paupers only, but impartially to all; and when the division of the produce of labour, instead of depending, in so great a degree as it now does, on the accident of birth, *will be made by concert on an acknowledged principle of justice.*" Having this ideal, he "regarded all existing institutions and social arrangements as merely provisional, and welcomed with the great-est pleasure and interest all Socialistic experiments by select individuals." In short, the study planted by Adam Smith and watered by Ricardo had, in the third quarter of the nineteenth century, imbibed a full measure of the spirit of Saint-Simon and Owen,—and that in England, the home of what the Germans call "Manchesterthum."
>
> I do not mean to suggest that those who learnt Political Economy from Mill's book during this period went so far as their teacher in the adoption of Socialistic aims. This, no doubt, was far from being the case. Indeed—if I may judge from my own experience—I should say that we were as much surprised as the "general reader" to learn from Mill's *Autobiography* that our master, the author of the much-admired treatise "On Liberty," had been all the while looking forward to a time when the division of the produce of labour should be "made by concert."[45]

Note, too, that while Mill remains a utilitarian to the end of his life, utilitarianism itself undergoes in his hands a sort of transformation. The principle of utility, or the greatest-happiness principle, which was taken to be a maxim of self-interest, becomes a precept of self-sacrifice, and the doctrine which teaches that every man must of necessity pursue his own happiness is made to lead to the conclusion that a good man of heroic mould will be willing to serve the happiness of others by the absolute

45. Sidgwick, *Miscellaneous Essays and Addresses,* pp. 241, 242. Compare particularly L. Stephen, *English Utilitarians,* iii. pp. 224–237.

sacrifice of his own.[46] Whether this conclusion can be justly drawn from utilitarian premises may be left for the discussion of moralists. Thus much is certain, that the principle of utility, as expounded by Mill, is somewhat difficult to grasp, and is a very different thing from the simple and absolutely comprehensible notion that every man is by his own nature impelled to pursue his own happiness, and that the intelligent pursuit by each man of his well-understood interest will inevitably secure the greatest happiness of the greatest number. One may well wonder whether Bentham would have recognised his own doctrine in the exposition of it provided by the most eminent and faithful of his disciples.

Whether in this instance, and in others, Mill really succeeded in the attempt to reconcile principles, each of which he thought contained half the truth, may be doubtful. To some even of his admirers it may seem that he effected rather a juxtaposition or combination than a fusion or reconciliation of apparently opposed convictions. But however this may be, it is clear that John Mill was a teacher created for, and assured of a welcome in, an age of transition. The lucidity of his style, which may sometimes surpass the clearness of his thought, and the matchless skill in the arrangement of arguments, which occasionally disguises both from himself and from his readers a weakness in the links of his reasoning, his patent honesty, and his zeal for truth, constituted the intellectual foundation of his influence over the youth of 1860–1870. But other qualities of a different order enhanced his authority. His susceptibility to every form of generous emotion, combined, as it almost must be, with intense desire for, and appreciation of sympathy, made an author known to most Englishmen only by his writings something like the personal friend of his readers. His immediate influence is a thing of the past, but for the purpose of these Lectures it possesses a peculiar importance. The changes or fluctuations in Mill's own convictions, bearing as they do in many points upon legislative opinion, are at once the sign, and were in England, to a great extent, the cause, of the transition from the individualism of 1830–1865 to the collectivism of 1900. His teaching specially affected the men who were just entering on public life towards 1870. It prepared them at any rate to accept, if not to

46. *Utilitarianism*, p. 23.

welcome, the collectivism which from that time onwards has gained increasing strength.

II. As to the dependence of legislative opinion on the general tendencies of English thought.

In considering the manner in which legislative opinion has, especially between 1830 and 1900, been affected by the general movement of English or rather of European thought, a student should divert his attention from many eddies or cross-currents of opinion which, interesting though they be, are of minor consequence, and fix his mind resolutely upon those leading features of modern thought which, just because they are easily recognised, seem to be obvious and commonplace, but are in reality the governing characteristics of a particular age.[47] Among these traits he will certainly note the increasing freedom of discussion and the disintegration of beliefs, that increasing importance given to the emotional side of human nature which has been called the apotheosis of instinct, and the growth of the historical method. Each of these three tendencies has had a share in shaking the authority of Benthamism or individualism.

Freedom of discussion and the disintegration of beliefs are so closely inter-connected that they may well be considered as two sides or aspects of one phenomenon. Of the immense increase, in England at least, of freedom of discussion (miscalled freedom of opinion) during the nineteenth century it is difficult to form an adequate conception. In 1800 the free expression of opinion was strictly limited by positive law, by social custom, and by prevalent habits of thought. We indeed habitually think of England as the home of free thought, no less than of free speech. But in this matter we are the victims of a natural delusion, due to the circumstance that in 1800 and for many years later there was more of liberty in England than elsewhere, whence one is apt to conclude that Englishmen enjoyed an absolutely large amount of intellectual and moral freedom. True indeed it is that Englishmen possessed more freedom than existed on the Conti-

47. For Mill's influence see *Henry Sidgwick, A Memoir*, p. 36. [Editor's note: This footnote was added in the second edition.]

nent, but the extent of this freedom was merely comparative. Could any Englishman of to-day be carried back to the reign of George III. he would feel himself choked by a moral and intellectual atmosphere which stifled the expression of every kind of heterodoxy—that is, of all thought opposed to the prevalent beliefs of the time. Conflicts between judge and jury over the law of libel, and one State trial after another raising the question, what were the lawful limits to freedom of speech and writing, show that even in the political world freedom of opinion, as we now understand it, was far from well established. In other spheres it was in practice limited by custom even where it was not curtailed by law. Occasional protests of innovators or free-thinkers bear witness to the tightness of the restraints placed upon free discussion. But we are not to suppose that this was generally felt as a grievance. Bondage imposed in the main by social opinion, just because it coincided with public sentiment, met with acquiescence, if not (as was generally the case) with active approval. Bold was the reformer who between 1800 and 1820 avowed his sympathy with so-called Jacobinical principles, even though his Jacobinism went no farther than a desire for the representation of Birmingham and the disfranchisement of Old Sarum. Bolder far was the theologian who applied historical criticism of the most moderate character to the Biblical records.[48] Reckless rather than bold was the avowed opponent of fundamental beliefs whether social or religious. Nor was his bravery likely to elicit sympathy, for the majority of English men and English women enjoyed in the early part of the nineteenth century, as nearly always, just the amount of freedom in matters of thought or opinion which met their desires.

The widespread confusion between freedom of opinion and freedom of discussion, logically erroneous though it be, is not without excuse. It arises from a fact well worth notice. Where men cannot express their thoughts freely and openly, and especially where this want of liberty is sanctioned

---

48. As late as 1830 Milman's *History of the Jews* shocked English opinion. "In this unpretending book for the first time 'an English clergyman treated the Jews as an oriental tribe, recognised sheiks and emirs in the Old Testament, shifted and classified documentary evidence, and evaded or minimised the miraculous.' Consternation, which the author had not anticipated, spread among the orthodox; the sale of the book was not only stopped, but the publication of the series in which it appeared ceased."—Milman, *Dict. Nat. Biog.* xxxviii. p. 3, by R. Garnett.

by public opinion, freedom of thought itself ceases to exist. Men think little about things of which they cannot speak.

It is necessary to get rid of the notion that liberty of opinion as now understood was really characteristic of England in the earliest years of the nineteenth century, in order that we may realise the full extent of an intellectual and moral revolution which, because it has not been accompanied by outward violence or startling political changes, is apt to escape notice. To-day, at the beginning of the twentieth century, the expression of opinion has in England become all but completely free. One or two facts may serve as sign-posts to mark the stages of this revolution.

By the middle of the nineteenth century the restraints imposed by law on free discussion had all but vanished. Statutes or common law rules which, except on the ground of sedition or defamation, interfered with liberty of speech or writing were, in practice at any rate, obsolete. Even in 1841 the trials of Hetherington and Moxon—oddly connected as they were—for the publication of blasphemous libels were felt to be anachronisms. The maxim that Christianity is part of the common law[49] was derided by eminent lawyers. In 1859 the whole tone of Mill's *Liberty* implies that the discussion of all political and even of most social topics was little checked by law. Buckle's injudicious denunciation of the imprisonment inflicted on Pooley, a half-witted Cornish labourer, for writing up in public places language offensive to every Christian, as a gross instance of legal persecution proves that such persecution was in reality all but unknown; whilst the general feeling that the severe punishment of a semi-maniac, for the indecency rather than the blasphemy of his language, was a mistake, shows the tolerant spirit of the time. Later legislation[50] has removed such trammels on the freedom of the press as existed in 1859. The necessary vagueness of the law of libel is now open to objection, if at all, on the score only of its inefficiently protecting the possible victim of defamation.

49. Whether the publication of an attack on Christianity made in a serious spirit and in decent language might not still theoretically expose a man to prosecution, is uncertain. See Stephen, *Digest Crim. Law,* 5th ed. Art. 179, p. 125; and compare Odgers, *Libel and Slander,* pp. 475, 490. It is certain, however, that in practice such an attack on Christianity would now not expose any man to punishment.

50. See Stephen, *Comm.* iii. ch. xvi. (14th ed.), pp. 229–234; the Newspaper Libel and Registration Act, 1881, the Law of Libel Amendment Act, 1888.

Even in 1859 Mill's *Liberty* denounced the hostility, not of the law but of social opinion, to independence of conduct and originality of thought. But this complaint, whatever its reasonableness in Mill's day, sounds in 1905 nothing better than a paradox. Before the end of the nineteenth century the expression of opinion had become all but completely free. At the present time there are no political, and very few social, moral, or religious theories to the maintenance whereof is attached that kind of reprobation which would deter a man of ordinary firmness from freely speaking his mind. The silence which, among the family of James Mill, concealed religious scepticism would now be an absurdity. Avowed agnostics or the adherents of new and strange creeds suffer nothing in public estimation. Bradlaugh was, before the close of his life, a respected member of Parliament, and popular, it is said, among his fellow members, yet Bradlaugh's atheism would have shocked such deists as Franklin or Tom Paine. Clergymen, it is true, still subscribe to, and are supposed to be bound, in some very indefinite sense, by the doctrine of the Thirty-Nine Articles. But the clergy of the Church of England in practice enjoy the right to express their opinions on all matters of religion and theology with nearly as much freedom as the laity. Not only upon Biblical history but upon doctrines which have often been supposed to be the fundamental dogmas of Christianity, preachers whom every man respects may utter criticisms which, in the days of Dr. Arnold, would hardly have been whispered by a minister of the Church of England to his most intimate friend, and which in 1860 would have amazed, if not scandalised the authors of *Essays and Reviews,* and might well have given rise to proceedings in the Ecclesiastical Courts.

Englishmen, then, of all classes have obtained, and practically exercise the right to say or print whatever they like, provided they are not guilty of sedition or defamation. We are witnessing a freedom of thought and of discussion more complete than has ever permanently existed among the whole people of any country known to us by history. This statement is not equivalent to the assertion that the English world of to-day is characterised by any special vigour or originality either of intellect or of character. Mill and others held, and with truth, that vigorous persecution, either legal or social, may destroy the capacity for free thought. They thence concluded that absolute freedom would stimulate originality and individuality. This inference is of most dubious validity. All men hate trouble and the discovery of truth or the detection of error involves a laborious process of thought, whilst few are the men to whom the attainment of truth is an object of keen desire. Add to all this that man is far more of an imitative than inventive animal, and inventiveness or originality is the rarest of all gifts. What ground is there, then, for holding that human beings, simply because they are left free to think and act as they like, will in fact like to labour in the search for truth, or to strike out new paths for themselves rather than pursue the pleasant and easy course of imitating their neighbours? Whether, however, freedom of opinion or discussion be the parent of originality or not, the one thing which is past a doubt is that such liberty exists in modern England.

My reason for insisting upon this point with perhaps excessive emphasis is, that the development of freedom of opinion has in England been in the closest way connected with, and indeed has been one main cause of, that singular phenomenon which is best described as the disintegration of beliefs or, in other words, the breaking up of established creeds, whether religious, moral, political, or economical.[51]

This characteristic of modern England has attracted special attention in the field of theology, where, with some inaccuracy of thought, it has been identified with scepticism. In reality, whether in the realm of religion or elsewhere, it means simply the breaking up or dissolution of large and coherent systems of opinion. This break up of any dogmatic system no more results of necessity in scepticism than it does in increased belief or faith. Its one indubitable effect is to weaken some body of opinion and thus leave room for the growth of other forms of belief. The open avowal of Agnosticism, the increased authority in the Church of England of High

51. This need excite no surprise. Free discussion does in the end favour the establishment of indisputable truths, but its immediate effects are first to direct attention towards the weak points of any existing body of beliefs, and next to reveal an unexpected amount of dissent from received formulas. Now, as an ordinary man's faith in any moral or intellectual doctrine depends in part on its coherence, in part on the authority of experts, and greatly also on the sympathy of others with his faith, anything which shows that a creed is not entirely consistent, that even experts are not agreed as to its truth, or that many persons dissent from it, inevitably shakes the faith of ordinary believers. See on this subject Tarde, *Les Lois de l'Imitation.*

Church doctrine, the revival in England of Roman Catholicism,[52] and the creation of the Salvation Army are all facts belonging to the present time; they have all been equally fostered by the disintegration of beliefs.

In any case this dissolution of dogmatic systems is clearly traceable in provinces of thought which border upon and run into the domain of legislative opinion. Faith, for instance, in the English Constitution was, fifty years ago, the common characteristic of almost all our statesmen. This was a creed of no sudden growth. It had been preached by the genius of Burke, it was enforced by the arguments and learning of Hallam, it colours every page of Macaulay. It explains Wellington's celebrated declaration[53] that the nature of man was incapable of creating, by any effort, institutions of such paramount excellence as the constitution which England enjoyed under the unreformed Parliament of 1830. The Whigs never desired to do more than to repair the revered fabric of the constitution. Many of them held that the policy of reform was nothing but the strengthening of the original foundations on which rested the institutions of England. Lord John Russell—to call him by the name by which he will always be remembered—was the most rigid of Whigs; Lord Palmerston was a man of the world and a flexible statesman, little hampered by any general principles or formulas. But both Russell and Palmerston believed, and acted on the belief, that Frenchmen, Germans, or Italians might all of them put an end to any grievances under which they suffered by the adoption of the form of Government which existed in England; a constitutional King, a House of Lords and a House of Commons, and the whole English party-system, must, it was thought, be enough to ensure the happiness of any nation.

This was, in the main, the creed of at least two generations. Hence the enthusiasm[54]—which in 1905 has become almost incomprehensible—for

52. Any one whose memory of past phases of opinion stretches back over sixty years will acknowledge that at a time to be remembered by men still living, Roman Catholicism seemed to ordinary Englishmen to be, as far as England was concerned, a thing of the past. It was to them, like Jacobitism, a dead faith. One may find a record of this state of feeling in *Father Clement,* a not unimpressive religious tale, which, published in 1823, had by 1860 reached thirteen editions. Its aim was to show, from an Evangelical point of view, that a Roman Catholic priest might, in spite of all his superstitions, be a man of deep personal piety.

53. See Walpole, *Hist.* ii. p. 12.

54. Compare the language of James Martineau, in a letter to a friend, September 9, 1830.

the three glorious days of July which, as in 1830 all Englishmen believed, would close the era of revolutions, by endowing France with the blessing of constitutional monarchy. But from 1830 onwards attacks began to be made on the popular faith in the English Constitution. Benthamites led the way. Place, who carried the doctrines of his teachers to absurdity, pronounced the Constitution to be nothing better than a nose of wax which could be twisted in any way one pleased. In 1838 Richard Cobden contemned the "great juggle of the *English Constitution*—a thing of monopolies, and Church-craft, and sinecures, armorial hocus-pocus, primogeniture, and pageantry," gravely suspected that for the great mass of the people Prussia possessed "the best government in Europe," and would gladly have given up his taste for talking politics to secure for England an administration as good as that of Prussia.[55] Carlyle, between whom and the great Free-Trader there were many unsuspected points of sympathy, derided all the favourite formulas of constitutionalists as shams, and accustomed his readers to see in Cromwell and Frederick the Great the sort of heroes who, in defiance of constitutional or democratic principles, could govern a people vigorously for the people's own good. Still faith in constitutional government died hard. Between 1860 and 1870 Matthew Arnold's satire was directed against that stolid belief in English institutions which to his mind was still strong enough to present a formidable hindrance to the intellectual and moral improvement of his countrymen.

Times have changed. Where shall we now find the ardent believers in the constitution of England? If they exist at all they belong in spirit to the past. One consolation indeed may be tendered to the Whigs of an old type who still remain amongst us as interesting survivals of another age. If belief in constitutionalism has all but vanished, the faiths or heresies which were

---

"'France! glorious France! Has there ever been a week since the Resurrection which has promised such accumulated blessings to our race, as that week of national regeneration? Where will it end? The invigorating shock must pass through the Netherlands, Spain, Italy. When that revolution is compared with any period of history, in what an encouraging light does it exhibit modern character and mind. The whole struggle has been conducted in a spirit of disinterestedness which to me is impressive in the highest degree. Such a people must be almost within sight of the value of religious truth.'"—Cited *James Martineau*, by J. Estlin Carpenter, p. 67 (*n.*).

55. Morley, *Life of Cobden,* i. pp. 130, 131.

its rivals are rapidly becoming the ghosts of dead ideals. Who is there who now expects political salvation from any heaven-sent hero? An autocrat who aspired to play the part of a modern Caesar ruled France for some eighteen years, but his reign ended with the disaster and ignominy of Sedan. The King of Prussia, that "good and just man who," in Cobden's eyes, "shattered the sceptre of despotism, even in his own hand," by his zeal for popular education, has been succeeded by a combined King of Prussia and German Emperor, whose power is based on the fact that Prussia is, as it always has been, and Germany is fast becoming, a military state in which the whole nation is a trained army.

Nor has democratic republicanism fared better than other political creeds. The vast Republic of the West, and the Third Republic of France, which has now lasted longer than any constitution welcomed or endured by the French people since 1789, are both forms of government which may to a certain extent satisfy the judgment, but do nothing to gratify the imagination or kindle the enthusiasm of mankind. Neither at Washington nor at Paris can the most enthusiastic of democrats discover an ideal Commonwealth. Republicanism, it has been said by an eminent Frenchman, has ceased to be a heresy, but it has also ceased to be a faith. This is the epitaph which, with the necessary verbal changes, must be inscribed over the tomb of more than one political system which, during the nineteenth century, has for a time commanded more or less confidence. To no political and social faith is it more applicable than to the Benthamite liberalism of 1830. Utilitarianism in its turn has been shattered by the disintegration of beliefs.

This fact need excite no surprise. Benthamism was a coherent system; its ethics, its constitutional theories, its jurisprudence, and its political economy were indissolubly linked together, and were indeed different aspects of one and the same theory of life and human nature. The creed owed its power in part to the large element of truth, now much underrated, which it contained, in part to its self-consistency and to the clearness and precision of its dogmas, and in part also to the unbounded faith of its adherents. As long as utilitarian doctrine remained clear and dogmatic, and was preached by teachers who could put forth the truth as they saw it without hesitation or limitation, the authority of utilitarianism waxed great; but the gradual disintegration of beliefs, the result of that freedom of discussion which had been gained by the efforts of the Benthamites, told against the Benthamite faith. Utilitarians, as has been shown by the example of John Mill, became infected with candour and eclecticism; but the breadth and indefiniteness of an eclecticism which attempts to combine in one whole the half truths to be found in different systems cannot excite enthusiasm or stimulate men to action. Open-mindedness, candour, and the careful sincerity which forbids all exaggeration, even of the truth, are admirable qualities, but they are not the virtues which obtain for a faith the adherence of mankind. It is the definiteness not the vagueness of a creed, as it is the honest confidence of its preachers, which gains proselytes. As utilitarian doctrine became less definite, and as its exponents stated it with less boldness and with more qualification, the authority of Benthamism suffered a decline. The influences which dissolve a creed told alike upon preachers and hearers.

Consider from this point of view the side of utilitarianism which bore most closely on legislation, and note the change, not so much in the principles as in the tone of political economy. This is a matter rather of history than of economics, and thus fairly open to the consideration of persons who make no pretension to be economists. Between 1830 and 1845[56] the common run of political economists, of whom Miss Martineau and Cobden may be taken as types, showed a marked tendency to treat political economy as a definite and recognised science, the laws whereof were as well established as, and possessed something resembling the certainty of, the laws of Nature.[57] Some apparently dogmatic writers may indeed have

---

56. See especially Mill, *Autobiography*, pp. 246, 247. Compare Austin's attack on Dr. Friedrich List's *Das nationale System der politischen Oekonomie*, in *Edinburgh Review*, lxxv. (July 1842), p. 515. This examination by Austin of our author's pretended system is well worth notice. The attack on protection is powerful, but the tone is obviously different from that which a writer of half Austin's ability would, in 1905, adopt in the criticism of the views held by an eminent opponent. The dogmatic tone is the more remarkable since Austin was by no means a narrow Benthamite, and, as we have seen, professed great disrespect for what he called the "universal principles of human nature of the political economists." (See p. 117, *ante*.)

57. "The political economists, in many instances at least, wrote as if an attempt to alter the rate of wages by combinations of workmen was like an attempt to alter the weight of the air by tampering with barometers. It was said that the price of labour depended, like the

introduced limitations or qualifications hardly noticed by their readers; but what we are here concerned with is the effect on the outside public; and it can scarcely be disputed that between 1830 and 1845 political economy was received by the intelligent public of England as a science containing very definite and certain principles from which were logically deduced conclusions of indisputable and universal truth. In Mill's *Political Economy* one can already perceive a modification, if not exactly of doctrine, yet certainly of tone and feeling. The doctrine of *laissez faire*, for example, and the mode of looking at life, and above all at legislation, loses a good deal of its rigidity and of its authoritative character;[58] and this modification is at any rate a step towards the conclusion which some later writers favour, that in determining the cases in which the intervention of the State (*e.g.* in the control of labour) may be beneficial we ought not to place reliance on any definite maxim or presumption in favour of respecting individual freedom, but must consider in each particular instance how far the action of the State is likely to be more beneficial than unrestricted competition.

"It is futile," writes Jevons in 1882,

> to attempt to uphold, in regard to social legislation, any theory of eternal fixed principles or abstract rights. The whole matter becomes a complex calculus of good and evil. All is a question of probability and degree. A rule of law is grounded on a recognised probability of good arising in the opinion of the lawgiver from a certain line of conduct. But as there almost always occur cases in which this tendency to good is overmastered by some opposite tendency, the lawgiver proceeds to enact new rules limiting, as it is said, but in reality reversing, the former one in special cases. Lawgivers, as well as philosophers, delight in discovering euphemisms adapted to maintain the fiction of universal principles. When the principles fail to hold good, it is said that the cases are exceptional. It is a general principle that a man may do as he likes with his own property. It is an exception when a railway company forcibly takes possession of his land.
>
> I venture to maintain, however, that we shall do much better in the end

---

price of other commodities, solely upon supply and demand, and that it could not be altered artificially" (Stephen, *History*, iii. p. 211). Compare for the tone of economists, the preface to Miss Martineau's *Political and Economical Tales*.

58. See Mill, *Political Economy*, Bk. v. ch. xi.

if we throw off the incubus of metaphysical ideas and expressions. We must resolve all these supposed principles and rights into the facts and probabilities which they are found to involve when we inquire into their real meaning.[59]

On the soundness of this modification or denial of the doctrine of *laissez faire* there is no need to pronounce any judgment. The matter to be here insisted upon is that any introduction by competent teachers of modifications or qualifications into the doctrines of political economy inevitably deprives these doctrines of much of their popular authority. Absolute precepts may command absolute belief and obedience. But a rule originally supposed to be without exception true, is certain, when qualified by even the fairest of exceptions, to lose far more of weight with the general public than ought in reason to be taken from it. When once it is taught that there is no rule, or hardly any presumption in favour of *laissez faire,* every man will in practice hold that wherever a law will get rid of what he deems an evil, by which he and his fellows suffer (*e.g.* the unlimited competition of aliens), the intervention of the State is beneficial.[60] A creed which has lost

59. Jevons, *The State in Relation to Labour,* 3rd ed. (1894), by M. Cababé, pp. 16–17. See also Intro. pp. vii, viii, xiii, xiv.

Contrast this with the language of Austin, *Edinburgh Review,* lxxv. "There is always . . . a general presumption against the expediency of such an interference," *i.e.* an interference of a Government with the concerns of its subject (p. 527). "We are not bound to prove, in an affirmative or direct manner, the expediency of freedom of trade, since there is a general presumption against the interference of governments with the interests and concerns of their subjects" (p. 528, and see his general argument in favour of universal freedom of trade, *ibid.* p. 529).

60. Note the language of an Ulster working man who on July 7, 1903, writes to the *Times,* stating, and probably with truth, that the workmen of America are better off than the workmen of England, and then proceeds: "Now there is something wrong here. You will, no doubt, agree that it should be the object of every statesman and of every Government to promote the welfare of the people, and to improve their conditions. How is it, then, that the British Government has not succeeded in placing us working men in anything like the splendid position that the American Government has placed its working men? Britishers should, I submit, be second to none. Our workmen are, without doubt, the finest and most intelligent men in the world; they should therefore receive the highest wages, and no Government, in my opinion, ought to experience any difficulty in securing the highest remu-

authority has of necessity left room for the rise of new and opposed beliefs. Add to this that economists themselves seem sometimes to dread that the attempt to treat economical problems in a scientific spirit should deprive them of that sympathy which they not only give to others but themselves require.[61]

Here we touch upon the apotheosis of instinct. That reaction of the nineteenth against the eighteenth century, the influence whereof streamed in upon John Mill and his contemporaries,[62] and thus deeply affected the generation which came under their teaching, was by no feature character-ised more distinctly than by the new importance attached to the emotional as contrasted with the rational side of human nature. This reliance on or appeal to feeling or instinct would have appeared to Bentham and his school little better than a roundabout way of declaring that the merit or demerit of any course of action, *e.g.* the passing of a law, depended upon the feeling of the person making the appeal. All reference, in short, to emotions, which could not be justified on utilitarian grounds, would have seemed to the Benthamite school a specimen of that *ipse-dixitism* (to em-ploy one of their master's own expressions) which he and his disciples held in special abhorrence.

We may think that this dread of sentimentalism was connected with an incomplete view of human nature, but it ought to be admitted that utili-tarian Liberals possessed, from their own point of view, two justifications for regarding with suspicion that appeal to instinctive feeling which has since their time played so marked a part in the public life of England.

The reform, in the first place, of law and society in accordance with the principle of utility depended on the possibility of calculating, not indeed

---

neration for such men; yet the British Government has been unable to do it, and I for one would like to know the reason why."

The singular assumptions on which this argument rests are made by many persons, but are rarely put forward with as much openness as by the Ulster workman.

61. Is it conceivable that Ricardo or Malthus would, after the manner of a distinguished living economist, have favoured his readers with a confession of faith, beginning and ending with *credo in unum Deum?* This declaration of religious belief sounds in a treatise on political economy as much out of place as the historical creed of St. Athanasius.

62. See Mill, *Autobiography,* p. 161, and compare Mill, *Three Essays on Religion,* pp. 44, 45. [Editor's note: The second half of this footnote was added in the second edition.]

with anything like mathematical but with a certain sort of rough accuracy, the effect of a given law in increasing or diminishing human happiness. But in order that such a calculation may be possible, it is essential that a law or an institution should be criticised on assignable grounds—as, for instance, that it will increase or diminish the security of property, or that it will lower or raise the price of food. For if once the defenders or censors of a legal or other innovation desert such definite grounds of criticism, and appeal to their own instinctive feelings of approval or disapproval, the application of the Benthamite method to the law of a country becomes an impossibility. How can one reason about the advantage, for example, of allowing or forbidding divorce, if *A* simply asserts his sympathy with freedom of affection, and *B* retorts that his instinct or conscience bids him respect the sanctity of marriage? There is in reality no common ground of argument.

Then, in the second place, strong and natural sentiments most sincerely entertained, come into conflict with one another. It is difficult to make emotion, however respectable, the basis of sound legislation. It is absolutely certain that utilitarian reforms, of which every one now admits the benefit, have often been achieved in defiance of popular sentiment. In any case it is clear that the apotheosis of instinct has, whether for good or bad, tended to produce results which would have startled the reformers of 1830.

Consider the growth of English imperialism.[63]

In no part of our public life did the principles of utilitarianism obtain at one time more complete acceptance than in everything which regarded the relation of England to her colonies. Bentham's *Emancipate your Colonies,* published in 1793, was addressed to the French National Convention. It urged upon France, and upon all other countries which possessed a colonial empire, the expediency and the duty of bringing about a peaceable

---

63. The word "imperialism" has, it has been well remarked by my friend Mr. Bryce, undergone a change of signification. In 1865 imperialism meant Caesarism (*i.e.* an autocracy like Louis Napoleon's), as opposed to constitutional government, and was always used with an unfavourable connotation. In 1905 imperialism means the wish to maintain the unity and increase the strength of an empire which contains within its limits various more or less independent States. The expression is as applicable to the inhabitants of the United States as to the subjects of the British Crown. It is used sometimes with a favourable, sometimes with an unfavourable connotation.

separation from their dependencies. This counsel did not obtain the assent of Frenchmen, but whether accepted or not, it became to them of little practical importance owing to the success of the English navy in stripping France of possessions outside Europe. Nor did *Emancipate your Colonies* produce any immediate effect in England. But this application of *laissez faire,* first published for sale in 1830, gradually gained the approval of English public opinion. Obvious facts told for more than argument. The contest with the American Colonies and its issue had never been forgotten. No revenue could be raised from Englishmen living outside the United Kingdom. The possibility of monopolising colonial trade became doubtful. Hence it was increasingly difficult to prove that England gained any pecuniary advantage from the possession of dependencies. Towards the middle of the nineteenth century *laissez faire* was the order of the day. In no sphere of action was the trouble saved by leaving things alone more obvious than in England's government of colonies, which, if distance be measured by time, were much farther off from the mother-country than they are at present, and which assuredly desired to govern themselves.

In 1841, Sir George Cornewall Lewis published his *Government of Dependencies.* He was a disciple of Austin; he belonged in spirit to the Benthamite school; he was a statesman versed in administrative affairs, and possessed a high reputation not only for philosophic enlightenment, but for practical soundness of judgment. His book is the application to our colonial policy, by a man of good sense and political experience, of the tenets propounded by Bentham. Lewis's teaching represented the opinion entertained between 1840 and 1860 by all sensible Liberals. To such men it seemed obvious that the course of prudent statesmanship was to leave our colonies as much as possible alone, to be prepared at any moment for their desiring independence, and to be careful only that separation, when it came, should be peaceable and take place under feelings of mutual goodwill and friendship. Some statesmen of repute considered our colonial empire itself a matter of regret. Brougham in 1839[64] described Wolfe's capture of Quebec as an operation "which crowned our arms with imperishable glory, and loaded our policy with a burden not yet shaken off." He cites also, with the keenest approval, the view of Lord St. Vincent in 1783, that Canada

---

64. Brougham, *Historical Sketches,* Lord St. Vincent, p. 307.

ought to be surrendered, and his opinion that by not then surrendering it we were retaining "a running sore, the source of endless disquiet and expense," and that "if this fair occasion for giving up Canada is neglected, nothing but difficulty, in either keeping or resigning it, will ever after be known."

Disraeli was not indifferent to the power of England; he stands in popular imagination, and not quite without reason, as the forerunner of imperialism, but he wrote in 1852 to Lord Malmesbury, "These wretched colonies will all be independent in a few years, and are a millstone round our necks."[65] The leaders of the Manchester school, who represented the ideas of Benthamite liberalism, assuredly deplored the existence of our colonial empire. If proof of this be needed, read these extracts from the writings of Richard Cobden:

> If it could be made manifest to the trading and industrious portions of this nation, who have no honours or interested ambition of any kind at stake in the matter, that, whilst our dependencies are supported at an expense to them, in direct taxation, of more than five millions annually, they serve but as gorgeous and ponderous appendages to swell our ostensible grandeur, but in reality to complicate and magnify our government expenditure, without improving our balance of trade,—surely, under such circumstances, it would become at least a question for anxious inquiry with a people so overwhelmed with debt, whether those colonies should not be suffered to support and defend themselves, as separate and independent existences.[66]

> The Corn Laws are a part only of a system in which Whig and Tory aristocracy have about an equal interest. The colonies, army, navy, and church are, with the corn laws, merely accessories to our aristocratic government.[67]

> It is customary, however, to hear our standing army and navy defended as necessary for the protection of our colonies, as though some other nation might otherwise seize them. Where is the *enemy*(?) that would be so good as to steal such *property*? We should consider it to be quite as necessary to arm in defence of our national debt.[68]

65. *Memoirs of an Ex-Minister* (ed. 1885), p. 260.
66. *The Political Writings of Richard Cobden*, 1886, pp. 24, 25 (1835).
67. *Ibid.* p. 2, Letter of 1836.
68. *Ibid.* pp. 242, 243.

Cobden's language was more trenchant and his mode of thinking more logical than the words or thoughts of ordinary politicians. But his expressions if they exaggerated, on the whole represented the sentiment of the time. Conduct rather than words is the true test of men's convictions. One feature of English policy is sufficient to show the slight importance attached at one time to the connection between the mother-country and her dependencies. From 1855 onwards Victoria, New South Wales, and other colonies, received from the Imperial Parliament powers of self-government as wide as were compatible with their remaining part of the British Empire. Belief in free trade had at that date risen to an ardent faith that free exchange was an unquestionable benefit for all countries at all times and under all circumstances. Yet statesmen who held this creed made no attempt to prevent the self-governing colonies from adopting a protective tariff even against the mother-country. Two explanations of this conduct may be suggested. The one is the expectation of free-traders that when once England had renounced the heresy of protection its fallacies would cease to delude the rest of the world. The other explanation is that between 1850 and 1860 English statesmen hardly considered the British colonies as a permanent part of the Empire. It was doubtful, they thought, whether either England or English dependencies gained anything by forming one State; colonial self-government seemed only a stage towards national independence. Separation would be merely the dissolution of a partnership which prevented the colonies from carrying on their own affairs in their own way, and which imposed upon England heavy and unprofitable burdens.

A thorough change has during the last thirty years come over the whole spirit of our colonial policy.[69] The sincerity of our imperialism is shown

---

69. In nothing is this change more visible than in the difference between the tone of Lewis's *Government of Dependencies*, published in 1841, and the tone of the Introduction to the same work, in the excellent edition published by my friend, Mr. C. P. Lucas, in 1891. Among the possible advantages of possessing dependencies, Lewis mentions the "glory which a country is supposed to derive from an extensive colonial empire," but he dismisses this point at once in a few contemptuous sentences. His editor can hardly understand this contempt, and finds the answer thereto in the assertion that the use of a colony to England cannot be measured by its present or marketable value. The contrast is the more instructive

by our action. The war in South Africa was as surely waged by England and her self-governing colonies to maintain the unity of the British Empire as the war against the Southern States was waged by the Northerners to maintain the unity of the United States. Neither the British people nor the citizens of the Northern States were prepared to acknowledge the right of secession. The determination of the English people to resist the dismemberment of the Empire seems to myself, as it must have seemed to every Englishman who gave his moral support to the war with the Boers, fully defensible on grounds of good sense and of justice. Nor was there any difficulty in defending the war in South Africa on grounds which would commend themselves to any utilitarian who took an extended view of national interest. The maintenance of the British Empire makes it possible, at a cost which is relatively small, compared with the whole number of British subjects, to secure peace, good order, and personal freedom throughout a large part of the world. In an age, further, of huge military States it is of the highest importance to safeguard against foreign aggression one of the two greatest free commonwealths in existence. The day of small States appears to have passed. We may regret a fact of which we cannot deny the reality. Great empires are as much a necessity of our time as are huge mercantile companies.

These and other like considerations, to which even the most utilitarian of statesmen could not refuse attention, may be urged, and ought to be urged, in support of English imperialism, but an imperialist ought not to hesitate to make two concessions. The one is that it is difficult to prove that the individual happiness of a citizen, say of London, is, because of the maintenance of the British Empire, either greater or less than the happiness of a citizen of Switzerland, whose country can boast of no dependencies. The other concession is that, though valid utilitarian arguments may be adduced for resistance to the aggressions of the Boers, the spirit which enabled the United Kingdom and its colonies to carry an arduous war to

---

because both the writer and the editor of the *Government of Dependencies* must be held men of cool judgment and of sound sense, and write with the advantage of practical acquaintance with our colonial administration. A sane imperialist joins issue with a sane Benthamite; the difference in their point of view marks the opposition between the ideas of 1841 and the ideas of 1905.

a successful end owed its force not to these arguments but to a sense of the greatness, to the memory of the achievements, and to faith in the future, of the British Empire. The yearly crowning of Nelson's column, the influence exerted by the writings of Froude, of Seeley, and above all of Mahan, the tales and the verses of Rudyard Kipling, with their glorification of British imperial sway, and the echo which the teaching of all these writers finds in the hearts of the English people throughout the United Kingdom and our self-governing colonies, all tell their own tale. They all bear witness to the power exerted by a kind of sentiment which it is extremely hard to express in terms of utilitarian philosophy. Imperialism is to all who share it a form of passionate feeling; it is a political religion, for it is public spirit touched with emotion. No sane imperialist should care to deny that this is so. He may well admit the dangers while vindicating the essential reasonableness of a policy founded in part on feeling. He will, however, unhesitatingly contend that enthusiasm for the maintenance of the British Empire is a form of patriotism which has a high absolute worth of its own, and is both excited and justified by the lessons of history. But here we pass from a striking illustration of the influence exerted in the public life of modern England by a sentiment hardly understood or appreciated by the Benthamite school, to the influence of historical tradition, which is connected with and stimulated by historical habits of thought.

This historical method,[70] or the habit of looking at ideas and institutions in the light of history and as part of the growth of society, was foreign to

70. This expression has at least three meanings, or aspects, all of which are combined in the minds of its devotees:

1. The habit or practice of examining the growth or history of laws, institutions, customs, or opinions.

2. The desire and attempt to make discoveries in the history of mankind analogous to the discoveries made by means of investigation and experiment in the sphere of natural science.

Historical and scientific investigations may run easily into one another: an examination into the early history of civilisation, on the one hand, may throw light upon the Darwinian theory, and, on the other hand, Darwin's speculations may be looked upon as inquiries into the early history of all living beings, including man.

3. The habit of looking upon men, not as separate individuals but as members or parts of the social organism.

the prevailing spirit of the eighteenth century, and was especially repugnant to Bentham, in this, as in all things, the true son of his age. Read carefully this passage from his note-books:

> He [Chamberlain Clarke] ridiculed Panopticon; he had admiration for all that is ancient, dislike for all that is modern; he had a theory that law should descend from generation to generation, because law is *weighty*, and ought, therefore, naturally to descend: he put me on the wrong scent in my studies; prevented my getting forward by always driving me back, back. He sent me to read indifferent accounts of law as it was; he so filled my mind with notions of the merit of looking backwards, that I took to Anglo-Saxon inquiries, studied their language, and set myself to learning laws that had passed away.
>
> I remember joining him to deplore the loss of Lord Mansfield's manuscript by the mob; I should now think such a loss a gain.[71]

We are apt to smile at the grotesque naïveté with which our philosopher rejected counsel which would now be pressed upon a student by the most learned and capable of the teachers of law both in England and in the United States, and to regret,[72] in a patronising manner, that Bentham should have lacked the historical spirit. Meanwhile we often fail to observe, what is a matter of some consequence, that the indifference of Bentham and his school to merely historical inquiries was grounded on a sound instinct. In many departments of life, and certainly in the province of law reform, the analysis of human nature as it exists is of infinitely more importance than research into the annals of the past.[73] Nor does the matter end here. The historical spirit, and still more the turn of mind which it

71. Bentham, *Works,* x. p. 51. Note, however, Bentham's appreciative comment on Montesquieu, *ibid.* p. 143.

72. It is more than doubtful whether the world would have gained any real advantage by Bentham having been inspired with enthusiasm for legal archaeology. Time spent on the exploration of legal antiquities would have been so much time and energy deducted from study of the principles which should guide a reformer in the amendment of the law. What at the end of the eighteenth century England needed and found in Bentham was not a legal historian but, to use the expression of Brougham, a legal philosopher.

73. No discovery, for instance, as to the true character or constitution of the Witenagemót would have been of material aid to the writers of the *Federalist* in planning a constitution for the United States.

produces, may well be hostile to rational reform of the Benthamite type; and this in more ways than one.

Interest in the origin of laws or institutions shifts the aim of legal study. To Bentham its object was the promotion of salutary legislation which might benefit mankind. To Maine and his disciples the study of law had as its aim, not the reform of legislation, but the knowledge of legal history as one of the many developments of human thought. To Benthamites the promotion of human happiness, to enthusiasts for research the extension of historical science, is the true end of thought and study. As research becomes more important than reform, the faith that legislation is the noblest of human pursuits falls naturally into the background, and suffers diminution. By this change science may gain, but zeal for advancing the happiness of mankind grows cool.

An historical inquirer again has, as such, no reason for disliking an abuse. The institutions, such as slavery, which have added to the miseries of mankind, have a history, and a very important one, no less than have the movements which have conferred the greatest blessings upon humanity. There is then no reason why the effort to understand the development of an abuse should not to the zealot for research be at least as interesting as the labour necessary for its removal. Insistence, indeed, upon the historical grandeur of a constitution, which is full of patent defects, may become, even with a man endowed with the genius and the philanthropy of Burke, a plea for strenuous opposition to its practical improvement.

Historical research, further, just because it proves that forms of government are the necessary outcome of complicated social conditions, first, indeed, leads to the true conclusion that the wisest legislation can do far less than both philanthropic philosophers[74] and the ordinary public sup-

---

74. "One ought not to complain of the wickedness of man, but of the ignorance of legislators who have always set private interest in opposition to public."

"The hidden source of a people's vices is always in its legislation; it is there that we must search if we would discover and extirpate their roots."

"Moralists ought to know that as the sculptor fashions the trunk of a tree into a god or a stool, so the legislator makes heroes, geniuses, virtuous men, as he wills: ... reward, punishment, fame, disgrace, are four kinds of divinities with which he can always effect the public good."

These are the words of Helvetius (1715–1771). See Sidgwick, *Miscellaneous Essays*, p. 152. They embody the creed of Bentham. The historical method has made such language and

pose, for the immediate benefit of mankind, but next suggests the less legitimate inference that it is a waste of energy to trouble one's self greatly about the amendment of the law.

The opposition, moreover, between Benthamite schemes for the benefit of mankind, and the spirit engendered by historical research may with advantage be looked at from a wider point of view. Individualistic liberalism, whatever may be the form it takes, rests upon a strong and even an excessive appreciation of the characteristics which are common to all men, but historical research, especially if it be carried back to, or even beyond the earliest stages of civilisation, brings into prominence and exaggerates the dissimilarities between different classes and especially between different races[75] of mankind, and thus tends, not indeed to remove the reasonable grounds for securing to all men, as far as may be possible, an equality of rights, but to quench the confident enthusiasm necessary for the carrying out even the most well approved and the most beneficial among democratic innovations.[76]

The historical spirit, in the last place, often suggests to thinkers ideas of

---

such a faith impossible to-day for any man of education or ability. But has it not also made all but impossible that passionate enthusiasm for the amendment of the law which inspired the efforts of every reformer who had come under the influence of Bentham?

75. "Ce qui est réellement abusif . . . c'est l'acceptation élastique prêtée par beaucoup de socialogues naturalistes au mot *hérédité*, qui leur sert à exprimer pêle-mêle avec la transmission des caractères vitaux par génération, la transmission d'idées, de moeurs, de choses sociales, par tradition ancestrale, par éducation domestique, par imitation-coutume." [What really goes too far . . . is the elastic way in which many social scientists interpret the word "heredity." They use it, as needed, to suggest that along with biological characteristics, ideas, morals and social views are transmitted—by ancestral tradition, upbringing, and imitation—from one generation to the next.]—Tarde, *Les Lois de l'Imitation* (2nd ed.), p. ix. [Editor's note: The translation was added in the Liberty Fund edition.]

It is no mere accident that Maine, who in his *Ancient Law* undermined the authority of analytical jurisprudence, aimed in his *Popular Government* a blow at the foundations of Benthamite faith in democracy.

76. The abolition of negro slavery was not only justified but absolutely required by the principle of utility and by the conscience of mankind; for negro slavery was a disgrace to civilisation and an obstacle to progress. But could the Abolitionists either in England or in the United States have fought with success their desperate battle against oppression had they not been strengthened by an unswerving faith in the essential similarity and equality of all human beings whether blacks or whites?

great speculative value which tell upon the feelings of whole peoples who know not whence they derive their thoughts, but in whom these thoughts, being transformed into passions, may work out results very different from those aimed at by any philosophical reformer and results of which the good and the evil may be nearly equally balanced.

Nationalism, for instance, or the enthusiastic belief that the inhabitants of a country ought to be ruled exclusively by men of, or supposed to be of, their own race, has undoubtedly been intensified by the prevalence of the historical spirit, and has in turn lent new prestige and vigour to the use of the historical method. But nationalism has assuredly created an atmosphere in which utilitarian ideas cannot easily flourish. The greatest-happiness principle no doubt suggests that the inhabitants of a country may be better or, so to speak, more comfortably governed by native than by foreign rulers. Austrian administrators, though capable enough, were more likely to outrage Italian feeling than the grossly incompetent but Italian kings of the two Sicilies. Napoleon, the greatest administrator of his time, offered worse outrages to the sentiment of Spain than the vilest of the Spanish Bourbons. But who can deny that the administration of Lombardy may have been as good under the Austrians as now under the rule of an Italian monarch, or that Napoleon might have conferred upon Spain an administrative system which, from a utilitarian point of view, would have been far preferable to any scheme of government which has for centuries existed in the Spanish Peninsula? And if it be urged that, since Spaniards or Italians would not acquiesce in the rule of foreigners, it was impossible for alien rulers to establish good government either in Spain or in Lombardy, a thorough-going Benthamite would retort that this assertion, even if true, is irrelevant, for the resistance was caused by nationalism, and the question under consideration is whether the happiness either of Italians or Spaniards was promoted by yielding to the spirit of nationality.

However this may be, it can hardly be disputed that nationalism, connected as it often is with historical traditions belonging to a past age, may, and often has become a hindrance to what any Benthamite Liberal would account good government. What is even more to be regretted, a narrow spirit of nationalism, fostered, as it often is, by historical traditions, has in more States than one produced racial divisions and animosities, which are not only in themselves a gigantic evil and an impediment to all true progress, but, since they depend upon feeling rather than upon any wish for good government, cannot be composed by any merely rational reform of laws or of institutions. Here, in short, the historical spirit unites disastrously with the apotheosis of instinct. Happy, from a Benthamite point of view, is the nation which is not haunted by the dream or nightmare of past or traditional glory. The singular absence in England of all popular traditions causes some natural regret to poets and even to patriots. Yet it has assuredly favoured the growth and the preservation of English freedom. Forgetfulness is in politics akin to forgiveness. The absence of historical hatreds has at any rate delivered England from the spurious patriotism which

> Visits ancient sins on modern times
> And punishes the Pope for Caesar's crimes.

The enthusiast for nationality can indeed hardly deny that nationalism has often been a hindrance to various kinds of improvement, but he will of course plead that the spirit of nationality is of more value than any material or even than some kinds of moral progress. Whatever be the truth of this plea, the opposition between Benthamism and nationalism[77] is obvious. The historical spirit, therefore, in giving prominence to the idea of nationality has told against the authority of utilitarian liberalism.

The disintegration, then, of beliefs has weakened the authority of Benthamite doctrine; the apotheosis of sentiment has rendered difficult the application of the utilitarian theory to the amendment of the law; the historical method has fostered a spirit foreign to the ideas of Benthamite

---

77. Sympathy with national resistance to Napoleon in Spain and Germany was felt keenly by Tories and very slightly, if at all, by Whigs and Radicals.

Every creed, political no less than religious, if it is to be effective, must become a faith; but a faith is the alliance of thought with some strong and cognate feeling. Every form of political belief, therefore, seeks to connect itself with some appropriate emotion. This held good of Benthamite liberalism. It became a faith, but it could not naturally blend with the sentiments now known as imperialism or nationalism, though in 1830 they had hardly received definite names. Benthamism—just because the fundamental idea of utilitarian morality is that the proper aim of human action is the greatest happiness of the greatest number—had a real affinity, and in fact became closely allied with the sentiments of philanthropy and cosmopolitanism.

philosophy. Three tendencies pre-eminently characteristic of our time have, therefore, diminished, to say the least, the power of individualism and favoured, or at any rate cleared the ground for, the growth of collectivism. But we have already passed into a field of thought which lies beyond the limits of these lectures. An English lawyer ought not to trespass further upon the province of historians, moralists, or philosophers. He will do well to direct attention as far as possible to the close and demonstrable connection during the nineteenth century between the development of English law and certain known currents of opinion. He should insist upon the consideration that the relation between law and opinion has been in England, as elsewhere, extremely complex; that legislative opinion is itself more often the result of facts than of philosophical speculations; and that no facts play a more important part in the creation of opinion than laws themselves. He must above all enforce the conclusion at which every intelligent student must ultimately arrive, that each kind of opinion entertained by men at a given era is governed by that whole body of beliefs, convictions, sentiments, or assumptions, which, for want of a better name, we call the spirit of an age. "Deeper than opinions lies the sentiment which predetermines opinion. What it is important for us to know with respect to our own age or any age is, not its peculiar opinions, but the complex elements of that moral feeling and character in which, as in their congenial soil, opinions grow."[78]

78. Pattison, *Essays,* ii. p. 264.

Appendix

NOTE I. *The Right of Association*

(See pp. 68–74, 109–113, 136–143, 189–193, *ante;*
Pic, *Traité Élémentaire de Législation Industrielle, Les Lois Ouvrières* (2nd ed.);
Hauriou, *Prècis de Droit Administratif;*
Trouillot and Chapsal, *Du Contrat d'Association;*
Loi 14–17, juin 1791 (Loi Chapelier);
Code Pénal, arts. 414–416; *Loi 25 mai 1864; Loi 21 mars 1884; Loi 1er juillet 1901.*
See especially Duguit (Léon). *Les Transformations du Droit Public* (1913); *Les Transformations Générales du Droit Privé* (1912); *L'État, Le Droit Objectif et la loi Positive* (1901).)

> *(A) The problem raised in every civilised country by the right of association.*

Of the nature of the right of association and its peculiarities enough has been already said (pp. 109–113, *ante*).

The point to note is that at the present day its exercise raises difficulties in every civilised country. In England, as elsewhere, trade unions and strikes, or federations of employers and lock-outs; in Ireland, the boycotting by leagues and societies of any landlord, tenant, trader, or workman, bold enough to disobey their behests or break their laws; in the United States, the efforts of mercantile Trusts to create for themselves huge monopolies; in France, the real or alleged necessity of stringent legislation in order to keep religious communities (*congrégations religieuses*) under the control of the State—in almost every country, in short, some forms of association force upon public attention the practical difficulty of so regulating the right of association that its exercise may neither trench upon each citizen's individual freedom nor shake the supreme authority of the State. The problem to be solved, either as a matter of theory or as a matter of practical necessity, is at bottom always and everywhere the same. How can the right of combined action be curtailed without depriving individual liberty of half its value; how can it be left unrestricted without destroying either the liberty of individual citizens, or the power of the Government? To see that this problem at the present day presents itself everywhere, and has nowhere received a quite satisfactory solution, is of importance. The fact suggests at least two conclusions: The one is, that the difficulty felt in England of dealing with our combination law arises, to a great extent, neither from the greediness of employers nor from the unreasonableness of workmen, but from the nature of things; the other is, that the most which can be achieved by way of bringing into harmony two essentially conflicting rights, namely, the right to individual freedom and the right of association, is to effect a rough compromise between them. Such a practical solution of a theoretically insolvable problem is sometimes possible. That this is so is proved by our existing law of libel. It is a rough compromise between the right of X to say or write what he chooses, and the right of A not to be injured in property or character by X's free utterance of his opinions. The compromise is successful; it substantially allows freedom of discussion, and at the same time protects Englishmen against defamation.

(B) *Comparison between the development of the combination law in France and in England during the nineteenth century.*

The expression "combination law," though peculiar to the law of England, may conveniently be used as describing a particular part of French no less than of English law. It means the body of legal rules or principles which regulate the right of workmen, on the one side, to combine among themselves for the purpose of determining by agreement the terms on which, and especially the wages at which, they will work, or, in other words, sell their labour; and the right of masters, on the other side, to combine among themselves for the purpose of determining by agreement the terms on which, and especially the wages at which, they will engage workmen, or, in other words, purchase labour.

The development of the combination law in France and in England has been, during the nineteenth century, marked by curious similarities and differences. This will be seen to be so if we take the law of France and compare it with the law of England at different parts of the nineteenth century.

As to Similarities.

I. The combination law of France, no less than that of England, passed during the last century through three stages; these three stages of development in each country roughly correspond in character and in sequence, though not in date.

First Stage, 1800–1864. During this period trade combinations, whether temporary or permanent, either of men or of masters, were under the law of France unlawful, and the persons taking part in them were liable to punishment; a strike was a crime, a trade union (under which term we may include a combination of employers) was an unlawful association. (See Pic, pp. 185, 186, and 211–229; Hauriou, 5th ed. pp. 100, 101, and compare Hauriou, 3rd ed. pp. 155–158.) This was the effect of both revolutionary and Napoleonic legislation. In 1789 the National Assembly had dissolved all trade guilds, corporations, or unions. The *Loi Chapelier,* 14 *juin* 1791, imposed penalties on persons taking part—to use English expressions—in strikes or lock-outs, or becoming members of trade unions (see Pic, pp. 185, 186, 213). The *Code Pénal,* arts. 291, 292, prohibited all societies or associations of more than twenty persons (except mercantile partnerships) which were not authorised by the Government, and articles 414–416 punished with severe penalties combinations (*coalitions*) either of masters or of workmen; and the *Code Pénal,* though it did not come into force till 1810, more or less codified or represented the spirit of earlier revolutionary legislation. The combination law of France, moreover, was till 1849 not even nominally equal as between men and masters. It pressed heavily on combinations of workmen, and lightly on combinations of employers (see *Code Pénal,* arts. 414–416). In practice, a law which was felt to be oppressive by artisans was looked upon with favour by their employers. The law remained in substance unchanged till 1864; its severity as against workmen was increased during the reign of Louis Philippe (*loi* 10 *avril* 1834), and the law, though in 1849 it was so amended that combinations of workmen were placed nominally in exactly the same position as combinations of masters, still pressed with far greater severity on the employed than on employers.

The French combination law then from 1800 to 1864 bore, as regards its practical effect, a strong resemblance to the English combination law from 1800 to 1824 (see pp. 68–74, *ante*). Under French law it was impossible, under English law it was, to say the least, extremely difficult, for any workman to take part in a strike or to join a trade union without committing a crime. In France a trade union was an unlawful, in England it was at best a nonlawful association. In each country the combination law which prevailed there in the corresponding stage of its development originated in fact in legislation earlier than 1800. In each country enactments directly applying to combinations, whether of masters or of workmen, were supplemented by other parts of the law. Behind the combination law of France lay the extensive power conferred upon the Government (*Code Pénal*, arts. 291, 292) of refusing to authorise, or putting an end to the existence of whole classes of associations among which trade unions appear to have been included. Behind the English Combination Act of 1800 lay the law of conspiracy.

Second Stage, 1864–1884. The law of 1864 (*loi* 25 *mai* 1864) so amended the *Code Pénal*, arts. 414–416, as to make strikes lawful proceedings. The general effect of the law, with the details whereof we need not trouble ourselves, appears to have been this: Temporary combinations (*coalitions*) for the purpose of raising or lowering wages, or, as we should say, strikes or lock-outs, ceased to be punishable. On the other hand, various unlawful acts, such as acts of violence, assaults, menaces, or fraudulent manoeuvres, when done by any one for the purpose of maintaining a strike or lock-out, or generally interfering with the free exercise of a man's business or work (*exercice de l'industrie ou du travail*) were made severely punishable, and the punishment was increased if these offences, *e.g.* an assault, were the result of a combination (*plan concerté*) (see *Code Pénal*, amended articles 414, 415), and the new crime was created of combining to interfere with the free exercise of a man's business or work by the imposition of fines, prohibitions, and the like. No doubt the new crime might be committed as well by masters as by men, but it is obvious that the general effect of the amended law was to punish severely every unlawful act, and a good number of acts not in themselves unlawful, which interfered with free trade in labour. When we remember that a trade union still remained an unlawful society, the general result of the legislation of 1864 must have been that whilst a strike was no longer in itself an unlawful proceeding, it remained hardly possible to use any of the means which render a strike effective without a breach of the law, or, in other words, without the commission of a crime (*Code Pénal*, arts. 414–416, as amended by *loi* 25 *mai* 1864).

The general likeness between the French combination law of 1864 to 1884 and the English combination law of 1825 to 1875 (see pp. 136–143, *ante*) is patent. In each country the law was intended to establish free trade in labour. It allowed to masters and to men such an amount of combined action among themselves as the legislature deemed necessary for ensuring such freedom of trade. It punished severely various unlawful acts, *e.g.* assaults, menaces, etc., when used, speaking broadly, for the purpose of interfering with an individual's right to carry on his business in such manner or to work on such terms as he pleased. It in effect limited the right of combination whenever it interfered with freedom of trade in labour. It was in each country a law which, though it did not make strikes unlawful, made it an extremely difficult matter to carry out an effective strike without the commission of crime. The likeness between the combination law of France and of

England during the second stage of its development must indeed not be over-pressed. No comparison can possibly be fair which does not take into account, among other considerations, the far greater power always possessed by a French than by an English Government. The authority of the Executive in France is even now not adequately realised by most Englishmen. All that can safely be asserted is that the French legislation of 1864 gave expression to ideas very similar to the beliefs which underlay the English Combination Act of 1825. It is at least a noticeable coincidence that Napoleon III., who in 1860, under the influence of Cobden, pro-moted free trade in goods, did, in fact, by the legislation of 1864, try to promote free trade in labour as understood by political economists.

Third Stage, 1884 to the end of the nineteenth century. The law of 1884 (*loi du 21 mars* 1884) includes much of what Englishmen understand by the combination law, but deals with a wider subject than the right of combination as exercised by employers or by workmen. Its object is to legalise all professional associations (*syndicats professionnels*)—that is, societies of whatever kind (not being trade part-nerships, which have always been fully legal) for the promotion or the protection of the interest of any profession or trade (*loi du 21 mars* 1884, *art.* 3). It repeals, as regards all such professional associations, all earlier laws, *e.g. Code Pénal,* arts. 291–294, and 416, which might restrict their freedom of action. With the wider aspects of the law we are not concerned; what we need chiefly note is that trade unions, whether of masters or of men, come within the class of professional associations, and therefore profit by the law of 1884. The French combination law of to-day would appear, as far as an English lawyer can judge, to be much as follows: Strikes have been since 1864 in theory, and are now in practice, if properly conducted, entirely lawful proceedings. Trade unions are, like other professional associations (*syndicats professionnels*), lawful societies. The *Code Pénal* still punishes severely assaults, menaces, and the like, used as means for interfering with a man's right to carry on his business or to work as he sees fit. The law, therefore, imposes heavy punishment upon conduct, which is illegal in itself, when used as a means for rendering a strike effective; but, otherwise, combinations between masters on the one side, or men on the other, for regulating the terms of the labour contract, are lawful, and a strike may be carried on without any necessity for breaking the law.

The likeness between the combination law of France since 1884 and the com-bination law of England since 1875 at once arrests attention. In France and in England the law is intended to allow to employers and employed as unlimited a right of combination as is compatible with the respect due to the freedom of individuals, whether masters or workmen. In each country strikes and lock-outs are lawful; in each country a trade union is a lawful society; in neither country does a trade union need for its legal existence the sanction of the Government. In each country masters and workmen stand, as regards their right to combine, on a complete equality; in each country the law allows combinations for the purpose of regulating the terms of the labour contract. Both in France and in England the law protects the liberty of individuals by imposing special penalties on any man guilty of certain unlawful acts, *e.g.* assault, intimidation, and the like, for the purpose of interfering with his neighbour's freedom of action; in other words, the law of each country specially punishes acts of coercion likely to be committed in furtherance of a strike. (Compare *Code Pénal*, arts. 414, 415, and the Conspiracy and Protection of Property Act, 1875, s. 7.) The practical similarity between the combination law of each country is increased if we take into account the abolition, under modern French law, of restraints on the liberty of the press and on the right of public meeting which used to hamper attempts to carry out a strike, and if we at the same time remember that the celebrated law on associations (*loi du 1ᵉʳ juillet* 1901) has very widely extended the right of association. We are naturally then led to the conclusion that the combination law of France and the combination law of England not only bear a great similarity to one another, but have at last reached exactly the same goal. This idea does not entirely harmonise with facts, but does contain a large element of truth.

II. In France as in England judicial legislation, or judicial interpretation which comes very near to legislation, modifies the combination law.

French Courts, it is true, are far less bound than our English tribunals by precedent, and different Courts will in France occasionally on one and the same question of principle pronounce inconsistent decisions. Still, French judges must from the nature of things interpret the law of 21st March 1884 in accordance with principle, and interpret it so as if possible to respect at once the rights of trade unions (*syndicats*) and the rights of individual masters or workmen. That they have tried to do this is manifest. It is also clear that they have had to deal with just the kind of questions which have perplexed our judges. They have been or may be called upon, to consider the questions whether a trade union can lawfully put on a black list, or boycott (*mettre à l'index*), a workman because he is not a member of a union; or, on the other hand, whether a master can lawfully discharge a workman because he is a member of a union? And French Courts apparently would in such cases at any rate protect individual freedom, and hold the action both of the union and of the employer to be unlawful, because it, in fact, interfered with the right of the workman to stand apart from, or to belong to, a trade union as he thought fit. Such decisions as these would greatly resemble in spirit some recent judgments pronounced by our Courts. What further appears to be clearly established in France is that in such cases the person aggrieved has a right of action for damages against the wrong-doer. (See Pic, pp. 232–235.)

III. Both in France and in England a severe combination law did not at any time fully attain its object.

Even during the first stage of the French combination law (1800–1864) trade combinations, certainly among employers, and in some cases among workmen, grew up and existed not only by the toleration, but with the approval of the Government. The administrative power of the Executive could do a good deal to mitigate the severity of the combination law, and it would rather seem that, at any rate during the second stage of the combination law (1864–1884), workmen, no less than employers, did in fact exercise the power of association with considerable freedom. To what extent this freedom may have been used, no English lawyer can pronounce with certainty. In England, at any rate, the severity of the combination law, even between 1800 and 1824–25, did not suppress the combined action of workmen. The Combination Act of 1825 certainly was not inconsistent with the existence both of trade unions and of strikes.

As to Differences.

I. At the beginning of the nineteenth century the combination law of France and the combination law of England, though they aimed at the same object, namely, the suppression of trade unions and strikes, rested upon essentially different principles.

The French combination law as it then existed was the work of men who were both lawyers and individualists. As lawyers they inherited from the traditions of the *ancien régime* the belief (characteristic of French law) that the right of association was dangerous to and ought to be strictly controlled by the authority of the state (Trouillot and Chapsal, *Du Contrat d'Association*, pp. 5–11). As individualists they were thoroughly imbued with the conviction, handed down to them by Turgot and other philosophic reformers, that corporations and, above all, trade guilds, and the like bodies, were hostile to the freedom and the interests of individuals, and that whilst the rights of individual citizens and the rights of the State deserve recognition, no account at all ought to be taken of the supposed interest or rights of corporate bodies (Pic, pp. 184–186, 211–213; Hauriou, pp. 100, 101). This conviction held by the lawyers who, either as revolutionary statesmen or as Napoleonic officials, remodelled the law of France, is well expressed in these sentences in the Report of Chapelier in favour of the law which bears his name.

"Il doit sans doute être permis à tous les citoyens de s'assembler; mais il ne doit pas être permis aux citoyens *de certaines professions* de s'assembler *pour leurs prétendus intérêts communs.* Il n'y a plus de corporation dans l'Etat. Il n'y a plus que *l'intérêt particulier* de chaque individu et *l'intérêt général.* Il n'est permis à personne d'inspirer aux citoyens un intérêt intermédiaire, de les séparer de la chose publique par un esprit de corporation." [All citizens should enjoy the right of assembly, but citizens from certain professions who wish to congregate in support of claimed common interests should not be allowed to do so. There are no longer any guilds (corporations) in this nation. There is only each individual's particular self-interest, and then the common interest. No one is permitted to rally the citizens to an intermediate cause, to distance them from the public interest by calling upon a guild spirit.]—Pic, *Tràité Elémentaire de Législation*, p. 212. [Editor's note: The translation was added in the Liberty Fund edition.]

Hence, though the French combination law in its earliest stage treated strikes and trade unions with special severity, it nevertheless placed associations, whether temporary or permanent, either of masters or of workmen, in theory at least on the same footing as other professional societies (*syndicats professionnels*). All such societies were looked upon with jealousy or disapproval as intended to promote the interest of particular professions, and, therefore, presumably hostile to the interest of the public. The combination law of France, in short, though it no doubt pressed with special heaviness on such societies as trade unions, was, after all, inspired by a conviction that it was necessary to place strict limits on the general right of association. It thoroughly harmonised with French opinion of the day and with the general spirit of French law.

The authors of the Combination Act of 1800 were Tories. They were in no special sense individualists, but they accepted the ideas of the common law. From the common law they learned that men might lawfully combine together for the attainment of any object which was neither unlawful nor opposed to public interest; but from the common law they also learned that any combination in restraint of trade was opposed to the public interest, and might possibly make any man who took part in it a conspirator. They perceived, further, truly enough that a strike or a trade union did aim at the restraint of trade. They therefore, while by no means denying the common law right of Englishmen to combine together for any lawful purpose, passed an Act quite in harmony with the legislative opinion of the day, which aimed at the suppression of strikes and trade unions (see pp. 68–74, *ante*).

Hence, though the French combination law and the English combination law were at the early part of the nineteenth century equally severe, yet there has always been this difference between them. The French combination law has always rested on the general principle, till quite recently admitted by almost all Frenchmen, that the right of association ought to be very strictly controlled. Thus a trade union was treated as one of that large number of professional associations on all of which the Government ought to keep a watchful eye. The French combination law was severe, but it was hardly exceptional legislation. The English Combination Act of

1800, and to a certain extent the Combination Act of 1825, behind which (as already noted) stood the law of conspiracy, were specimens of exceptional legislation; for they rested on the idea that while all men ought in general to enjoy what one may term the right of association, yet that combinations of workmen and, in theory, of masters, since they tended towards the restraint of trade, ought to be the object of special watchfulness on the part of the Government, and generally to be the subject of special and peculiar legislation. Thus the combination law of England was opposed to the general spirit of the common law, and had from the first the defects which inevitably attach to all law-making of an exceptional character.

II. Till 1884 the existence of trade unions lay in France at the mercy of the Government (see *Code Pénal*, arts. 292–294). In England, even in 1800, the members of trade unions might be liable to punishment under the Combination Act of 1800, or under the law of conspiracy, and a trade union which was certainly a non-lawful, was possibly an unlawful society, but it could not be dissolved at the will of the Government. English workmen, like all other Englishmen, fell under the rule of law, not of arbitrary power.

III. The existing combination law of France differs in character from the existing combination law of England.

A comparison, no doubt, of the French law of 1884 (*loi* 21 *mars* 1884) with the Combination Act of 1875 and the Trade Union Acts 1871 and 1876 (see pp. 189–193, *ante*) suggests, as already pointed out, that the combination laws of France and of England are now of a fundamentally similar character. But this idea is erroneous, and leads us to overlook an essential difference which may be thus stated: The right of association has in France under the law of 1884 and the law of 1901, as well as under other laws, been vastly extended. By these changes trade combinations, whether in the shape of strikes or trade unions, have been made thoroughly legal; they have profited and were intended to profit by changes in the general law of the land which have favoured every kind of combined action. But trade combinations are not in France regulated by exceptional legislation. A trade union is a lawful society, but it is so in virtue not of any special legislation or of any special privilege, but because it falls within the body of professional associations, the position whereof is regulated by the *loi du* 21 *mars* 1884. In England, on the other hand, though as in France a strike is a lawful proceeding and a trade union is a lawful society, the position of men on strike and of a trade union is still to a certain extent exceptional. Thus a combination to do an act in contemplation or furtherance of a trade dispute between employers and workmen may escape from criminality, where a combination to do the same act for some other purpose may be a crime, and a trade union itself, though a legal society, stands in some respects in an exceptional situation (see pp. 189–193, *ante*). England has still a special combination law, whilst trade combinations are in France governed entirely, or all but entirely, by the general law of the land. The cause of this difference is seemingly to be found in a fact to which attention has already been directed. The law of France was at the beginning of the nineteenth century as much opposed as was the law of England to trade combinations, and in truth was more severe, but it was not in strictness exceptional legislation. The law of England in regard to trade combinations was not only severe but was also exceptional. The result is curious. The feeling has grown up in England which has apparently not grown up in France, that trade combinations for the regulation of labour must be treated exceptionally. Severity has given place to favouritism: the denial of equality has by a natural reaction led to the concession of, and promoted the demand for, privilege.

NOTE II. *The Ecclesiastical Commission*

The rapidity which between 1836 and 1850 marked the reform of the Church Establishment (see pp. 243, 244, *ante*), though due in the main to a general improvement in the tone of public opinion, must be ascribed in part to the whole body of legislation of which the Ecclesiastical Commissioners Act, 1836, forms the best known and by far the most important portion.

This legislation, some part of which was of earlier and some of later date than 1836, produced the following (among other) effects:

(1) The efficiency of episcopal supervision was increased.

This resulted from the abolition of peculiar and anomalous jurisdictions and the rearrangement of diocesan areas, as well as the creation of the new sees of Manchester and Ripon. All this was effected soon after the Act of 1836. Some of the sees were vacant. Bishops of other sees waived their vested interests and assented to the proposed changes.

(2) The stringent provisions of the Pluralities Act, 1838, with regard to pluralities, non-residence, and so forth, tended to put an end to the abuses at which they were aimed, and worked quicker than might have been expected. The operation of the Act was delayed only by the vested interests of incumbents who were in possession at the date of the Act and had already taken advantage of the greater license of the law. Death, resignation, or preferment, each year diminished their number.

(3) A large increase was rapidly effected in church accommodation.

The Church Building Commissioners were created in 1818; by 1835 they had, by aid of parliamentary grants of £1,500,000 administered by them, and of private donations called forth to meet their allotments out of these grants, built 212 additional churches, which provided additional accommodation for 283,555 persons.

The Incorporated Church Building Society was at the same date credited with having spent on the enlargement of churches, etc., £196,770. This was raised by private subscription, and, it was believed, caused the expenditure on the same objects, by persons locally interested, of £900,000. Provision was thus made for the church accommodation of 307,314 persons.

(4) The creation of new parochial districts and the endowment thereof, as also the improvement of the parsonage houses and of the incomes of underpaid incumbents, was carried on with vigour.

Between 1818 and 1850, the Church Building Commissioners created 764 new parishes or separate ecclesiastical districts. Between 1843 and 1850 the Ecclesiastical Commissioners had under the New Parishes Acts, 1843, 6 & 7 Vict. c. 37, and 1844, 7 & 8 Vict. c. 94, created, in addition, 228 ecclesiastical districts; and in order that their operation might be carried on with the greater rapidity, the Commissioners were permitted by the New Parishes Act, 1843, to borrow, and they did borrow, a sum of £600,000, which they were allowed to spend as income in anticipation of their own rapidly increasing income. As early, further, as 1850 the Commissioners' funds had enabled them to provide, in the case of necessitous benefices, large capital sums for the provision of parsonage houses, and as much as £50,000 per annum (in addition to some £30,000 for the new districts above mentioned) for the perpetual augmentation of the incomes of under-paid incumbents.

(5) Much was done to reapportion and equalise the revenues of parochial benefices.

The Ecclesiastical Commissioners have never possessed any power of general reapportionment of such revenues, similar to that which was given them in relation to the revenues of bishoprics, but under several enactments, such as the Ecclesiastical Commissioners Act, 1840 (3 & 4 Vict. c. 113), s. 74, extended by the Augmentation of Benefices Act, 1854, s. 8, the Ecclesiastical Leasing Act, 1842, s. 13 (and see 21 & 22 Vict. c. 57, s. 10), they had been enabled, with the required consents of bishops and patrons, to do a great deal indirectly to equalise the incomes of benefices, and their action in increasing the incomes of necessitous benefices has all told in the same direction. To this add, that under the Augmentation of Benefices Act, 1831, the incumbent of a mother parish is able, with the consent of his bishop and patron, to charge the revenues thereof in favour of the incumbent of a daughter parish formed wholly or partly out of the mother parish. Legislation, in fact, had by 1850 done a good deal, though it has since done more, towards the equitable apportionment of parochial revenues, and towards raising the income of the poorest class of incumbents. Here, as elsewhere, one reform added to the effect of another. The want, for example, of parsonage houses, and the under-payment of incumbents, was an excuse, or even at times a justification, for pluralism or non-residence. As parsonage houses were built and something done towards equalising clerical incomes, and thus alleviating the poverty of the poorer clergy, the excuses for pluralism and non-residence lost their force.

The details of a reform as rapid as it was effective cannot be here pursued further, but they deserve consideration since they enforce two conclusions directly bearing on the relation between law and opinion.

First. The rapid internal reform of the Established Church between 1830 and 1850 owed both its origin and its effective working to the active support it derived from the moral opinion of the day.

Secondly. Public opinion was, in this instance, unmistakably affected by legislation of which public opinion was itself the author. When the law had been strenuously directed towards the putting down of pluralism and non-residence, good men began to perceive that practices which they had through habit come to look upon with easy tolerance were in reality unbearable abuses.

NOTE III. *University Tests*

(A) *Movement for Abolition from 1772.*[1]

1772. Feathers' Tavern petition rejected in the House of Commons by 217 to 71, but followed by the substitution, at Cambridge, of a declaration of *bonâ fide* church membership for the subscription to the three Articles of the 36th Canon.

1803. Oxford Examination Statute enacted by Convocation, whereby an examination in the Thirty-nine Articles was added to the existing conditions of a B.A. degree.

1834. Petition from 63 members of the Cambridge Senate, followed by long debates in both Houses, and counter-petitions.

Mr. G. Wood's Bill, to open the University to Dissenting undergraduates, and to abolish the restriction of degrees to Churchmen, passed the House of Commons by majorities of 185 to 44, 371 to 147, and 164 to 75; but was rejected in the Lords by 187 to 85.

1835. Attempt by Lord Radnor in the Peers to abolish subscriptions on matriculation, defeated by 163 to 57. The Heads of Houses at Oxford had recommended this alteration, but it was rejected by Convocation.

1. Use has been made, with permission, of Note M to Sir George Young's pamphlet on University Tests.

Abolition of Unnecessary Oaths Act passed, clause 8 giving power to the Universities to substitute declarations, in certain cases, for oaths.

1836. Substitution accordingly at Cambridge of declarations for oaths of obedience to statutes, and such like.

1838. Similar substitution at Oxford.

1843. Mr. James Heywood's petition presented by Mr. Christie, and Bill moved to abolish certain oaths and subscriptions, and extend education to persons not members of the Church of England. Rejected by 175 to 105. Attempts were made in the two succeeding years to revive the question, but without success.

1850. Mr. Heywood's motion for a Commission to inquire into the state of the Universities and Colleges carried by 160 to 138, after six nights' debate, with the consent of the Ministry, and issue of Commissions accordingly.

1852. Commissions reported.

1854. Oxford University Act (17 & 18 Vict. c. 81) passed, abolishing all religious tests on matriculation, or on taking an ordinary bachelor's degree.

1856. Cambridge University Act (19 & 20 Vict. c. 88) passed, throwing open all ordinary bachelor's degrees, all endowments tenable by undergraduates, and the nominal title of M.A. By this Act the declaration of *bonâ fide* church membership received for the first time a legislative sanction, and was employed to keep the Nonconforming M.A.s out of the senate and the parliamentary constituency.

1860, 1861. The Senior Wrangler for two years in succession prevented from sitting for a fellowship at Cambridge by the restrictions in the Act of Uniformity.

1862. Petition from 74 Fellows of Colleges at Cambridge actually resident, praying for the repeal of the "Conformity to the Liturgy" clause in that Act, on the ground of injury to the University.

1863. Bill introduced by Mr. Bouverie to give effect to the prayer of the petitioners, and read a first time by 157 to 135.

Petition from 106 of the Heads, Professors, and present and former Fellows of Colleges and College Tutors at Oxford, alleging the futility and pernicious effect of the restrictive system, and praying for the opening of degrees.

1864. Mr. Bouverie's Bill rejected by 157 to 101.

Bill introduced by Mr. Dodson to place degrees at Oxford on the same footing as at Cambridge; read a second time by 211 to 189, but defeated finally by 173 to 171.

1865. Bill introduced by Mr. Goschen to throw open degrees at Oxford, and read a second time by 206 to 190. Degrees in Divinity were excepted from its operation.

1866. Mr. Bouverie's Uniformity Act Amendment Bill (208 to 186) and Mr. Coleridge's Oxford University Tests Bill (217 to 103) read a second time in the

House of Commons. An attempt to reduce the latter to the dimensions of "the Cambridge compromise" was successfully resisted in Committee.

1867. Mr. Coleridge's Bill was extended in Committee to Cambridge (253 to 166), and passed through the House of Commons without a division; but was defeated in the Lords by a large majority. Mr. Bouverie's Bill read a second time by 200 to 156, but lost on a third reading by 41 to 34, at the very end of an exhausting session.

1868. The two Bills amalgamated, and made complete by the insertion in the repealing schedule of certain special Acts disqualifying Roman Catholics. The Bill completely enfranchised the University with the exception of degrees in Divinity; which exception is due to the unfortunate condition of Holy Orders attached to them. As to the Colleges, its action was permissive; it removed the impediments to free election imposed by the State; and these were in some cases the only legal restriction; but in others a new statute, framed by the College with the consent of the Queen in Council, and (in some) of the visitor, would have been necessary to render the removal effectual.

This Bill, though read a second time by 198 to 140, did not reach the House of Lords.

The Universities Tests Act, 1871, 34 Vict. c. 26, in effect abolished tests in the Universities of Oxford and Cambridge;[2] it relieved persons taking lay academical degrees, or taking or holding lay academical or collegiate offices, from being required to subscribe any article or formulary of faith, or to make any declaration of religious belief, or profession (sec. 3).

But the general effect of the Act was subject to several restrictions.

(1) It did not apply to degrees or professorships of divinity.

(2) It did not open to any layman, or any person not a member of the Church of England, any office which was, under any Act of Parliament, or University or collegiate statute in force at the time of the passing of the Act, *i.e.* on 16th July 1871, restricted to persons in holy orders, or affected the person appointed thereto with the obligation to take orders.

(3) It did not apply to any college not existing on the 16th July 1871, *i.e.* it did not apply to colleges created after 16th July 1871. (See *R. v. Hertford College* (1878), 3 Q.B.D. (C.A.), 693.)

The Universities of Oxford and Cambridge Act, 1877, 40 & 41 Vict. c. 48, created commissions for carrying out various reforms in the Universities, and especially for the modification of college statutes. The Act did not directly affect religious tests, but it in fact led to the abolition of clerical restrictions on the tenure of almost all headships and fellowships of colleges.

2. As also of Durham.

(B) Observations.

(1) The nationalisation of the English Universities has, like most other great reforms, been carried out with extraordinary slowness (see pp. 21–24, *ante*). The presentation of the Feathers' Tavern Petition, 1772, is separated from the Universities Tests Act, 1871, by a year less, and from the Universities of Oxford and Cambridge Act, 1877, by five years more, than a century.

(2) Delay in the execution of a necessary reform has, as in other instances, been here equivalent to a change in the character and the effects of the reform itself (see pp. 28–30, *ante*). The petitioners of 1772 aimed at a wider and a different kind of revolution from the change accomplished either by the Liberals who carried the Universities Tests Act, 1871, or by the statesmen, whether Conservatives or Liberals, who planned and carried the Universities of Oxford and Cambridge Act, 1877. Nor is it possible to doubt that the opening of the national universities to Nonconformists in 1834 would certainly have been a different thing from the tardy nationalisation of the universities in 1871.

(3) This nationalisation is still incomplete.[3] The Established Church still, as a matter of fact, occupies at Oxford and Cambridge a position of pre-eminence and predominance (see p. 250, *ante*). The correctness of this statement may possibly, I know, be disputed, but seems to me, after the most careful consideration, undeniable. If none but Roman Catholic priests had access to the university pulpits; if no one but a Roman Catholic could at Oxford or Cambridge take a degree in divinity; if in both universities every theological professorship were in fact held, and almost every theological professorship were tenable only by a Roman Catholic, and at Oxford only by a Roman Catholic priest; if, whilst a Roman Catholic might be the head of any college and many Roman Catholics occupied that position, the headships of some two, or possibly three colleges were restricted to priests of the Church of Rome; if in every college chapel Roman Catholic services, and Roman Catholic services alone, were, during term, daily celebrated; if, to sum up the whole matter, the Church of Rome possessed by law at Oxford and at Cambridge the privileges, and no more than the privileges, now in fact retained by the Church of England, could any man for a moment deny that Roman Catholicism did, in fact, in our national universities hold a position of pre-eminence? But if this question contains its own answer, how is it possible to argue that the Church of England is not at the present moment predominant in the Universities both of Oxford and of Cambridge? It is, of course, arguable that a church, acknowledged with the assent

---

3. See letter of H. Sidgwick, April 25, 1898, in *A Memoir*, pp. 564, 565. [Editor's note: This footnote was added in the second edition.]

of the country to be the Church of the nation, must hold a position of superiority at the national universities. With this point, be it noted, we are here in no way concerned: my only wish is to insist upon the fact that, whether wisely or unwisely, whether rightly or wrongly, the nationalisation of the English universities is still left incomplete.

NOTE IV. *Judge-made Law*

(See pp. 257–259, *ante;* Pollock, *Essays in Jurisprudence and Ethics,* p. 237, and *First Book of Jurisprudence* (2nd ed.), Pt. ii. c. vi.)

A. Origin of Judge-made Law

The existence of judge-made law—that is, of laws or rules created by the Courts of a country in the course of deciding definite cases—arises from the general acceptance in such country of two ideas.

The one is that a judge or a Court—the two expressions may be here treated as equivalent—when deciding any case must act, not as an arbitrator, but strictly as a judge; or that it is a judge's business to determine not what may be fair as between *A* and *X* in a given case, but what, according to some definite principle of law, are the respective rights of *A* and *X*. Hence it follows that every Court in deciding a case must tacitly, or expressly, apply to it some definite principle which is often indeed so clearly known that no special mention need be made of it, but which may be difficult to discover; and when this is so the Court must lay down the rule which guides its decision.

The other idea is that a Court or a judge must follow precedents, by which expression is really meant that a Court having once decided a particular case on a given principle (such *e.g.* as that an employer is liable to make compensation for damage arising from the negligence of his servants in the course of their employment) must decide all really similar cases in accordance with the same principle, or, to put the same thing in other words, that a Court is bound, as the expression goes, by its own judgments.

One may add that from this very respect for precedents it logically follows that when the judgments of an inferior Court are on a matter of law set aside (*i.e.* are either reversed or overruled) by a superior Court, the inferior Court must henceforth follow the judgment of, *i.e.* the principle laid down by the superior Court, and that a final Court of Appeal, such as is in England the House of Lords, is bound by its own judgments, *i.e.* must apply the principle laid down by itself for the decision of a particular case to all similar cases, until and unless the principle itself is declared to be no longer law by the Legislature, *i.e.* in England by an Act of Parliament.

Now these two ideas—namely, that Courts must act as judges, not as arbitrators, and that the duty of a Court is to follow precedents—though to a limited extent admitted in all civilised countries, have obtained more complete acceptance in England than in any continental, and perhaps in any other existing, State. For English Courts, and it may be said the English Legislature, have now for a length of time accepted not only these two fundamental ideas, but all the consequences that follow from them; and the best way to understand the nature of these fundamental ideas, and the way in which they actually produce judicial legislation, is to examine one or two examples of the steps by which English Courts have even in recent times created rules which, as they really have the force of law and are made by the Courts, may rightly be termed judge-made law.

Not many years have passed since *A* brought an action against *X* and *Y*, directors of a company, for damage caused to him by a fraudulent misrepresentation published by them in a prospectus of the company. The statement published was false. *X* and *Y*, however, thought the statement to be true, but their belief in its truth was due to their own gross negligence in omitting to examine whether it was true or not. The following question of principle then called for decision: Could gross negligence be treated as equivalent to fraud? The uncertainty of the law may be seen in the disagreement of eminent judges. A judge of the Chancery Division held that negligence was not the same thing as fraud—that carelessness, in other words, was not mendacity (*Peek* v. *Derry* (1887), 37 Ch. D. 541). The Court of Appeal reversed his decision, and held that gross negligence was under the circumstances equivalent to fraud (*ibid.* at p. 563). But the House of Lords reversed the judgment of the Court of Appeal, and held with the Court of first instance that carelessness is not the same thing as deceit (*Derry* v. *Peek* (1889), 14 App. Cas. 337). And this principle, which the House of Lords could not itself depart from, became in 1889 part of the law of England, and was loyally and fully accepted by the very judges of the Court of Appeal who had held a different view of the law. It is, further, at this very moment a rule of English law, except in so far as it has been modified, as regards directors of companies, by the Directors' Liability Act, 1890, 53 & 54 Vict. c. 64. This case is worth careful study. We here see every step in the formation of judge-made law. That *X* and *Y* had acted with blamable carelessness was clear; but a judge had nothing to do with this point: his duty was to determine whether on principle their negligence rendered them guilty of fraud. As a matter of fact, we must say that, where good judges differed, the question of principle was doubtful. The Court of first instance laid down one law, the Court of Appeal another, and the House of Lords, agreeing with the Court of first instance, at last established a rule to which every Court, including the House of Lords itself, was bound to adhere, *i.e.* which became the law of the land, and this law was finally modified by the only power which can change every law—namely, the Imperial Parliament.

Just about fifty years ago the Court of Queen's Bench decided what was then assuredly a doubtful point, that where *X* induced *N* to break *N*'s contract with *A*, the latter had a right to recover damages from *X* (*Lumley* v. *Gye* (1853), 2 E. & B. 216). The validity of this rule, and certainly its extent, remained open to doubt. Some twenty-eight years later it was affirmed and somewhat extended by *Bowen* v. *Hall* (1881), 6 Q.B.D. (C.A.) 333. It has of recent years been distinctly affirmed both by the Court of Appeal (*Temperton* v. *Russell* (1893), 1 Q.B. (C.A.), 715), and by the House of Lords (*Quinn* v. *Leathem* (1901), A.C. 495).

Fifty years ago, again, it was doubtful whether, if *X* had entered into a contract with *A*, and before the time for performing the contract had arrived, informed *A* that he would not perform it, *A* had a right then and there to sue *X* for breach of contract (*Hochster* v. *Delatour* (1853), 2 E. & B. 678). Eminent judges were here again in some doubt. The law was in truth uncertain. But later decisions (*Frost* v. *Knight* (1872), L.R. 7 Ex. 111 (Ex. Ch.); *Mersey Steel* & *Iron Co.* v. *Naylor* (1884), 9 App. Cas. 434) have affirmed the principle of *Hochster* v. *Delatour;* the Courts or the judges have then in reality made it a law.

It would be difficult to find a better instance of judge-made law than the rule laid down by the House of Lords itself, that the House is bound by its own decisions (*London Street Tramways Co.* v. *London County Council* (1898), A.C. 375; *R.* v. *Millis* (1844), 10 Cl. & F. 534; *Beamish* v. *Beamish* (1861), 9 H.L.C. 274). Some competent critics, indeed, have argued that this rule or law has only of recent years been firmly established. If this view be correct (which may be doubtful) it only makes the establishment of the rule with which we are dealing all the more striking as an example of legislative authority exerted by the final Court of Appeal. The rule, however, is in any case one towards which the decisions of the House of Lords and the dicta of eminent lawyers have pointed. It is in strict conformity with the respect for precedent which is the parent of judge-made law. It is in any case now part of the law of the land, and therefore forms an impressive instance of a law indirectly though surely enacted by the final Court of Appeal. These illustrations of such judicial law-making may suffice. It would be easy to multiply them; they sufficiently, however, prove the conclusion on which it is here necessary to insist— that the legislative action of the judges is the necessary consequence of ideas which underlie our whole judicial system.

B. Amount of Judge-made Law

It is hard to give to any person not versed in English law an adequate notion of the extent to which our law is the creation of the Courts (see pp. 257–259, *ante*). As already stated, by far the greater part of the law of contract—one might almost say the whole of the law of torts, all the rules or doctrines of equity, several outlying branches of the law—such, for example, as the principles embraced under the head of the conflict of laws—either originally were, or still are, to be deduced from judicial decisions or, what is in reality the same thing, from the doctrines of writers such as Coke, whose dicta are accepted by the Courts as law. Statutes themselves, though manifestly the work of Parliament, often receive more than half their meaning from judicial decisions. And this holds good not only of ancient, but sometimes also of modern Acts of Parliament.

It is at least a curious fact, that by an odd paradox our rules of procedure, which seem from their nature to belong naturally to the sphere of judicial legislation, derive their ultimate authority at the present day from the Judicature Acts. But here, as elsewhere, *exceptio probat regulam.* No doubt the authority of the Rules of Court is derived from the Judicature Acts, but Parliament has most wisely, under these Acts, given to the judges direct, though admittedly subordinate, legislative authority. The Rules of Court are framed by judges, though they require for their validity the tacit sanction of Parliament; and these Rules of Court are as truly laws as any part of the Judicature Acts under which they are made. They decide matters of great importance. If they deal only with procedure, it is absolutely impossible to handle procedure freely without immediately trenching upon substantive law. Where there is no remedy there is no right. To give a remedy is to confer a right. Thus the rules which determine the limits of the High Court's jurisdiction do in truth often determine how far any person has a remedy against, *e.g.* a breaker of a contract or a wrong-doer who is not in England—*i.e.* they in reality, though not in form, determine the effective rights of *A* against *X*, who is not in England, in respect of a contract broken or a wrong committed by *X*.

It is a common notion with us, countenanced by the general expressions of French writers of authority, that judicial legislation is unknown to, and indeed cannot exist in countries such as France, where the law is reduced to the form of a Code (see Berthélemy, *Droit Administratif,* p. 12). But this idea, if accepted too absolutely, is misleading. True it is that in countries where precedent is of less weight than in England, where there are several independent Courts of Appeal, where there exists no one final Court of Appeal (in the sense in which we use that term), and where the Executive has a good deal to do with the interpretation of the law, the sphere of judicial legislation is less extensive than in England; but it is certainly not the case that in modern France, at any rate, you will find no judge-made law. Precedent (*la jurisprudence*) tells with French judges, and wherever precedent has weight there one will always find case-law, which, in the modern world, is almost necessarily judge-made law. We have already seen (see pp. 335–336, *ante*) that the French combination law has been expounded and modified by the judges (see Pic, pp. 198–201) in much the same way as the combination law of England has been explained and modified by our Courts. Judicial decisions (*la jurisprudence*) have extended the property rights of a married woman under the Code (see *Le Code Civil*, 1804–1904; *Livre du Centenaire*, pp. 287–289). And generally, if we are to believe French authorities, reported judgments have in France told considerably upon the whole character of the Code (*ibid.* pp. 175–204). What is less obvious at first, but on investigation turns out even more certain, is that the whole of French *droit administratif*, which is gradually being transformed into a regular part of French law, is wholly or almost wholly based upon case law; it no more depends upon any law passed by the French Legislature than did equity in the time of Charles II. depend upon any Act of Parliament (see Dicey, *Law of the Constitution*, 7th ed., pp. 369, 370).

C. Characteristics of Judge-made Law

(1) Judge-made law is real law, though made under the form of, and often described, by judges no less than by jurists, as the mere interpretation of law.

Whoever fairly considers how large are the masses of English law for which no other authority than judicial decisions or reported cases can be found, will easily acquiesce in the statement that law made by the judges is as truly law as are laws made by Parliament. In what sense, if at all, the function of the judges can be described as merely interpretation of the law is considered in a later part of this Note.

(2) Judge-made law is subject to certain limitations.

It cannot openly declare a new principle of law: it must always take the form of a deduction from some legal principle whereof the validity is admitted, or of the application or interpretation of some statutory enactment.

It cannot override statute law.

The Courts may, by a process of interpretation, indirectly limit or possibly extend the operation of a statute, but they cannot set a statute aside. Nor have they in England ever adopted the doctrine which exists, one is told, in Scotland, that a statute may become obsolete by disuse.

It cannot from its very nature override any established principle of judge-made law.

A superior Court may, of course, overrule any principle of law that derives its authority merely from the decisions of an inferior Court. Thus the House of Lords may, and occasionally has, set aside or treated as not being in reality law a rule which, though of considerable antiquity and long received as law, has not been confirmed by the sanction of the House itself; and the Court of Appeal is not bound to follow principles in favour of which nothing can be cited but judgments of the King's Bench Division or of the older Courts of which the King's Bench Division is the successor. But no Court—not even the House of Lords—will directly invalidate a rule sanctioned by that House.

Even this statement must be taken subject to some slight limitation. The House will occasionally limit the operation of a well-established legal rule either by subtle distinctions or by "refusing to carry a rule further," as the expression goes. By this is really meant that the House, while recognising the validity of some well-recognised legal principle, and applying it to cases which indubitably fall within it, will not apply it to other cases which can be brought within it only by some process of logical argument. Nor is there anything in this course inconsistent with sound logic and good sense. It is a mere recognition of the undoubted fact that a sound principle may, even as expressed in authoritative judgments, cover cases to which it was never meant to apply, and which were not before the mind of the Court which enunciated the principle. When this is so, a Court of final appeal rightly gives effect to the real meaning rather than to the mere words of a rule of law. This, at any rate, is the way in which our Courts sometimes deal with rules resting upon judicial decisions. The freedom with which they interpret such rules is a virtue. What is to be regretted is that our Courts have felt themselves less at liberty, in modern times at least, with regard to the interpretation of statutes, and are apt to pay more attention to the words than to the spirit of an Act of Parliament.

(3) The incapacity of the Courts to change a rule on which they themselves have conferred the character of law leads to the important result that the legislative powers of the Courts, unlike in this to the authority of Parliament, become gradually in particular spheres exhausted.

Their capacity, for example, to carry out further reforms in regard to the property rights of women had early in the nineteenth century all but reached its final limit (see pp. 267–273, *ante*). Before 1870 it was exhausted. The field for innovation or reform was filled or blocked by rules which, whether created by statute or by judicial legislation, neither the Court of Chancery nor any other Court had the power to modify or change; and what happened in this particular instance must always happen whenever a given department of law has been made the subject of much legislation, whether parliamentary or judicial; the way towards change or reform has got blocked by laws which, under the English Constitution, can be changed or amended only by the sovereign authority of Parliament. From this fact it might be inferred that the sphere of judicial legislation must gradually become narrower and narrower, and judicial legislation itself come at last completely to an end. This conclusion contains this amount of truth, that no modern judges can mould the law anything like as freely as did their predecessors some centuries ago. No Lord Chief-Justice of to-day could occupy anything like the position of Coke, or carry out reforms such as were achieved or attempted by Lord Mansfield. There are whole departments of law which no longer afford a field for judicial legislation. But for all this the judicial authority of the Bench, though subject to restriction, is not likely to be reduced to nothing. The complexity of modern life, in the first place, produces new combinations of circumstances, which, in so far as they give rise to legal disputes, bring before our tribunals what are in reality new cases— that is, cases which must be determined either by applying to their solution some new principle, or, what more often happens, by the extension of some old principle which is found to be really applicable. The interpretation, in the second place, of statutes will always exercise the ingenuity of our judges. In either case there is room for the exercise of what is in truth judicial legislation.

(4) Judge-made law is apt to be hypothetical law.

A clear rule, supported by a judgment of the House of Lords, is in reality as much a law as any Act of Parliament, and this holds *a fortiori* true of a rule supported by many judgments both of the House of Lords and of other Courts. But there may well be rules established by the judgments, say, of the King's Bench, of the old Court of Exchequer Chamber, or of the present Court of Appeal, which have been generally acquiesced in, but have never been brought before the House of Lords. This was till quite recently—to recur to an illustration already used—the state of things with regard to the rule that *A* had a right of action against *X*, who induced *N* to break his contract with *A*. Till a year or two ago it depended for its authority wholly upon a judgment of the Queen's Bench, reinforced by a later decision of the Queen's Bench Division. Was it good law or not? Not the most learned of lawyers could give an absolutely conclusive reply; no one could in reality say more than that the rule in question was hypothetical law. And a good deal of such hypothetical law is, it should be observed, always in existence, and may continue to exist for a length of time. For many years it was a matter of real uncertainty whether the Divorce Court had jurisdiction to divorce persons permanently resident though not domiciled in England. A decision of the Court of Appeal showed that such jurisdiction might exist (*Niboyet* v. *Niboyet* (1878), 4 P.D. (C.A.) 1). But many of the best lawyers entertained grave doubts whether the decision of the Court of Appeal was good law. It was in truth hypothetical law. The doubts of critics have at last been justified. The decision of the Court of Appeal in *Niboyet* v. *Niboyet* has been virtually overruled, and we now know with something like certainty that domicil must be taken to be in England the basis of divorce jurisdiction. This tendency of judicial legislation to foster the existence of hypothetical law is its worst defect. The public, it may be suggested, would gain a good deal if a power were conferred upon the House of Lords of calling up for the House's decision (say on the motion of the Attorney-General, and, of course, at the public expense) cases determined by the Court of Appeal, and involving the determination of an important principle of law which had never come before the House of Lords.

D. Objections to or Criticisms on the theory of Judge-made Law

The view of judge-made law here propounded is exposed to three different objections or criticisms.

First objection. There is no such thing, it is sometimes objected as judge-made law; Courts or judges are never the creators of law; they always act, as long at any rate as they discharge their proper duty, as interpreters of the law and not as legislators; the law which they interpret may be statute law, or it may be a rule of law created by custom, but in any case it exists and is known to the people of a given country before the judges undertake to interpret it. The validity, it is added, of this objection is proved by the fact that Courts invariably profess to explain a law which already exists and needs only explanation.

Now, in replying to this objection, which may be put in various forms, it is well to make one or two admissions. If the critic means only that the very elastic term "interpretation" may be so extended as to cover everything which is done by an English judge when performing his judicial duty, it may be admitted that this is so. A mere dispute about the right use of a word which easily admits of almost indefinite extension is an idle piece of logomachy which it is wisdom to avoid. If, further, it be meant that in many cases a judge or a Court does act merely as an explainer of the law, this again may easily be conceded. Nor can it be disputed that the explanation of a rule may, especially where the rule is followed as a precedent, so easily glide into the extension or the laying down of the rule, or in effect into legislation, that the line which divides the one from the other can often not be distinctly drawn. And to these admissions may be added the further concession, that in modern times, when an immense number of fixed rules established either by Parliament or by the Courts are in existence, it rarely happens that a judge, consciously at any rate, does more than expound what one may well call established legal principles. But all these concessions do not get rid of the fact that a great deal of law has been, and a good deal still is from time to time, the result of, and in effect created by, the action of the Courts. The very rules which modern judges only interpret or explain can in many cases be drawn only from the judgments of their predecessors. A judge who applies to a particular case the principle that a promise made without any consideration, or in popular language a promise for which the promisor gets no advantage, is void, certainly may do no more than apply or interpret a well-known legal principle. But the principle itself does not originate in any statute. The long and intricate process by which it was thought out and established affords a singular instance of judicial legislation. When a judge applies the words of a statute to a particular case he may well do no more than follow a rule which he in no way creates, but, as the history of all our older statutes and of many of our modern statutes shows, judges who interpret statutes and whose interpretation become precedents in reality legislate. To say that all inter-pretation is legislation is, no doubt, to maintain a paradox. But this paradox comes nearer the truth than the contention that judicial law-making is always in reality interpretation. Nor does our objector gain anything by insisting that judge-made law often is what it assuredly is not always, the mere recognition or interpretation of custom. The same thing may be said of many statutes. The motives which induce either parliaments or judges to treat certain customs as laws do not invalidate the fact that when parliaments or judges give effect to a custom they legislate. Here again it is well to avoid arguments turning mainly upon the meaning of words. Whether and in what sense custom is to be considered the source of law, or whether it be or be not true that judge-made law or judicial legislation are expressions open to criticism, are questions which a reasonable man may well treat with some in-difference. If an objector admits, what with regard to English law he can hardly dispute, that great portions of it are recorded only in and derive their authority from the judgments of the Courts, the objection that there is no such thing as judge-made law has received a substantial answer.

Second objection. Judges, it has sometimes been maintained, have undoubtedly in fact made law, but have accomplished their end by the fraudulent pretence that they were interpreting a law which, without any moral claim to do so, they were in fact creating.

This contention, that laws are the result of judicial frauds is nearly akin to the delusion that religions are the growth of priestly imposture. Both of these notions are ideas belonging to an obsolete mode of thought. In neither case do they deserve careful confutation. The notion that judges pretended to expound the laws which they really made is based upon ignorance of the fact that fiction is not fraud, and that legal fictions are the natural product of certain social and intellectual condi-tions. Nor, be it added, has the progress of civilisation as yet enabled us to get rid entirely of something very like legal fictions, or at any rate of the tendency in some departments of law to confuse facts with fictions. This habit is still very traceable in the field of constitutional law. It is convenient—perhaps necessary—to consider the will of the majority as the will of the whole nation. But it is perfectly clear that this identification, whatever its convenience or its necessity, is a political fiction. What, again, are we to say about the powers ascribed by English constitutionalists to the King? In some instances, no doubt, the fiction is a mere figure of speech. Few, one trusts, are the men who seriously believe that the millions raised by taxes are granted to or spent by the King. Most persons probably know that the King himself takes no share in the administration of justice. But what part does he or can he take in the appointment of ministers, or in moulding the policy of the country? The wisest constitutionalist is the man who on such matters keeps a judicious silence. One may conjecture that those who minimise and those who "maximise" (if we may use a term invented, like minimise, by Bentham) the action of the Crown are in equal danger of error. Fiction and fact are here probably blended. The artificial ascription of almost unlimited power to the King is a means of concealing the fact that powers which are not unlimited are indefinite.

Third objection. The Courts, it is sometimes said and still more often thought, though they certainly do legislate, never ought to legislate at all.

This is an idea constantly put forward by persons who, rightly or wrongly, object to some principle established by judicial decisions. Such critics urge not only that the rule which they condemn is a bad one, on which point they may perfectly well be in the right, but also that the rule, whether wise or unwise, whether right or wrong, ought never to have been laid down at all by the Courts, and this on the ground that it is the business of the Courts to decide cases and not to make laws.

The answer to this line of criticism is that the person who pursues it has in no case a right to blame the judges. His argument may mean that the whole English judicial system, with its respect for precedent, is a bad one. So be it. But, even if this be so, English judges cannot be blamed for acting in accordance with a system which they are appointed to administer. Our objector's argument, on the other hand, may mean that, the English system being what it is, judges can, if they choose to do so, always avoid judicial legislation. But, if this be the critic's meaning, he distinctly ascribes to judges a liberty of choice which they do not in fact possess. To simplify the matter, let us confine our attention to the House of Lords. A case comes before the House which can only be decided by either affirming or denying the application or validity of some principle. But either affirmation or denial will equally establish a precedent, or in other words, a legally binding rule or law. How under this state of things can the House by any possibility avoid judicial legislation? Return to the case already noted of *Derry* v. *Peek*. The question to be determined was, whether gross negligence when unaccompanied by deceit could be treated as equivalent to fraud. There was much to be said in favour of an affirmative answer, and the Court of Appeal said it with great force. There was much also to be said in favour of a negative answer, and this, too, was said by Lord Herschell and other eminent lawyers with the greatest vigour. The House of Lords did, as a matter of fact, give a negative reply, and laid down the law that carelessness was a different thing from lying. It is not necessary to decide or to intimate which of two possible rules was the more logical. All that need here be contended is that the House was compelled to lay down one rule or the other, and that whichever rule was laid down would in effect become law. In this case, as in a thousand others, the House, though acting as a Court, was compelled to legislate; and what is true of the House of Lords applies in a measure to every Court throughout the land. A critic who objects to the rule, or in reality the law established by a judgment of the House of Lords may maintain that the House committed an error. He may maintain that the rule which the Lords established was not a logical deduction from the principles they intended to follow, or that the rule, though logical, was inexpedient, or, if he pleases, that the rule was both illogical and inexpedient. But if he has mastered the nature of judge-made law he will hardly commit himself to the contention that the House of Lords was to blame simply because its judgment established a fixed rule of law. This was a result over which the House had no control, and for which, therefore, it deserved neither praise nor blame.

NOTE V. *Proposed Collectivist Legislation of 1905**

At the moment when the last pages of this book are passing through the press four measures have already been received with favour by the House of Commons. They are the Trades Dispute Bill, the Aliens Bill, the Unemployed Workmen Bill, and the Relief (School Children) Order.

These proposals suggest more than one observation strictly germane to the subject of these lectures.

First. They mark the distance which divides the democratic collectivism of today from the Benthamite liberalism of 1830–1870. The Trades Dispute Bill and the Aliens Bill are inroads upon individual liberty as understood by the Liberals say of fifty years ago; the Unemployed Workmen Bill and the Relief (School Children) Order strike a blow at the foundations of the great Benthamite reform embodied in the new poor law of 1834.

* [Editor's note: Note V was included in the 1905 edition but was deleted in the 1914 edition.]

Second. A legislative revolution is clearly due to a change of public opinion. If any opponent imputes it—which is certainly not my intention—to the selfishness or recklessness of politicians, and asserts, unfairly enough, that English statesmen have no other desire than to please the electors, he may rightly be asked why it is that the electors themselves approve in 1905 of laws which they would not have approved of in 1875 or 1885? He can give but one answer—"a change of public opinion." But it must in fairness be remembered that political leaders are themselves affected by alterations in the moral or social atmosphere which tell upon their followers, and that there is no reason to suppose that English politicians are either more or less rash or selfish in 1905 than in 1875.

Third. A revolution of opinion which is going on before our eyes is assuredly not in the main caused by the strength of argument. The arguments for and against say the Unemployed Workmen Bill are the same which must have been employed in favour of or in opposition to a similar measure in 1875. But to-day the weight of argument is thought by thousands of Englishmen to tell conclusively for the acceptance of the measure, whilst thirty, or twenty, or even ten years ago the weight of argument would have been thought to tell conclusively for its rejection. Opinion has been changed, not by argument, but by circumstances.

Fourth. The rapidity with which collectivist legislation now makes way excites astonishment. It need surprise no one who thinks it worth while to study, and accepts the conclusions arrived at in these lectures. The socialistic laws of to-day are not to be ascribed to any sudden change. They are forced on by a current of opinion which has been gathering force for at least forty years.

Introduction to the Second Edition

Aim of Introduction

THIRTEEN YEARS HAVE PASSED since the nineteenth century came to an end. In England they have been marked by important legislation of a novel character. The aim of this Introduction is to trace the connection, during these opening years of the twentieth century, between the development of English law and the course of English opinion. The task is one of special difficulty. An author who tried to explain the relation between law and opinion during the nineteenth century undertook to a certain extent the work of an historian, and yet was freed from many of the impediments which often beset historical inquiry. His duty was to draw correct inferences from admitted facts, or at any rate from facts easily to be discovered. They could be ascertained by a careful study of the Statute Book and of legal decisions, and also of the letters and memoirs written by statesmen, teachers, or writers who had affected the legal doctrines of their time. Then, too, such an author, writing of a time not long past, was almost delivered from the difficulty with which an historian of eras removed by the lapse of many years from his own time often struggles in vain, the difficulty, namely, of understanding the social and intellectual atmosphere of bygone ages. The writer, on the other hand, who deals with the development of law and opinion in England during the earlier years of the twentieth century feels, all but instinctively, that he has entered upon a new kind of work which is encompassed with a new sort of perplexity; he is no longer an historian, he is in reality a critic. He is compelled to measure by conjecture the sequence and the tendency of events passing before his eyes, and of events in which he is to a certain extent an actor. Also he cannot as to contemporary events possess knowledge of their ultimate results; yet this knowledge is the instrument on which an historian of good sense mainly relies in forming his judgments of the past. Time tests all;[1] but this criterion cannot be applied by the contemporary critic of his

---

1. Tocqueville thus sums up the result of a vehement discussion immediately after the

own country and its laws. A little research will soon prove to him that few indeed have been the men who have been able to seize with clearness the causes or the tendencies of the events passing around them.[2] Rare indeed are the anticipations before 1789 of the revolution impending over France. Among modern writers known to Englishmen, three alone occur to me who can justly claim to have foreseen the course of contemporary history. They are Burke, Tocqueville, and Bagehot. Burke assuredly studied the contest between England and her American Colonies with an insight, and therefore with a foresight, unknown to his generation. He saw through the follies and foresaw the crimes of French Revolutionists with all but prophetic power. But his argument throughout the conflict with the Colonies is weakened by his blindness to the fact, visible to men of far inferior genius to his own, that American independence would not deprive England of her trade with America; and, while he saw all that was contemptible and detestable in the revolutionary movement, his eyes were closed to most of its causes and to all that may now be said in favour of its effects. Tocqueville uttered in January 1848 words which are strictly prophetic of the Revolution of February 1848.[3] He, at least forty years ago, predicted that socialism, derided in his own day, might in later years assume a form in which it would obtain a wide and favourable hearing.[4] But his unrivalled power of analysis did not reveal to Tocqueville the intellectual capacity of Louis Napoleon, at any rate as a conspirator, or the hold which the Napoleonic tradition had on the memory and the sympathy of the French peasantry and of the French army. Bagehot in early manhood grasped by his power of thought, what, by the way, Palmerston had also perceived through his experience in affairs, the readiness with which an ordinary Frenchman would condone or applaud the crime of December 1851. Bagehot again analysed the principles and the working of the English Constitution during the mid-Victorian era with an insight not attained by any Englishman or by any foreigner during the nineteenth

---

Revolution of February 24, 1848, between himself and an intimate friend: "Après avoir beaucoup crié, nous finîmes par en appeler tous les deux à l'avenir, juge éclairé et intègre, mais qui arrive, hélas! toujours trop tard." [In the end, after much shouting, we both appealed to the future, that sincere and enlightened judge who, alas, arrives always too late.]—*Souvenirs d'Alexis de Tocqueville,* p. 98. [Editor's note: The translation was added in the Liberty Fund edition.]

2. Tacitus, it has been pointed out, though endowed with extraordinary sagacity, exhibits little or no insight into the progress of the gigantic revolution which culminated in the establishment of Christianity throughout the Roman Empire.

3. See Tocqueville, *Souvenirs,* pp. 15, 16, and *Law and Opinion,* p. 180, *ante.*

4. Tocqueville, *Souvenirs,* p. 111.

century. But Bagehot, even in 1872, did not, as far as I can perceive, fully anticipate that rapid growth or misgrowth of the party system which has now been admirably described and explained by A. L. Lowell in his monumental *Government of England.* Who can hope to attain anything like success in contemporary criticism of English legislation and opinion when he knows that such criticism has, in the hands of Burke, Tocqueville, and Bagehot, produced only partial success, and success in some cases almost overbalanced by failure? This question supplies its own answer. My aim in forcing this inquiry upon the attention of my readers is to make them perceive that an Introduction, which may appear to be simply a lecture added to my speculations on Law and Opinion during the nineteenth century, is written under conditions which make it rather an analytical than an historical document, and introduce into every statement which it contains a large element of conjecture. In the treatment of my subject I have pursued the method to which any readers of my *Law and Opinion* have become accustomed. I treat of (A) The state of legislative opinion at the end of the nineteenth century; (B) The course of legislation from the beginning of the twentieth century; (C) The main current of legislative opinion from the beginning of the twentieth century; (D) The counter-currents and cross-currents of legislative opinion during the same period.

(A) Legislative Opinion at the end of the Nineteenth Century

Let the reader who wishes to realise the difference between legislative opinion during the period of Benthamite liberalism and legislative opinion at the end of the nineteenth century first read and consider the full effect of a celebrated passage taken from Mill's Essay *On Liberty,* and next contrast it with the description of legislative opinion in 1900 to be gathered from Lectures VII. and VIII. of the present treatise.[5]

"The object of this Essay," writes Mill in 1859,

is to assert one very simple principle, as entitled to govern absolutely the dealings of society with the individual in the way of compulsion and control, whether the means used be physical force in the form of legal penalties, or the moral coercion of public opinion. That principle is, that the sole end for which mankind are warranted, individually or collectively, in interfering with the liberty of action of any of their number, is self-protection. That the only purpose for which power can be rightfully exercised over any member of a civilized community, against his will, is to prevent harm to others. His own

5. See pp. 150–214, *ante.*

good, either physical or moral, is not a sufficient warranty. He cannot rightfully be compelled to do or forbear because it will be better for him to do so,
because it will make him happier, because, in the opinions of others, to do
so would be wise, or even right.

These are good reasons for remonstrating with him, or reasoning with him,
or persuading him, or entreating him, but not for compelling him, or visiting
him with any evil in case he do otherwise. To justify that, the conduct from
which it is desired to deter him must be calculated to produce evil to some
one else. The only part of the conduct of any one, for which he is amenable
to society, is that which concerns others. In the part which merely concerns
himself, his independence is, of right, absolute. Over himself, over his own
body and mind, the individual is sovereign.[6]

The importance of this "simple principle," whatever its intrinsic worth, arises
from the fact that at the time when it was enunciated by Mill it obtained, at any
rate as regards legislation, general acceptance, not only by youthful enthusiasts,
but by the vast majority of English Liberals, and by many Liberal Conservatives.
It gave logical expression to convictions which, though never followed out with
perfect consistency, were shared by the wisest among the writers and the statesmen
who, in the mid-Victorian era, guided the legislative action of Parliament. In regard
to interference by law with the liberty of individual citizens, it is probable that a
Benthamite Radical, such as John Mill conceived himself to be, differed little from
a Whig, such as Macaulay, who certainly did not consciously subscribe to the
Benthamite creed,[7] and it is probable that the late Lord Salisbury (then Lord Robert
Cecil) would not on this matter have disagreed essentially with either the typical
Benthamite or the typical Whig.

Mill himself tacitly, though grudgingly, admitted that there was little in the law
of England which in 1859 encroached upon individual liberty. The object of his
attack was the alleged tyranny, not of English law, but of English habits and opinion. Macaulay laid down no rigid rule limiting the sphere of State intervention,
but he clearly held that, as a matter of common sense, government had better in
general undertake little else than strictly political duties. English statesmanship was
at the middle of the Victorian era, in short, grounded on the *laissez faire* of common sense. From this principle were drawn several obvious inferences which to

---

6. Mill, *On Liberty,* pp. 21 and 22.

7. Compare Mill, *On Liberty,* with Macaulay's review of *Gladstone on Church and State.*
Mill indeed entertained in his later life a sympathy with socialistic ideals foreign to Macaulay's whole mode of thought. Leslie Stephen, *English Utilitarians,* iii. pp. 224–237.

enlightened English politicians seemed practically all but axiomatic. The State, it was thought, ought not as a matter of prudence to undertake any duties which were, or which could be, performed by individuals free from State control. Free trade, again, was held to be the only policy suitable for England, and probably the only policy which would in the long run benefit the inhabitants of a modern civilised State. It was further universally admitted that for the Government, or for Parliament, to fix the rate of wages was as futile a task as for the State to undertake to fix the price of bread or of clothes. In harmony with these views one principle was not only accepted but rigidly carried out by every Chancellor of the Exchequer according to his ability; it was that taxation should be imposed solely for the purpose of raising revenue, and should be imposed with absolute equality, or as near equality as was possible, upon rich and poor alike. Hence the ideal Chancellor of the Exchequer was the man who, after providing for the absolutely necessary expenditure of the State, so framed his Budget as to leave the largest amount possible of the national wealth to "fructify," as the expression then went, "in the pockets of the people." Gladstone exactly satisfied this ideal. In 1859, hardly any man who occupied a prominent position in public life (except here and there a few belated Protectionists, among whom Disraeli must not be numbered) dissented greatly from Mill's simple principle, at any rate as regards legislation. In other words, Benthamite liberalism, as interpreted by the rough common sense of intelligent politicians, was, when Mill published his treatise *On Liberty,* the predominant opinion of the time.[8]

Contrast now with the dominant legislative opinion of 1859 the dominant legislative opinion of 1900, as described in Lectures VII. and VIII.[9] The general effect of these lectures may be thus summed up: The current of opinion had for between thirty and forty years been gradually running with more and more force in the

8. It is a curious question how far Bentham's own beliefs were directly or logically opposed to the doctrines of sane collectivism. He placed absolute faith in his celebrated "Principle of Utility." He held that, at any rate in his time, this principle dictated the adoption of a policy, both at home and abroad, of *laissez faire.* But it is not clear that Bentham might not in different circumstances have recommended or acquiesced in legislation which an ardent preacher of *laissez faire* would condemn. (See Lect. IX. p. 215, *ante.*) It may be suggested that John Mill's leaning towards Socialistic ideals, traceable in some expressions used by him in his later life, was justified to himself by the perception that such ideals were not necessarily inconsistent with the Benthamite creed, which was his inherited, and to his mind unforsaken faith. See pp. 302–307, *ante.*

9. See pp. 150–214, *ante.*

direction of collectivism,[10] with the natural consequence that by 1900 the doctrine of *laissez faire*, in spite of the large element of truth which it contains, had more or less lost its hold upon the English people. The laws affecting elementary education, the Workmen's Compensation Act of 1897, the Agricultural Holdings Acts, the Combination Act of 1875, the whole line of Factory Acts, the Conciliation Act, 1896, and other enactments dwelt upon in the lectures to which I have referred, though some of them might be defended on Benthamite principles, each and all if looked at as a whole prove that the jealousy of interference by the State which had long prevailed in England had, to state the matter very moderately, lost much of its influence, and that with this willingness to extend the authority of the State the belief in the unlimited benefit to be obtained from freedom of contract had lost a good deal of its power. It also was in 1900 apparent to any impartial observer that the feelings or the opinions which had given strength to collectivism would continue to tell as strongly upon the legislation of the twentieth century as they had already told upon the later legislation of the nineteenth century.[11] To any one further who had studied the weight given to precedent by English Parliaments, no less than by English Courts, it must have been, or perhaps rather ought to have been, certain in 1900 that legislation already tending towards collectivism would in the earlier years of the twentieth century produce laws directly dictated by the doctrines of collectivists, and this conclusion would naturally have been confirmed by the fact that in the sphere of finance there had occurred a revival of belief in protective tariffs, then known by the name of a demand for "fair trade." With the perennial controversy between free-traders and protectionists a student of law and opinion has no necessary concern; he may however note that socialism and protection have one feature in common: they both rest on the belief that the power of the State may be beneficially extended even though it conflicts with the contractual freedom of individual citizens. The protectionist and the socialist each renounces the trust in *laissez faire*. From whatever point of view our subject be looked at, we reach the conclusion that by 1900 the doctrine of *laissez faire* had already lost its popular authority.

(B) Course of Legislation from Beginning of Twentieth Century

My immediate object is to show that certain well-known Acts of Parliament belong in character to, and are the signs of the power exercised by, the collectivist movement during the first thirteen years of the twentieth century. I venture indeed here

---

10. Compare especially Lect. IV. pp. 46–50, and Lect. IX. p. 215, *ante*.
11. See pp. 183–198, *ante*.

to remind my readers that throughout this Introduction, as throughout the whole of this treatise, I am not primarily concerned with stating or commenting upon the often complicated provisions of definite statutes, *e.g.* the Old Age Pensions Act, 1908, or the National Insurance Act, 1911; my aim is always to trace, and as far as I can demonstrate, the close connection between English legislation and the course of legislative opinion in England.

The laws which most directly illustrate the progress of collectivism are the following Acts, taken in several cases together with the amendments thereof: The Old Age Pensions Act, 1908. The National Insurance Act, 1911. The Trade Disputes Act, 1906. The Trade Union Act, 1913. The Acts fixing a Minimum Rate of Wages. The Education (Provision of Meals) Act, 1906. The Mental Deficiency Act, 1913. The Coal Mines Regulation Act, 1908. The Finance (1909–10) Act, 1910.

The Old Age Pensions Act, 1908. By the Old Age Pensions Act, 1908, any man or woman who has attained the age of 70 years, and who has been a British subject for 20 years up to the date of the receipt of the pension, and who has resided in the United Kingdom for at least 12 years in the aggregate out of such 20 years, and whose yearly means do not exceed £31 : 10s., is, subject to certain disqualifications, entitled to receive at the cost of the State a weekly pension of an amount which varies according to his or her means of from one shilling to five shillings a week.[12]

This right to a pension is indeed subject to certain disqualifications,[13] the principal of which are that a person is in general not entitled to a pension when he is actually in receipt of poor relief, or while he is actually *undergoing* imprisonment for some serious crime,[14] or for ten years after the date on which he has been released from imprisonment for such crime, and that a person is not entitled to a pension if before he becomes so entitled "he has habitually failed to work according

---

12. The scale is as follows:

Where the yearly means of the pensioner as calculated under this Act—	Rate of Pension per week.	
	s.	d.
Do not exceed £21	5	0
Exceed £21, but do not exceed £23 : 12 : 6	4	0
Exceed £23 : 12 : 6, but do not exceed £26 : 5 : 0	3	0
Exceed £26 : 5 : 0, but do not exceed £28 : 17 : 6	2	0
Exceed £28 : 17 : 6, but do not exceed £31 : 10 : 0	1	0
Exceed £31 : 10 : 0	No pension.	

See sects. 1, 2, and Schedule.

13. For the details as to disqualification see Old Age Pensions Act, 1908, sect. 3, and Old Age Pensions Act, 1911, sect. 4.

14. Sect. 3, sub-sect. 1 (*c*), and sub-sect. 2.

to his ability, opportunity, and need, for the maintenance or benefit of himself and those legally dependent upon him."[15] This disqualification, if strictly pressed, might beneficially cut down the number of qualified pensioners, but one may doubt whether, under the present condition of popular feeling, this disqualification will be often enforced.

From the provisions and the tendency of the Old Age Pensions Acts several conclusions worth attention may be drawn: A person, in the first place, may have a full title to a pension though he is an habitual pauper in frequent receipt of poor relief, but prefers to vary the monotony of the poorhouse by occasionally, say in the summer, coming out of the house and relying for support upon his pension and his casual earnings. Then, again, the Old Age Pensions Acts inculcate, by the force both of precept and of example, the belief that the pensioner is in a very different position from a pauper; for sect. 1, sub-sect. 4, enacts that "the receipt of an old age pension under this Act shall not deprive the pensioner of any franchise, right, or privilege, or subject him to any disability." An old age pensioner, therefore, may even now in conceivable circumstances be entitled to vote for a Member of Parliament and join with friends who are counting on old age pensions after the age of 70, in voting that the title to a pension shall commence with the age of 60. Nor does the evil end with such an exceptional case. It is reasonable to anticipate the establishment in England, as now in our self-governing colonies, in the United States of America, in France, and in the German Empire of Manhood or Universal Suffrage. Now the Old Age Pensions Act is the bestowal by the State of pecuniary aid upon one particular class of the community, namely, the poorer class of wage-earners. It is in essence nothing but a new form of outdoor relief for the poor. Surely a sensible and a benevolent man may well ask himself whether England as a whole will gain by enacting that the receipt of poor relief, in the shape of a pension, shall be consistent with the pensioner's retaining the right to join in the election of a Member of Parliament?

The amendments, further, of the Old Age Pensions Act, 1908, tend towards relaxing the terms under which a person becomes entitled to an old age pension. Residence in the United Kingdom for 20 years is now reduced to residence for an aggregate of 12 years during such 20 years; and in some cases residence outside the United Kingdom is sufficient. Hence the following important result: The title to an old age pension hardly depends at all upon the character of the pensioner. The Old Age Pensions Acts, as they now stand, are based upon the belief that in the United Kingdom a really poor man, if he is permanently resident here, is morally entitled to outdoor relief at the rate of five shillings a week on attaining the age of

15. Sect. 3, sub-sect. 1 (*b*).

70. This may or may not be sound moral doctrine, but it is absolutely opposed to the beliefs of the Benthamite Liberals, who, by the enactment in 1834 of the New Poor Law, saved the country districts of England from ruin.

The National Insurance Act, 1911.[16] The attention of my readers ought to be directed exclusively to the aim of the Act and to the administrative methods of the Act.[17] They each illustrate the influence of collectivism or socialism on English legislation.

Aim of Act. The Act[18] aims at the attainment of two objects: The first is that, speaking broadly, any person, whether a man or a woman, whether a British subject or an alien,[19] who is employed in the United Kingdom under any contract of service, shall, from the age of 16 to 70, be insured against ill-health,[20] or, in other words, be insured the means for curing illness, *e.g.* by medical attendance. The second object is that any such person who is employed in certain employments specified in the Act[21] shall be insured against unemployment, or, in other words, be secured support during periods of unemployment.[22]

The whole drift of the statute, and especially the conditions, exceptions, and limitations contained therein, show[23] that the Act founds a system of insurance solely for the advantage of persons who, in popular language, would be described as servants or workmen. The Act is, therefore, on the face of it a piece of legislation which is intended to benefit wage-earners, and especially the poorer classes of wage-earners, who have no income sufficient for their support independent of their power to earn it by personal labour.

Thus under the National Insurance Act the State incurs new and, it may be,

---

16. Students who need information on the details of the Act should consult the *Law relating to National Insurance,* by G. H. Watts.

17. The mode in which the cost of health insurance and unemployment insurance is in part undertaken by the State, and in part imposed upon employers and upon the workmen or servants who are insured, has a socialistic character. But this feature in the Insurance Act has been amply noticed, and it is hardly worth while here to insist upon it.

18. As amended by the National Insurance Act, 1913, and applied by numerous regulations.

19. An alien does not in all cases get the same advantage from insurance as a British subject. See Act, sect. 45, and Watts, *National Insurance,* pp. 45, 46.

20. See Act, Part I. sects. 1–83.

21. *Ibid.* sect. 84, and Sixth Schedule.

22. For unemployment insurance see Part II. sects. 84–107.

23. *E.g.* by the fact that the Act does not in general, at any rate as to health insurance, benefit any one who has an income of £160 a year and upwards, though it does apply to any person who by way of manual labour earns an income however large, *e.g.* £200 a year. See First Schedule, Part II. (*g*), and Watts, *National Insurance,* p. 280.

very burdensome, duties, and confers upon wage-earners new and very extensive rights. The State in effect becomes responsible for making sure that every wage-earner within the United Kingdom shall, with certain exceptions, be insured against sickness, and, in some special cases, against unemployment. Now before 1908 the question whether a man, rich or poor, should insure his health, was a matter left entirely to the free discretion or indiscretion of each individual. His conduct no more concerned the State than the question whether he should wear a black coat or a brown coat.

But the National Insurance Act will, in the long run, bring upon the State, that is, upon the tax-payers, a far heavier responsibility than is anticipated by English electors. Part I. of the Act, which creates a system of national health insurance, has excited much attention and attack. Part II. of the Act, which introduces for a few trades a system of unemployment insurance, has been little noticed by the public, and has met with little censure; yet national unemployment insurance may well turn out to be a far more hazardous and a far more important experiment than is national health insurance. The risks of ill-health are calculable, the risks of un-employment are hard to calculate. No man prefers illness to health, but many men may prefer unemployment money to wages for hard work. But the importance of unemployment insurance does not end here. It is in fact the admission by the State of its duty to insure a man against the evil ensuing from his having no work. This duty cannot be confined permanently to workmen employed in some seven kinds of work. The authors of the Insurance Act know that this is so; they have provided the means by which the Government of the day can, at any moment, without the need for any Act of Parliament, increase the number of the insured trades. The National Insurance Act admits the so-called right to work. There are men still living whose political memory carries them back to 1848. They will recollect that the *droit au travail* was then one of the war-cries of French socialists, and was in England deemed to be one of the least reasonable of their claims. Nor is it easy to forget the saying attributed to Archbishop Whately, "When a man begs for work he asks not for work but for wages." However this may be, the statesmen who have introduced unemployment insurance supported by the State have, whether they knew it or not, acknowledged in principle the *droit au travail* for the sake of which socialists died behind the barricades of June 1848. The National Insurance Act is in accordance with the doctrines of socialism, it is hardly reconcilable with the liberalism, or even the radicalism of 1865.

Administrative Methods of Act. The methods by which the objects of the Act are to be obtained is marked by characteristics which harmonise with the principle or the sentiment of collectivism.

The National Insurance Act greatly increases both the legislative and the judicial authority of the Government or of officials closely connected with the Government of the day.

Legislative Authority. Under Part I. of the Act the administration of national health insurance is ultimately placed in the hands of, or controlled by, a new body of insurance commissioners who are appointed by the Treasury. These governmental officials have the power to make regulations for the carrying out of the Act which, if not annulled by the King in Council, become part of the Act itself. The width of this authority can only be realised by considering the language of the National Insurance Act, sect. 65, which runs as follows:

> The Insurance Commissioners may make regulations for any of the purposes for which regulations may be made under this Part [I.] of this Act or the schedules therein referred to, and for prescribing anything which under this Part of this Act or any such schedules is to be prescribed, and generally for carrying this Part of this Act into effect, and any regulations so made shall be laid before both Houses of Parliament as soon as may be after they are made, and shall have effect as if enacted in this Act.

This power to make regulations is probably the widest power of subordinate legislation ever conferred by Parliament upon any body of officials, and these officials, namely, the Insurance Commissioners, are appointed by the Treasury, *i.e.* by the Government, and are part of our whole governmental system. The regulations made by them come into force immediately after they are made. Any regulation indeed must be laid before each House of Parliament for twenty-one days, and may be annulled by the King in Council on a petition that it shall be annulled being presented within that twenty-one days by either House.[24] But any one will note that even such annulling is without prejudice to the validity of anything previously done under the annulled regulation. Practically, and with regard to any matter within the terms of Part I., a regulation made by the Commissioners is in reality part of the Act, and noncompliance therewith is made an offence as if it were part of the Act.[25]

Part II. of the Act contains the law as to unemployment insurance. The administration and management of this part of the Act are placed in the hands of the Board of Trade, or, in other words, of the Government. Now the Board of Trade has a power of making regulations for any of the purposes for which regulations may be made under that part as wide as the power conferred upon the Insurance

24. See sect. 65, proviso.

25. Sect. 69, sub-sect. 2. Compare further as to legislative powers of the Commissioners, Act, sects. 7, 15, 27, and Insurance Act, 1913, sect. 19.

Commissioners for making regulations with regard to health insurance.[26] But the Board of Trade has a further and most important power of adding to the number of insured trades.[27] Hence it follows that the Government of the day can of their own authority increase indefinitely the number of insured trades, and apparently extend the provisions as to unemployment insurance to every trade throughout the United Kingdom.[28]

Judicial Authority. As to many questions concerning health insurance which may arise under Part I. of the Act, the Insurance Commissioners have judicial authority.[29] Any person aggrieved by their decision may appeal to the County Court, with a further right of appeal on any question of law to a judge of the High Court. But this right of appeal has, I am told, been made little or no use of. Under Part II.[30] any claim by a workman for unemployment benefit, and any question arising in connection with such claim, are, in the first instance, to be decided by one of the insurance officers, *i.e.* by officials appointed by and in the service of the Board of Trade. Such decision is subject to an appeal, on the part of the workman making the claim, to a Court of Referees.[31] A Court of Referees consists in general of three persons—one drawn by rota from a panel of employers' representatives, another drawn by rota from a panel of workmen's representatives, and a Chairman (who must be neither an employer nor a workman in an insured trade)[32] appointed by the Board of Trade. On an appeal the Court of Referees may make to the insurance

26. See sect. 91.

27. See sect. 103, and Sixth Schedule. Nor does the proviso to sect. 103 materially restrict the power of the Government to make an order including a new trade, unless indeed it should happen that the person holding an inquiry with relation to the order reports that the order should not be made.

28. See sect. 113 as to the necessity of the order being laid before either House of Parliament.

29. See sects. 66, 67. Compare, however, Regulations of June 5, 1912, in App. I., Watts, p. 299.

30. "All claims for unemployment benefit under this part of this Act, and all questions whether the statutory conditions are fulfilled in the case of any workman claiming such benefit, or whether those conditions continue to be fulfilled in the case of a workman in receipt of such benefit, or whether a workman is disqualified for receiving or continuing to receive such benefit, or otherwise arising in connection with such claims, shall be determined by one of the officers appointed [under Part II.] of this Act for determining such claims for benefit (in this Act referred to as 'insurance officers')." Act, sect. 88 (1).

31. Act, sect. 88, proviso (*a*). There are about seventy such Courts constituted under the Act.

32. See Act, sect. 90, and Parliamentary Paper (B 16).

officer such recommendation as they may think proper. The insurance officer, unless he disagrees with the recommendation, must give effect to it. If he disagrees he must, if requested by the Court, refer the recommendation to the umpire. The umpire is a permanent official appointed by His Majesty, *i.e.* by the Government of the day. The decision of the umpire is final and conclusive, *i.e.* the jurisdiction of the law Courts is apparently excluded. One such umpire has now been appointed for the whole United Kingdom. An insurance officer however may, if he considers it expedient, instead of determining any claim or question, refer it at once to a Court of Referees, whose decision will be final and conclusive. The result seems to be that this course of procedure by the insurance officer excludes both the jurisdiction of the umpire and of the law Courts.

Neither the Chairman of a Court of Referees, nor even the Umpire, has the security of tenure conferred on every judge of the High Court under the Act of Settlement.

These summary statements of the authority, both legislative and judicial, given to persons or bodies either closely connected with, or subject to, or part of the Government of the day, are enough to prove that the Insurance Act creates in England a system bearing a marked resemblance to the administrative law of France.[33] Now administrative law has, it must be admitted, some distinct merits. A law Court is not a body well suited for determining the number[34] of disputes or claims which are certain to arise under the National Insurance Act. Legal proceedings, even in the County Courts, must always be slow and relatively expensive. Official proceedings may be rapid and may be rendered not costly to litigants. But administrative law has two defects which have till very recent years forbidden its existence in England. Administrative tribunals always tend to exclude the jurisdiction of the ordinary law Courts. Administrative Courts are always more or less connected with the Government of the day. Their decisions are apt to be influenced by political considerations. Governmental officials cannot have the thorough independence of judges. Both these defects are apparent in the administrative system framed by the authors of the National Insurance Act. We may be certain that the Regulations made or sanctioned by the Government of the day will, whatever party be in office, be occasionally dictated by the desire of every English Ministry to conciliate the goodwill of the electors. It is incredible that quasi-judicial decisions pronounced by the Insurance Commissioners or by the Courts of Referees will not

33. See, as to French *droit administratif, Law of the Constitution,* ch. xii.

34. The number of claims to unemployment benefit may vary from, *e.g.* 20,000 to 40,000 claims in each week, involving payments at the rate of seven shillings for each week of unemployment.

sometimes be influenced by the same desire. There exists special reason to fear the effect of political bias on decisions with regard to unemployment insurance. The question whether workmen are or are not entitled to unemployment benefit may conceivably become very closely connected with their power to carry on a strike with success. A slight legislative change in the terms of one enactment in the National Insurance Act[35] might make it possible for strikers to support a contest with their employers by means of money in part supplied by the State. The constitution of the Court of Referees shows that Parliament felt the difficulty of obtaining an impartial decision of the questions which might come before such a Court. It is not equally clear that Parliament has excluded the risk that the action of such an official Court may be swayed by the political principles of the Government which takes part in constituting the Court. An administrative Court is never a completely independent tribunal.

The Trade Disputes Act, 1906. To a student interested in the course of law and opinion during the twentieth century the character and scope of this statute is summed up in an enactment which runs as follows:

> An action against a trade union, whether of workmen or masters, or against any members or officials thereof on behalf of themselves and all other members of the trade union in respect of any tortious act alleged to have been committed by or on behalf of, the trade union, shall not be entertained by any Court.[36]

The direct effect of this enactment is that a trade union, whether of workmen or masters (which may be a very wealthy society), is now absolutely protected from liability to an action for any tort or wrong by or on behalf of the trade union.[37] Thus if a trade union possessed, say, of £20,000, causes a libel to be published of *A,* an employer of labour, or of *B,* a workman who refuses to join the union, or

---

35. See sect. 87 (1), and as to the claim made by workmen to unemployment benefit during a strike, the *Times,* January 27, 30, and February 3, 1914. The insurance officer in this case did not allow the claim, and his decision was, rightly it would seem, upheld by the Court of Referees. Note further that from an insurance officer's decision in favour of a claim by a workman to unemployment benefit there is no appeal.

36. Sect. 4 (1). I have purposely criticised the Trade Disputes Act solely with reference to this enactment. Sections 1, 2, and 3 are (it is submitted) based on an erroneous principle, but one's judgment of the Act must depend upon one's approval or condemnation of sect. 4.

37. Whether an action might not be maintained against trustees of the Union? (see *Linaker* v. *Pilcher* (1901), 17 T.L.R. 256). But the funds could not be got at if the tort was committed in contemplation or furtherance of a trade dispute.

excites some fanatical ruffians to assault *A* or *B,* neither *A* nor *B* can maintain an action against the union for the tort, and thereby either vindicate his character or recover a penny of damages.[38]

This enactment therefore confers upon a trade union a freedom from civil liability for the commission of even the most heinous wrong by the union or its servants, and in short confers upon every trade union a privilege and protection not possessed by any other person or body of persons, whether corporate or unincorporate, throughout the United Kingdom. This is assuredly a very extraordinary state of the law;[39] it points towards indirect results which have not yet been fully apprehended by the English public.

1. It makes a trade union a privileged body exempted from the ordinary law of the land. No such privileged body has ever before been deliberately created by an English Parliament.

2. It is highly probable that the legal immunities conferred upon trade unions[40] may soon be claimed by, and must be conceded to bodies which may not be now technically within the definition of a trade union. Suppose that a tenants' union were created for the purpose of lowering rents, or a labourers' union for the purpose of raising the wages of agricultural labourers. It would be difficult indeed to give any sound reason why such union should not, in common with trade unions, be protected against actions for libel or for any other tort.

3. A tort will sometimes, though not always, involve the wrongdoer in the commission of a crime. A sufferer who finds that he cannot bring an action against a trade union for a gross libel, may be tempted to try whether he may not obtain at least protection by substituting a prosecution for an action. Nothing could from a public point of view be more disastrous. Criminal proceedings are, as compared with civil proceedings, ineffective. For their very severity detracts from their utility.

38. *Vacher* v. *London Society of Compositors* [1913], A.C. 107. He might possibly vindicate his character by bringing an action against the actual publisher, *e.g.* a penniless printer, from whom he could recover neither damages nor the costs of the action.

39. My learned friend, Professor Geldart, who is one of the ablest and the fairest of the commentators upon our Combination law, and who does not agree with most of my strictures upon the Trade Disputes Act, has expressed his opinion that the enactment in question (*i.e.* sect. 4, sub-sect. 1) is "contrary to justice and expediency." (See the *Times,* March 18, 1912.)

40. See the Trade Union Act, 1913, sect. 2, for a new definition of trade union and for power of Registrar of Friendly Societies to register a combination as a trade union, and to give a conclusive certificate that a trade union is a trade union within the meaning of the Act.

A jury will often hesitate to convict an offender who may have acted from more or less good motives where they would be ready to make him pay damages for the injury done, *e.g.* by a libel, to an innocent person, and judges rightly frown upon the attempt to turn a tort into a crime. Then, too, punishment for crime falls inevitably within the control of the Crown, or in other words of the Government. Suppose that the leaders of a trade union were convicted as criminals of libel: Is it at all certain that a Government fearing the displeasure of a Labour Party, might not use the Crown's prerogative of pardon to put an end to the imprisonment of men whom trade unionists held to be martyrs?

4. An enactment which frees trade unions from the rule of equal law stimulates among workmen the fatal delusion that workmen should aim at the attainment, not of equality, but of privilege. The Trade Disputes Act as a whole, and especially the fourth section thereof, is best described in the words of Sir Frederick Pollock: "Legal science has evidently nothing to do with this violent empirical operation on the body politic, and we can only look to jurisdictions beyond seas for the further judicial consideration of the problems which our Courts [up to 1906] were endeavouring (it is submitted, not without a reasonable measure of success) to work out on principles of legal justice."[41] This is the conclusion of an impartial jurist. Historical fairness requires me to add one reflection. Our Combination law has been from beginning to end vitiated by the delusion that the relation of workmen and masters ought to be regulated by exceptional legislation.[42] The unjust severity towards workmen which was embodied in the Combination Act, 1800, is the explanation, though not the excuse, for the unjust favouritism enjoyed by trade unionists under the Trade Disputes Act, 1906.

Every objection which lies against the Trade Disputes Act has received increased force from the passing of—

The Trade Union Act, 1913. In 1909 the Courts unhesitatingly decided that the funds of a trade union[43] could not lawfully be applied to the furtherance of political objects.[44] This judgment, though approved of by sound lawyers, excited the censure of trade unions. The Trade Union Act, 1913, was passed to reverse or to annul that decision. A trade union has thus power to become an avowedly political association. It is difficult to suppose that men of justice and common sense could maintain that such an association can prudently be relieved from all liability to an action

---

41. Pollock, *Law of Torts* (8th ed.), p. v.

42. See pp. 188–193, *ante.*

43. The position of an unregistered union is not quite clear.

44. *Amalgamated Society of Railway Servants* v. *Osborne* [1909], A.C. 87.

for tort, *e.g.* for the publication during an election of some gross libel on a candidate whose politics meet with the disapproval of a trade union.[45]

Acts fixing Minimum Rate of Wages. Up to the last quarter of the nineteenth century it was the firm conviction of English economists, and of English Liberals, that any attempt to fix by law the rate of wages was an antiquated folly. This belief is no longer entertained by our Parliamentary statesmen. Under the Trade Boards Act, 1909, Trade Boards[46] have wide powers for the establishment of minimum rates of wages in certain trades,[47] *e.g.* the trade of ready-made and wholesale bespoke tailoring, and the Board of Trade has power by an order which needs confirmation by Parliament, to extend the Act to other trades.[48] By the Coal Mines (Minimum Wage) Act, 1912, Parliament has itself fixed a minimum wage for workmen employed underground in coal mines.[49]

The influence of collectivism on legislation in the twentieth century is curiously traceable in laws enacted since 1900, which, though to a certain extent defensible on Benthamite grounds, would hardly have been passed when Benthamite liberalism was the dominant opinion of the day. The meaning of this statement can be best shown by a few illustrations.

The Education (Provision of Meals) Act, 1906. The Elementary Education Act, 1870, was the work of Liberals, and even of Conservatives, who were not consciously influenced by any ideas which could be called socialistic. Whether the Education Act, 1891, which practically relieved parents from the necessity of paying for any part of their children's elementary education, would have been approved of by the statesmen who passed the Education Act, 1870, may be open to doubt. It is certain that they would have condemned the Education (Provision of Meals) Act, 1906. No one can deny that a starving boy will hardly profit much from the attempt to teach him the rules of arithmetic. But it does not necessarily follow that a local authority must therefore provide every hungry child at school with a

---

45. The Act of 1913 not only authorises trade unions under considerable restrictions to pursue political objects, but authorises them without any restriction to devote their funds to any other lawful objects whatever. In the pursuit of these objects they would be entitled to the immunity given them by the Trade Disputes Act, 1906, sect. 4, from actions for torts.

46. Trade Boards Act, sect. 1.

47. *Ibid.* sect. 4.

48. *Ibid.* sect. 1, sub-sect. 2.

49. I have purposely omitted details as to the mode in which minimum wages are to be fixed by law. For my present purpose the importance of any Minimum Wage Act is the admission of Parliament that wages can rightly be fixed by law and not by the mere haggling of the market.

meal;[50] still less does it seem morally right that a father who first lets his child starve, and then fails to pay the price legally due from him for a meal given to the child at the expense of the rate-payers should, under the Act of 1906, retain the right of voting for a Member of Parliament.[51] Why a man who first neglects his duty as a father and then defrauds the State should retain his full political rights is a question easier to ask than to answer.

Take again *The Mental Deficiency Act*, 1913. Most of its provisions for the protection of defectives, both from themselves and from their neighbours, recommend themselves to common sense. They would probably have been welcomed by a humanitarian and a jurist, such as Bentham. Yet the Act would hardly have been passed by the Parliament, say of 1860. The interference which it involves with the dangerous liberty of defectives would at least have raised suspicion in the minds of men who had hailed the individualism of Mill's *Liberty* with indiscriminating applause. They would have felt that the measure was open to one serious objection. The Mental Deficiency Act is the first step along a path on which no sane man can decline to enter, but which, if too far pursued, will bring statesmen across difficulties hard to meet without considerable interference with individual liberty.

The Coal Mines Regulation Act, 1908. The long line of Factory Acts stretches back to 1802,[52] when Toryism was dominant. Factory legislation for the protection of children and women was made an essential part of English law at the time when individualistic liberalism was the received creed of educated Englishmen. Even here modern collectivism has given a new turn to old legislation. The Factory Acts interfered little, if at all, with the right of a workman of full age to labour for any number of hours agreed upon between him and his employer. But the Coal Mines Regulation Act, 1908, prohibits, subject to certain limitations, the employment of workmen in coal mines for more than eight hours during any consecutive twenty-four hours, and imposes a penalty upon any man, including the workman himself,[53] who contravenes the provisions of the Act.

The Finance (1909–10) *Act*, 1910. From, at any rate, 1845, till towards the close of the nineteenth century a taxing Act was generally held open to censure if it imposed a special burden upon one class of the community; it was still more generally agreed that taxation should be imposed mainly, one might almost say exclusively, to meet the financial wants of the State.[54] Retrenchment and economy

---

50. See Act, 1906, sect. 3.
51. *Ibid.* sect. 4.
52. See pp. 156–170, *ante.*
53. See Act, 1908, sect. 7.
54. Compare Bernard Mallet, *British Budgets, 1887–1913*, Preface, p. vii.

in short were considered to be the appropriate virtues of a Chancellor of the Exchequer. Now the Finance Act, 1910, imposed various new taxes, such as Increment Value Duty, or Income-tax in the shape of Super-tax on incomes over £5000; but the essential characteristic of the Act lies not in its imposition of a heavy burden of taxation, but in its violation of the two principles which had been on the whole respected by Chancellors of the Exchequer during the greater part of the nineteenth century. It imposes specially heavy taxes upon the rich, and upon landowners. It is also an Act passed not for the mere purpose of raising needful revenue, but with the aim of promoting social or political objects. Undeveloped land duty, for example, is imposed, partly at any rate, for the purpose of compelling or inducing a landowner to erect dwelling-houses or buildings which may be useful as habitations or places of business, though he might himself prefer to leave his land open as a field or garden. Whether such filling up of open spaces might always be an advantage to the public I do not care to consider; all I insist upon is the plain fact, that the Finance Act, 1910, is a law passed not merely to raise the revenue necessary for meeting the wants of the State, but also for the attainment of social ends dear to collectivists.

This feature in the Act may give rise to serious reflection. It sets a precedent for the use of taxation for the promotion of political or social ends. Such taxation may easily become the instrument of tyranny. Thus revolutionists bent on the nationalisation of land might, by heavy taxation, beat down its value in the hands of a private owner till he is willing to sell it far below its real worth. Revolution is not the more entitled to respect because it is carried through not by violence, but under the specious though delusive appearance of taxation imposed to meet the financial needs of the State.

(C) The Main Current of Legislative Opinion from the beginning of the Twentieth Century

The main current of legislative opinion from the beginning of the twentieth century has run vehemently towards collectivism.

When the last century came to an end belief in *laissez faire* had lost much of its hold on the people of England. The problem now before us is to ascertain what are the new causes or conditions which since the beginning of the present century have in England given additional force to the influence of more or less socialistic ideas.[55] These causes may be thus summed up:

---

55. A critic should never forget that the truth of a belief is not necessarily demonstrated

1. *The Existence of Patent Facts which impress upon ordinary Englishmen the Interdependence[56] of Private and Public Interest.* Mill's "simple principle"[57] depends wholly upon the assumption that in a civilised country, such as England or France, the conduct of an individual may be strictly divided into conduct which concerns or interests himself alone, and conduct which concerns mainly the State or, in other words, his neighbours. It is also tacitly assumed by Mill that by far the greater portion of the conduct pursued by an ordinary and well-meaning citizen concerns mainly himself, and that therefore by far the greater part of such a man's action ought to be guided by his own opinion or judgment, and certainly ought not to be interfered with by the force of law.[58] But since 1859 almost every event which has happened has directed public attention to the extreme difficulty, not to say the impossibility, of drawing a rigid distinction between actions which merely concern a man himself and actions which also concern society. The perplexity indeed of modern law-makers, as indeed of the public, has been of late indefinitely increased by several circumstances, each of which tends to blur the distinction between matters which concern only an individual and matters which concern the public.

Thus the whole course of trade tends rapidly to place the conduct of business in the hands of corporate or quasi-corporate bodies. The railway companies, for instance, of England are wholly in the hands of masses of shareholders who for some legal purposes may well be considered one person, though they constitute in reality many thousands of persons, and of persons who in practice never take any effective part in the management of the concerns from which they derive their income. These companies, moreover, carry on a business the successful management whereof assuredly affects the prosperity, and even the safety, of the United

---

by its wide acceptance. Half the history of human thought is the tale of human errors. The belief that a crusade by Christians for the recovery of the Holy Land and the Holy Sepulchre was commanded by reverence for Christ was entertained for centuries in the leading countries of Europe, and by the best and wisest of men. This faith was at best a generous delusion. The Crusaders, it has been well remarked, sought for the living among the dead.

56. This interdependence is, I believe, at bottom the meaning of the technical expression "solidarity" which, with writers such as Duguit, is an almost sacramental term.

57. See p. 361, *ante.*

58. Mill qualifies, or rather extends, his simple principle by the remark that, where he talks of conduct which affects only a man himself, he means conduct which affects "only himself . . . directly, and in the first instance." Mill thereby all but admits that hardly any conduct of a human being can be named (except conduct which does not go further than the realm of thought) which, strictly speaking, affects "only himself." See Mill, *On Liberty,* p. 26.

Kingdom. Hence the antithesis between the individual and the State is with difficulty maintainable. A modern strike again, whether it be a strike against one employer, or a body of employers, turns out more often than not to involve social or public interests. But when once this is granted the application of Mill's simple principle becomes no easy matter. An impartial observer may doubt whether the principle itself can really govern the complex transactions of modern business.

The advance, again, of human knowledge has intensified the general conviction that even the apparently innocent action of an individual may injuriously affect the welfare of a whole community. The first man who carried a few rabbits with him to Australia and set them loose there to propagate their offspring at will, was no criminal; he no doubt felt that he was doing a thing beneficial to himself, and, if he thought about his neighbours at all, not injurious to the public. But few malefactors have ever given more trouble to, and imposed more expense upon, a respectable community than this ill-starred importer of rabbits brought upon his adopted country. Almost every addition, again, to that sort of knowledge, which is commonly called science, adds to the close sense of the interdependence of all human interests. The discovery, for instance, that the health of a nation depends, or may depend, on the general observation of certain rules of health, not only increases this sense of interdependence but also suggests that the fancies, the scruples, or the conscientious objections of individuals, or, to put the matter shortly, individual liberty must be curtailed when opposed to the interest of the public.

2. *The Declining Influence of Other Movements.* Various political, social, or even theological movements or beliefs, which during the nineteenth century occupied the thoughts of statesmen, patriots, and philanthropists, have ceased to interest deeply Englishmen of the twentieth century. Hence half the attractiveness of socialism. It is a system which has not as yet been tested by experience; it has not as yet achieved in practice even that half-success which, to ardent believers in plans for the improvement of mankind, is equivalent to something more disappointing than failure.

That many movements which seemed full of infinite promise have, even when successful, disappointed the hopes of their adherents is certain. The belief, for instance, in the untold benefits to be conferred upon mankind by merely constitutional changes, such, for example, as the establishment of Republics, or of Parliamentary Monarchies, is hardly comprehensible to the Englishmen of to-day. The passion for nationality, again, no longer commands in England, or indeed throughout Europe, the enthusiasm aroused by Mazzini, by Kossuth, by Cavour, and by Garibaldi. The men of the twentieth century find it hard to understand how aged statesmen, such as Palmerston and Lord John Russell, became fervent believers in the principle of nationality, and such modern critics of mid-Victorian ideas are specially puzzled when they find a belief in nationalism to have been combined with a desire to found throughout Continental Europe constitutional monarchies after the English model. Nor is this diminution of interest in the cause of nationalism a result of its failure. It were truer to assert that the success of nationalism has in England destroyed enthusiasm for nationality. Italy has achieved freedom, unity, and independence. But the resurrection of Italy has lost its romance. Germany has for the first time become a united and powerful State. But then the creation of the German Empire has not fulfilled the hopes of English constitutionalists. It has imposed upon the world the all but unbearable burden of huge standing armies. The unity of Germany has involved the dismemberment of France. We can at any rate now see that national independence is nothing like a cure for all the evils under which a country may suffer. No foreigner tyrannises over Spain or Portugal, yet it may be doubted whether independence has brought immense benefit to Spaniards or to Portuguese. This state of feeling explains, though it does not justify, a singular phenomenon. Englishmen of to-day have witnessed the victories gained by the Greeks over the Turks with an apathy or indifference which would have amazed many of our grandfathers, even though they were high Tories.

Where, again, can we find the generous enthusiasm for raising backward races of the world, such as the negroes of America, to a position of freedom and equality? The spirit of Garrison seems to be dead in Massachusetts. That hatred of slavery, which well-nigh eighty-one years ago compelled the emancipation of the West Indian slaves, seems for the moment unknown to English electors, though we may trust that this decline in public virtue is a merely transitory phenomenon.

An observer, further, who is anxious to treat a serious matter with fairness, can hardly help suspecting that preachers and divines of to-day have lost to some extent the belief, held by most of their predecessors in England, that human beings individually, or society as a whole, can be reformed by the teaching of doctrine which the preacher holds to be religious truth. The nature of the possible change or contrast on which it is necessary to insist may be most fairly shown by means of historical examples. Nobody for a moment doubts that the teaching of Wesley, and the Methodist movement generally, did produce a great and most beneficial effect upon the social condition of thousands among the miners, the labourers, and the artisans of England. Religious conversion of men, whom ignorance and want of moral guidance had left in a condition of something very like Paganism, produced a body of good men and of good citizens, and of persons therefore who in a country like England did as a rule obtain material prosperity.[59] It has been indeed not

59. See Leslie Stephen, *English Thought in the Eighteenth Century,* ch. xii. pp. 409–425.

unreasonably suggested[60] that the rise of Methodism diverted the ablest men among the wage-earners of England from sympathy with the revolutionary doctrines of 1789. But however great the benefits conferred by Methodism on large bodies of Englishmen, it is clear that the primary object of the early Methodists was to inculcate what they held to be the saving truths of Christianity. Social reform was the happy but secondary result of their teaching. The same remark holds good of the Evangelicals, though happily their religious fervour made them the champions of humanitarianism. The High Churchmen and Tractarians of eighty years ago were certainly, and, from their own point of view quite rightly, much more occupied in vindicating or asserting the Catholic character of the Church of England than in any kind of secular reform. That every sincere minister of religion inside and outside the Church of England has laboured and is labouring to promote, according to his lights, charity, peace, and goodwill among mankind, even a cynic would hesitate to deny. The language of Richard Baxter—

> I preached as never sure to preach again,
> And as a dying man to dying men—

describes the sincere purpose of the best and the most pious among the preachers of England up to the middle of the nineteenth century: but it hardly describes the attitude or the aim of the best and the most sincere preachers of to-day. This assertion does not imply any change of creed on the part of ministers of religion, still less does it point at any kind of dishonesty. My statement is merely the recognition of an admitted fact. Good and religious men now attach less importance to the teaching of religious dogma than to efforts which may place the poor in a position of at any rate comparative ease and comfort, and thus enable them to turn from exhausting labour to the appreciation of moral and religious truth. This is a change the existence whereof seems hardly deniable. It gives to the preachers of to-day a new interest in social reform; and, it may be added, the declining interest in the preaching of religious dogma in itself opens the minds of such men to the importance of social improvement. But to speak quite fairly, this change produces some less laudable results. It disposes zealous reformers to underrate the immense amount of truth contained in the slow methods of improvement advocated by believers in individualism and *laissez faire,* and to overrate the benefits to be gained from energetic and authoritative socialism. The fervent though disinterested dogmatism of the pulpit may, moreover, in regard to social problems, be as rash and misleading as the rhetoric of the platform. It is specially apt to intro-

---

60. Lecky, *History of England in the Eighteenth Century,* ii. ch. ix. pp. 635–638.

duce into social conflicts the intolerable evil of "thinking fanatically,"[61] and therefore of acting fanatically. However this may be, the altered attitude of religious teachers in regard to social reform has, in common with the other changes of opinion on which I have insisted, added strength to the current of collectivism.

3. *The General Acquiescence in Proposals tending towards Collectivism.* Wealthy Englishmen have made a much less vigorous resistance to socialistic legislation than would have been expected by the statesmen or the economists of sixty years ago. This acquiescence in proposals opposed to the apparent interest of every owner of property, has led at least one ingenious writer[62] to fancy he had discovered some unknown law of human nature which compelled the rich men of England to perform acts of otherwise inexplicable unselfishness. In truth a somewhat curious phenomenon is amply explained by the combination of an intellectual weakness with a moral virtue, each of which is easily discernible in the Englishmen of to-day. The intellectual weakness or failure is the indolent assumption that the effect of apparently great legal or political changes is, in the long run, very small. This view is suggested by the superficial reading, or the still more superficial memory, of English political history from the accession of George III. (1760) to the accession of George V. (1910). During these one hundred and fifty years almost every legal change, whether entitled reform or revolution, has produced far smaller results than were anticipated by their advocates or by their opponents. Catholic Emancipation, 1829, the Reform Act, 1832, the establishment of Free Trade, 1845, the line of Factory Acts, extending from 1802 to the present day, the democratic extensions of the Parliamentary suffrage, which received their latest, though not probably their final, development in 1884, have not to all appearance revolutionised the condition of England. They have not led to deeds of sanguinary violence, nor given rise to the reactionary legislation which has done so much to delay the course of peaceful progress in France. Hence the homely and comfortable but delusive doctrine that in the political world "nothing signifies."[63] The high moral virtue, which tends accidentally in the same direction as a kind of intellectual apathy, is the daily increasing sympathy in England with the sufferings of the poor. Benev-

61. See an admirable letter by the Dean of Durham, *Times,* November 27, 1913.

62. See Benjamin Kidd, *Social Evolution,* and compare "Political Prophecy and Sociology," in *Miscellaneous Essays and Addresses,* by H. Sidgwick, p. 216.

63. Such easy-going confidence on the part of ordinary Englishmen in the infinitely small effect of legislation, whether good or bad, may be pardoned when we reflect that a systematic thinker such as Herbert Spencer, in many of his strictures on the failure of legislation to achieve its avowed object, makes far too little allowance for the long latent period which often elapses before results appear. See W. Bateson, *Biological Fact and the Structure of Society,* p. 28 (n.).

olence is quite as natural to man, and in fact is far more common, at any rate with civilised men, than outrageous selfishness or malevolence. An Englishman of the middle classes who is freed from the necessity for all-absorbing toil in order to obtain the means necessary for acquiring the independence or the comforts of his life, is more often than not a man of kindly disposition. His own happiness is diminished by the known and felt miseries of his less wealthy neighbours. Now, for the last sixty years and more, the needs and sufferings of the poor have been thrust upon the knowledge of middle-class Englishmen. There are persons still living who can recall the time when about sixty years ago the *Morning Chronicle* in letters on London Labour and the London Poor revealed to the readers of high-class, and then dear, newspapers the miserable condition of the poorer wage-earners of London. These letters at once aroused the sympathy and called forth the aid of Maurice and the Christian Socialists. For sixty years novelists, newspaper writers, and philanthropists have alike brought the condition of the poor constantly before the eyes of their readers or disciples. The desire to ease the sufferings, to increase the pleasures, and to satisfy the best aspirations of the mass of wage-earners has become a marked characteristic of the wealthy classes of Englishmen. This sentiment of active goodwill, stimulated no doubt by ministers of religion, has spread far and wide among laymen, *e.g.* lawyers, merchants, and others not specially connected with any one religious, theological, or political party. There is nothing in all this to excite surprise, though there is much to kindle hope. It may be expected that, as has happened again and again during the history of England, the power of opinion may, without any immense revolution in the institutions of the country, modify and reform their working. No doubt there is something also in the present condition of public sentiment to arouse fear. The years which im-mediately preceded the French Revolution witnessed the rapid development of benevolence and philanthropy in France and throughout the civilised countries of Europe. These feelings were not unreal though coloured, under the influence of Rousseau, with too much of rhetoric to suit the taste of the twentieth century, and were connected with speculative doctrines which, in common with modern col-lectivism, combine some important truths with some at least equally important delusions. No criticism, in any case, of public opinion in England is worth anything which fails to take into account the goodwill of the richer classes of Englishmen towards their less prosperous neighbours.

4. *The Advent in England of Parliamentary Democracy.* Democracy, if the word be used in the way it should always be employed, as meaning a form of government, has no necessary connection with collectivism.[64] It is nevertheless true that the extension of the Parliamentary suffrage (1866–1884), combined with the existing

64. See Lect. III. pp. 36–44, *ante.*

conditions of public life in England, has increased, and often unduly increased, the influence of socialists, and for the following reasons:

It has, in the first place, made known and called attention to the real or the supposed wishes or wants of the poorer electors.

It has, in the second place, increased the power of any well organised Parliamentary faction or group, which is wholly devoted to the attainment of some definite political or social object, whether the object be the passing of socialistic legislation or the obtaining of Parliamentary votes for women. For such a group may certainly come to command a vote in Parliament sufficient to determine which of the two leading parties, say, speaking broadly, of Conservatives or of Radicals, shall hold office. In such circumstances one of these two parties is almost certain to form an alliance with a faction strong enough to decide the result of the great party game. Hence it may well happen that socialists may for a time obtain the active aid, and to a certain extent the sympathy, of a great party whose members have no natural inclination towards socialism. This possible tyranny of minorities is a phenomenon which was hardly recognised either by the statesmen or by the thinkers of 1860 or 1870, but it is a fact to which in the twentieth century no reasonable man can shut his eyes.

The course of events, in the third place, and above all the competition for office which is the bane of the party system, have at last revealed to the electorate the extent of their power, and has taught them that political authority can easily be used for the immediate advantage, not of the country but of a class. Collectivism or socialism promises unlimited benefits to the poor. Voters who are poor, naturally enough adopt some form of socialism.

5. *The Spread of Collectivism or Socialism in Foreign Countries.* Englishmen have rarely been directly and consciously influenced by the example of foreign countries. English political or social movements have been influenced far less by logical argument than by the logic of facts, and of facts observable in England. English collectivism and socialism owes its peculiar development in England mainly to the success of English trade unionism, but every part of the world is by means of railways and electric telegraph being brought nearer to each other. It may therefore be taken for granted that the progress of socialistic legislation and the trial of socialistic experiments in English colonies, such as the Australian Commonwealth, or in the United States, or even in an utterly foreign country, such as France, have promoted the growth of collectivism in England. In 1914 events occurring in France are better known to an English artisan than in 1814 they were known to an English squire or merchant.

It is worth while in this connection to observe how nearly the French Legislature has, whether consciously or not, entered upon the path followed by the Imperial

Parliament of the United Kingdom. The resemblance between the development of social legislation in France and in England may be thus illustrated: The laws of March 21, 1884, and of July 1, 1901, have established in France the "right of association" (to use a French term), and thereby conferred upon trade unions, whether of workmen or of masters, and also upon all other professional associations, rights closely resembling, though not identical with, the rights possessed since 1875 by English trade unions. In France provisions for the support of the poor have received a development which at any rate recall the English poor law.[65] In both countries the law confers old age pensions on the poor, though in France both the employer and the employed contribute to the pension. In both countries there exists a body of factory legislation, though it is far less developed in France than in England. In France as in England accidents befalling a workman in the course of his employment entitle him to compensation from his employer.[66] In each country the law prohibits the truck system of payment, and the law secures for workers in factories and shops a weekly day of rest.[67] The English Parliament has in the case of some employments established a minimum wage in favour of workmen.[68] Proposals in favour of the same policy have been laid before the French Parliament, and, it is said, may probably find acceptance. The reacquisition in 1908 by the French State of a whole railway system is a considerable step towards the nationalisation of railways.[69] In none of these cases does the law of the two countries coincide, but in these and in many other instances English public opinion and French public opinion are clearly flowing in the same direction. As far as Englishmen can judge, the law of England has, in its unsystematic way, gone further in the direction of socialism than has the law of France. I can discover no French law giving to any association the privileges conferred on English trade unions by the Trade Disputes Act, 1906. A foreign critic may conjecture that the influence of small landowners, or so-called peasant proprietors, in France checks the progress of socialism. The comparison between the social legislation of the two countries has this special point of interest: In each country you have a real system of popular government; in each country Parliament is supreme; in each country parliamentary government means party government. The Third Republic of France more closely resembles, and can

---

65. See Pic, *Les Lois Ouvrières* (3rd ed.), sects. 1404–1411.

66. *Ibid.* sects. 1077–1138; law, April 9, 1898; law, July 18, 1907.

67. *Ibid.* sects. 777, 808, 825.

68. See p. 375, *ante.*

69. *Rachat des chemins de fer de l'ouest,* law, July 13, 1908. See Duguit, *Droit Constitutionnel,* i. p. 428.

more easily be compared with, the constitutional monarchy of England than can any other system of government now existing on the European Continent.

6. *The Existence of Industrial Discontent or Warfare.* "The industrial situation . . . in the world at large has not improved during the last twenty-five years. On the contrary, it has become more exasperated and more dangerous. What is the way out of the prevailing condition of industrial warfare? It amounts to warfare, this incessant conflict within the political body between the employed and the employers—and in many cases it becomes an actual physical contest."[70] Thus writes the *President Emeritus* of Harvard University: he is no socialist; he represents the energetic character of New England; he is imbued with the sanguine temperament of every born citizen of the United States. "Social discontent is by universal admission the distinctive character of our age; and the rapid spread among the European populations of doctrines which presuppose a more or less violent transformation of society provides no distant parallel to the ardent Messianic expectations of Christ's contemporaries."[71] These are the words of the Dean of Durham in a sermon on the Kingdom of God. They are certainly not meant to encourage hopes grounded on revolutionary transformations of our social condition. Who can doubt that discontent among the wage-earners is a distinctive characteristic of the present time?

In any attempt to explain this state of feeling we must bear in mind one consideration. It is that discontent or even violent indignation aroused by an existing state of society is often due far less to the absolute amount of the suffering endured among men prepared to rebel against the most fundamental laws of social existence than to the increased vividness of the contrast between given institutions and the desires of persons who suffer, or think they suffer, from the existing state of things. Thus it is quite possible that the wage-earners of England may be relatively better off than were their fathers or their grandfathers fifty or a hundred years ago. But yet the contrast between the rich and the poor in England may press more heavily upon the thoughts and the imaginations of English working men than it did towards the beginning of the nineteenth century. Whether from an economical point of view the existence of millionaires does great harm, or any harm, to the mass of the people, may be a matter of doubt. What is absolutely certain is that the existence of millionaires emphasises the difference between rich and poor, and also kindles among all classes an exaggerated desire for wealth.

Then, too, it is a highly probable opinion that the poorer citizens of all civilised countries have arrived at a stage of education which makes it easy for them to

---

70. *Successful Profit-Sharing,* by Charles W. Eliot, *President Emeritus* of Harvard University.
71. See the *Guardian,* November 7, 1913, p. 1398, Sermon by the Dean of Durham.

perceive the possible benefits for wage-earners to be derived from the interference of the State, and at the same time to be victims to the easily propagated delusion that all wealth possessed by the rich is so much stolen from the poor. One lesson of experience should never be absent from the mind of any student engaged in investigating the history of opinion. Revolutions are not by any means always due to increasing or to new oppression. It would be ridiculous to assert that the citizens, for example, of the Australian Commonwealth suffer from oppressive laws; they enjoy high wages, they can if they wish become landowners, they can at their pleasure repeal any law which they deem to be unjust, or enact any law which they deem to be necessary to the prosperity of their country. Yet socialistic legislation and experiment have been carried to a greater length in Australia than in England. The discontent, in other words, with the inequality between rich and poor is, whatever be the reason, felt with special force in a very prosperous English Colony. The history of the French Revolution presents a somewhat similar phenomenon. Hostility to the *ancien régime* was felt more keenly by Parisians, who from the nature of things could not suffer much from "feudal institutions," than by peasants living in the country districts of France. The privileges of the nobility had, before 1789, a far more real existence in La Vendée than in any great town, yet the peasants of La Vendée supported the throne and the altar when Paris supported or tolerated the Reign of Terror.[72]

(D) Counter-Currents and Cross-Currents of Legislative Opinion from the Beginning of the Twentieth Century[73]

The progress of the more or less dominant collectivism[74] of 1914, or in popular language of socialism, will certainly be delayed, and quite possibly be arrested,[75] by different though closely interconnected counter-currents of opinion.

72. Sir Alfred Lyall inferred from Tocqueville's writings that it was the prosperity and the enlightenment of the French people that produced the great crash of the Revolution.

73. As to the meaning of counter-currents and cross-currents of opinion see Lect. X. p. 211, *ante.*

74. For the meaning of collectivism see p. 46, *ante.*

75. Prophecy is the vainest of pursuits, but a thoughtful reader should bear in mind that, while on the one hand guesses as to the future course of social development are of no value unless they are grounded upon actually observed facts, yet on the other hand a forecast of what is likely to happen is a legitimate kind of argument if, in spite of its predictive form, it is an analysis of existing and observable tendencies.

First Counter-current. The surviving belief in the policy of *laissez faire.*[76]

The exaggerated faith once placed in the wisdom of leaving things alone, has brought *laissez faire* into discredit. Yet a candid observer will note that the distrust of State interference is still entertained by the mass of English citizens. It is not my business to argue that this sentiment never produces bad results. My sole contention is that it has still a very strong hold upon Englishmen, whether rich or poor. Benthamite liberalism owed half of its triumph to its coincidence with the individualism of the common law,[77] and independently of the belief in any philosophic theory, the dogma of *laissez faire* has commended itself, and does commend itself to hundreds of Englishmen, and for very obvious reasons. It has stimulated energy of action. It has left room for freedom of thought and individuality. It has fostered the trust in self-help. It has kept alive emphatically the virtues of the English people. But at this point trust in individual liberty runs into and forms part of a second counter-current, which deserves separate examination.

Second Counter-current. The inconsistency between democracy and collectivism.

In England a democrat is nowadays more than half a socialist, and a collectivist, or in popular language a socialist, is generally a democrat. As a democrat each of them holds that the best form of government for any civilized country, and certainly for England, is a constitution under which the wish of the majority of the citizens ultimately determines the course of legislation. Popular government, in short, means to such a man, even though he be more or less a socialist, government in accordance with popular opinion.[78] This democratic conception of government contains the important truth that it is impolitic if not impossible, at any rate in a civilised State, to found institutions or to enforce laws which the citizens thereof detest. It is further true that honest representative government is the best arrangement hitherto invented for averting legislation which the people of a given country are unwilling to accept. This is the strength of the democratic creed. But it is also true that a modern democracy, while it protects the people from unpopular laws, gives inadequate security for the passing of laws which are in themselves wise and good. So much as to the creed of a thorough-going English democrat who looks, as do most of our Radicals, with some favour upon socialism. A socialist who is secondarily, so to speak, a democrat, believes that any civilised country, and certainly England, should be governed in accordance with socialistic principles, as

76. See p. 104, *ante.*

77. See p. 125, *ante.*

78. See *Public Opinion and Popular Government*, by A. Lawrence Lowell. This book contains the most subtle analysis of public opinion and the best account known to me of its relation to popular government.

being the principles which tend to promote the welfare of the people. Now the strength of socialism is that a socialist is saved from the delusion which, though childish, is not uncommon, that whatever the people desire is, because they wish for it, right and wise; and that the granting of such wish will always conduce to the welfare of a country. Most persons further, though not all, will concede that the socialistic ideal contains in itself some elements of truth, and also is the expression of an honest and laudable wish to better the position of the wage-earners in every civilised country. This concession, however, does not involve the belief that law can benefit the people as much as does the maintenance of personal freedom. The weak point of the socialistic ideal is that it is a dogmatic or authoritative creed and encourages enthusiasts who hold it to think lightly of individual freedom, and suggests the very dubious idea that in a democracy the wish of the people may often be overruled for the good of the people. The ideal of democracy, in short, is government for the good of the people by the people, and in accordance with the wish of the people; the ideal of collectivism is government for the good of the people by experts, or officials who know, or think they know, what is good for the people better than either any non-official person or than the mass of the people themselves. Each of these two ideals contains something of truth, but each of these ideals may sooner or later clash with each other. This conflict may take various forms. But beliefs marked by essential inconsistency are certain to give rise to most serious and, it may be, very practical and embittered dissension.

In England our socialistic democrat or our democratic socialist is, naturally enough, blind to this inconsistency. He is convinced that socialism will promote the welfare of England. He therefore assumes that socialism when put into practice will become popular. He sees that the progress of democracy has for the last thirty years coincided with the passing of socialistic laws. He forgets that the existence of a democracy prevents any sagacious collectivist from pressing upon English electors any law which is not, apparently at least, beneficial to the poor. The Old Age Pensions Act certainly offers a pecuniary benefit to most wage-earners. Whether the working men of England will ultimately gain by relying on the State for their support in old age, is a question which you can hardly expect men who have been able to save nothing for the wants of their declining years to consider. A country labourer will never be offended by the offer of the nation to give him five shillings a week from the day he has reached the age of 70. The inconsistency between democracy and socialism will never be fully recognised until earnest socialists force upon the people some law which, though in conformity with socialistic principles, imposes some new burden upon the mass of the voters.

My aim is to prove that even now such inconsistency exists. Look at things passing before our eyes. A collectivist never holds a stronger position than when he advocates the enforcement of the best ascertained laws of health. Disease inflicts injuries upon men of all classes. Its appearance gives the most striking example of the way in which different members of the community are bound together by that mutual interdependence for which French writers use the term "solidarity." One would have thought it therefore impossible that a large body of Englishmen should be found to resist measures commended by sound knowledge for the resistance to the spread of disease. That vaccination, if rigidly enforced, would banish small-pox from England is believed by the vast majority of experts competent to form an opinion on such a matter. Yet the Radicals of Leicester, in the name of freedom or of conscience, claim the right and, with the connivance of politicians who are fishing for votes, exercise the power to propagate small-pox. We have here, at any rate for the moment, an instance of conflict between democratic and socialistic enthusiasm. Take again the Mental Deficiency Act, 1913. It approved itself to both Houses of Parliament; it approves itself to almost every person throughout the United Kingdom who possesses the not always united qualities of humanity and of good sense, still it met with strenuous opposition from ardent democrats.

Take quite a different instance of the opposition between democracy and socialism. No one until recent times has disputed that democratic institutions are strengthened by the existence of a large number of small and independent land-owners. Whether it be possible to create anew a body of yeomen in a country where, mainly from economical causes, such yeomen have disappeared is a question which need not here receive any answer. No man, however, can dispute that the existence of such a territorial democracy contributes in Switzerland, in France, and in the United States to the prosperity and the effectiveness of popular institutions. But the modern socialist does not desire the maintenance or the production of a large class of independent yeomen. He desires property, and especially property in land, to be owned by the State. He perceives, truly enough from his own point of view, that the existence of a large number of independent landowners, each of whom can call a comparatively small piece of land his own, will be a serious and possibly an insuperable obstacle to the nationalisation of land. The peasant proprietors of France in 1848 rallied round Louis Napoleon because he promised protection against socialists. In truth the opposition between the democratic desire for an independent yeomanry and the socialistic passion for the nationalisation of land is not accidental. The owners of small estates feel more strongly than any other class the joy of ownership. It is among them that the possession of property exercises the magical effect attributed to it by Arthur Young. But a sincere socialist condemns the passion for individual ownership. He wishes to substitute for it the passion for common ownership by the State. Here again the democratic ideal as understood by Englishmen is inconsistent with the ideals of socialism.

Another difference between the ideals of an English socialist and an English democrat is to be found in the attitude which they respectively take up towards scientific experts. The socialist's ideal is a State ruled by officials or experts who are socialists. The democrat's ideal is a State governed by the people in conformity with the broad common sense he attributes to ordinary citizens. Hence the socialist escapes the folly of idolising the people. But it were foolish to suppose that democratic suspicion of experts or officials always originates in popular ignorance. Respect for experts ought always to be tempered by the constant remembrance that the possessors of special knowledge have also their special weaknesses. Rarely indeed does reform come from even the best among professional men. Bentham gained the ear of some eminent lawyers, but the conception of Benthamite reform did not come from the leaders of the Bar, nor generally from the judges. Pasteur was no doctor, and the doctors of France for a long time slighted his discoveries and resisted his suggestions. Lister showed, what no one doubts, that professional eminence is not inconsistent with originality and genius, but he was attacked with vehemence by one among the most famous of Scottish physicians, and for many years could not gain the credence or the support of some eminent English surgeons. And this blindness of experts is no accident. A man's minute knowledge and interest in a certain class of facts, however important in themselves, is, owing to limitations of the human intellect, often balanced by ignorance, in no way disgraceful, of other facts which though they may have a direct bearing upon the prosperity of mankind, do not happen to interest or perhaps to be known to our scientific expert. Canning, we are told by a very distinguished man of science, did not learn till late in life that tadpoles turned into frogs, and thought that a schoolboy who gave him that information was fooling him. This "portentous ignorance" suggests to our scientific instructor that a man capable of it is disqualified from safely exercising high functions of statesmanship. It is happy for England that the unscientific Englishmen of the early nineteenth century had not adopted any such disqualifying dogma. The insight, the foresight, and, above all, the rapid resolution of Canning achieved for England a deliverance from danger hardly less important than the security conferred upon her by the victory of Trafalgar. Our democrat, if he is a man of sense, ought to have one inestimable virtue. He may lack the knowledge possessed by the ablest of specialists; but he knows and feels that the prosperity of men and of nations has its source in self-help, energy, and originality. He is thus saved from that belief in formulas which has now and again wrecked the plans of enthusiastic socialists.

Let us examine the opposition between democracy and socialism from a slightly different point of view. It will then be seen that some of the most energetic movements of the day are closely connected with beliefs which, whether true or false, are naturally adopted by democrats and not easily accepted by socialists. Take, for instance, the agitation in favour of giving parliamentary votes to women. Many arguments worth consideration may be adduced in support of this movement. But its real strength lies in the acceptance of the dogma, that every human being of full age has *prima facie* an innate or natural right to the full political powers of a citizen. This doctrine is congenial to democrats who at times have treated the claim to manhood suffrage as a natural right. Its fallaciousness has indeed been proved again and again by Burke, by Bentham, and by Comte. It is opposed also to the assumption always latent in socialistic teaching that the will of the people may be overruled by socialists for the people's good. No existing institution, again, is more democratic, and may possibly turn out more conservative, than the referendum. It lies at the very basis of popular government in Switzerland; but the intelligent socialist fights very shy of the referendum, for he fears, not without reason, that the vote of the people might be adverse to a policy of socialism. On no point, again, is public opinion more divided than on the question of divorce. With the theological beliefs which give special bitterness to this controversy we need not here concern ourselves. The noticeable fact for our present purpose is that the difference of opinion as to the terms, if any, on which divorce ought to be allowed, arises from the difference between the individualistic, or democratic, and the socialistic view of life. If marriage be looked upon mainly as a contract between man and wife it is obviously reasonable to put an end to a marriage of two persons when it causes deep unhappiness to both, or when it causes misery to the one party and gives very little happiness to the other. This consideration seems to many democrats all but conclusive in favour of allowing divorce. Hence in every democratically governed country divorce is made year by year more easily obtainable. But if divorce be looked upon mainly from the point of view of a sane collectivist, the question whether divorce should be facilitated becomes an inquiry far more difficult to answer. Marriage, he will argue, when treated as a union which hardly admits of dissolution, confers great benefits upon the State. The interest of the community therefore is the only test which can decide whether the right to divorce should be extended or restricted; the relief which divorce may give to an individual suffering from an unhappy marriage cannot be a decisive consideration.

Such thinkers are certainly themselves coming to perceive the possible conflict between democratic and socialistic ideals. The devices by which they try to explain away this opposition are sometimes more startling than reassuring. One writer maintains that the whole misery of modern life consists in the conflicting interests of classes, and that when the State substitutes for the existence of different classes one uniform class of citizens all the members whereof are equally governed with equity and in accordance with the principles of enlightened socialism, selfishness and the conflicting interests it produces will disappear.[79] To an ordinary man who knows something of history, and has not shut his eyes to human nature as it actually exists, it must seem that the love of self, whether justifiable or unjustifiable, is due to causes deeper than any political or social reform will ever touch. A nation or a State means, conceal it as you will, a lot of individual selves with unequal talents and in reality unequal conditions, and each of these selves does—or rather must—think not exclusively, but primarily of his own self. The old doctrine of original sin may be totally disconnected from the tale of Eve and her apple, or any other religious tradition or theological dogma, but it represents an undeniable fact which neither a statesman nor a preacher can venture to ignore. It is urged again that the need for individuality or originality, which is fostered by democratic freedom, is of trifling importance, and that civilisation owes much less to creative genius than to the collective endeavours of mankind. This is the grossest of blunders. Tarde in his *Lois de l'imitation* has emphasised with extraordinary subtlety and vigour the debt which we all owe to human imitativeness, but he never overlooks the fact that unless for the occasional appearance of a genius and an inventor, there would be little in existence worth imitation. The very ablest of socialistic or semi-socialistic jurists removes the conflict between the power of the State and the freedom of the individual by, at the same time, thrusting into prominence the notion of solidarity, and asserting in language, which might almost be taken from John Mill, the duty of the State to foster individuality of character. He, however, confers upon the State the right of compelling an individual to take any course of action whatever which the State deems conducive to the welfare of the citizens whereof it is composed.[80] Englishmen will readily acknowledge that there are many cases in which the interference of the State really increases the personal liberty of a citizen, but, to any one brought up under the influence of John Mill and Tocqueville, it will be very difficult to believe that it is possible to deny that there may be, and in a socialistic state always will be, a conflict between the freedom necessary for the full development of individuality and the power of a government which has to enforce upon individuals deference to the principles of authoritative socialism. Despotism may continue to be tyranny, even though it may have become both popular and benevolent.

From whichever side the topic is approached, there will appear to be a real inconsistency between democratic government, *i.e.* the government of public opinion, and the rule of socialism, *i.e.* the enforcement of principles which, whether true or false, will sometimes assuredly conflict with the public opinion of the time.

79. Hillquit, *Socialism in Theory and Practice*, p. 120.
80. See Duguit, *L'État, le droit objectif et la loi positive*, p. 49.

A Cross-current. The opposition to the expensiveness or the financial burdens of collectivism.

Socialistic government is expensive government. And this is no accidental characteristic. For the true collectivist or socialist does not leave a penny which he can help to "fructify in the pockets of the people." The reason of this is clear. Our socialist believes that money not taken hold of by the State fructifies, if at all, in the pockets of the rich, such as millionaires and Dukes, and that it never reaches the overworked and underpaid wage-earner until it is seized by the tax-collector and dealt out to the worthy poor—and the poor are always worthy—by the action of the State. This line of reasoning or of feeling, of course, leads to the collection of huge revenues to be used for profuse expenditure directed by the superhuman wisdom of Government to the benefit of wage-earners.

The following statements are meant to show the immense increase in the amount of taxation imposed upon the tax-payers and rate-payers of England (including Wales):

The Burden of Taxation. The tax-payers and rate-payers of England bear the weight of a double system of taxation.

(1) *National Taxation, or Taxes, in the Strict Sense of that Term.* Such taxation is imposed directly by Act of Parliament and falls upon all the tax-payers of the United Kingdom. The whole revenue of the United Kingdom, in so far as it is raised by taxation,[81] for each of the five years 1908–1909 to 1912–1913, inclusive, may be thus stated:

1908–1909	£125,550,000
1909–1910	105,230,000
1910–1911	175,162,000
1911–1912	155,040,000
1912–1913	154,753,000

81. The whole revenue of the United Kingdom, including revenue arising from non-tax sources, such, *e.g.* as the postal service, and the receipts from the Suez Canal Shares, has been stated for the same years as follows:

1908–1909	£151,578,295
1909–1910	131,696,456
1910–1911	203,850,587
1911–1912	185,090,285
1912–1913	188,802,000

See Finance Accounts of the United Kingdom, 1912–1913, and *Whitaker's Almanack*, 1914, p. 500.

In other words, the revenue raised by taxes has increased during the last five years (1908–1909 to 1912–1913) by £29,203,000.

Now the meaning of these facts is made clearer by a comparison of the revenue of the United Kingdom to-day with the revenue of the United Kingdom in 1885–1886. In 1885–1886 the revenue raised by taxation was £74,927,000, whereas the revenue for 1912–1913 was £154,753,000. In twenty-seven years taxation has increased by £79,826,000, that is to say, it has increased, on an average, of slightly under £3,000,000 a year. The revenue, in short, from taxation was in 1912–1913 at least double the revenue in 1885–1886.[82]

The date 1885–1886 is noticeable. The last great Act of Parliamentary reform was passed in 1884, and established democratic government based on Household Suffrage throughout the whole of the United Kingdom. From 1885 it is possible to trace the gradual increase in the revenue raised by taxation, though this increase does not become very noticeable till some ten years later. The contrast between the £74,927,000 raised in 1885–1886 and the £154,753,000 raised in 1912–1913 is noteworthy. It can hardly be overlooked, whatever may be the inference which is rightly drawn from it. But, as already pointed out, the inhabitants of England are taxed not only as tax-payers but also as rate-payers.[83]

(2) *Local Taxation or Public Rates.* Such taxation is imposed directly by some of the numerous local bodies authorised in England by Act of Parliament to impose rates.[84] If we want to see the weight of taxation imposed upon Englishmen by the national taxes with which we have already dealt, and by public rates, it will be convenient to add together the national taxes and the public rates[85] for the following four years, 1907–1908, 1908–1909, 1909–1910, 1910–1911. In such a comparison

82. In 1885–1886 the persons subject to income-tax paid £15,160,000; in 1912–1913 they paid £44,806,000. The tax has increased by more than £29,500,000. Nor is there the least reason to expect the least diminution in the weight of taxation. The notice officially sent round to tax-payers estimates the national expenditure for 1913–1914 at £195,640,000.

83. Of course this is true also of the inhabitants of Scotland and Ireland, who also pay their share of the taxes imposed on the tax-payers of the United Kingdom. But as I am dealing with the law and the public opinion of England, it in many ways simplifies the treatment of my subject if we confine ourselves as much as possible to laws affecting Englishmen.

84. See for the nature and number of local authorities who can impose Public Rates, *Local Taxation Returns,* 1910–1911, Part VII., Summary, p. 3. The number of such separate local authorities in the year 1910–1911 were 25,614. The year 1910–1911 is the last for which returns have been furnished.

85. The public rates raised in England for the years 1907–1911 were: 1907–1908, £59,627,577; 1908–1909, £61,218,203; 1909–1910, £63,261,164; 1910–1911, £65,073,131.

it will be best to omit altogether from our computation of the amount raised for the national revenue any non-tax revenue.[86] Hence the following results:

In 1907–1908 the burden of taxes and rates together amounted to £189,947,577, in 1908–1909 to £186,768,203, in 1909–1910 to £168,491,164, and in 1910–1911 to £240,233,131.[87]

As there is not as yet available any complete return of the rates collected in England since 1910–1911, it is impossible to state authoritatively, how much the rate-payers of England have paid by way of local taxation or rates, in addition to payment of public taxes, in the years 1911–1912 and 1912–1913. If, however, we assume that the rates imposed for the year 1912–1913 were not greater than the rates collected for the year 1910–1911, that sum at least must be added to the amount raised as taxes for that year, with the result that the taxes and rates together amounted to at lowest the sum of £218,013,940. But it may be taken as morally certain that the rates for 1912–1913 will turn out to exceed the rates for 1910–1911 by more than a million,[88] and hence the whole amount of taxes and rates for 1911–1912 will come to at least £220,826,131. From the huge amount drawn from tax-payers and rate-payers some inferences may at any rate be drawn with a good deal of probability.

Thus the burden of taxes is gradually forming an immense restriction upon individual freedom, for it must always be remembered that a tax, whatever its form, is always levied upon definite assignable persons with whose means of free action it interferes. The old liberalism of sixty years ago meant cheap government, and encouraged the individual energy which is the life-blood of true democratic government. Then again heavy taxes are a source of public danger. In the case of a foreign invasion an over-taxed England might be found in the course of a very few months to be, even if well provided with Dreadnoughts, an indefensible England. This peril would be greatly increased if the mass of the people and of the voters had come more and more to depend for their prosperity on the aid of the State. A recent *Life of Cobbett* records that the Peace of Amiens (1803) was so popular with the London mob that they drew the carriage of the French envoy in triumph to his house. No one can doubt that it might be very difficult to carry on even a strictly defensive war, if it became necessary to cut down the amount of old age pensions or of insurance and unemployment benefit. But here we come across

86. See p. 394, note 81, *ante.*

87. The apparent lightening of the burden for the year 1909–1910 was due to the dispute of the two Houses over the Budget, and its rejection by the House of Lords. A large amount of taxes was not then collected, within the financial year 1909–1910, but it swelled the amount collected in the following year.

88. It will be observed that between 1907–1908 and 1910–1911 the rates have risen by more than £5,445,550.

the consideration that quite possibly the gradually increasing dislike to excessive taxation might bring not only the richer classes, but also the large middle class of tradesmen and skilled artisans who may feel that they are being pressed down under the load of taxes into the ranks of the strictly poor, to cry halt to any further socialistic and costly experiments. Thus patriotism and imperialism may well reinforce impatience of excessive taxation, and in effect create new cross-currents of opinion hostile to the progress of socialism. Englishmen of wisdom and public spirit may well forbid the squandering upon even benevolent experiments of resources which ought always to be preserved for the defence of our national greatness and independence.

Conclusions

What then are the inferences which can be drawn from the rapid growth of collectivism and the force of the circumstances, feelings, or beliefs which in England oppose its further progress?

One assertion may be made with confidence. It is that the prevalence of inconsistent social and political ideals (which often by the way co-exist in the mind of one and the same person) is full of peril to our country. For it is more than possible that English legislation may, through this inconsistency of thought, combine disastrously the defects of socialism with the defects of democratic government. Any grand scheme of social reform, based on the real or supposed truths of socialism, ought to be carried out by slow and well-considered steps taken under the guidance of the best and the most impartial of experts. But the democratic idea that the people, or any large number of the people, ought to have whatever they desire simply because they desire it, and ought to have it quickly, is absolutely fatal to that slow and sure kind of progress which alone has the remotest chance of producing fundamental and beneficial social changes. Democratic legislation, on the other hand, ought to have the advantage of harmonising with, or at any rate not going much beyond, the public opinion of a given time. But this harmony between law and sentiment is easily contemned by socialists, who feel that they know better than do the electors of England what is really for the good of the English people. Hence it is all but certain that great changes planned by enthusiasts will, if they seem to be popular, be carried out with haste and without due consideration as to the choice of means proper to obtain a given end, and, on the other hand, that on some occasions a party of self-called reformers will force on the electors changes which, whether good or bad, are opposed to the genuine convictions of the people. All that it is necessary to insist upon is that either blunder is likely to cause huge loss, and it may be ruin, to England. This is a matter of ominous significance.

Another line of reflection is absolutely forced upon a student of recent legislation. The socialists of England who desire "the abolition of the wage system,"[89] are, he will see, aiming at a fundamental revolution in the whole condition of English society. The change may be the most beneficial of reforms or the most impracticable of ideals. But in any case it will involve a severe conflict, and a conflict which may last not for years, but for generations. The arduousness of the fight is certain. Englishmen, and especially that class of Englishmen who will have to pay the immense sums, and make the large sacrifices required for carrying out the revolution longed for by enthusiastic socialists, will offer the most stubborn opposition to a change which touches the very foundation of existing society. To Englishmen at least it is one thing to assent to the removal of definite and assignable grievances, it is quite another thing to sanction a course of unlimited innovation justified rather by the feelings and the hopes than by the arguments of its advocates. It is equally certain that the revolution to which socialism points cannot be worked out until the lapse of a long period of time. The social transformation of the modern world must be compared both in its importance and in its difficulty with the Reformation of the sixteenth and seventeenth centuries, or with the French Revolution. The Reformation represented a conflict extending over at least 130 years, the French Revolution can hardly even now be said to have reached its close, and, if we consider it as ended, has covered more than 100 years. In 1789 the best and wisest men in Europe expected from political reforms results as fundamental and as beneficial as any Englishman with leanings towards socialism can expect from social reforms.[90] In the one case we know, and in the other case we may conjecture that the expectations of reformers have been based to a large extent on the failure to understand the nature of man.

The last reflection which I will venture to suggest inevitably takes the form of a question. What are the hopes which a reasonable man may cherish with regard to the progress of collectivism in England? Unless he be a person of astoundingly sanguine temperament it would be difficult for him not to perceive that the combination of socialistic and democratic legislation threatens the gravest danger to the country. One may go a step further than this, and point out that if you look to the course of English history, founded as it is on individualism, or to the actual condition of English society, based, as it is, on the ideas suitable to the greatest of commercial communities, the transformation of England into a socialistic State

89. See *Industrial Unrest and Trade Union Policy,* by Charles Booth, pp. 15–21.

90. Englishmen of the twentieth century can hardly believe in the wildness of the hopes originally excited by the French Revolution. The shortest and by far the most impressive picture of the boundless expectations "of better days to all mankind" formed by men of sense and judgment is to be found in Books IX–XI of Wordsworth's *Prelude.*

looks like an absolute impossibility. But this fact does not preclude—it really fa-vours—the anticipation that definite reforms of law or custom, and still more of feeling, which are now advocated on more or less socialistic grounds, may be adopted with success by Englishmen. The possible fulfilment of this hope rests upon the assumption that democracy in its best form can become a government which at any rate tries to look, not to the interest of a class, even though the class be made up of the greater number and the poorest among the inhabitants of England, but to the interest of the whole nation. We must assume, we must indeed hope, that the socialists of England will accept the profoundly true dictum of Gabrielle Tarde that "a socialist party can, but a working man's party cannot, be in the great current of progress."[91] For a party of socialists may aim at the benefit of the whole State, a labour party seeks the benefit of a class. English democracy now knows its power, as English kings knew their power in the Middle Ages, as the English nobility knew its power after the Revolution of 1688, as the middle class knew its power between 1832 and 1866. This historical retrospect suggests much hope. The best of our kings, the most sagacious of our nobility, the most humane and the most prudent of our middle class did, though they each often displayed gross ignorance and marked selfishness, try honestly to govern with a view to the welfare of the whole country. It is to be hoped rather than expected that the English democracy may, under great temptations to err, display as much public virtue as the nobles of 1688 or the ten-pound householders of 1832. On the question whether our hope is well founded the opinion of intelligent and not unsympathetic foreigners is better worth attention than can be the judgment of any Englishman affected, as it must be, by the political sympathies and conflicts of the day. Mr. Lowell has studied the English Constitution more thoroughly than have most Englishmen. He has also carried the analysis of public opinion in En-gland and in the United States a step further than any recent writer. Now of our country he says, "the political system of England, which was never that of an absolute monarchy, and has never become quite a democracy of the traditional type but has ever carried the forms of one age over into the next, and thus com-

---

91. Tarde, *Les Transformations du pouvoir*, p. 258. "Toute politique qui se propose le tri-omphe exclusif d'une classe ou d'une caste, fût-ce de la classe ou de la caste la plus nombreuse et la plus déshéritée, est rétrograde au premier chef. Un parti *socialiste* peut être dans le grand courant du progrès; un parti ouvrier non." [Any political movement whose aim is the exclusive triumph of any one class or caste, even if it is the largest and most deprived, is entirely retrograde. A socialist party can be seen as part of the great current of progress; a workers' party cannot.] [Editor's note: The translation was added in the Liberty Fund edi-tion.]

bined some of their virtues."[92] These words hint at the aspirations of a reasonable Englishman; it may be hoped that we may carry the individualistic virtues and laws of the nineteenth century into the twentieth century, and there blend them with the socialistic virtues of a coming age. Mr. Charles W. Eliot, the eminent predecessor at Harvard of President Lowell, suggests to a certain extent the mode by which this end may be accomplished. He believes and preaches that, without any tremendous legal change, the social unrest, the existence whereof every one acknowledges, can gradually be put an end to, if we come to the conclusion arrived at by him after studying for a good many years the question of content in labour, that "the conditions of content in labour, which I have enjoyed personally, are those which all labouring people ought to enjoy."[93] Weigh now the words of an eminent German professor who has carefully studied the economic history of England and recognises the development of socialistic ideas among modern Englishmen:

> Economic liberalism taught England to believe in the rights and greatest possible development of the individual; to regard each man as equal before the Law, and to display toleration towards the opinions of others, whether in politics or in religion; to place the same social value on all professions, and to respect what other nations and races hold holy. To other nations these and other characteristics of Liberal culture are still novel and unfamiliar. The Englishman will not lose them even under a new social system, for they have become an integral part of his national character.[94]

The hopes suggested by these foreign observers of our public life are confirmed by the whole history of England. It has condemned violent revolution, but has favoured the gradual reform or abolition of admitted defects in a tolerable state of society. Englishmen are likely, therefore, to favour the gradual amendment of a social condition as good as, and possibly sounder than, the condition of any other large European country. To this consideration may be added the confidence that the increased sympathy assuredly now felt by the best men and women of England with the wants of the poorer classes will facilitate wise legislation, and create or restore "the conditions of labour under which the labourer may reasonably be expected to be contented, efficient, and happy." Here, however, we approach the

---

92. A. L. Lowell, *Public Opinion and Popular Government,* p. 295.

93. *Successful Profit-Sharing,* by Charles W. Eliot. The same view seems to me practically adopted in *Industrial Unrest and Trade Union Policy,* by Charles Booth.

94. *Economic Liberalism,* by Hermann Levy, Ph.D., p. 124.

realm of prophecy. A prudent man will in these circumstances do well to adopt as his conclusion the words of Alexis de Tocqueville:

> Le socialisme restera-t-il enseveli dans le mépris qui couvre si justement les socialistes de 1848? Je fais cette question sans y répondre. Je ne doute pas que les lois constitutives de notre société moderne ne soient fort modifiées à la longue; elles l'ont déjà été dans beaucoup de leurs parties principales, mais arrivera-t-on jamais à les détruire et à en mettre d'autres à la place? Cela me paraît impraticable. Je ne dis rien de plus, car, à mesure que j'étudie davantage l'état ancien du monde, et que je vois plus en détail le monde même de nos jours; quand je considère la diversité prodigieuse, qui s'y rencontre, non seulement parmi les lois, mais parmi les principes des lois, et les différentes formes qu'a prises et que retient, même aujourd'hui, quoi qu'on en dise, le droit de propriété sur la terre, je suis tenté de croire que ce qu'on appelle les institutions nécessaires ne sont souvent que les institutions auxquelles on est accoutumé, et qu'en matière de constitution sociale, le champ du possible est bien plus vaste que les hommes qui vivent dans chaque société ne se l'imaginent.[95]

---

95. *Souvenirs d'Alexis de Tocqueville* (Paris, 1893), pp. 111 and 112.

"Will socialism remain buried in the disdain with which the socialists of 1848 are so justly covered? I put the question without making any reply. I do not doubt that the laws concerning the constitution of our modern society will in the long run undergo modification; they have already done so in many of their principal parts. But will they ever be destroyed and replaced by others? It seems to me to be impracticable. I say no more, because—the more I study the former condition of the world and see the world of our own day in greater detail, the more I consider the prodigious variety to be met with not only in laws, but in the principles of law, and the different forms even now taken and retained, whatever one may say, by the rights of property on this earth—the more I am tempted to believe that what we call necessary institutions are often no more than institutions to which we have grown accustomed, and that in matters of social constitution the field of possibilities is much more extensive than men living in their various societies are ready to imagine."—*Recollections of Alexis de Tocqueville,* English translation, by de Mattos, pp. 100, 101.

Index

voting rights (*continued*)
114–17; for women, 114n37, 392. *See also* household suffrage; universal suffrage

wages for workmen in early-nineteenth-century England, 73–74. *See also* Minimum Rates of Wages Acts
wage system abolition, 398
Walpole, Robert, 9–10
war in South Africa, 323–24
Warren, Samuel, 233
Wedderburn, Alexander (Earl of Rosslyn), 215–16
Wellington, Duke of, 149, 312
Wesley, John, 287
Westcott, Bishop Brooke Foss, 290
Whigs: of the age of George the Third, 59; anticlerical leanings, 222–23; and ecclesiastical reform, 226–28, 237; freedom of discussion and religious beliefs under, 145; point of similarity with Benthamites, 362
Wilberforce, William, 288
women: factory regulations protecting, 168–69; legal restrictions on individual freedom, 185; social class and legal rights, 273–75; the vote for, 114n37, 392; women's rights, 32. *See also* married women's property rights; Ten Hours Bill

Wordsworth, William, *Prelude,* 398n90
working class: changed attitudes toward, in mid nineteenth century, 170–72; Collectivist legislative reforms on behalf of, 195–201, 202–3, 204–6, 209–12; discontent within, 386–87; ecclesiastical support for, 290–91; education of children, 82–83, 195–98; Harriet Martineau on, 297; hours of labor regulation, 376; John Stuart Mill on Parliament's relationship with, 177–78; legal restrictions on individual freedom of, 185; legal rights contrasted with tenant's rights, 189; legal rights relative to customer's rights, 199–201; legal rights relative to domestic servant's rights, 200n49; and matters ecclesiastical, 236; relief for workingmen in early nineteenth century, 73; representation by and power in Parliament, 215–20; similar legislation in France and England, 385; viewed as disadvantaged in competition with capitalists, 188. *See also* health insurance for workers; trade unionism; unemployed workmen
Workmen's Compensation Acts: *1897,* 200–201; *1897* and *1900,* 50, 185
workmen's compensation for injury on the job, 199–200

This book is set in 10.5/14 Minion, designed by Robert Slimbach in 1992.
Minion is a digital face inspired by late Renaissance fonts.

The book is printed on paper that is acid-free and meets the
requirements of the American National Standard for Permanence
of Paper for Printed Library Materials, z39.48-1992. ♾

Book design by Erin Kirk New,
Watkinsville, Georgia
Typography by Apex Publishing, LLC,
Madison, Wisconsin
Printed and bound by Worzalla Publishing Company,
Stevens Point, Wisconsin